Conflicting Worlds

New Dimensions of the American Civil War

T. MICHAEL PARRISH, EDITOR

BROTHERS ONE AND ALL

Esprit de Corps in a Civil War Regiment

MARK H. DUNKELMAN

LOUISIANA STATE UNIVERSITY PRESS

BATON ROUGE

*540 82124

DESIGNER: AMANDA McDONALD SCALLAN
TYPEFACE: WHITMAN
TYPESETTER: COGHILL COMPOSITION CO.
PRINTER AND BINDER: THOMSON-SHORE, INC.

Library of Congress Cataloging-in-Publication Data

Dunkelman, Mark H.
Brothers one and all : esprit de corps in a Civil War regiment / Mark H. Dunkelman.
    p. cm.—(Conflicting worlds)
    Includes bibliographical references and index.
    ISBN 0-8071-2978-X (hardcover : alk. paper)
1. United States Army. New York Infantry Regiment, 154th (1862–1865) 2. United States Army—Military
life—History—19th century. 3. Fellowship—History—19th century. 4. United States—History—Civil War,
1861–1865—Social aspects. 5. Soldiers—New York (State)—Social conditions—19th century. 6. Soldiers—United
States—Social conditions—19th century. 7. New York (State)—History—Civil War, 1861–1865—Regimental
histories. 8. United States—History—Civil War, 1861–1865—Regimental histories. I. Title. II. Series.
E523.5154th.D855   2004
369'.15'09747—dc22

2004000585

In loving memory of my parents, Harold and Irene

CONTENTS

ILLUSTRATIONS

Map

Photographs

following page 247

Acknowledgments

First and foremost, my sincere thanks go to the many descendants and friends of the 154th New York cited in the bibliography and illustration credits for sharing letters, diaries, memoirs, photographs, relics, and other materials with me. I wish I could name each and every one of them here and thank them individually, but the list would be too long. Without their devotion to our ancestors' memory, my ongoing work could not be accomplished. I cannot overstate my appreciation of their kind, generous, and invaluable help.

Thanks are also due to the archivists and librarians at the various institutions that provided materials. Three deserve special mention. Lorna Spencer, Curator of the Cattaraugus County Memorial and Historical Museum in Little Valley, New York, has steered information to me for years, and always has a ready answer to my questions. Daniel Lorello, Associate Archivist at the New York State Archives in Albany, was helpful beyond the call of duty during my research trip to that repository. And Lorna Knight, Curator of Manuscripts, Division of Rare and Manuscript Collections, Carl A. Kroch Library, Cornell University, Ithaca, New York, and the library staff enabled me to reach a longstanding goal by making available the Edwin Dwight Northrup Papers, and photocopying hundreds of pages from the collection.

My two trips to Ithaca were made much more enjoyable by Judy and Charles Scott of Lansing, New York, who provided me with a pleasant home away from home during my research at Cornell. Their hospitality was most welcome.

I have another home away from home in Fairfax, Virginia, courtesy of my longtime friend Christopher L. Ford and his wife, Michelle, and son, Wesley. Chris is always ready to accompany me to a battlefield or a bookstore, and I treasure the times I am together with my oldest Civil War friend.

Dr. Thomas P. Lowry and his wife, Beverly, of Woodbridge, Virginia, have done Civil War scholars a great service by indexing the massive Union court-martial records at the National Archives in Washington. The Lowrys provided me with the references to 154th New York court-martial files.

Mark A. Snell, Director of the George Tyler Moore Center for the Study of the Civil War at Shepherd College in Shepherdstown, West Virginia, kindly invited me to make a presentation at the Center's 2000 seminar on "The Legacy of the Civil War." My talk became the framework for chapter 11 of this book.

My thanks to Michael J. Winey, former Curator of Special Collections at the U.S. Army Military History Institute at Carlisle Barracks, Pennsylvania, for thirty years of partnership in the hunt for the legacy of the 154th New York.

My deep appreciation goes to four expert historians of the Civil War's common soldiers—Edwin C. Bearss, Chief Historian Emeritus of the National Park Service and battlefield guide extraordinaire; Earl J. Hess of Lincoln Memorial University in Harrogate, Tennessee; James M. McPherson of Princeton University; and Reid Mitchell of New Orleans, Louisiana—who took time from their pressing schedules to read my manuscript, make valuable comments and suggestions, and provide endorsements for the book. I am also grateful to T. Michael Parrish, editor of the Conflicting Worlds: New Dimensions of the American Civil War series, for a close reading of the manuscript and several constructive suggestions for its improvement. While I have incorporated many of the readers' suggestions, the final analyses and conclusions are mine alone, as are any errors.

Special thanks—and love—to my aunt Floris Sarver of Getzville, New York, who ties me to my ancestors and gives me a home when I return to western New York. And extra special thanks and love to my wife, Annette, and son, Karl, who let me be me, and make me most happy.

This book is dedicated to my late parents, Harold and Irene, who always encouraged my efforts in artwork, writing, music, and historical research. It was my father's stories about his grandfather that inspired my study of the 154th New York, and led all these years later to this book. I would like to think that Dad and Great-Grandpa Langhans know what they have wrought.

INTRODUCTION: *This Little Band*

On June 23, 1865, approximately 325 members of the 154th New York Volunteer Infantry gathered before their commander, Lieutenant Colonel Lewis D. Warner, at a military depot in Elmira, New York. The Civil War was over; the victorious Union armies were disbanding. The soldiers of the 154th were about to receive their final pay and discharges and board a train for the journey to their home counties, Cattaraugus and Chautauqua, in the western part of the state. Before those last military procedures, before the men were re-transformed from soldiers to civilians, they engaged in several minutes of solemn recollection and introspection when their colonel delivered his farewell address.

Warner acclaimed the end of the war, recalled their lives together as soldiers, and remembered the many comrades who were no longer in the ranks. He spoke of the anticipated release from irksome military discipline and the homey pleasures they were about to enjoy. After thanking the men for their obedience to orders, he closed by urging them to be good citizens, as they had been good soldiers. "May no act of yours, either individually or collectively," Warner declared, "sully the reputation of the Regiment, which is now equaled by few, and excelled by none."

At the heart of Warner's speech to the regiment were "a few words with regard to the time in which we have been so closely connected, as members of the 154th." The men had answered their country's call, the colonel proclaimed, "actuated only by motives of patriotism," seeking only the restoration of peace, the crushing of the "monster Rebellion," and the plaudits of a grateful nation. Thus motivated, they had been "*brave noble* and *true*" soldiers, as proved by the history of their many battles and campaigns: Chancellorsville, Gettysburg, Lookout Valley, Chattanooga, Rocky Face Ridge, Resaca, Pine Knob, Peachtree Creek, Atlanta, Savannah, and the Carolinas. "Fellow Soldiers," Warner declared, "the 154th needs no eulogist to portray its deeds; they are inscribed in enduring characters upon the annals of the past three years:—and there, while our Nation exists, they will remain, and will be held in remembrance by a grateful people."

He then made a most remarkable statement: "Standing here, as I do now, with your achievements fresh in my memory, I would not exchange my three years' connection with this little band for all the rest of my life together; for I feel that, in after years, I can look upon these as of more value than them all."[1]

Warner was in the prime of his life when he uttered those words; three days later he observed his forty-third birthday. In the antebellum years he had married and fathered two young sons, established himself as a carpenter, joiner, and lumberman in his Cattaraugus County home town of Portville, and won the respect of the community, serving as justice of the peace and town supervisor. Now he was about to return to his home, to add two children to his family, to maintain an active involvement in his town's civic and fraternal organizations, to serve more terms in elective office, to be revered as a hero of the war, and to survive to be one of Portville's oldest and most esteemed citizens. But he was ready to dismiss all the years he had spent, and all the unknown years to come, as lesser than the three years he served with the 154th New York in a terrible war. He was ready to place the love of his family circle and the friendship and admiration of his townspeople as secondary to the bonds that tied him to his comrades of the 154th. He knew that he could never match what he had been through with the regiment in the war, that he and his fellow soldiers had survived an ordeal that bound them together indissolubly, that their service would define them for the rest of their lives, that they were leaving something irreplaceable behind as they parted.[2]

Warner observed that the 154th had entered the field nearly a thousand strong; now they numbered about a third of that amount. The depleted ranks "tell their own tale of battles, marches, exposures, privations, hardships, and all that tends to exhaust the physical powers, and shorten the life of man." The missing soldiers had fallen on the battlefield, died of wounds or disease, "starved and rotted in *Southern Prisons*," been discharged for disabilities, or been transferred to the Veteran Reserve Corps. And yet, the colonel averred, among the survivors, "I do not believe there is one now within the sound of my voice who regrets that he became a *Soldier Boy*; or who would not, were our Country again in danger,—were the war-cry again to resound from the hill-tops and along the valleys of old Cattaraugus and Chautauqua—buckle on, as before, his armor, and rally 'round the Old Flag, shouting the battle-cry of Freedom."[3]

More than forty years later, Marcellus W. Darling, an old soldier boy of the 154th, wrote his memoirs, which—significantly—largely centered on his Civil War service. Remembering that long-ago June day in Elmira, Darling clearly recalled Warner's farewell address as an emotional event for both the colonel and his listeners alike: "The brave and stalwart colonel was more broken up than I ever saw him in battle, where he was always cool and brave. Tears flowed, but there was a strong effort at self-restraint, thinking how we had marched and fought side by side for so long a time, trusting in each other, supporting each other, dividing rations, caring for wounded and dead and sick. Mutual hardships had made us brothers, one and all. And now all this was to come to an end. We parted, even from these hardships, with a sense of pain around the heart."[4]

Another of the soldier boys of the 154th New York who listened to Colonel Warner's farewell address was my great-grandfather, Corporal John Langhans of Company H. A twenty-one-year-old native of the German duchy of Lauenburg, he had immigrated with his parents and younger brothers to the United States in 1857, landing in New York City in 1858 and proceeding directly to Cattaraugus County, where the family worked on a farm in East Otto until they saved enough money to buy their own land on Jackman Hill, in the neighboring town of Ellicottville. John enlisted at East Otto in September 1864, joined the 154th in Atlanta, and marched with the regiment across Georgia to Savannah, through the Carolinas, and to Washington, where he proudly paraded in the Grand Review of Major General William Tecumseh Sherman's army.

John Langhans had no regrets that he became a soldier. He stood his service well and was promoted to corporal at the end of the war. After the Grand Review, while the regiment was waiting to be mustered out near Bladensburg, Maryland, John summarized his military experience in a letter home. "It is just 9 month ago to day when we left East Otto," he wrote. "When we then looked ahead it looked rather dark, but things look better now, since then we have made a greate circle in the United States and have seen many a hard day or night, but still I have seen lots of good times and I have had lots of fun, I would not have missed this chance for 1,000 dol-l[ars]." For John, the war had been a great adventure in his new land.[5]

He returned to his family's Jackman Hill farm and lived for sixty-four more years. It was largely a contented life. The family increased its land holdings and built a substantial farmhouse to replace their log cabin. John married and fathered three children, who in turn gave him sixteen grand-children. As the years passed, he added the newest conveniences to his pros-perous dairy farm: indoor plumbing, electricity, a telephone, a Victrola, a radio, an automobile. He was active in his Lutheran church and in Republi-can politics, serving as Ellicottville's tax assessor and clerk of his local school district. He traveled frequently. He enjoyed generally good health through-out his long life.

He died on September 19, 1929. Six days later the weekly *Ellicottville Post* carried a front-page obituary and account of his funeral, accompanied by a portrait photograph. The headline was revealing:

JOHN LANGHANS, CIVIL WAR VETERAN, DIES
Was Corporal In Old 154th and Was On Famous March
With Shreman [*sic*] To Sea.[6]

His long and active life of eighty-five years was compressed in summary to the nine months he had served with the 154th New York in General Sher-man's campaigns. In the bold headline, he was once again a young man marching with his regiment through Georgia. It was how he wanted to be remembered. Indeed, during his lifetime, John had made sure that autobio-graphical sketches published in two local history books both stressed his Civil War service—and that his children and grandchildren were familiar with his tales of Sherman's marches. Like Colonel Warner and Marcellus Darling, John Langhans had found soldiering with the "old 154th" to be the central experience of his life.[7]

Mementos preserved by generations of my great-grandfather's descen-dants trace a line from his service in the closing year of the war to the final years of his life. There is a wealth of stuff. Relics from the war include a carte-de-visite portrait of him taken by a Washington photographer; the bay-onet from his Enfield rifled musket; the silver star badge of the Twentieth Army Corps, engraved with his name, rank, company, and regiment; the cot-ton bolls he was said to have picked as souvenirs during the March to the

Sea; and his "housewife," a small sewing kit made for him—according to a note in his hand—by the women of East Otto and given to him prior to his departure to the front.

Other memorabilia reveals how his service remained essential to his identity in the postwar decades: the brass buttons from the uniform coat he wore as a member of the great Union veterans' organization, the Grand Army of the Republic (GAR); tasseled and embossed ribbons and badges he wore at GAR events and reunions of the 154th New York Regimental Association; souvenirs and postcards from his postwar trips with other veterans of the 154th to Gettysburg, Chattanooga, and Georgia; photographs of him and his comrades of Ellicottville's GAR post during cemetery ceremonies on long-ago Decoration Days. Considering these keepsakes, it is evident that his nine months' service with the 154th New York echoed resoundingly throughout the six and a half decades of his later life. As the headline of his obituary indicated, he ever after remembered himself as a member of the old 154th, marching with Sherman to the sea.

John Langhans, Lewis Warner, Marcellus Darling, and hundreds of their comrades of the 154th New York—like the soldiers of thousands of Civil War regiments, of North and South—were bound together in a special fashion by their lifelong devotion to their regiment. This regimental allegiance is best defined by the French term *esprit de corps*: the common spirit existing in the members of a group, a spirit that inspires enthusiasm, devotion, and strong regard for the honor of the group.[8]

Esprit de corps existed among Civil War soldiers to varying extent at the several levels of military hierarchy: company, regiment, brigade, division, corps, army. But the strongest organizational esprit was found at the regimental level. When asked to name his unit, a Civil War soldier almost invariably responded by naming his regiment. His regiment tied him to his closest comrades and inspired his deepest organizational pride and staunchest unit loyalty—the essence of esprit de corps. If the men themselves were the heart of a Civil War regiment, esprit de corps was its soul.[9]

Regiments were the core of larger military units, from brigade to army. As the elementary component of Civil War forces, their stability and efficiency were crucial to the success of the larger organizations. In General Sherman's perceptive definition, "The regiment is the family." Strengthened by esprit de corps, regimental families banded together in the face of uncertainty and adversity, stuck together through years of hardships and horrors, and persevered for the cause until the war came to a close. And after a regiment dispersed at the war's end, esprit bonded its veterans through the postwar decades. As the years passed, veterans held their old regimental comrades in a special fraternal regard, an attachment they carried with them to their graves.[10]

Esprit de corps was built into the makeup of a typical Civil War regiment. Recruited within the confines of a single city or county or state legislative district, a regiment's identity was tied to its home community. Those community ties were interlaced with familial, ethnic, and professional ties among the volunteers, which further strengthened regimental identity. A constant flow of communication kept the home folk informed of the doings of their regiment, and the regiment apprised of goings-on at home. As time passed, a regiment learned who in its home community supported the war effort and who were lukewarm or in outright opposition. The soldiers' empathy and sympathy, naturally, clung to the former. In Union regiments a growing political awareness often fostered a political consensus. The men looked to home for unambiguous support at the ballot box, the soldiers' aid society, and the recruiting station.

At the front, meanwhile, camaraderie grew among the men. As they endured the vicissitudes of army life together, they became devoted to their regiment. Separation from the regiment made them long for a return to their comrades. But esprit was not universal. Shirkers and deserters peeled away from the regiment, leaving a core of survivors more tightly bound then ever. Ineffective officers were weeded out and replaced by competent men promoted from the ranks, who instilled enough discipline to mold the regiment into an effective military machine. As they struggled through hardships and sickness and battle and death, caring for each other, amusing each other, surviving with each other, the soldiers' sense of regimental identity coalesced and their esprit de corps blossomed into a regimental pride that would transcend the war.

Regimental esprit de corps was a central factor in Civil War military history. Esprit bonded the members of a regiment into a tightly knit unit filled with pride, bound to uphold its reputation, and determined to endure until victory was won. Esprit de corps consequently was the essence of regimental cohesion. Esprit-charged regiments were the backbone of Civil War armies, the muscle and sinew that enabled those armies to withstand the hardships of camp and campaign, to march great distances, to strike the enemy with deadly effect, to be beaten by the enemy and recuperate to fight again—and to do it all over and over during four years of war.

In addition to its organizational importance, regimental esprit de corps played a significant role in the motivation of individual soldiers. The esprit-charged soldier stuck to his regiment through good times and bad, cared for his sick, wounded, and dying comrades, and followed the colors into the maelstrom of battle time and time again. Men volunteered to serve and fight in the Civil War for a variety of reasons, but as their careers as soldiers evolved and lengthened, regimental esprit de corps solidified as a motivational factor.

The impact of regimental esprit lasted well beyond the war's end. Like John Langhans, many veterans devoted considerable time and effort to commemorative activities. Closest to their hearts were activities involving their old regiments. Veterans erected monuments, visited old battlefields, wrote their memoirs, and reunited at regimental association reunions. Committees oversaw the writing and publication of regimental histories. An esprit developed among veterans as a whole, even among former foes. As veterans formed organizations that grew into political power brokers in the postwar decades, the country elected a string of former Union officers as president. By 1921, the federal government had paid more than $5.7 billion to Civil War pensioners, and plenty of veterans and their descendants were still receiving checks. Every village and county in the country had its veteran activists, many of them prominent in civic and political affairs. The aging Boys in Blue and Gray passed their prime of life wielding a potent sway on American political, social, and cultural currents.[11]

Surprisingly little has been written about Civil War regimental esprit de corps. Modern historians of the war's common soldiers have generally acknowledged the strength of regimental esprit, but few of them have analyzed it to any considerable extent, and their comments on the subject are remarkably brief. In his groundbreaking 1943 study of Confederate soldiers, the genre's pioneer, Bell Irvin Wiley, noted Johnny Reb's deep-seated pride in his regiment. Nine years later, in his book about Union soldiers, Wiley wrote, "The regiment figured prominently in Billy Yank's loyalties." But Wiley confined his assessment of Union regimental esprit to two short paragraphs of observations about regimental pride. He noted that a soldier's "fierce loyalty" to his regiment caused him to become extremely protective of his unit's reputation, that rivalries between regiments sometimes went beyond friendly banter to fisticuffs, and that proposals to consolidate depleted regiments led to protests by their members. Wiley offered no commentary on esprit's development or attributes or its importance to regimental cohesion and soldier motivation.[12]

In an excellent but often overlooked study of Union soldiers published in 1960, Francis A. Lord wrote, "The regiment was the most important organizational element of the Federal army." Lord noted the soldiers' strong identity with their regiments and pointed to the hundreds of postwar regimental histories as indicative of unit loyalty, but like Wiley he neglected to analyze esprit in any depth or to comment on its significance.[13]

Some succeeding historians have been equally terse. "Perhaps in no other war was the 'esprit' of the regiment more vital or apparent than in the Civil War," wrote E. B. Long, but other than mentioning community ties within regiments, he merely noted, "While there was pride in nation, army, corps, division, and brigade, it was the regiment which usually counted most." Wiley's closest disciple, James I. Robertson Jr., remarked on the great allegiance of Civil War soldiers to their regiments, without elaboration. Randall C. Jimerson similarly declared the importance of the regiment to a soldier's identity, but did not amplify his comment.[14]

Other historians have skirted the issue. In a provocative study which argued that the idealistic motivation of Civil War soldiers eroded as the war dragged on, Gerald F. Linderman cited comradeship as an essential bond among the men, but centered it in the mess rather than the company or regiment. Larry M. Logue also found comradeship strongest among messmates. Comradeship, however, is not synonymous with esprit de corps—it is rather a component of esprit de corps, and in discussing comradeship rather than esprit, Linderman and Logue did not address the larger topic.[15]

In studies of the armies of the war's western theater, two historians considered esprit de corps at higher levels. Writing about the men who marched through Georgia and the Carolinas, Joseph T. Glatthaar referred to their great pride in belonging to Sherman's army and discussed pride and rivalries among corps, but made no mention of regimental esprit. (To my own great pride and satisfaction, Glatthaar chose a wartime portrait of John Langhans as one of three representative soldier's images to illustrate his book.) In a study of Confederate soldiers of the Army of Tennessee, however, Larry J. Daniel observed that regimental and brigade esprit eclipsed that felt for division, corps, or army, and noted the dissatisfaction which resulted when depleted regiments were consolidated.[16]

Some historians have scrutinized regimental esprit more closely. Writing about the Union soldier in battle, Earl J. Hess cited "the mutually supportive interaction among members of the small, tight, intimate community of the regiment" as probably the most significant source of battlefield morale. According to Hess, bonds of trust and affection "knitted the regiment into a military family," and those regimental families were "a vessel in which hundreds of thousands of Northern men survived the storm of war." Soldiers were so loyal to their regimental families, Hess asserted, that they felt guilty at the thought of leaving them before the war was over.[17]

Other historians have looked to modern studies of combat motivation by military sociologists to support their brief commentaries on Civil War regimental esprit de corps. In a study of raw troops at the Battle of Shiloh, Joseph Allan Frank and George A. Reaves pointed to esprit as a source of combat motivation. "Men may fight because of personal attachments to their comrades or their regiments," Frank and Reaves contended, and they identified several factors that contributed to regimental esprit de corps: social and economic homogeneity, close ties to home communities, and the shared experience of battle. In a later study, however, Frank argued that political motivation was paramount to soldiers over other ideologies, and paradoxically rejected camaraderie as a significant motivating force. Frank even went so far as to state that volunteer troops did not "develop strong ties to their units and . . . foster the type of regimental pride that motivated professional armies."[18]

Following a similar tack to that steered by Frank and Reaves, two other historians have linked regimental esprit with primary group (or small-unit) cohesion, a term coined by social scientists studying World War II soldiers to denote the bonding of a small group of comrades. Reid Mitchell and James M. McPherson saw primary groups as Shakespearean "bands of brothers," and found them common among Civil War soldiers. Mitchell offered familial companies and regiments as examples of Civil War small-unit cohesion. Mitchell also examined Union soldiers' ties to their home communities, but only tenuously linked those ties to regimental esprit de corps. Basing his conclusions on evidence provided by tens of thousands of soldiers' letters, James McPherson wrote, "The pride and honor of an individual soldier were bound up with the pride and honor of his regiment." McPherson also noted rivalry among regiments and observed that disgrace befell regiments that performed poorly. He sketched the influences of territorial recruitment, family ties, and friendships on unit loyalty, and noted that combat experience strengthened esprit and dissolved petty factions and rivalries in some regiments. Ultimately, however, McPherson found that regimental esprit de corps was "related to but not precisely the same" as the primary group cohesion of military sociologists. A soldier's primary group—as defined by the sociologists—was the small circle of men closest to him: his mess or squad. The soldier's regiment, however important, was a secondary group.[19]

In a history of the Union Army of the Ohio, Gerald J. Prokopowicz referred repeatedly to regimental esprit de corps. "The regiment, more than any other unit," he wrote, "was a self-aware community, held together by bonds based on common geographic, social, cultural, or economic identities, strengthened by months of training and campaigning as a unit. Organizational loyalty and cohesion at the regimental level was thus extraordinarily strong." Prokopowicz described locally recruited companies as families that banded together to form regimental home towns. He touched on several aspects of regimental pride and observed that for most soldiers the regiment was "the source of their military identity" and the object of "almost mystical loyalties."

But to Prokopowicz, regimental esprit de corps was a two-edged sword. "The devotion that soldiers felt for their regiment," he wrote, "contrasted with their relative indifference toward other regiments and toward the army as a whole, would have long-lasting effects, both positive and negative, on the performance of the Army of the Ohio." In contrast to regimental esprit, Prokopowicz argued, "Bonds of organizational identification and loyalty rarely extended throughout larger units. Frequent reorganization and sheer size meant that brigades, divisions, corps, and armies did not have the permanence or human scale that might have allowed such bonds to develop. . . .

As long as its members identified themselves primarily with their regiments, the army remained a decentralized aggregation of military communities." This concentration of unit loyalty at the regimental level made Civil War armies "so elastic that they could not be broke, yet it also made them into awkward weapons that their leaders could not yield with decisive effect." Prokopowicz asserted, "The regiment-based culture of the army . . . determined how well or poorly the Army of the Ohio fought." In the end, the army survived "because its individual regiments maintained their organizational identity."[20]

"Students of Civil War battles have long recognized the primary place of the regiment in the hearts and minds of Civil War soldiers," Gerald Prokopowicz wrote. As the above overview indicates, historians in pioneering works have acknowledged the importance of regimental esprit de corps, but their analyses have been tentative and inconclusive. This is primarily a result of perspective. Previous historians have commented on regimental esprit as a fact of common soldier life, as a facet of soldier motivation, and as a factor in the performance of larger units. Consequently they have neglected to adequately address esprit's essential elements—its causes, development, expression, and power. To date, no historian has thoroughly examined Civil War regimental esprit de corps from the most logical perspective—that of a single regiment.[21]

This book is drawn from that perspective. Its evolution can be traced to my childhood in western New York. Fascinated by my father's stories of his grandfather John Langhans's Civil War service, and stimulated by the wartime letters and relics our family had saved, I was inspired to begin what has become a lifelong study of the 154th New York. This is my third book of 154th New York history. The first, coauthored with Michael J. Winey, then curator of Special Collections at the U.S. Army Military History Institute, was a straightforward regimental history, chronicling the 154th's camps, campaigns, and battles. The second told the best-known individual story to emerge from the regiment's history: that of Sergeant Amos Humiston, who was killed at Gettysburg and was identified by means of a photograph of his three children he clutched in his hand as he died—a poignant fate that bestowed on him and his bereaved family national and lasting fame.[22]

Brothers One and All returns to the collective history of the 154th New

York. Using the 154th as an archetype, it attempts to answer several basic questions about Civil War regimental esprit de corps. Why and how did regimental esprit develop? How did esprit manifest itself? What threats did esprit have to overcome? What shape did esprit assume in the postwar years?

For answers, I have turned to the soldiers of the 154th themselves. Their testimony is contained in more than thirteen hundred wartime letters and two dozen diaries of members of the regiment, which I have located, copied, and transcribed over more than a quarter-century of research. This material includes the observations of more than a hundred members of the regiment, approximately one-tenth of the total who served. I have let them express themselves through liberal quotations from their writings. (In doing so, I have let their ofttimes erratic spelling and punctuation stand uncorrected; words or phrases they emphasized by underlining have been rendered in italics.) More often than not, the quotations are only a few examples of many similar observations by the men on a particular topic. My task has been to give the soldiers' voices a careful and thorough hearing, to heed their commentary on a wide range of themes, to identify the themes that provide answers to the questions posed above, and to place those themes in a sensible sequence.

Although this study confines its examination of esprit de corps to a specific regiment, I believe its conclusions are largely applicable to most other regiments of both the North and the South—especially those regiments that saw active duty at the front, as the 154th New York did. Esprit de corps in the 154th most likely formed and revealed itself in much the same way as it did in a regiment from Maine or a regiment from Mississippi. Exceptions to that general assertion have been duly noted.

Regimental esprit de corps was a powerful force. It rang strongly in the 154th New York during three years of war, and echoed forcefully throughout the rest of the lives of survivors like John Langhans, Lewis Warner, and Marcellus Darling. It filled the regiment's men with a common spirit, and made them "brothers, one and all."

PART ONE

Home Ties

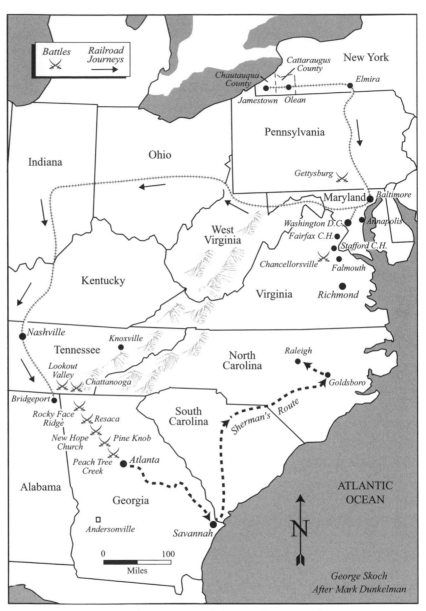

Area of operations of the 154th New York.

CHAPTER 1

Demographics and Identity

On the night of July 31, 1862, a crowd of more than three hundred citizens of East Otto, New York—about a quarter of the township's population— jammed the Baptist church at a crossroads hamlet, filling the pews and blocking the aisles and stairways. They had assembled to attend a "War Meeting," to listen to the promised speakers, and to demonstrate to the rest of Cattaraugus County and the nation at large that "the great heart of East Otto still beats true to the Union."

The meeting opened with an election of officers, after which one of the principal speakers was introduced. Reuben E. Fenton, the Republican U.S. congressman representing Cattaraugus and its western neighbor, Chautauqua County, spoke for more than an hour to a rapt audience. Frequently interrupted by hearty applause, Fenton outlined the cause and progress of the Southern rebellion, lauded the labors of President Abraham Lincoln's administration in combating the insurrection under great difficulties, and promised that in the future a more vigorous policy was to be adopted—one which would make the Confederacy realize the horrors and burdens of war. Fenton's oration, a reporter noted, "raised the enthusiasm of the audience to the highest pitch."

Fenton was followed to the pulpit by Addison G. Rice, a lawyer and state assemblyman from nearby Ellicottville, the Cattaraugus County seat. Applause and occasional uproarious laughter greeted Rice's remarks as he denied rumors of a lack of patriotism in East Otto and expressed complete confidence that the town, in response to a recent call for volunteers, would furnish her full quota of recruits and provide them with adequate bounty money.

It was nearly midnight when Rice finished his speech, but not a person had left the church. Now the assembly got down to its primary business. A flood of financial pledges poured in, and a bounty of forty dollars was promised to any man who enlisted. Then, amid deafening cheers and the blare of patriotic tunes from a brass band, volunteers were called for. Five young men responded immediately and signed the enlistment roll under the supervision of Dan B. Allen, a twenty-three-year-old lawyer recently admitted to the bar. Seven others promised to enroll in the next few days, enabling East Otto to meet its quota. A committee of wealthy citizens was assigned to solicit additional bounty subscriptions, and at about one o'clock in the morning the meeting adjourned with nine cheers for the volunteers, and three more for the speakers.[1]

A few weeks later, a twenty-year-old student at the Westfield Academy in Chautauqua County found himself unable to concentrate on his study of Latin, German, geometry, and physics. That afternoon Newell Burch returned home, ate his supper, and, without a word to his parents, went to the stable and saddled a horse. As he was riding out of the yard, one of his sisters spotted him and asked where he was going. To the village of Portland, to enlist, Burch replied. "Don't you do anything of the kind!" his sister yelled after him as he rode out of sight.

On his way to the village, Burch was joined by an elderly neighbor, also bound to the war meeting scheduled that night in Portland. The young man hitched his horse to the old man's buggy and they rode on together. Have you talked with your father about enlisting? the neighbor asked. No, Burch replied, it wasn't necessary—he was going to enlist, no matter what. On reaching Portland, the two found a wildly enthusiastic crowd. Joseph B. Fay, a forty-five-year-old farmer from the nearby village of Brocton, brandished an enlistment roll, and five dollars was offered to the first volunteer. "If you're bound to enlist, take that five dollars," whispered Burch's neighbor. "I am not enlisting for five dollars, but for the war," Burch replied, and after two or three men had enrolled, he stepped forward and signed the roll to exuberant cheers. Altogether, Fay recruited twenty-nine men that night in Portland.[2]

In the midst of their neighbors, family, and friends, the men enlisted—committing this very personal act in the very public forum of the grassroots community war meeting. The volunteers were leaving the bosom of their home towns and villages and counties, but they would never cut their ties to the home folk. At the heart of regimental esprit de corps was the soldiers' constant identity as members and representatives of their home communities. Such strong communal identity was possible because the typical regiment was formed within relatively narrow geographic confines. Like hundreds of other Civil War regiments, the 154th New York was deeply rooted in the communities from which it grew.

Government mandates set the recruiting process in motion. Six days after President Lincoln issued his July 1, 1862, call for 300,000 three-year volunteers, the federal War Department set New York State's quota at twenty-eight regiments. The state immediately ordered most of its thirty-two senatorial districts to constitute regimental districts and form a regimental rendezvous in each. Prominent citizens in each district were requested to establish committees to supervise recruiting in their area. The response in the Thirty-Second District, composed of Cattaraugus and Chautauqua counties, was rapid. On July 12 at Mayville, the Chautauqua County seat, delegates from the two counties met in the court house and resolved to raise the regiment apportioned to them, six companies to come from Chautauqua, the remaining four from Cattaraugus. Five days later, at a similar meeting in Ellicottville's court house, committees of three from each Cattaraugus County township were appointed to superintend recruiting in their respective communities.

A final preliminary meeting was held at a hotel in Dunkirk, Chautauqua County, on July 19. A committee of prominent men from both counties, appointed by Governor Edwin D. Morgan and the state adjutant general, petitioned Morgan to grant recruiting authorizations to twenty individuals. A military depot was authorized in the Chautauqua County city of Jamestown, and a civic-minded businessman was named commandant. Camp James M. Brown, named after a martyred local officer, was established at the county agricultural society's fairgrounds in Jamestown's outskirts. Within days, the score of men selected to raise recruits had received their gubernatorial authority. The work then began in earnest.

In late July and early August, war meetings like those in East Otto and Portland were held at churches, schools, and halls in every town in Cattaraugus and Chautauqua. By mid-August, the district's allotted ten companies were reported to be full. But more work was yet to come. On August 19, gubernatorial committeeman Addison Rice sent a telegram from Albany to the editor of the *Cattaraugus Freeman*, the Republican newspaper published in Ellicottville: "Cattaraugus has [permission to raise] a whole Regiment of Volunteers—10 Companies." Rice was appointed colonel by Governor Morgan, with authority to recruit the proposed Cattaraugus regiment. Ten more companies were to be raised; Chautauqua and Cattaraugus counties were each to have their own distinct regiment. When the gubernatorial committee reconvened in Jamestown on August 21 and approved the plan to raise a second regiment in the district, another round of war meetings opened in the two counties.[3]

Towns vied with each other to be the first to complete raising their quota of volunteers. According to one of her committeemen, Perrysburg was the first town in Cattaraugus County to reach the goal. He boasted about the achievement in a letter to the *Cattaraugus Freeman*: "Men, women and children turned out *en masse* at Rugg Town, at Versailles, and tonight we close the series at Cooper's. Money runs like water. Fifty Dollars and the sustenance of the family was paid by the Town to each Volunteer, and from $5 to $25 was paid by individuals as bounties. *We have enlisted five men over and above our quota!* We march forth 50 strong, and report at Camp Brown on Tuesday. We challenge competition in Old Cattaraugus."[4]

Other towns found other reasons to brag. When Salamanca filled her quota, a citizen noted, "Ten of our men from one street have volunteered— neither use profane languages or intoxicating liquors. Can so much be said of any Town in Cattaraugus?" When volunteers from several adjacent towns were formed into companies, more braggadocio was heard. A member of one of the Cattaraugus companies, soon to be Company A of the 154th New York, declared, "It is sufficient to say that we have the *best* Company in Camp. This is conceded by all." A member of Company G countered by declaring his comrades to be "as intelligent and brave a class of young men as Cattaraugus affords." Company esprit de corps was inherently strong.[5]

Towns outdid themselves to show support for the cause. At an immense war meeting held in the Chautauqua County village of Delanti a crowd of three thousand gathered around a huge bonfire, and the town of Stockton's quota was filled on the spot. Daily war meetings were held in the villages of Dunkirk and Fredonia until their quotas were met. Ladies and gentlemen donated diamond rings, watches, gold chains, and cows to be auctioned off for bounties. With such war fever raging, the second ten companies were readily raised.[6]

The task of enrolling volunteers fell to the gubernatorially authorized recruiters. Almost all of them, like Dan Allen and Joseph Fay, called their neighbors to the cause while personally pledging to lead them to the front. On reaching Camp Brown, the volunteers in turn rewarded the enrollers by electing them as company officers. Two or three men generally worked at enrolling a company of about ninety men, appearing at war meetings or canvassing independently in as few as three or as many as a dozen neighboring towns. Dan Allen, for example, assisted by the Reverend Ransom L. Blackman of the Perrysburg Methodist Episcopal Church, enrolled men in nine towns in the northeast quadrant of Cattaraugus County. Those recruits formed Company B of the 154th and elected Allen captain. (Blackman did not join the regiment.) Joseph Fay, assisted by Isaac T. Jenkins and another man, raised Company E in Chautauqua County's Lake Erie shore towns of Portland, Westfield, and Ripley. Fay became captain, Jenkins his first lieutenant. The work of one enrolling officer was exceptional. Harrison Cheney, a thirty-two-year-old farmer and former teacher, enrolled all ninety-four men of Company D on his own. The recruits came from Cheney's home town of Freedom and five other towns in the northeast corner of Cattaraugus County. Naturally they elected Cheney their captain. (Three decades after the war, a biographical sketch of Cheney in a county history claimed that "he was the only man who recruited, personally, every man of a company in this State.")[7]

While the three committeemen from each of Cattaraugus County's thirty-one townships generally confined themselves to support work—arranging war meetings and procuring bounty money—with no intentions of enrolling men or serving themselves, there were some exceptions. In addition to serving as a committeeman, Perrysburg's Reverend Blackman helped Dan Allen raise Company B and also enrolled many of the men of Company K from the same geographic area. Ellicottville committeeman Samuel C. Noyes Jr., while not an enrolling officer, was nonetheless commissioned as the 154th's adjutant. John F. Nelson of Great Valley served on his town's committee and was elected captain of Company H after recruiting it, with the help of two assistants, in nine southwestern Cattaraugus County towns.[8]

Imbued with community pride and led by respected townsmen, company after company arrived at Camp Brown. Even before they were banded together into regiments, the companies possessed strong esprit de corps based on common geographic ties. Friends, neighbors, and townsmen instinctively became tent mates and formed messes together. In the future, their letters home would frequently contain news of "the boys" from their home town: "Our Otto boys are mostly in the hospital." "All the boys from Leon are well except Del. He has the fever again." "All of the Olean boys are safe with the exception of Ben." "I am the only one from our Town with the company out of eighteen that came from our Town with it Having out winded all the rest." Until the day they died, the soldiers referred to themselves as boys no matter what their age.[9]

By mid-September, the Thirty-Second District had completed raising twenty companies, twelve from Chautauqua County and eight from Cattaraugus, along with an extra company of sharpshooters. On September 11, ten Chautauqua companies were mustered into the U.S. service as the 112th New York. The following day that regiment departed Camp Brown for the front, accompanied by the company of sharpshooters. Three days later, the two surplus Chautauqua companies reported to Colonel Rice for duty. They and the eight Cattaraugus companies formed the second regiment—the 154th New York. The Chautauqua minority consisted of Joseph Fay's lakeshore men of Company E and Company F, raised largely by Captain Thomas Donnelly and First Lieutenant John C. Griswold in four inland towns.

Here was a potential threat to esprit de corps in the newly formed 154th. The two Chautauqua companies must have been disappointed not to be included in the 112th Regiment. The *Jamestown Journal* reported that they "endeavored to get into the [112th] Regiment, but were not able to do so, only ten companies of infantry being allowed to march with the Regiment." So the Chautauquans were fated to form a distinct minority in the 154th. But members of Companies E and F are strangely silent about the matter in their surviving letters and diaries. Nor has any comment about the situation been found in the writings of Cattaraugus men. Indeed, the Chautauqua County men seem to have overcome any initial disappointment and blended quite seamlessly into the 154th Regiment alongside their Cattaraugus County neighbors. The ten companies were mustered in on September 24 and 25, the field and staff, noncommissioned staff, and line officers mustered the next day, and three days later the 154th New York left Camp Brown for Virginia.[10]

By the time of the formation and departure of the 112th and 154th Regiments, many soldiers from Cattaraugus and Chautauqua counties were already serving at the front. But those veterans for the most part were spread throughout many regiments, with a company or two here or there and individual soldiers widely dispersed. Exceptions were the 64th New York Infantry, which contained six Cattaraugus companies and was known as the Cattaraugus Regiment (a name the 154th would come to share), and the 9th New York Cavalry, containing eight companies wholly or partially raised in Chautauqua and Cattaraugus and referred to as the Westfield Cavalry. As recruiting began in the Thirty-Second District in the summer of 1862, a Washington correspondent of the *Cattaraugus Freeman* lamented the dispersal of the two counties' veteran soldiers and its ill effects on them: "Our citizens should take the utmost pains to have our brave boys enlist in the regiment to be formed in that district. Cattaraugus boys are scattered through no less than forty regiments; the same is true of Chautauqua. By the scattering process the credit of their heroism and valor in arms is lost to these counties; they are connected with commands that share not in their local pride, nor sympathize with them individually."[11]

In the 154th and 112th New York, Cattaraugus and Chautauqua sent their most representative regiments to the war. County pride consequently was a major factor in esprit de corps in the 154th—and in support for the regiment back home. County pride also placed a burden on the new soldiers: the expectation by the home folk that the regiment would uphold the honor of Cattaraugus. As the *Cattaraugus Freeman* put it after the 154th left for the front, "It is said to be one of the finest Regiments that has yet been mustered into the service from this State, and, judging from the character of both officers and men—many of whom we are personally acquainted—it will reflect additional luster upon the already well established fame of our Cattaraugus Volunteers." Reading those words when copies of the *Freeman* reached camp in Virginia, the men of the 154th understood that the actions of their regiment would be closely scrutinized back home.[12]

That the regiment faced the task with optimism and bravado was best expressed by three poetic entrepreneurs from its ranks. Second Lieutenant Philander W. Hubbard of Company K and Private Andrew G. Park and Sergeant James Byron Brown of Company B all wrote and published poems as cheap broadsides or stationery for sale to their fellow recruits at Camp Brown. Hubbard's verses, titled "The Friends I Left Behind Me," anticipated a joyful return to loved ones at home after crushing the rebellion. The lieutenant imagined himself blinded by smoke and dust on the battlefield, slaying and capturing Southern traitors while cannons roared and he shouted his battle cry—*"The Empire State!"* In "The Brave Soldier," Park was even more bloodthirsty, assuring the reader that the 154th had enlisted "to rush on the foeman, wherever they are, to drive, take and slaughter, and give utter despair," and, ultimately, to dig and fill Confederate graves.

The prolific and aptly named Byron Brown—"Brown the Poet" to his company comrades—published at least three of his compositions during the war. He issued two broadsides at Jamestown. The first, "The Soldier's Farewell," was an acrostic that spelled "Written in Camp J. M. Brown." In it Brown vowed to rush warlike to reclaim the seceded states, wielding steel (his bayonet) to "break down the traitor's form." Brown cleverly published his second poem in two versions—"Army Song of the Cattaraugus [or Chautauqua] Boys"—to enlarge his potential audience. It was "a Song for our own, for our brave noble boys, a greeting to those Cattaraugus employs." Once again Brown promised doom to the foe. There was no thought of defeat for his Cattaraugus boys:

> We'll stand by each other and fight till we fall,
> United in mind we'll strike terror to all;
> And turn not like cowards our backs on the foe,
> For the God of our battles shall guide as we go.[13]

More than community ties bound the Cattaraugus and Chautauqua boys of the 154th. In their ethnic and occupational backgrounds they had much in common. Family relationships were extensive among them. Taken together, those similarities created a fertile field for the growth of regimental esprit de corps.

Around the time of the regiment's muster-in, each company was required to fill in a descriptive book listing the name, age, height, complexion, eye and hair color, birthplace, occupation, and date and place of enlistment of every one of its enlisted men. Company G's book was improperly filled out, omitting the personal descriptions of the men. But the other nine company books, including some additional listings of subsequent recruits, provide descriptions of 892 members of the regiment. From that sample, a detailed demographic portrait of the 154th New York can be drawn.

The men were overwhelmingly native-born Americans, primarily of British descent, the sons and grandsons of pioneer settlers of Cattaraugus and

Chautauqua counties. Western New York was well settled by the time of the Civil War; the 1860 population of Cattaraugus County was 43,886, Chautauqua counted 58,422. Virtually all of that population had immigrated to the counties in the previous six decades, most of it moving westward from New England, with many families sojourning in central New York State for a generation or two.[14]

Almost half of the men of the 154th New York, 431 of them (roughly 48 percent), were natives of Cattaraugus or Chautauqua County. They brought into the regiment a truly innate county pride. About 28 percent (253 men) were born elsewhere in New York, making more than three-quarters of the 154th natives of the Empire State. Approximately 12 percent of the men were born in other states, including Connecticut, 5; Illinois, 1; Maine, 4; Massachusetts, 5; Michigan, 3; New Hampshire, 1; New Jersey, 1; Ohio, 7; Rhode Island, 1; Vermont, 23; and Pennsylvania, 54 (Cattaraugus and Chautauqua's southern neighbor provided more than half of all such recruits). All were born in the northern states but one, Private James W. Randolph of Company A, a native of Louisiana. The birthplaces of four men were not listed.[15]

About one-quarter of the soldiers of the Union armies were foreign-born. Fewer were found in the 154th; only about 11 percent of the regiment's members were born in other countries. Of them, more than half came from either Ireland (28) or Germany (27). The others were natives of England (11); Europe (1); France (5); Canada (9); Holland (1); Prussia (1); Scotland (4); Sweden (2); and Wales (9). The foreign-born were generally scattered throughout the regiment, their company affiliation depending on where they had enlisted. The group of nine native Welshmen were the exception. Recruited by one of their number, William Charles, from a thriving Welsh community centered in the town of Freedom, they somehow found themselves assigned to Company F. In that Chautauqua company they formed both an ethnic minority and a Cattaraugus County minority. In his frequent letters to his wife, Charles often relayed news of the "Welsh boys."[16]

Although immigrant soldiers sometimes sought the companionship of their native countrymen, there is no evidence that they closed themselves off from their American-born comrades. Indeed, the letters of William Charles and other foreign-born soldiers indicate that the process of assimilation, already well under way in their previous civilian life, was if anything accelerated by their army service. One of the few times the Welshmen socialized en masse was on Christmas Day 1862, when they made and enjoyed a special dinner together. Charles described it as an unusual occurrence: "In the morning I spoke to the Boys (that is the Welsh Boys), to know if we could not have a dinner all to gether for once," he informed his wife. "They all said *we could*."[17]

Welsh, British, Irish, German—arrayed in line, the 154th Regiment presented a sea of white faces. But a closer look revealed a few men of color. Three privates of Company B, Ransom Russell, Abraham Wright, and Ora Wright, were mulattoes. Russell was heartily disliked by some officers and men, primarily (it seems) because he was argumentative, pugnacious, insubordinate, and a general disturbance in the company—not because he was part black. Abraham Wright, on the other hand, was described by his white company comrade and fellow prisoner of war Thomas R. Aldrich as a "No. 1 fellow," and "one of the best fellows I ever saw." From the little evidence available, it would seem the mulattoes of the 154th were judged on their character, not their skin color.[18]

Nothing is known about how Private Jacob Winney was treated by his comrades of Company K. Winney was the only known Native American to serve in the 154th—a Mohawk from the Six Nations Reserve in Canada who had married a Seneca and was living on one of the two large Seneca reservations in Cattaraugus County when he enlisted. Soon after arriving in Virginia, Winney injured himself by falling into a deep ditch during a night march. The resulting disability led to his discharge less than three months after his muster-in. Only one passing reference to Winney survives in a comrade's letter; it makes no mention of his ethnicity.[19]

The ethnic and racial makeup of the 154th New York was only minimally diverse. The vast majority of the men were of British ancestry and natives of the state they now served. Racially the regiment was virtually monolithic. Ethnic differences would not hinder esprit de corps in the 154th.

About 48 percent of the soldiers in the Union army as a whole were farmers when they enlisted. In the 154th New York, 74 percent of the men (658) were farmers. Numbers of men in other occupations included thirty-four lumbermen; thirty-three mechanics; twenty-four laborers; fifteen carpenters; thirteen blacksmiths; ten joiners; eight clerks; eight shoemakers; seven masons; six sailors; five wagon makers; four painters; four saddlers; four students; three harness makers; two each of merchants, cabinet makers, farriers, millers, millwrights, physicians, printers, shingle makers, and teachers; and one each of the following: artist, boatman, brewer, butcher, carpenter and joiner, carriage maker, clergyman, cooper, dealer, dentist, fisherman, hotel keeper, machinist, medical student, musician, physician and surgeon, porter, sawyer, shingle weaver, stonecutter, stove maker, tailor, teamster, telegraph operator, theological student, and tobacconist. Eleven men's occupations were not listed.[20]

Historian Earl Hess, who cited the 154th as atypical because of its high proportion of farmers, argued that the work habits of the many manual laborers in the Union army enabled them to cope with the dangers of battle. According to Hess, phlegmatic rural workers approached their duties as soldiers in much the same fashion that they regarded their tasks on the farm—with steady certainty about what had to be done, with the necessary determination and endurance to finish the assigned job, and without giving the whole dangerous business undue worrisome thought. The 154th New York's many farmers also were used to working together, as they had in communal logging and husking bees back home. Common work habits were just what was needed to help mold an efficient regiment. With its heavy concentration of farmers, the 154th was well equipped to tackle the chores of military life.[21]

The average age of the 154th's volunteers was 25.8, exactly the same as the Union army at large. But that figure was skewed by an unknown number of men who lied about their ages to enlist. At least thirty-one underage boys swore they were over eighteen years old in order to enroll in the regiment. More than half of them were seventeen; some of them observed their eighteenth birthdays within a month or two after mustering in. There was a substantial number of sixteen-year-olds. Three fifteen-year-old members of the 154th have been documented. Privates Philip Mason and Devillo Wheeler of Company I both turned sixteen soon after the regiment reached Virginia. Mason was still with the 154th at its muster-out in 1865. Wheeler was captured at Gettysburg and apparently died as a prisoner of war. Private Charles W. McKay of Company C, born in Cattaraugus County on January 25, 1847, was the youngest known member of the regiment. The fifteen-year-old flourished as a soldier. By the end of the war McKay was a sergeant, and in the postwar years he was awarded a Medal of Honor for heroism in the battle at Dug Gap, on Rocky Face Ridge, Georgia.[22]

At the other end of the scale were at least twenty men who prevaricated by claiming they were younger than forty-five, the regulation maximum age. Among them was the Indian, Jacob Winney, who turned fifty-four sometime in 1862. Like Winney, most of the senior soldiers were eventually discharged for disability. The oldest documented member of the 154th was a tough old native Irishman, Private Barney McAvoy of Company G, who was about sixty-six years of age when he enlisted. According to company comrades, McAvoy dyed his hair as part of his subterfuge. Despite his advanced years, McAvoy stuck with the regiment and fought at Chancellorsville and Gettysburg before he was hospitalized with rheumatism and discharged in Tennessee in February 1864.[23]

Kinship was common among the soldiers of the 154th. At least fifty-eight pairs or trios of brothers, totaling 126 men, have been documented as serving in the regiment. Brothers therefore formed more than 11 percent of the 1,065 total membership; in other words, one out of every ten men was brother to another member of the 154th. Very likely there were more. How many sets of cousins, uncles and nephews, brothers-in-law, and fathers- and sons-in-law were in the regiment's ranks is unknown, but indications are they were plentiful. (Many of the men also had brothers and other relatives serving in other regiments.) Loyalty among the members of the 154th must have been strongly bolstered by the widespread family ties.[24]

Brothers and other relatives often were parted by death. Five pairs of brothers lost their lives—imagine the heartbreak of those losses in their Cattaraugus and Chautauqua County homes. Austin and Henry A. Munger enlisted together in their home town of Arkwright, Chautauqua County, and were mustered in as privates of Company F. After less than two months in the service, Austin died of typhoid fever at a hospital in Alexandria, Virginia. It fell to Lieutenant John Griswold to tell the victim's brother. "The news of Austins death fel with crushing weight upon Henry," Griswold wrote. "The first burst of grief & afterwards his silent sorrow is sad to behold." About a year and a half later, Henry was shot through the neck at the Battle of Dug Gap. He died at an Indiana hospital in January 1865.[25]

Eight pairs of fathers and sons served in the 154th: Benjamin and Levant F. Barber; Asa and Calvin Brainard; Ebenezer M. and Charles H. Cooley; Walter and Norman H. Grey; Henry and Norman H. Hugaboom; Nathan and Ira L. Keech; Barzilla and Alva C. Merrill; and George Williams and George Jr. To them could be added Amos Pettit and his sons Joshua R. and George W. Pettit, although father Amos, as the 154th's first sutler, was not an official member of the regiment. Like the many brothers and other relatives, the filial pairs often met with tragedy. Ebenezer Cooley lost his son Charles to typhoid fever less than two months after they mustered in. Norman Grey lost his father, Walter, to disease in September 1863. When Benjamin and Levant Barber enlisted together as privates in Company I, both lied about their ages. Benjamin actually was fifty; Levant sixteen. According to William Charles, the elder Barber "could not let *his boy* go with out his going with him So they both came, and they were most always *together*." When Levant succumbed to typhoid fever at the regimental hospital near Falmouth, Virginia, in January 1863, the empathetic Charles wrote of Benjamin, "Oh dear who can tell the grieff and the sorrows of that poor old man. Indeed I am not able to look at him without shedding a tear and uttering a prayer to that Being who alone can comfort him."[26]

Barzilla Merrill, a forty-four-year-old farmer from the Cattaraugus County town of Dayton, followed his seventeen-year-old son Alva C. in enlisting as a private of Company K. On bidding her husband and eldest son good-bye, Ruba Cole Merrill was left behind on the family's farm to care for a crippled daughter and a younger son. Barzilla and Alva kept Ruba informed of their activities in voluminous letters, recording the various camps occupied by the regiment and the marches it made through the Virginia countryside. For seven months, father and son led a mostly placid but rugged life, accustoming themselves to army routine. They tented apart, each choosing messmates of their own age group. But father and son kept a watchful and loving eye on each other. Barzilla wrote proudly to Ruba that Alva's strength of character was uncorrupted by the rough elements common to camp. Alva reported with satisfaction that his father stood up well to the hardships of army life.

On the eve of another march, April 12, 1863, both sent letters home to Ruba. "We shall not (if we march) . . . have any chance to mail any letters," Alva informed his mother, "so you kneed not think it strange if you do not hear from us in quite a spell." Barzilla told his wife he placed his trust in God, "that things will be so arranged that we as a family may have the privileg of reuniting under the paterna[l] roof I look for this time to come and I expect it and further some times I feel that I have an evidence of it." He added one more line: "One thing I can say thy will o God be done."[27]

They were the last words Ruba received from her loved ones. Father and son marched with the regiment to a Rappahannock River ford, where for two weeks they picketed the shoreline and peered at enemy pickets on the far bank. Then one evening the 154th was abruptly loaded aboard pontoon boats to spearhead a crossing of the river. For the first time, Barzilla and Alva felt the sensation of being under fire, but the hasty shots fired by a few fleeing Confederates splashed harmlessly into the river. For the next several days the march carried the men into the heart of a dense forest, where they finally took position in a clearing near an old tavern.

That the enemy was near was evident by the distant rumble of artillery and musketry, but the regiment was posted on the army's extreme flank and seemed to be well out of harm's way. Nevertheless, the men's nervous anticipation grew as rumors of a Confederate thrust toward their position was met with indifference and inaction by their generals. By late afternoon of May 2, however, it appeared another day had passed safely. Barzilla and Alva and the others began cooking their suppers and preparing for the night's sleep. Suddenly the distant forest erupted with a mighty thunderclap of gunfire, accompanied by the piercing wail of the rebel yell.

As the massive Confederate attack approached, the regiment formed in a shallow rifle pit and the men watched with astonishment as a tangled mass of Union fugitives fled past their position into the woods to their rear. Then came the enemy, filling the fields as far as the eye could see, inexorably driving everything from their path. Barzilla and Alva fired their muskets with the rest of the regiment. The Confederates staggered, then came on again, sweeping past the 154th's flank and nearing the breastwork. An order to retreat was shouted. As the soldiers raced for the woods behind them, many fell. A shot hit Barzilla in the shoulder, wounding him slightly. Moments later another bullet struck him in the head and he fell dead.

Alva and the other survivors scrambled though the woods, the enemy in hot pursuit. After a harrowing night, young Merrill and a small group of other comrades, having separated from the regiment during the chaotic retreat, fell in with other Union units. That morning, Alva shared some coffee with Private Marcellus Darling of his company. "As it was making it began to boil over," Darling later recalled. "I ran to take it off the fire, when behold, the rebel line was advancing on us, and leaving the coffee we fell into line, began firing, and so kept up the hot fight till nearly noon. . . . Merrill was killed by my side. . . . With terrible destruction from rebel shell men lay dead and wounded all about us."[28]

About a month after the 154th New York was shattered at Chancellorsville, Ruba Merrill received a letter from the regiment's assistant surgeon, Corydon C. Rugg, and read these searing words: "I am compelled to furnish you with the sad and to you painful knowledge of the death of both your Husband and Son. . . . Their remains cannot be obtained We were not allowed the privilege of burying our dead. . . . You might as well look for a gold dollar in the sea as to try to find either of them."[29]

CHAPTER 2

Lines of Communication

A pall, never to be lifted, fell over the Merrill homestead in Dayton on the news of the killing of Barzilla and Alva. Over the years of the war, many homes in Cattaraugus and Chautauqua would plunge into mourning on receiving similar tidings of death from the 154th Regiment. Many families in the two counties would anxiously await word from their menfolk after another great battle was fought. Any word from loved ones at the front, at any time, was avidly sought—to learn that a father or brother or cousin was alive and well and still with the regiment. For their part, the soldiers of the 154th New York would typically take every opportunity they were offered to assure the home folk of their well-being—or to let them know they had been wounded, or were sick, or were otherwise broken down.

A great tide of communication flowed back and forth between the front and home. In writing to their friends and families, the soldiers referred to themselves in both the first person singular and first person plural. I am, I was, I will, wrote the soldiers about their individual health, humor, and hopes. We are, we were, we will, they wrote about the activities of their regiment—the new collective identity they had all assumed on mustering in. More often than not, what they had to relate was written in the plural. Infused with esprit de corps, an individual's persona yielded to regimental allegiance.

Communication between soldiers and loved ones took many forms. A vast correspondence in letters was the chief lifeline that tied front and home together. A lesser but still important traffic in goods, artifacts, and souvenirs was mailed and expressed back and forth in great numbers. Photographs sent to and from the front provided loved ones with a tangible and precious visual image of their distant beloved. An enormous amount of money was exchanged, often after aggravating waits. Those long-distance transactions were occasionally supplemented by in-person contacts, as soldiers returned home and home folk visited the front.

Members of the 154th went to war as representatives of their home towns and counties. Constant contact between the soldiers and their home folk—when the military situation allowed it—kept the regiment's home ties knit tightly.

"You ought to see the excitement that it creates when the mail comes into camp," Private James D. Emmons of Company F wrote to his sister from the 154th New York's camp near Fairfax Court House a few weeks after the regiment reached the Virginia front. "It generally comes in about breakfast time they all leave their meals until they have read their letters." Writing a day later, Private Charles W. Abell of Company E told his "Dear Dear Mother," "You do not know with what eagerness I listen to the names as they are read hoping that every mail will bring news from some one to me from home and you never can know how much good it did me to get that first letter that you wrote." At the regiment's 1862–1863 winter camp near Stafford Court House, Virginia, First Sergeant George A. Taylor of Company F visited Chaplain Henry D. Lowing, who acted as the regimental postmaster, after the daily 8 P.M. roll call to pick up his company's mail. "There are always more or less of the company that will rush to my tent at this time," Taylor reported, "and will stay talking and reading letters until 'Tapps' (signal to put out lights) and as long after as we will keep open doors."[1]

Perhaps nothing satisfied the soldiers more than receiving letters. Over and over, from muster-in to muster-out, they expressed their pleasure at getting mail. "Nothing makes a soldier feel better than to hear from the loved ones at home," Private Marion Plumb of Company D wrote to his wife from Virginia in 1862, adding that he had read her latest letter twenty times. "A letter is the greatest comfort that a soldier has," Private John Dicher of Company B wrote from Alabama to a girlfriend in 1863. "No one but a soldier can fully appreciate a letter from home," First Sergeant Richard J. McCadden of Company G informed his mother and brother a month later. "You dont know how cheering it is to get a letter on the march or on the battlefield when we are tired and fatigued," Corporal Marcellus Darling of Company K wrote to his family from a Georgia battlefield in 1864. "Your letters are so full of interest better than eny thing else that you can bestow uppon me," Private Jesse D. Campbell of Company D told his home folk from Atlanta in 1864. "It does a soldier good to have a letter from old Cattaraugus," Private John Langhans of Company H informed his brother two weeks later.[2]

Hundreds of miles of separation could seemingly disappear when a soldier read a letter from home. Sitting by the fireplace in his winter hut, reading by candlelight the first letter he had received from his mother, Ruba, in more than a month, Alva Merrill declared, "I almost forgot I was a soldier for a few minutes." Reading a "truly refreshing" letter from his wife, Susan, Lieutenant John Griswold wished, "If I could only see your eyes snap the scene would be life like and exilerating." Sergeant Edgar Shannon of Company B observed that a letter from his girlfriend, Francelia Hunt, was just "a little paper with a few marks upon it yet what a power it possesses, it takes me back again to those happy times which we passed together. again I am with you in your room listening to the music of the melodean or your voice." To Private Emory Sweetland of Company B, disturbed by the "wicked companions" that surrounded him, his wife's letters were "the only visible link that binds me to virtue, honor, home & loved ones." He added, "Write often darling, write long." "It is a great source of gratification to be enabled to communicate with those we love when we cannot enjoy their presence," George Taylor assured his wife. He continued, "It makes the time seem shorter and the distance between us less to be enabled to sit down and read a few lines written by a loved hand."[3]

Hospitalized in the parole camp at Annapolis, Maryland, after his capture at Chancellorsville, Private Charles F. Allen of Company B was moved to a burst of grandiloquence on receiving a letter from his mother:

> O Mother you dont know how much good it does me to receive a letter from home stating that all is well. It relieves the mind of its anxiety & is A greater joy, A greater pleasure, Tis more welcome than a costly treasure. Money the Idol of mankind cannot purchase a prize valued so high. With what plesure I read your letter once twice & yet again. It seemed as I read as if you were talking to me. When I closed a tear would come forth & trickle down my cheek. I felt like thanking god that things at Home are as well as they are.[4]

Private Horace H. Howlett of Company K turned to verse to express his appreciation of his sister's letters:

> Home with all its joys is present
> when those letters come from thee

household faces bright and plesent
look with sunny smiles on me.[5]

Disappointment at not receiving letters could be bitter. Less than two weeks after arriving in Virginia, Private Ira Wood of Company A lamented to his wife, "O that I could get one Word from you I have rote 4 or 5 leters to you and got none How do you think I feel when I rite the tears fall from my eyes." Writing from a Washington hospital after suffering three wounds at Chancellorsville, Corporal Thomas R. Aldrich of Company B wrote to his mother, "I have not got a letter from any one yet the rest of the boys have got two or three why cant you write it makes me mad to think I cant get a letter under four or five weeks after writing." William Charles was jealous of his Company F comrade and fellow Welshman Corporal William E. Jones about the frequency of letters sent from their respective fathers. "Please tell Father that I should [like] to have a letter from him," Charles requested his wife. "Billy Jones' father writes to him very often But I never get a letter from my father just as if I had no *father on earth*." Henry Van Aernam, the 154th's surgeon, related a distressing incident to his wife: "I was sorely disappointed tonight in not receiving a letter from you. I had looked for it so anxiously and so long that I could hardly believe our mail boy when he told me there was nothing for me tonight. I thought he was mistaken and had him look the mail over again and with a little ill concealed petulance he announced the result of the search 'I told you there was nothing.' I turned away disappointed and heartsick."[6]

Edgar Shannon inadvertently expressed regimental esprit de corps when he received a letter from Francelia Hunt after a long lapse: "I was pleased to get a letter for it has been so long since I had had one that I began to think that I had not got a friend outside of the 154th regiment."[7]

The men did not hesitate to voice complaints about the infrequency or brevity of their correspondents. "It has been 3 weeks since I have heard from home," griped Richard McCadden to his brother. "I should think you must write as often as I can." Marcellus Darling had a suggestion for his parents regarding a younger brother: "Take him by the coat collar and tell him you will whip him if he does not write to me and see what effect that will have." "I am very impashent wateing for a letter from you," Private James D. Quilliam of Company E complained to his wife. "I do not see why i do not get more letters i sent you five or six this month and have recieved but two which is it you or the post ofis is in fault i dont know." On another occasion, Quilliam groused about the shortness of her letters. "I dont like the stile of your half sheat letters," he wrote. "It seems to bad to send just a half a sheat more than 1000 milds when you can send 3 or 4 sheats just as well."[8]

Back in Cattaraugus and Chautauqua counties, mail from soldiers caused similar feelings of joy and anxiety. "How I should like to come into your tent and see you and talk with you about old times," Martha James wrote to her boyfriend, Private Samuel R. Williams, one of the Welsh boys of Company F. "Well I cant do that but I can talk with you through the pen and ink and paper." Months later, Martha expressed concern that Samuel had not received two of her letters. "I am afraid that some of the boys takes them out and keep them as I cant guess what comes of them." In reply, Samuel wrote, "I dont think that eney of the Boys has taken eney of the letters for i hav bin hear most all time when the male came in so i think they have stopt on the rode somewhare."[9]

"You need not think that I am going to stop writing because I don't hear from you," Francelia Hunt assured Edgar Shannon. "I am going to write all the more. If you were not a Soldier I hardly think I should do this way," she teased. "I presume I should write once or twice a *year*." Other women were less composed when mail failed to arrive from their loved ones. "I dont know why you dont write oftener," Ann Eliza Jane Green wrote in 1864 to her husband, Private Stephen R. Green of Company E. "You was good about writing when you first went to the army but you neglect me now in stead of to letters a weak one letter in tow weaks. . . . I get so lonesum and uneasy if i dont here every weak you no where i am but i dont know whare you are i think you had aut to be more perticeler about writing."[10]

Writing to her husband, John, from their home in Arkwright, Chautauqua County, Susan Griswold expressed a conflict: she was uneasy not to hear from him, yet she understood his inability to write regularly. Unbeknownst to her, Griswold had been wounded and captured at Chancellorsville just three days before she composed her letter:

> If you knew how anxious I am to hear from you you would drop a few
> lines to me if it was posable but I do not know as it is when you are
> on the moove then is the time that I feel the most anxiety about you

to think you are in battle & then not to hear from you it seames some of the time I can not endure it but I suppose it is imposable for you to send letters at all times so I lay no blame to you knowing you will remember us as often as you can.[11]

Mary Jane Chittenden of Yorkshire, Cattaraugus County, wife of Private William F. Chittenden of Company D, gently prodded her husband to follow the example of his townsman and company comrade, Private George W. Bailey, and write more often: "Mrs Bailey gets letters oftener than I do & I write almost two to her one I send one nearly every mail do not think me complaining but your being in danger makes me far more anxious about you." "You complained of not getting my letters often enough," Chittenden responded. "I do not know as you get them all or as I write as many as Mr Bailey but I think he has no stronger regards for his family than your humble servant W. F. C." Months later, Mary Chittenden was feeling fortunate compared to other Yorkshire soldiers' wives. "Some of the women in this neighborhood do not hear from their Husbands oftener than once a week or fortnight," she informed William. "I should almost go wild if I could not hear from you oftener."[12]

Sometimes soldiers intended their letters to be shared by loved ones with extended family and friends; other times they wrote confidentially. Marcellus Darling addressed a letter to "Dear parents, brothers, sisters, comrades, friends, School mates, Sweet hearts, neighbors and gentlemen and ladies." But Barzilla Merrill notified his wife, Ruba, "Some time I will write so that you may let the neighbors read it and some times it wont do read first your self and see." Like other married couples, the Merrills occasionally tucked into their regular missives a separate slip of paper containing "choice news." This consisted of gossip and racy innuendoes—"matters that we would not talk about in company," as Barzilla defined it. "I dont know but you think that I write improper or impolite," he admitted to Ruba about such private passages, "but I write about as I hapen to feel when I am writing."[13]

Mary Chittenden assured William that their correspondence was private. His parents had opened a letter addressed to her, but they "soon found out that would not answer." She informed her husband, "I have told all the folks yours & mine that Williams letters must never be opened by no one but me if this is wrong so let it be I will not allow it at any rate so do not fear to write to me just what you wish & do tell me what ails you and how you are do not refuse me this."[14]

Other soldiers' letters, however, were written expressly to the public at large as correspondence to the dozen or so newspapers published in Cattaraugus and Chautauqua counties. (Unfortunately, few runs of those papers survive.) Sometimes such letters contained the opinions of the writer on the progress of the war, or political issues, or other abstract matters. More often, however, they were straightforward chronicles of the doings of the regiment. As such, they were an expression of esprit de corps, as Second Lieutenant Alanson Crosby of Company A indicated in the inaugural letter of a series he sent to the *Cattaraugus Freeman*: "It is now nearly a month since the 154th Regiment left Jamestown for the seat of war, and no account of its progress has yet been publicly given to the friends of the brave boys who compose it. As almost every family in your vicinity has a representative here, it may be of interest to some of your readers to know how we reached our destination, and some of the incidents connected with our Journey, and our soldier-life in the sunny land of Dixie."[15]

Several other members of the regiment became regular newspaper correspondents. Corporal Joel M. Bouton of Company C, a former typesetter for the *Olean Times*, wrote regularly to that paper and one in Cuba, New York. During the Atlanta campaign, Major Lewis D. Warner reported weekly on the 154th's activities for the *Olean Times*. Letters to home newspapers were welcome even if late. Prefacing a two-month-old letter describing the Chattanooga and Knoxville campaigns, the editor of the *Fredonia Censor* wrote, "The following letter, written by Milon J. Griswold, a member of the 154th, to his relatives in Arkwright . . . although written some time since, will still prove of interest to all the friends of our gallant boys in the field." Sometimes, however, a soldier's letter to a newspaper never saw print. When a letter he sent to the *Cattaraugus Freeman* failed to appear, Emory Sweetland speculated, "Maybe like many Soldiers letters it never reached its destination. but far more likely the editor did not consider it worthy of a place in his paper."[16]

Writing a letter was not always the simple matter it might seem. "I can tell you that it is not a very pleasant duty for one to write here with all the inconveniences we have to put up with," Musician Thaddeus L. Reynolds of Company I informed his family, citing the regiment's frequent moves. When they did settle in camp, the men had to improvise their writing desks. "You would smile seeing me here writing," George Taylor told his wife, "sitting on my wool blanket on one stone big as a wagon box and writing on my rubber blanket folded on another great stone in front of me just high enough, another behind me is just right to lean against." Barzilla Merrill described his methods to Ruba: "I set flat on my bottom on the ground in the shade of a tree with my Knapsack on my lap which serves for a table sometimes I write in the evening in my tent in the same way and my gun bayonet stuck in the ground which serves for a candle stick and so the thing goes." Straining to see what he was doing, Private Eason W. Bull of Company D wrote to his brother, "It is 11 o'clock and I am writing this by moonlight as I believe you will know when you try to read this."[17]

Other hindrances frustrated writers. Horseplay by comrades disrupted concentration and spilled bottles of ink. Pens leaked great blots. Ink froze during cold weather. Soldiers ran short of writing supplies. Alva Merrill asked Ruba to send him the ingredients (extract of logwood and a potash compound) to mix with water to make ink. First Sergeant Francis Strickland of Company I sent his wife a letter written on cartridge paper. And over and over and over again, the soldiers asked the home folk to send them stamps. Soldiers' letters could go through the mail without a stamp, but the recipient had to pay the postage and the soldiers wanted to spare their correspondents that trouble.[18]

Self-consciousness about their limitations as writers—especially as spellers—gave some men pause. "The reason I have not writen before is that I am ashame to write for I cant spell nor write so enney one can read it," Private Lyman Wilber of Company G explained to his uncle and aunt, "but I thought that I would write and if you can't read it jist send it back and I will read it for you." James Quilliam insulted his wife while admitting his own shortcomings in orthography. "I am sory if I make as bad work spelling as you do for i can ask men that knowes how to spell any hard word and it is neglect if i spell bad." Sergeant Amos Humiston of Company C urged his wife to overlook their mutual deficiencies as writers. "Thare is one thing I want you to stop," he told her, "that is finding so mutch fault with your letters if they please me it nead not trouble you if you do not I shal think that you are making fun of mine we will call it an even thing and make no apologies."[19]

Sometimes the press of duties or active military operations prevented the soldiers from writing. Responding to a complaint from his wife, Susan, John Griswold explained, "Thare are a hundred things continually arising to hinder one from writing at any time he would wish but I will try to keep even with you if I can." In North Carolina in 1865, the 154th was ordered to go out foraging with its brigade. "I wanted to write to you," Private Levi D. Bryant reported to his wife, "& so I went up to the doctor & got excused from going on account of rumatism in Left Leg. So you get this Letter By [that] means. you said I must write Longer Letters to you," he added. "If my time was my own I could."[20]

Much of the time, though, the men had plenty of opportunity to write. "A Soldier might just as well write one time as another," Quartermaster Sergeant Newton A. Chaffee informed a friend. The only thing to stop him was laziness. "As I have plenty of time that I have nothing to do," admitted Stephen Green, "I write as mutch to pass off a little time as anything for I have no news to write." Few of the soldiers would have agreed with Private Wilber Moore of Company H, who announced to his mother, "I hate to write I do." Most of them kept to a schedule like that of Surgeon Van Aernam: "I have always written home at *least* twice a week ever since I left home either sick or well and have generally done so every other day." In an effort to keep track of their extensive correspondence, some husbands and wives took to numbering their letters.[21]

On the eve of a march, Corporal Newell Burch of Company E recorded that he "consigned 40 or 50 letters to the flames to day." Burning accumulated letters was a common practice among the soldiers, albeit a regretted one. "I am sorry but I could not carry them," Barzilla Merrill wrote to Ruba after destroying her letters. After Corporal John N. Porter of Company H was captured at Gettysburg, his tent mate Wilber Moore wrote to Porter's sister, "I have no place to keep his letters and I take the liberty [of] open[ing] them before the Co. and burning them it is the way we have had to serve all the boys who were taken." Some men, however, refused to part with loved ones' letters and went to the expense of sending them home to be preserved. "I thought som of burning them but i did not like to do so for i thought they mint be some hurt in it," Samuel Williams confessed to Martha James. "I think that i will send som of them back to you before long." William Chittenden, finding his wife Mary's letters were "getting quite bulky for my blouse pocket," sent them home with a friend who was visiting the front. "I do not burn them as many do," he wrote, "and they might be lost."[22]

Soldiers demonstrated esprit de corps when they shared mail, forwarded mail, and wrote mail for their comrades. When Private Henry Cunningham of Company K offered a cousin the opportunity to add a postscript to a letter to Cunningham's parents, the fellow "took my pen and commenced scribbling as fast as possible." When he was sent from the regiment to a Washington hospital, William Chittenden assured Mary that "Nat will take care of what letters goes to the Regt and send them to me as soon as he knows where I am." And so Private Nathaniel S. Brown did, forwarding letters from camp to his brother-in-law Chittenden and other hospitalized Company D comrades. Horace Howlett wrote to the wife of a company comrade, Private George W. Newcomb, after the Battle of Chancellorsville to let her know Newcomb had survived "one of the almightes fights that was ever hird of." Newcomb "sent by George Bailey to have me write a few lines and let you know he was all right," Howlett informed Ellen Newcomb. Esprit de corps insured that Howlett would fulfill the request.[23]

"The Boys here gets most every thing you can think of by mail," wrote William Charles, "from love letters to a pair of Boots—and Stockings hankerchiefs Hats, Suspenders *and so fourth* &c." Repeating a request to his sister to send him a pair of boots, John Porter kidded, "You will find out there is as much inconvenience in having relation in the army as there is Honor." But the home folk were happy to oblige the requests of their soldier boys, and a great traffic of goods flowed from Cattaraugus and Chautauqua to the front.[24]

The men asked for stamps, stationery, newspapers, and diaries. They asked for thread and shoemaking tools and coffee pots and frying pans. They asked for satchels and combs. They asked for money. They asked for medicine. One soldier requested a hydropathic diarrhea treatment system. They asked for clothing: gloves, boots, shirts, suspenders, and socks ("Uncle Sam's socks don't last more than one day," Eason Bull observed). And they asked for food, any taste of home to break the monotony of hardtack, salt pork, and coffee: cakes, maple sugar, pies, peppers, catsup, crackers, cheese, dried fruit, doughnuts, butter, tea, and chewing gum.[25]

To guide their loved ones, the soldiers made specific lists of wanted goods and offered detailed packing, addressing, and shipping instructions. "Do up the hat in some papers," John Griswold ordered his wife, Susan, "put the gloves & suspenders inside of it & fill it up with dried apples so it will keep its place and then fill in around it with dried apples doughnuts or anything that will not stain or injure the hat." Second Lieutenant Salmon W. Beardsley of Company K, after requesting some items from his wife, directed her to "box them up in a small strong box and send them on having the Express Agent be sure to have them forwarded to the nearest Express office direct to Lieut. S. W. Beardley Co K 154th Regt. N. Y. Vols Washington DC to be forwarded by Express to Aquiai Landing you will pay the Express charges and take a bill of the box which you will forward to me by letter and that you will see [will] be my order for [picking up] the box."[26]

Tent mates and townsmen encouraged their families to pack up a box together. "Monroe [Young] and I have concluded to have each a few things sent from home," George Taylor informed his wife, "and you can send them in one Box and it will not cost any more scarcely for both than it would for one." When petty home squabbles prevented such arrangements from being made, the soldiers expressed their displeasure. A box that some of the Welsh boys received "was most likely intended as a *private consern*," William Charles noted to his wife, but the senders "did very wrong in not letting you and Mrs or Mr John Jones sending some little something to those they love so well." Charles later informed his wife that one of the Welsh boys was "very much ashamed that those silly women acted so foolish about that box."[27]

Soldiers greeted the arrival of a long-anticipated box with elation. John Griswold vividly described the excitement generated by the receipt of a box sent from Chautauqua County to the members of Company F at the 1863–1864 winter camp at Lookout Valley, Tennessee:

> As soon as it was landed here it was surrounded and every word of the mark read and reread the No. weight and freight examined and criticized the box heafted and one particular hemlock board in the cover was decided to have come from Arkwright. after they had sufficiently examined the box . . . I directed Sargent [Homer A.] Ames to make a hole in it and ascertain what was inside. with hatchet in hand he made them fall back in [a] ring and proceeded to nock of the cover, and now

comes a general overhauling article after article is draged from its resting place untill the bottom of the box is reached, and every thing exposed to view I then directed that the contents be divided as near as
equal as could conveniently be between the diferent bunks of the
company according to the No. of inmates, the Company being small
it gave to all quite a taste of the luxuries of home, which after a long
period of living on army rations is quite refreshing the Company appreciate this act of friendship and good will on the part of the donors
and desire to express to them their genuine and hearty thanks for
their generous donations and kind regards for our welfare.[28]

John's nephew Milon Griswold sent a formal letter of thanks for the box
on behalf of the company, to be published in Chautauqua newspapers. He
expressed the men's pride as representatives of "our kind friends at home in
old Chautauqua . . . who will ever be remembered by the soldiers of our little
company as friends of the Union and its liberties, and who will help to sustain the star spangled banner that it may float in triumph over all secession-
ism at last." Griswold assured the home folk, "Your names will be
remembered by us after 'this cruel War is over.' "[29]

When a box of clothing and hospital supplies arrived at the Lookout Valley camp from the Ladies Aid Society of East Randolph, Cattaraugus County,
Colonel Patrick Henry Jones replied on behalf of his command and voiced
the emotional as well as physical comfort such gifts granted: "The Regiment
desires to present to yourselves and the patriotic society which you represent
its sincerest thanks, and through me, to express its gratitude for your kindly
remembrance. . . . It is not material aid alone that is required to nerve the
Soldiers of the Republic. Your gift implies much more and we fully appreciate the tender spirit of the donors and assure you that the husbands, brothers, & friends of the Ladies Aid Society, treasure your good opinion, now and
hereafter, as one of its chiefest rewards, and will merit its continuance."[30]

Occasionally a box brought disappointment. Shipping times could take a
month or more, and if the senders had included perishable foodstuffs, the
results could be disastrous. One of the Welsh boys, Corporal William M.
Davis, received a box at Lookout Valley that had been five weeks on the road.
"Every thing in it was nearly spoiled . . . matted together with *mould*," reported William Charles, including "a Boiled chicken . . . in an *awful* state of

decomposition." Davis and Charles were "very much disapointed" that they "could [not] get a mouthful of any thing that *tasted good.*" James Emmons became angry with his company comrade Private Albert H. Goulding, who "knew that I expected a box and he was out there waiting and waching for the box and took it to the hospital and opened it and took all the sugar and the mince pie the most of the cheas and som berries." A couple of days later Goulding told Emmons his box had arrived, whereupon Emmons discovered the theft and Goulding received a rebuke. Marcellus Darling complained that the postmaster in his home town of Leon overcharged for items sent to soldiers and asked his family to use another post office. "I will not humor him to let him charge what he pleases," Darling wrote. "It makes me mad to think that he will try to nig a Soldier so."[31]

Goods were sent home as well. Members of the 154th shipped handicrafts, mineral and botanical specimens, revolvers, knives, hardtack, Confederate money, maps, and unneeded blankets and coats, particularly dress coats. Some of the items, such as souvenir walking sticks cut from Lookout Mountain, were commemorative in nature. Such mementos of the regiment's service were tangible symbols of esprit de corps. From Savannah, Emory Sweetland sent his wife "some articles from different battle fields, all labeled." Some battle relics were deeply personal. Captain Matthew B. Cheney of Company G sent to his wife the point of his sword, broken off by a piece of shell at Chancellorsville, along with an account of the incident. Private Addison Shafer of Company C preserved the bullet that wounded him at Gettysburg. Private Asa S. Wing of Company G made the bullet extracted from his neck during the Atlanta campaign into a watch fob. Private Charles E. Whitney sent the bullet cut out of his thigh after Chancellorsville to his family in care of a comrade returning home on furlough. Sergeant John A. Bush of Company D kept the piece of shell and the fragment of bone removed from his right arm at Gettysburg. When Corporal Job B. Dawley of Company K was shot dead by his Confederate captors in North Carolina in March 1865, Private Joseph Cullen of Company B opened Dawley's coat, saw the bullet embedded under the skin of his chest, and excised it. Cullen eventually gave the grisly memento to a comrade, who in turn forwarded it to the slain soldier's brother, former corporal John M. Dawley of Company K. The surviving brother was linked to his slain brother by a chain of esprit de corps.[32]

One type of item sent back and forth in the mail held a special place in soldiers' hearts: photographs. And one of those pictures was to have a unique destiny. "I got the likeness of the children and it pleased me more than eney thing that you could have sent me," Amos Humiston wrote to his wife in May 1863. Little did he know that within weeks he would grasp the ambrotype for his final sight as he died at Gettysburg, that it would be the means of his identification, and that it would become one of the most famous photographs of the war, reproduced widely when his story inspired an outpouring of prose, poetry, and song.[33]

Although none of them achieved the fame of the Humiston children's image, hundreds, perhaps thousands, of other ambrotype, tintype, and carte-de-visite photographs were associated with members of the 154th New York. Like the picture that propelled the Humistons to celebrity, all of the photographs received and sent by the soldiers and their loved ones were treasured. When the 154th scattered in retreat at the Battle of Chancellorsville, the knapsack of Private Truman D. Blowers of Company G became unhooked as he ran, sweating and panting, to the rear. "Throw it in the ditch," a comrade yelled. "Oh, I can't do that," Blowers replied, "my wife's picture is in that!" Unlike Blowers, Private William P. James of Company F, one of the Welsh boys, abandoned his knapsack, which contained his wife's portrait. "Sue will have to send Bill another *likeness of her face,*" William Charles noted, "*for the Rebels* have got the *one he had.*"[34]

From the first days at Camp Brown in Jamestown to the last days in camp outside of Washington, members of the 154th posed for photographs to send home to loved ones—when they had the cash and a photographer was available. The men fussed about the price and quality of their photographs, made wry or wistful comments about their portraits, worried about whether the images reached home, and instructed the home folk about the proper care of the pictures. And they repeatedly requested likenesses of their loved ones. Letters soldiers wrote on receiving or viewing photographs from home offer some of the most moving passages in their entire correspondence. "I take a look at my little picture very offten and it does me good every time I look at my Dear boy," William Charles wrote about a portrait of his son. "I wish he was here to play with me." Months later, Charles wrote, "Please tell Tommy that Dat has those Pictures, But they are some what broken up from being carried in the pocket so long. Dat looks at them *very* offten. Wonder if *any body* ever looks at *Dats Picture*!!!" Emory Sweetland had a deeply emotional response when he received an ambrotype of his wife and daughter:

> How my heart came up in my throat as I looked at the shadows of those two loved & loving ones, that God has blessed me with. you don't know what a comfort it is to me to even look at your portraits. How I long to clasp you both in my arms. You spoke of my sending it back. I can not think of that not at present at least. . . . I value it above rubies. . . . I haven't ripped all the glazing off the ambrotype yet but I think I've looked a little of the shine off. I've looked at it by the hour since I've got it.[35]

Some photographs demonstrated the bonds of esprit de corps. Regimental comrades swapped and posed for portraits with each other, and soldiers sent pictures of regimental friends to their home folk. "You said a while ago that you wanted some pictures to put in your Book," William Charles wrote to his wife. "I have three that I am very proud of. Doctor Vanernum has been very kind to me. . . . Major L. D. Warner is also a very cleavor man, and Quarter Master [Timothy A.] Allen is a good friend to me. Do you not think that they are good pictures. I will have more by and by maybe." In coming months Charles did indeed send home portraits of other 154th friends. Other members of the regiment sent loved ones portraits of the popular regimental surgeon. "Dr. Vanaernam gave me his photograph to day," Emory Sweetland notified his wife. "It is a good one & I prize it verry much. I will try & get an album for you to put our photographs in." Not surprisingly, Van Aernam himself swapped and sent home photographs. Sending his wife a portrait of Colonel Jones, the surgeon noted, "I hope to have a lot of Photos of friends here to send you in a few days."[36]

Most expressive of the regiment's esprit was a commemorative souvenir created by the officers of the 154th at the end of the war. Pictures of twenty-seven of them were collected and copied as a large, composite photograph, with the individual bust portraits arranged in two concentric ovals around a central image of Lewis D. Warner, commander of the regiment for the last year of the war. Comrades through three years of strife were depicted together forever in copies of the memento.[37]

Like letters, boxes, and photographs, money tied the army to the home front. Before the 154th New York left Camp Brown for the seat of war, each volunteer who chose to do so signed an allotment roll, designating a certain amount of his pay to whomever he chose to receive it. Richard McCadden, who as a sergeant was to be paid seventeen dollars per month, explained the arrangement in a letter to his mother: "I signed when I was at Jamestown to send home $12. per month of my pay I will receive a check evry pay day to that amount which I can send home . . . and if the check is lost they will furnish me with another it dus not cost a sent I signed it to [his brother] Billy and he is the only one that can draw on it and he will have to endorse it before he can get the money on it."[38]

Most of the men, like McCadden, allotted substantial amounts of their pay to their families, keeping only a few dollars of each month's pay for their personal use. Altogether, the 948 officers and enlisted men originally mustered into the 154th allotted $9,284 to their families—slightly less than ten dollars per man. With most of the soldiers allotting most of their pay, penury was their usual lot in camp—especially since payday was chronically late. Complaining frequently, the regiment waited four months, until February 1, 1863, for its first payment. Young Devillo Wheeler sent his allotment check to his father the following day and noted, "I Could of Sent you some [more] money this time but most of the boys sined the alotment to send there money home so they Dident have much to pay there Debts."[39]

"A large share" of the soldiers "dont save much," Emory Sweetland noted. The men often used the back pages of their diaries to tabulate their financial accounts, a multitude of debts, loans, clothing expenses, purchases of food and sundries, and payments received. Entrepreneurial soldiers devised ways to make money on the side. William Charles and Emory Sweetland earned substantial amounts of extra cash selling trinkets they crafted—artifacts that appealed to their comrades' sense of esprit de corps. Charles fashioned corps badges out of coins; Sweetland whittled commemorative pipes out of laurel root. Both proved to be immensely popular with the men. Others turned to more mundane enterprises. "I cannot tell just how mutch I have earned cobling," Stephen Green informed his wife, "but I think about 10 or 11 Dollars including what you sent in taps &c." In another letter, Green noted that his Company E comrade Private Charles Anderson "does Washing and earnes a good many dimes in that way he has sent home more money than any other private in our company."[40]

A family member was less likely to receive extra cash, however, than a request like one Alva Merrill sent to his brother and sister: "I want you should get that money that Mr Dawley owes me and send it to me in the next letter I want to get me a ruber blanket."[41]

Soldiers and home folk occasionally exchanged visits. The men returned to Cattaraugus and Chautauqua on furlough, and civilians from the two counties visited the front. Such visits served to preserve home ties and bolster esprit de corps, although the granting of furloughs presented some problems.

"There is great strife in Our Regt now to see who shall have furloughs," Thaddeus Reynolds wrote from the 154th's winter camp near Stafford Court House in February 1863. A recent order stipulated that two (later three) out of every hundred soldiers in a regiment could be furloughed at a time, for up to ten days each. Soldiers receiving furloughs were to have exemplary records, and married men were to have preference. Regiments judged to be below standard in appearance and soldierly conduct were denied furloughs; the 154th New York was fortunately not among them. Company or regimental officers generally chose the recipients of furloughs, but the first furlough in Company C was decided by a "one-sided cast-lot game," and lucky Private Harris Lamb happily left camp for a visit with his family in Portville.[42]

During much of their service, campaigning prevented members of the 154th from receiving furloughs. (Those hospitalized away from the regiment found it easier to be granted a leave.) When furloughs became available during periods of inactivity, many of the men eagerly sought them. This sometimes caused difficult situations. Strings were sometimes pulled for an advantage, and feelings were hurt. "I had the promise of [a furlough] for some time and expected to [have] been home before this," George Newcomb reported, "But there has been some cheating going on And I may not be able to get one." Men overstayed their leaves, aggravating their comrades. Private Frank Smith of Company F was absent for twenty-four days on a ten-day furlough. Smith "is fizzling out," George Taylor observed when he failed to reappear on the scheduled day. Smith's tardiness was "a poor joke" for Taylor's tent mate, Corporal Monroe Young, who was next in line for a furlough and had to await his comrade's return before he could leave for home. William Charles's wife protested when one of the Welsh boys, Private David J. Williams, received his second furlough, whereas Charles had yet to receive one. Responding to her complaint, Charles was philosophical about the situation. "You know that I must take things as they come and I never try to grumble or find fault," he wrote.[43]

Despite their desire to return home, many of the men decided not to apply for a furlough for practical reasons: lengthy travel times to and from western New York left little actual time at home, and furloughed soldiers had to pay their own transportation expenses, which were considerable. "How would you like to see me for 6 or 8 days at the expense of $30 or $40," Charles Abell asked his parents and siblings. "I hardly think it would pay me or any one else." Private Dwight Moore of Company H agreed. "I presume I could get a furlough if I tried," Moore informed his mother, "but I guess it wouldnt pay for I could only get one for 10 or 15 days and it would cost about 25 dollars to go and come." An emotional factor gave William Charles pause when he considered a furlough, as he explained to his wife: "You seem to wonder why I do not come home on furlough. . . . One reason that I do not come is this. That there are those there I love so much that it would allmost break my heart to come and remain with them a few days and then part with them again, 'perhaps for ever.' you see it would only tear open the old wounds afresh and make us all more wreched then we now are."[44]

Wives experienced the same psychological misgivings. Mary Chittenden wrote to her husband, William, "I dreamed a few nights ago that you came home on a short furlow and the thoughts of your leaving so soon again spoiled my visit. . . . I had rather wait longer than to have you come home to leave me again for the seat of war."[45]

Leaving for home and returning to camp, furloughed soldiers toted numerous items for their comrades. When Monroe Young finally left Company F on furlough for his Sinclairville home, he carried some shirts, a commission, and a specimen of petrified wood to Susan Griswold for his lieutenant. When First Sergeant Stiles B. Ellsworth of Company K was furloughed, Marcellus Darling "concluded to send home my Overcoat and one shirt, which I have packed up and shall send by Stiles." When First Sergeant Almon L. Gile of Company C returned home to Hinsdale, Cattaraugus County, Private James W. Washburn of that town instructed his parents, "If you have any little thing to send send it to me [with Gile.] he will bring it I guess he is a pretty good fellow."[46]

Homecomings of course were joyous. "Captain Harrison Cheney says that the people of Sandusky gave him a very warm reception" when he arrived home on leave, William Charles noted. After ten months as a prisoner of war, Thomas Aldrich returned home on furlough in March 1865. "I tell you I was a happy fellow," Aldrich recalled in the postwar years. "I did not think that anyone cared much for me, but in less than half an hour, every man woman and child in the village of Versailles were there to see me." Demonstrating esprit de corps, soldiers made sure to see relatives of their comrades while at home on furlough. William Charles notified his wife that a fellow Freedom resident, First Sergeant Ambrose F. Arnold of Company D, was to receive a furlough: "He says that he will come and make you a visit himself and wife," Charles wrote. He added, "Ambrose is a good boy a good soldier and a good friend." When Charles Whitney was at home on furlough after being released from Andersonville prison, the parents of Privates Charles Allen of Company B and David W. Travis of Company C—both incarcerated at Andersonville—visited Whitney to learn about their sons. Emory Sweetland notified his wife about the imminent arrival of a comrade. "I told him to go see father S. & you & make you a visit," Sweetland wrote. "I told him that any friend of mine from the 154th would be welcome at either one of my fathers. . . . He has no home & no one to welcome him on his arrival. he is a good fellow & I know that my sweet wife will treat him kindly."[47]

Private George Real of Company B left the 154th's camp at Stafford Court House on furlough at 10 A.M. on February 23, 1863, and arrived at his home in Dayton at 6 A.M. on February 25. It was a rainy day, but Real and his wife nevertheless went to visit their neighbor, Ruba Merrill, and deliver letters (including a hardtack and two dollars) from Barzilla and Alva. "Was extremely glad to see him," Ruba noted of Real's visit in her diary. Two weeks later, Real was back in camp and delivered goods to several Dayton men, including a new pair of boots to Barzilla. "I think that it made him look just fresh to go home and sleep with his wife," Barzilla commented.[48]

Returning from furloughs was a bittersweet experience for at least two members of the 154th—and an occasion for them to express their esprit de corps. Lewis Warner returned to Stafford Court House in April 1863 and found the 154th's camp deserted. The regiment had left on campaign. "This much for going home," Warner lamented in his diary. "Regt gone, perhaps already engaged with the Rebells and I not with them to share in the dangers or honors of the occasion. Had I known this I should have staid in camp, much as I wished to see home, with all its endearments." Weeks after the 154th New York was decimated at Gettysburg, Edgar Shannon returned to a Washington hospital after a furlough and reflected: "I had a very pleasant time while at home but . . . when I got on the cars oh, how lonely I felt such a dread uncertainty lay before me where would I be another year from this time & when should I meet with my friends & live over those pleasant times again which I had just passed through. Then I thought of my regiment & how it was scattered not hardly a boy that I knew left. these thoughts made me very sad."[49]

Civilians crowded Camp Brown in Jamestown prior to the departure of the 154th New York. "I wish you could be here and see them," William Chittenden wrote to his wife. "Here is a young soldier with his sweet heart prephaps the one chosen to share lifes joys and sorrows. here annother with his young wife by his side and in his arms he carries a little one annother picture shows a family group the father and Mother leading the little ones entrusted to their care and Brothers and Sisters and in fact all with some preasent for the loved ones shortly to leave them prephaps forever."[50]

At the front, however, visits from the home folk were rare. Trips from Cattaraugus and Chautauqua to the South often were occasioned by misfortune. When Austin Munger died and his brother Henry lay sick, their father journeyed from Arkwright to the front to get his surviving son into a Washington hospital so as to procure a discharge for him. When Private William Wellman of Company F was sent sick to a Washington hospital, his townsman Private Dennis A. Brand of Company D sent a letter to Wellman's brother back home in Yorkshire. Fred Wellman left home the morning he received the letter and rushed to his brother's side. William had been the sickest of all the 154th men at Harewood Hospital, but he recovered nicely under Fred's attentive care.[51]

Other visits were impelled by curiosity as well as the desire to see a loved one. "We had a visit from T D Phillips last week," John Griswold reported, possibly referring to the father of Private Thomas S. Phillips of Company F. "He thought the sight of the elephant well paid the expense." In November

1862, George Newcomb wrote, "Mr Chapman of Versailes arrived here to day," perhaps referring to a relative of Private Eugene Chapman or First Lieutenant William F. Chapman of Company K. Newcomb continued, "He intends to stay with us some time." Some visits were serendipitous. William Charles was doing detached duty at Ringgold, Georgia, in the spring of 1864 when he was surprised to encounter a friend from Freedom. The two "talked pretty fast for a while," sharing news from home. "It did me much good to see him," Charles reported. "It was almost as good as a letter from Home." The regiment was camped at Goldsboro, North Carolina, in April 1865 when it was visited by an Ellicottville man, John W. Meloy, an employee of the federal military railroad system. "I came up here to see the boys of the 154 Regt.," Meloy wrote, noting the men were "all well and hearty as bucks."[52]

Visits made by certain individuals probably had the imprimatur of their home community. Norman M. Allen, a prominent citizen of Dayton who served as town supervisor and held several appointive and elective offices during the war, visited his townsmen in Companies B and K in January 1863, bringing news of home in addition to the usual load of stuff for the men. George Newcomb reported, "Us Boys were all glad to see him and would [welcome] anny one who will visit us from Dayton." Other civilians engaged in errands of mercy on their own. After the Battle of Chancellorsville, Addison G. Rice—who had relinquished command of the 154th after delivering the regiment to the front—traveled from Ellicottville to Virginia to succor the wounded. "Col. Rice is entitled to great credit and the thanks of the Cattaraugus Regiment, for the interest he has taken in this matter," editorialized the *Cattaraugus Union*. "He went to the scene of battle, on his own expense, to relieve, if possible, the prisoners and wounded of the Reg't he so largely contributed in raising." After the Battle of Gettysburg, when word from the decimated 154th was scarce, a civilian named James W. Phelps from the Cattaraugus County town of Great Valley journeyed to Pennsylvania to ascertain the regiment's losses, visit the wounded, and notify relatives and hometown newspapers of the hospitalized.[53]

Not all the visitors to the front were male. "Quite a number of men & officers have sent for their families, & now it is nothing strange to see women and little children in Camp," William Charles wrote from Alexandria, Virginia, where the 154th New York bivouacked for much of August and September 1863. "But it is a little strange," Charles added, "to see a

Hoop skirt hanging in a soldiers tent." Quartermaster Timothy Allen's wife was one of the visitors; the couple stayed in rented rooms in a private house near camp.[54]

After the members of the 154th were dubbed "Hardtacks" when they engaged in some unscrupulous trading with other regiments of their brigade for that army staple, George Newcomb used the nickname in describing the visit of a wife to camp. He also used obscene language, rarely found in the soldiers' letters. "There is a young woman here that came here a few days ago," Newcomb wrote from the Stafford Court House camp. "She has got a Husband in the Regt She probably came down here to enjoy a hard tack f–k But her Husband must be in better trim than most of the Boys or I fear she will suffer for the want of f–k–g."[55]

"Some men have their wives come to see them occasionaly," Barzilla Merrill wrote from Stafford. He continued, "I see a nice yankee woman in camp and that does me some good." Merrill and his Company K tent mates, Privates Calvin S. Johnson and Bornt D. Shelmadine, discussed the possibility of a visit from their wives, but found one stumbling block: "We hant sleeping rooms enough in our house to lodge three couple," Merrill informed Ruba. "I hardly know whether we will send on that account." Other soldiers harbored reservations about visits from their wives. "I dont know what in tophet I could do with you here," John Griswold admitted to his wife, Susan, from Stafford. "You could not march & keep up & I have no idea they would let you ride one of the mules for they are so poor they can hardly carry themselves, so on the whole I guess you had better stay whare you are." Sergeant Stephen Welch of Company C refused to allow his wife to visit the Stafford camp: "She wants to come here very much," Welch noted in his diary, "but I cannot see it in that way. It is no place for an honest woman."[56]

Two wives of members of the 154th New York deserve special mention. Celia A. Bailey, wife of Private Levi D. Bailey of Company A, left her Carrollton, Cattaraugus County, home and accompanied her husband to the front, where she served the regiment as a volunteer nurse. Her tent was a fixture in the 154th's camps. Mrs. Bailey neither asked for nor received pay for her ministrations to the men. The wife of Private James Pollan of Company G, known to the men as Biddy, was a little Irishwoman who "kept with the Regt in all of its marches" throughout the war. Mrs. Pollan earned a considerable amount of money laundering and mending the men's clothes. Celia Bailey and Biddy Pollan were never carried on the muster rolls, but they were members of the regiment regardless.[57]

Worry, desperation, and anguish marked much of the communication between soldiers and the home front. The extreme danger the soldiers faced could not have made it otherwise. For example, forty-three members of the regiment have been quoted in this chapter. Of that random sample, thirty-one (72 percent) became casualties; four others were discharged for disability. Twenty of the men were fatalities, including eight who died as prisoners of war.

But numbers are a poor way to interpret heartbreak. It is far better to heed the words of people who experienced the torment. As the Battle of Chancellorsville wound down in Virginia, Susan Griswold wrote to her husband, John, from their Arkwright home: "I have got a head ache to day feel quite down for a few days not hearing any thing from you for so long & expecting you are in battle that I have cried my eyes amost out of my head but it is become allmost second nature for me to cry but being around amonst folks so much I have to put a doubble command over my feelings if I give way to my feelings I do not know what would become of me."[58]

Then came news of the battle, the list of the 154th's casualties published in the *Fredonia Censor,* and the shock: Lieutenant Griswold was reported killed. "You may judg how I felt," Susan wrote. She continued, "Oh my heart was allmost broke I cald on god to take me to it seamed that I could not live but the Lord put it into my heart that I must live for the sake of my child but oh the agony of mind that I past through for about a week I can not describe to you." Then a flurry of letters arrived from Company F. "In about a week some of the boys wrote home & they sayd you was wounded verry bad & they did not know what had become of you whether you wer dead or a Prisoner then it seamd I could not stand it I thought it would make me sick some of the time I was so weak I could hardly walk acroast the house." At last, a month after the battle, Susan received a letter from John—written in another man's hand—notifying her he had been wounded in the right arm, captured, imprisoned, released, and was hospitalized at Annapolis. She responded immediately. "I feel to day the deads alive," she wrote. "We have mourned you as dead."[59]

She wanted him to come home if he could; if not, she would go to him.

"Do come as soon as you can," she wrote. "If you can not com do let me know for I shall sertanly come down their for I can not stand it it is to bad to think of your being away afar whear I can not do anything for you nor see you." He would be pleased to see her indeed, John replied in another dictated letter, but he thought it unwise for her to travel to Annapolis because he might be sent elsewhere at any time. And while he desired a furlough home, the prospects of getting one were dim. Furthermore, he had heard from Company F. "I feal very anchious to visite the Company," his amanuensis wrote, "and shall do so as soon as i can git Permission."[60]

Susan replied: "Can I wait much longer [to see you?] I am afraid you will keep putting me off till you cant come home or you get well enough to go back to your company can you be so crull as not to come home or let me come & see you? . . . You say you are verry anxious to go to your company & shall do so I fear you are more anxious to go their than to come home you will say that I am a little jealous & I think I have reason to be."[61] To Susan Griswold, her husband's esprit de corps rivaled the matrimonial bond.

CHAPTER 3

Friends and Foes

After receiving some sort of slight from townspeople in Yorkshire Center a few weeks after her husband left for the front, Mary Chittenden sat down to compose a sad letter. "I had my feelings hurt very much this morning," she confided, "& O Wm. how my heart went forth to the absent one it seemed as if my heart would burst with grief but William I have made up my mind to let my neighbors alone as far as I can & live by my self till William comes home." Two weeks later, William Chittenden remarked to his wife, "Some are very unwilling to help a soldiers family little thinking how many inconveniences their families are subject to."[1]

Early in 1864, William Charles was incredulous to learn that the wife of his tent mate, David Williams, had taken in a disreputable boarder. "Can she be so foolish as to forsake her own husband bring woe and wretchedness upon her family and bring upon herself Eternal Damnation, for the sake of so vile a creature as Tom Rees," Charles asked his wife. If Williams knew what was going on, Charles declared, "it would kill him, I do believe." Later that year, Charles commented on additional scandalous news. "I understand that John Davis has been disgracing himself lately by conducting himself towards a *Soldiers Wife* in such a manner that would make any thing but a drunkard hate himself to *death*," he wrote. "It is well for him that some of the Soldiers that are here did not kech him at it they would [have] shot him as quick and with about the same feeling as they would a *skunk*."[2]

Unsympathetic neighbors and unfaithful wives were just two of many home front issues that worried the soldiers. Personal concerns were legion. Were their families enjoying good health? Were they able to keep up with work on the farm? Did they have enough money to get by? Beyond individual concerns, however, other apprehensions lurked. Did the people of Cattaraugus and Chautauqua counties support the war effort and the Lincoln administration? Would they continue to show that support as the war ground on? Would they offer their money, their votes, and their men for the

Union cause? To the soldiers of the 154th New York, imbued with esprit de corps, there was only one acceptable answer to those questions.

"It is one thing to sing rally Round the Flag and another thing to do it," Charles Abell observed. "I have found that out by experience." The men knew that home front support was essential to their well-being. "Do what you can for the benefit of the soldiers," Abell advised his parents, "for they need all that they get if I were at home I should Just go right in and give them a little lift *I reckon.*" "I intend to help pick the bone and I want the friends at home to do by [us] just as they agreed and then all will be well," Barzilla Merrill wrote. "Dont make us think that we are in straight opposition to our friends at home," First Sergeant James W. Baxter of Company I pleaded to one of those home friends.[3]

"Mother you have enough to see to at home without worrying or wishing you could help the wounded Soldiers," Marcellus Darling cautioned, but his sentiment was rare. The soldiers overwhelmingly sought and indeed expected the support of the home folk, and scorned those who refused or were reluctant to provide it. When William Charles's wife went around Freedom collecting "little comforts for the sick and wounded Soldiers," she met with some miserly responses. One neighbor donated only a couple of old shirts; a relative offered nothing. Charles was irate when he heard the news. "The man that cannot afford to give *anything* to a sick and wounded Soldier, is poor indeed," he wrote. "Cannot *give anything* to those who have *given their all.*"[4]

For their part, loved ones offered reassurances of fealty to their soldiers. "If I was a bird how quick I would fly down South to see you and all of our brave Soldiers boys," Martha James assured Samuel Williams. She continued, "I think of them evry day yes I think of thee when all is still." Mary Chittenden encouraged William to stay the course but be cautious. "I want you to keep up good courage & not worry about home any more than you can help for it will do no good," she wrote, "but do try & be careful of your health & life rush into no danger that can be avoided think of Mary & how she would stand even between you & the deathly missiles if possible, & be careful *O so careful.*" Renewing her subscription to the *Cattaraugus Freeman*, the wife of a member of the 154th sent a note along with her payment. "Inclosed is $4.50 which your bill calls for," she wrote. "May it help to print good news of victory, of right over wrong, and soldiers home from the war when peace is gained—an *honorable* peace—such as God will approve."[5]

When Sergeant Augustus A. Shippy of Company B was paroled after his capture at Chancellorsville, he was sent to the convalescent camp at Alexandria, Virginia. His mother, Isabella Shippy, wrote to the camp commander, requesting that her son be allowed to come home, as his father was ill with consumption and anxious to see him. She offered a strong guarantee that Augustus would return to the 154th after his visit: "You need have no fears but that he will return the moment he is exchanged. I have three sons in the army, and I would much rather they all fall on the battle field than to desert thier Country in this her hour of trial, or do one Cowardly act. they are true patriots Grandsons of one of the noble old heroes of the revolution inhaling patriotism with their first breath so you need have no fears. he will certainly come back to his regiment—from his mother."[6]

A poem written for Private David S. Jones of Company K by his brother Edward in Leon, Cattaraugus County, was sent to the *Cattaraugus Freeman* by a family friend, who thought that "the merit of patriotic sentiment will, doubtless, commend it to the *Freeman,* and its readers." The editor of the *Freeman* agreed, and ran it on the front page. The final two stanzas echoed Isabella Shippy's determination that beloved soldiers should see the fight through to the finish:

> Boys, when victory's crowned your efforts,
> And our flag in triumph waves,
> O'er the States that have seceded,
> And those Southern traitor's grave.
>
> When the States are all united,
> In the bonds our fathers tied,
> Then we'll welcome, gladly welcome,
> Brothers to our warm fireside.[7]

Cattaraugus and Chautauqua civilians often banded together in order to support the soldiers. They formed town "Loyal Leagues" to express their political support for the war effort, and relief societies to provide material aid to the soldiers. "Among the many patriotic organizations instituted in the Loyal States for the amelioration of the Soldiers hardships," Colonel Patrick H. Jones informed the East Randolph Ladies Aid Society, "none accomplishes its purpose more effectually than Societies kindred to yours." Among the items prepared and shipped by the Mansfield Female Association in Cattaraugus County were bandages, lint, quilts, socks, shirts, pillows, dressing gowns, and dried fruit. Home folk also contributed to the two largest national soldiers' relief organizations, the United States Sanitary Commission and the United States Christian Commission. More than a score of men (women were not allowed to serve), most of them clergymen, left Cattaraugus and Chautauqua for the front as Christian Commission delegates. And the home folk opened their purses for the Union cause. To provide bounties for its soldiers in 1862, the town of Mansfield raised more than a thousand dollars by private subscription and a specially levied tax. Citizens of Olean, Cattaraugus County's most populous town, raised more than $25,000 in private contributions during the war for bounties, aid to soldiers' families, and donations to the Sanitary and Christian commissions.[8]

Members of the 154th voiced their appreciation of such efforts. "The Christian Commission has done great things for the soldier," Edgar Shannon wrote. He continued, "God bless them and the fair ladies who have taken such an interest in the soldiers." James Quilliam crafted a ring from a shell and sent it to a Portland woman whom he "had heard of as a friend to the soldiers and had don much for the Sanatary and Christian Commission." Alanson Crosby was doing detached duty in Elmira, New York, when plans for the Southern Tier Fair, an event to benefit soldiers, were announced. Crosby sent the *Cattaraugus Freeman* a list of suggested items to be sold at the fair. "I presume there are many in Cattaraugus who would esteem it a pleasure to contribute some of the articles enumerated in the foregoing list," he wrote. "Cannot the ladies of Ellicottville and other towns levy contributions on the men for materials, and form Societies or circles for the working up of such articles as will be acceptable and saleable at the Fair?" When the great Metropolitan Fair to benefit the Sanitary Commission was held in New York City in April 1864, the 154th New York had a presence. Among the myriad items on display were photographs of Amos Humiston and his now-famous children, and a pencil sketch of the battlefield of Wauhatchie, Tennessee, drawn by Captain Arthur Hotchkiss of Company K.[9]

No individual did more to aid the men of the 154th than John Manley, universally known as "the Soldier's Friend." A native of Maine, Manley brought his family to the Cattaraugus County town of Little Valley in 1851.

At the outbreak of the war he was a clerk in the federal Interior Department in Washington. In the nation's capital, at nearby Virginia army camps, and back home in Cattaraugus County, Manley worked constantly and conscientiously on behalf of the county's soldiers, without seeking or receiving compensation. He mastered the intricacies of the War Department's bureaucracy and expeditiously cut red tape to obtain discharges, bounties, pensions, and back pay. "The doors and books of the Department fly open as if by magic at his approach," the *Cattaraugus Freeman* reported, "and he is treated with great respect and courtesy wherever he goes." Manley visited the camps on a regular basis and sent lengthy reports on Cattaraugus soldiers to the county press. During the war, he received more than four thousand letters from soldiers and their families. He helped organize the New York Soldiers' Relief Association in Washington and was secretary of its executive committee throughout the conflict.[10]

From the very start, Manley closely followed and abetted the fortunes of the 154th Regiment. "John Manley, 'the Soldiers Friend,' is here getting acquainted with the new levies," a soldier wrote from Camp Brown in Jamestown, "and it is only necessary to say 'John Manley' and the Soldiers are ready to give nine cheers and a tiger." On March 16, 1863, Manley arrived at the 154th's camp near Stafford Court House, bringing with him many boxes and packages sent from home folk to the regiment, "which, but for his watchfulness," wrote Adjutant Samuel Noyes, "would have been lost in the military whirlpool at Washington." Manley also brought a barrel of whiskey, for which the men cheered him lustily. At dress parade that evening, an order was read naming the 154th's camp in his honor. Manley responded with thanks, complimented the regiment on its fine drill, clean camp, and light sick list, and closed with an exhortation: "In the coming campaign . . . there can be no doubt that your gallant conduct will merit the plaudits of your friends and kindred on the far off hills of Cattaraugus and Chautauqua." Reporting on his visit in a letter to the *Cattaraugus Freeman*, Manley expressed confidence in the regiment. "From their strict attention to duty and zeal, the intelligence and discipline already displayed," he declared, "the 154th will share the honors of the coming campaign in a manner worthy of New Yorkers and Americans."[11]

In the following months, Manley presented every member of the regiment with two sheets of stationery bearing a "Camp John Manley" letterhead; wrote to Cattaraugus County newspapers about the regiment's fight at Chancellorsville; visited the regiment's paroled prisoners at the Alexandria convalescent camp; solicited and forwarded clothing and provisions for regimental officers incarcerated at Libby Prison in Richmond; instructed the home folk in how to address and send packages to their loved ones, whether in camp or in prison, either in care of him or to military freight depots; sent news of the 154th's enlisted men who had been paroled from the prison camp on Belle Island, in the James River opposite Richmond; obtained from the chief clerk of the Confederate commissary general of prisons a list of members of the 154th who had died in captivity; and disproved a rumor that Captain Edward Porter of Company I had been killed by bloodhounds in an attempted prison escape—all this in addition to his usual work of forwarding news of the regiment to the newspapers and carrying on his wide-ranging correspondence on behalf of the soldiers.[12]

As much as the soldiers of the 154th New York revered "the Soldier's Friend" and other supportive home folk, they reviled those who opposed the war effort—the compromise and peace advocates commonly known as Copperheads. "I think it is worse than useless to fight as long as the Rebels have so many friends at the north," William Charles wrote. Newton Chaffee declared, "When newspapers and political parties stop their petty quarrels, and all are together for upholding the Union and the Constitution, and especially for putting down this wicked rebellion, then is victory won. We fear not so much the rebels we have to face in battle, as we do those at home. . . . A traitor is ten thousand times worse than an open rebel, and should be dealt with accordingly." Realizing the adverse effect Copperheadism could have on the morale of soldiers' loved ones, James Quilliam cautioned his wife to avoid the naysayers: "Have nothing to do with those who air always got some bad story to tell about the war. They envent thousands of lies to make the friends of the soldier feel bad it makes them mad to think that we whip the rebs so and [they] try to get revenge by plagueing the soldiers family if they can do no more."[13]

In describing their Northern adversaries, the soldiers became as venomous as the reptiles that lent the Copperheads their name. Private Robert M. McKee of Company F, one of many members of the 154th to sound off on the subject in letters to hometown newspapers, vented the bitterness felt by the soldiers:

> "Copperheads" I am disgusted with, from their leaders . . . down to the lowest hangers-on of the scurvy poisonous set. Judge the feelings of thousands of men, who have left home and all that was dear to them, to fight the battle of their country, and to help crush out this wicked, unjust rebellion, and send traitors to the best Government the sun ever shone on, to their just doom, when looking back to their homes they have left, expecting at least the moral support of high-toned patriotism, they see the dagger-blade of treason, bloody treason drawn to stab them in the back.[14]

Many of the soldiers advocated violence toward Copperheads. "My opinion is, this war will not close during the present administration," McKee asserted, "unless an army is sent North for the express purpose of killing Copperheads." Newton Chaffee wrote, "I wish I had the whole of them here and could hold them where I want them. I would put them in front and make Breast Works of them for our men to shoot through." In Company A, Private Wilkes J. Miller reported, "Our Captain [Benjamin G. Casler] says: 'Boys, were shall we turn to fight—those North or South?' The cry was, 'Let us go *North!*' They are our greatest enemies, and deserve a severe punishment. Only give us a chance, and we will free New York of every vile Copperhead in it." Devillo Wheeler used sarcasm in castigating his town's malcontents. "I Could give them pick pockets around Allegany a piece of my mind," he wrote, "with their asses humped over the stove feat upon the stove pipe and saying why Dont our men Down there lick the rebels out and Come home why Dont they Come Down and help us I could shoot such men as them."[15]

When the deadly draft riots broke out in New York City in July 1863, shortly after the 154th was demolished at Gettysburg, members of the regiment universally condemned the unrest. "The boys in the army here think dreadful little of the idea of standing a wall of fire in front of the 'rebs' to save such traitors and miscreants as the rioters of New York City or their sympathizers in Cattaraugus," Surgeon Henry Van Aernam wrote. As the rioting ebbed, Emory Sweetland declared, "How ashamed I have been of my native state for the past few days. You might have heard curses long and deep against N.Y. if you had been here. it makes the old soldiers mad to think that the copperheads should be allowed to carry such things to such lengths in the north. I wish that our brigade & the battery that is with it could be sent to the citty. They would make short work of the riot They would not fire blank cartridges at the mob."[16]

"We have southern sympathizers here," Barzilla Merrill wrote in March 1863. He added, "Some dont feel afrade to advocate the doctrine here." But Copperheadism in the army seemed to wither quickly in the aftermath of the Gettysburg battle and the New York City riots. "It is difficult to find a soldier, as far as my experience goes," Private Colby M. Bryant of Company A wrote in July 1863, "but has a peculiar hatred to Copperheadism. Most all agree that if we are not now successful, it will be on account of that party North." By November of that year Edgar Shannon would write, "You'll not find many copperheads among the soldiers, they are home cowards & fools that are willing to be picked round by the southern chivalry."[17]

To Newton Chaffee, the Copperheads were as treacherous as their eponym: "They will be remembered by us as the most dangerous enamys we have to contend with. we respect the out spoken Rebbles of the south much more, for they tell us what we can depend on, but these copperheads are like snakes in the grass. they talk fair at your face, but turn and sting you in the back as you leave them. if justice was done them, a ration of hemp roap would be dealt out to them, and that to with out any mercy."[18]

For all the invective they hurled at their Northern enemies, the soldiers knew that the battle against the Copperheads would ultimately be decided in the political arena. Consequently, the men kept a close eye on national, state, and local politics, and were quick to offer their opinions of campaigns, candidates, and election results. In the 1860 presidential election, Cattaraugus County gave Abraham Lincoln a 64 percent majority over his three opponents. Although there is no way of knowing for certain, it might be safe to extrapolate from that percentage and guess that approximately six or seven out of every ten volunteers in the 154th New York were Republicans, the other three or four Democrats. Wartime elections in 1862 and 1864 revealed that support for Lincoln and the Republicans dipped slightly among Cattaraugus County voters, but it soared in the ranks of the 154th Regiment.[19]

The 1862 election for governor of New York pitted Republican and Union general James Wadsworth against Democrat Horatio Seymour. Cattaraugus

County gave Wadsworth 60 percent of its vote, but statewide Seymour prevailed. Reaction to the news varied in the 154th. "We have heared that Seymour is elected," William Chittenden wrote on November 7, and he added a lukewarm endorsement of the Democrat: "I hope it will be for the good of the country and that just and rightful measures may be adopted for the settlement of this useless war." "Of course we Republicans feel mighty sorry over it," William Charles acknowledged of Seymour's success, adding with half-hearted optimism, "Still it may be all the best. at least let us hope so." Charles was pleased to hear that his home town of Freedom had given Wadsworth a large majority (221 votes to 73). "I think that it is a great shame that he is not elected," he admitted. "The Rebels will now say that the north has owned itself to be in the wrong & are willing to settle up on any terms." Like Charles, Republican Lewis Warner tried to resign himself to Wadsworth's defeat. "Much as the result of the New York election is to be regretted by those who are really and earnestly for striking out by the strong arm of the Nation at every vestige of the rebellion," Warner wrote in a letter to a newspaper, "it is no time for useless regrets. Every patriot must buckle on his armor and press forward with renewed energy until the great end is attained."[20]

Colonel Patrick H. Jones and First Lieutenant Commodore Perry Vedder of Company G found that political expressions by soldiers could stir controversy. When Jones and Vedder, both staunch Democrats before the war, endorsed Wadsworth in letters to hometown Ellicottville friends, they were taken to task by the Democratic *Cattaraugus Union* in insulting terms:

> All the people ask of these officers is to have them attend strictly to their legitimate duties—to face and fight the enemy and suppress this unnatural rebellion, leaving political matters in the hands of those at home, who are more competent to judge of local matters than those distant from the scene of political strife. We have had already too much politics and too little military service in the army. Men, as a general thing, cannot attend to politics and fighting both at once. . . . We advise Col. Jones and Lieut. Vedder to turn their faces towards the south, and not longer look backwards toward home to regulate matters clearly not within the scope of their military calling.[21]

A week later, the editor of the Republican *Cattaraugus Freeman* berated his rival at the *Union* as a sour, savage, sore-headed Southern sympathizer,

and offered a defense of the two officers: "Colonel Jones and Lieutenant Vedder . . . knew that the election of Seymour would be hailed with unfeigned
joy by the Rebels and Rebel sympathizers everywhere; that it would encourage and strengthen the armies of Jeff Davis in their warfare against the Government, and aid in protracting this unnatural and wicked Rebellion. They
frankly and freely stated their opinions upon the subject, and urgently appealed to their political friends to rally to the support of Wadsworth. This is
the height of their offending."[22]

Using their respective presses as mouthpieces, spewing vituperative language, Republicans and Democrats vied for supremacy during the war. The
slightest pretense could initiate a political tirade. Thus when Captain Baker
Leonard Saxton of Company A returned to his Ellicottville home on a furlough, the *Union* was pleased to note, "Like most of our returned soldiers,
the Captain's political opinions have undergone a great change, having become convinced that the policy of 'nigger-ism' and radicalism, are 'making
things no better very fast,' and henceforth may be called a conservative,
square-toed Democrat." And when Commodore Vedder returned to Ellicottville on leave, the *Freeman* claimed, "The Captain is a firm supporter of
'Father Abraham.' His political sentiments have undergone somewhat of a
change since he entered the army, and we are reliably informed that he is
no longer able to discover the face of Washington in that of a Democrat."[23]

As time passed, voices were increasingly raised against the Democrats in
private letters from the ranks."I am no more of a Democrat than I was when
I left home," George Newcomb declared in March 1863, "and I do not think
I ever shall be." "I think that a man that voats the democrat ticket [is] just
as much an enemy as a rebble soldier," James Quilliam opined in December
1863, and the following February he railed against Portland's Democratic
candidate for town collector: "If such a man is to be elected even to a town
ofice thrugh the northern states we may expect a long war yet as the rebels
will think and know that they have many friends in the north which will
help them at every opertunity." In another February 1864 letter, Quilliam
wrote, "I have no doubt a democrat victory would cost the life of many thousand soldier and we have more to fear now from those we call our friends at
home then from all the rebel army since their only hope is in the democrat
party of the north." Wrote Horace Howlett, "I wont the democrats to under

stand they are plade out and thare is Not meny sound men will open thare head a bout democrats."[24]

When New York Democrats resolved at a mass meeting in the spring of 1863 that the war was unconstitutional and illegal and should not be sustained, Wilkes Miller responded bitterly: "It is enough to make one's blood boil to think, while we have been here to punish treason in the South, that a viler and more damnable monster . . . has been nursed and cherished by leading Democrats in the old Empire State, the place where we as soldiers have looked for sympathy and encouragement." He added, "Never could that polluted wretch, Seymour, have been Governor of New York if her best sons had not been in the army." Other soldiers—many of whom had not liked him much to begin with—soured on Seymour when he opposed the Emancipation Proclamation, resisted conscription, vetoed a soldiers' suffrage bill, and generally aligned himself with the most vehement opponents of the Lincoln administration. Inflammatory statements made by the governor in New York City on Independence Day 1863 were widely considered by the soldiers to have fed the discontent that erupted in the subsequent draft riots. "The Soldiers Dont think as much of him as they Did," James Baxter wrote of Seymour. "They give him the Credit of being the cause of that riot in New York. . . . I dont myself but the majority of Soldiers does."[25]

Consequently, Seymour received little support from members of the 154th New York when he ran for reelection in 1864 against Republican Reuben Fenton—the congressman representing Cattaraugus and Chautauqua counties who had helped recruit the 154th and was well known to its men. Adding much interest among members of the regiment to the political campaign that fall was President Lincoln's race for reelection against Democrat and Union general George B. McClellan, and the contest to fill Fenton's seat as U.S. representative from the Thirty-First Congressional District, featuring Democrat Jonas K. Button of Franklinville, Cattaraugus County, versus his Republican townsman Henry Van Aernam—the beloved surgeon of the 154th New York.

By the 1864 election, the 154th had developed an affectionate respect for the commander in chief. On April 10, 1863, the regiment had taken a memorable look at Abraham Lincoln when he reviewed the Eleventh Army Corps, to which the 154th belonged. A barrage of letters to the home folk described the pomp of the occasion—the clockwork maneuvers of the vast assemblage of troops, the brass bands, the large contingent of generals, the presidential entourage. In trying to describe Lincoln to their loved ones, members of the 154th often referred to his well-known portraits, and commented on his careworn appearance. "I had a fine view of the old rail splitter," Richard Mc-Cadden reported. "He is about as homely a man as you would wish to see altho he looks good natured you would know him by the picture you have seen so many times of him." Barzilla Merrill declared, "His portrate dont do him justice. He is a smarter looking man than that represents . . . but he looks care worn and palid." Henry Van Aernam disagreed with Merrill about Lincoln's portraits: "The pictures carry a good idea of how old 'Abe' looks— the most of them are exact likenesses—he looks careworn, anxious and fatigued."[26]

As the months passed, the soldiers repeatedly affirmed their devotion to the president. "I am a full believer in . . . old Abes Administration," declared James Baxter in November 1863. "I trust every Loyal man is in favor of Abe Lincoln how sweet the sound." Declared Horace Howlett in December 1863, "I would vote for him if I had to go five thousen milds to do it." "It looks as though Uncle Abe calculated to finish up the war whilst he is in the chair. . . . The army are unanimous for him," Emory Sweetland asserted after Lincoln issued a draft order in March 1864. Writing a week later, David Jones stated, "The more I see of old Abe the more I believe that Lincoln was raised like Washington for the especial salvation of his *Country*. . . . So far as I know Lincoln is the first and only choice of the soldiers." Wrote Newton Chaffee in September 1864, "The army is for Lincoln almost unanimous, and this is one of Uncle Abe's Regiments." Esprit de corps and political consensus had intersected.[27]

The 1864 Republican ticket of Lincoln, Fenton, and Van Aernam enjoyed virtually universal approval in the regiment. Support for the Democrats, Emory Sweetland averred, "will be about as scarce as Angels visits or Uncle Sam's green backs in the army." Former Democrat Commodore Vedder "is now a firm and enthusiastic supporter of 'Old Abe,'" the *Cattaraugus Freeman* reported. "He says that the nomination of Lincoln and [Andrew] Johnson gives great satisfaction to the whole army." Edgar Shannon wrote, "We are all very happy to learn that R. E. Fenton has been nominated for governor. The Regt. will vote for him unanimously. he has been a friend to the soldier, always ready to help him." Ignoring the *Cattaraugus Union*'s 1862 admonition against mixing soldiering with politics, the members of the regiment met to voice their support for Fenton and unanimously adopted resolutions to that effect, which they submitted for publication to the Republican newspapers of Cattaraugus and Chautauqua counties. Of course the soldiers of the 154th Regiment took pride in their own Surgeon Van Aernam's candidacy. "I am very glad to see the name of Doctor Henry Van Aernam on the ticket for Representative in Congress," William Charles wrote. "You know he is Chief Surgeon in our Regiment He is a first rate friend to me. . . . I do hope he will be elected."[28]

An act passed by the state legislature in April 1864 granted qualified New Yorkers serving in the military the right to vote by proxy over a period of sixty days. Soldiers signed a document empowering a civilian to vote on their behalf, and marked a ticket with their choices. Voting in the 154th took place during October. The results were a landslide. Approximately 150 votes were cast, with only five or six of the presidential ballots going for McClellan (and those were cast by diehard Democrats), Lewis Warner recorded. "Well, we can let Mc have those and still have enough to reelect Uncle Abram and that by a triumphant majority," Warner wrote. Horace Howlett reported, "Well I have sent my vote home for Old Abe and the union of corse. Who elce could a union man vote for that is a man." According to a regimental correspondent to the *Cattaraugus Freeman,* only three votes went against Fenton. First Lieutenant Horace Smith of Company H entered a ringing endorsement of the Republican slate in his diary: "The boys have all sent their votes home, but *Little Mac* gets a very small vote in this army. *Hurray for Old Abe! Fenton! and Dr. Van Aernam!*"[29]

Voting on November 8, the home folk in Cattaraugus and Chautauqua counties gave the Republican ticket about 61 and 69 percent of their vote, respectively. About a week later, Surgeon Van Aernam resigned his commission and left the 154th New York at Atlanta to take his congressional seat. "It was a sad day to our boys when he left," Horace Smith wrote. Fenton won the governorship; Lincoln was reelected. The soldiers could now expect all the political support they needed as they engaged in the campaigns that would help end the war.[30]

One of the few remaining Democrats in the regiment underwent a conversion two months after the election, when the 154th reached Savannah at the end of Sherman's March to the Sea. Corporal George P. Brown of Company A visited a family of former slaves in the city and was charmed by a teenaged girl who was of mostly white blood. On returning to the 154th's camp, Brown related his experience to his tent mate, Sergeant Andrew D. Blood. "Blood," Brown exclaimed, "I went away a Democrat but I have come back an abolitionist. When a party asks me to vote for to enslave such a people as the young lady I have seen today, then I cease to be one of their number any longer. I shall vote the ticket no more." With Brown's conversion, the 154th New York came one step closer to absolute political solidarity.[31]

The first regimental muster rolls completed in the field, dated October 31, 1862, less than a month after the 154th arrived in Virginia, recorded 947 officers and enlisted men present for duty. A year later, the October 31, 1863, rolls listed 257 present. By October 31, 1864, the number present had dwindled to 205—and 49 of them were new recruits who had joined the regiment in the previous few days, the only significant influx of recruits received by the 154th during its entire term of service. In round numbers, the regiment's strength had declined from 950 men to 150 in two years of service. As that great attrition eroded the ranks of the 154th, the surviving soldiers increasingly wondered where replacement manpower would come from.[32]

For a long time, conscription appeared to be the answer—and it was a perfectly acceptable answer to the soldiers. But the Enrollment Act passed by Congress in March 1863 set up a draft system that proved to be inefficient, corrupt, and riddled with two glaring loopholes: a draftee could hire a substitute or pay a $300 commutation fee and escape service. The veteran soldiers of the 154th New York were absolutely agreeable with the prospect of stay-at-home men being drafted—particularly the hated Copperheads, who, it was assumed, would take the cowardly way out and hire a substitute or buy a commutation. In letters home, the soldiers showed a constant interest in the draft, and who it would nab of the home folk.[33]

"Our Regt is quite small now, but I expect New York can fill it up if nessary," Richard McCadden wrote on the eve of Gettysburg. "I wish she would send us five or six hundred conscrips. I would like to march along with them a few days." For almost a year the soldiers had suffered hardships while able-bodied men enjoyed the comforts of home, and they were anxious to have the stay-at-homes join them in the ranks. "A draft . . . will probably relieve the town of a portion of its inhabitants," Dwight Moore noted, "and if it only takes the right ones, I shall be *very* happy to receive a visit from them in Virginia."[34]

But given the loopholes, the soldiers were not entirely sanguine that the draft would provide the needed men. "Pleas write and let me know who is drafted and all about it," Stephen Green wrote in a typical passage. He continued, "Al here want to no who the luccy ones are to draw a ticket we think that the most of the men in that town that are Drafted will pay the 300 Dollars or get a Substitut." William Charles inquired of his wife, "How does the Drafted copper Heads feel How do they like to pay their *little three hundred* Will Morgan Davis *come or pay*. . . . I wish it was so he would have to come down here himself. How I would Hoot *at him*." Opinions varied among the soldiers regarding the substitute and commutation stipulations. "If I were to dictate," Charles Abell declared, "No man should be exempt except by furnishing a Substitute or [if he] was himself Positively unfit for the service. No 300 or 600 Dollars would clear a man from the service." Advising his uncle, Private Oscar F. Wilber of Company G strongly recommended that the older man hire a substitute rather than serve if drafted: "Uncle Nathan if you are drafted you better hier a man to come in your place if it coasts you all you are worth to hire him for what is a mans property worth when he is dead."[35]

Richard McCadden mocked those males who remained at home. "When you hear those patriotic boys telling they would come into the Army if it was not for Pa or Ma or somebody els," he wrote to his sister, "just ask them if they would not come if it was not for the *bullets* I believe they have the most to do with them [not volunteering]." In a letter to his mother and brother, McCadden anticipated their pride in his voluntary service. "When this cruel war is over then I will return," he wrote, "and I am shure you will be much happier to see me than If I had stayed at home all the time or wated untill I was drafted." The scorn the soldiers felt for the stay-at-homes extended to those who were drafted. David Jones described the stigma that was attached to drafted men: "If I was a free man, and was liable for the or to the draft, and could not get off no other way I would enlist again. *never* would I come as a conscript, to be fooled at by the old soldiers and called 'conies' and have to put up with officers insolence that they dare not show us now." The soldiers' contempt for draftees was echoed by their loved ones. "They talk of drafting very strong . . . and the men are scart most to death," Martha James reported to Samuel Williams. "So I am glad that you enlisted when you did."[36]

But the draft proved ineffectual in getting men into uniform—aside from the many men who volunteered to avoid the dishonor of conscription—and not a single drafted man replenished the ranks of the 154th New York. Instead, the regiment looked to Cattaraugus and Chautauqua counties to reinforce its numbers with volunteers. "I am assured by the citizens of these Counties, that recruits could be raised quite rapidly provided we had officers there with proper authority to recruit them," Lieutenant Colonel Dan Allen wrote from the 154th's camp in Tennessee to the assistant adjutant general in Washington in February 1864. The 154th had been reduced to 464 enlisted men, with fewer than 300 present for duty, Allen explained. He requested that the War Department grant permission for a recruiting party to be sent from the regiment to Cattaraugus County to seek volunteers. Consequently, a detail consisting of Captain Commodore P. Vedder, First Sergeant Richard McCadden, and five enlisted men returned home in March 1864, but they met with little success. "I have the honor to report that I have up to date obtained only three recruits," Vedder wrote after two futile weeks of work, and the recruiting party returned to Lookout Valley on April 17 accompanied only by the trio of volunteers: Privates Fayette McClure and Sheldon A. Cobbet of Company D, and Sanford P. Kinyon of Company I (who would be killed exactly three weeks later at Rocky Face Ridge).[37]

A more successful effort occurred in September 1864, when fifty-six men enlisted to serve in the 154th and were sent to join the regiment at Atlanta. These recruits responded to a call by President Lincoln in July 1864 for 500,000 volunteers to serve one, two, or three years, "as they may elect." But they were also nudged to volunteer by a provision of Lincoln's proclamation—any town that did not meet its quota of volunteers would then draft the needed men on September 5, 1864. Reacting to Lincoln's call, the Cattaraugus County Board of Supervisors met in special sessions and resolved to appropriate more than $300,000 to recruit volunteers—some of whom would be sought by special agents out of state—and pay them fat $300 bounties. The money was to be raised by taxation. When the veteran soldiers of the 154th heard the news, they were incensed. Not only were they and their families to be taxed to support the measure, but the new recruits were to receive much larger bounties than the veterans themselves had in 1862.[38]

Wrote Emory Sweetland on learning of the appropriation:

The loyal & patriotic people of Catt. Co. resolved through their worthy supervisors to levy a Tax on the property of the county for the purpose of hiring negros, Jail birds & every thing & any thing to fill up the war worn & battle strained ranks of that noble old regt. the 154th N.Y. & save their own precious hides. now most of our boys own small pieces of land which from their being away . . . does not bring them but little profit & the idea of their being out here and enduring all the toll & danger & being taxed to exempt their friends & neighbors does not comport with our views of right. I must say that there has been much cussing & tall swearing since that our boys heard by the Freeman of the course that our county intends to persue & every one are hoping that the committee will not meet with success recruiting & the men have to be drafted yet.[39]

William Charles was also adamantly opposed to the legislation:

It certainly is too bad that Soldiers and Soldiers families should be compelled to pay such a heavy tax to those that enlist now. I do not see any justice in paying one Volunteer a thousand dollars now while those that have been in the field two and three years only get from twenty five to fifty dollars. Every Volunteer should be paid the same amount from the town be that sum little or much then no one would justly find fault. There are many a soldier in the army that has a little property at home but it takes all he can earn and more to pay the taxes on it, in order to pay others large bounties to do that which he is doing for nothing.[40]

The veterans' resentment indicated that assimilation of the new volunteers in the regiment would be a challenge to esprit de corps. Distaste for the new recruits' large tax-supported bounties was tempered, however, by awareness of the critical need for new men. Moreover, the new recruits were volunteers, not lowly conscripts, and they were Cattaraugus County men, not hirelings from elsewhere. The recruits were, after all, friends, neighbors, and kinfolk from back home, and they were better welcomed later than never. In a letter to his wife, William Charles expressed some of the ambivalence the veterans felt about their soon-to-be regimental comrades:

> You say that it is a time of sadness with you, for many of the boys have enlisted &c, &c. I think it ought to be a time of joy and rejoicings with you all to see men go to help their Brethren to gain the Victory, the Great Victory which sooner or later will crown our efforts. To be sure it is hard to go from ones family into the Army; to leave a comfortable home for the tented field, to leave the pursuits of peacefull domestic life for one of destruction and carnage Yes all that *is hard* and bad enough, but there are some things worse in this world than even that. To live a Coward at home or die a traitor abroad is ten thousand times worse![41]

Ultimately, the fate of esprit de corps in the 154th New York on the addition of the 1864 volunteers would depend on how the new men did their duties and endured the hardships they would face. As Newton Chaffee expressed it, "I hear that there is quite a number of our County enlisting for our Regiment. they should understand that if they come into this Regiment that they will have to work & fight, as this Regt does no Soft work, as work & fight is all they know." If any bitterness was shown by the veterans to the new recruits on their arrival at Atlanta, it went unrecorded by both factions. Indeed, one of the new recruits, Levi Bryant, wrote from Atlanta, "I got to my regament yesterday & found all the Boys & they was pleased to See us." It seems that hard feelings vanished or were repressed when the veterans finally greeted the new additions to their beloved regiment.[42]

Some of the 1864 volunteers did not even reach the regiment at Atlanta before they were waylaid with sickness; still others were weeded out and sent back from that city before the great march began. But a hardy bunch of the new men adapted to army life, survived their first active campaign, and stood their first fire during the siege of Savannah. "The recruits that came to us stand it well," Marcellus Darling wrote at the conclusion of the March to the Sea. They had worked and fought; they had met the veterans' criteria. Writing a few weeks later, one of the recruits made a remark that made him sound like a veteran. "We hear that their will be another draft at [home]," John Langhans wrote. "If there is it will make some fellows hop."[43]

PART TWO

War Ties

CHAPTER 4

Comrades, Cowards, and Survivors

When he reached Atlanta and joined the 154th New York in the autumn of 1864, new recruit John Langhans immediately looked up an old friend from home, veteran soldier John Dicher. Two years had passed since they last saw each other, but they quickly rekindled their friendship. "John Disher and I visit each other qiet often," Langhans wrote. "Our shantees are about 20 rods apart last night I was to his tent and we was talking about old times we enjoy our selfs verey well I have a grate deal better times than I ecspected so far."[1]

Already bound by community, occupational, ethnic, and family ties, friendship came easily to the soldiers of the 154th and offered a fertile ground for the growth of esprit de corps. "We have as much fun as we did cutting oats on the hill when the spider crawled on Fathers pie," Marcellus Darling informed his parents nine days after the regiment arrived in Virginia. "Some of the boys are home sick but they will get over that soon I am not I can say." Friendship certainly helped to dispel homesickness, as was the case with Alva Merrill and his tent mate, Horace Howlett. "You better believe that I and Horace takes a lot of comfort together," Alva informed his mother, Ruba. "If one gets any good thing the other has half I dont know what I should do without him I know I would be homesick if he was not here."[2]

Tied by friendship, messmates became families, tents or log huts became homes, and company streets became neighborhoods in a regimental village. "I will describe to you how our new home looks inside this evening," Barzilla Merrill wrote to Ruba from his winter hut near Stafford Court House in February 1863 as he offered a prose picture of himself and his tent mates, Calvin Johnson and Bornt Shelmadine, living in domestic harmony and peace: "I set on the foot of the bed . . . Calvin a little to my left loped over backwards on the bed and one foot up on the pile of night wood fast asleep. . . . Shelmadine is washing his cloths before the fire this makes our family our other tent mate [Hiram Vincent] is nursing to the hospital." A visit Barzilla made to some company comrades sounded much like a visit he and Ruba would have paid to neighbors back home in Dayton. "This evening our neighbors acrost the street gave me an invitation to come over and take supper with them and so I went," he reported. "They had some sweet potatoes and I had a good supper. . . . They had good chees to so you see that I have some friends here."[3]

In moments of introspection, the soldiers pondered the value of their friendships. "God has been verry merciful to me & has raised up many friends to me here," Emory Sweetland wrote. He continued, "I do not know as I have an enemy in the company. . . . I have good bunk mates. the Burroughs boys [brothers Daniel L. and George W. Burroughs, both privates of Company B] are steady boys, although not professors [of religion]." Fifteen months later, Sweetland reiterated his appreciation of comradeship: "I have always since that I have been with the regiment been treated with much kindness." Private Edwin R. Osgood of Company C, whose brothers Stephen and William W. Osgood were company mates, stated, "I do not think that i have got an enemy in the redgment thay are the best friends hear to me that i ever saw in my life evan the Curnal sed the other day that he shoud not like to have me go home for my folk Shoud not know me for i was as fat as a fooll."[4]

Comrades could not forsake comrades. "I should like some of your sweet apple sauce here," Marcellus Darling informed his family, "but [I] can not feel contented to come home & leave the rest of the boys yet." Furthermore, comrades became friends for life. On February 10, 1865, after a day of foraging in South Carolina, Andrew Blood noted in his diary an agreement he had made with his tent mate, George Brown: "One year from to day if all is well, G. P. Brown and wife is to make me a visit For [a] supper [of] chicken pot pie, in case I have a wife." Blood married five months after returning home at the end of the war, in November 1865, so he and Brown and their spouses might have kept their dinner date.[5]

As surrogate family members, comrades were frequently written about in intimate terms in letters to home folk. "George Real came and stuk his head into our tent this evening as I set writing," Barzilla Merrill informed Ruba. "He says tell them I am well george is fleshy and tough he and I walk out together we are trying to live in the enjoyment of religion." "The boys are all well," William Charles notified his wife. "Bill James has just come in and wish to be remembered Very kindly to you all. David Williams send his love and best wishes. David is some what low hearted but his *bodily health is improving.*" Marion Plumb instructed his wife, "Tell Mr Smith to give himself no unnecessary trouble about Horace he is one of the toughest Boys in the regiment."[6]

Not all of the men got along together, of course. Hiram Vincent was promoted to corporal in January 1863 and accepted an invitation to fill a vacancy as tent mate to Company K's orderly sergeant, Stiles Ellsworth, leaving his former tent mates Barzilla Merrill, Calvin Johnson, and Bornt Shelmadine. Vincent soon realized he had made a mistake. "Vinson says that he is sorry that he left us and shall try and get out again," Merrill reported. "He dont like his new company they sware drink and play cards our family are very quiet." Vincent was replaced in Merrill's tent by Private Taylor B. Vanderburgh (at age fifty-six, one of the regiment's senior soldiers), who fit in well. "Shelmadine is a good whole harted fellow so is Vanderburg," Barzilla wrote in March 1863. But his relationship with Calvin Johnson had become strained. "Calvin ant the man that I used to think he was," Merrill wrote. "He is verry selfish and over baring. . . . Calvin don't have any thing sent from home but he likes to eat what others get. . . . Say nothing about this," Barzilla cautioned Ruba. Like many of the men, he was reluctant to have criticism of his comrades spread among the home folk.[7]

Personal problems broke up messes and rearranged tent mates. Alva Merrill and Horace Howlett tented with privates William J. Hull and Theodore Wheelock in Company K until Hull and Wheelock became so "shiftless" and "nasty"—"and not only nasty but lousy [lice-ridden] to"—that the foursome broke up. "Horace and I tent alone now," Alva reported to his mother, Ruba. "We could not stand it with them. . . . You need not tell anybody so but it is a fact." Some men were described as general annoyances that nobody could get along with, among them Private Harvey Inman of Company K. "Harve Inman is quite wrathy," George Newcomb informed his wife. "He blows here the same as he did at home You need not say anny thing that I wrote about it for if his folks get hold of it they will write to him about it." Newcomb wanted no trouble with the pugnacious Inman. "Harvy Inman is known here about as well as he was to home and his repitation [is] about the same," Barzilla Merrill observed. "He has had two fights and got handled both times."[8]

Albert Goulding lost the respect of his comrades of Company F when he forged a letter, purportedly from his grandfather, to Second Lieutenant Dana P. Horton. It claimed that Goulding's mother was deathly ill and asked Horton to help Goulding get a furlough and to lend him money. Goulding was already in disfavor with his company comrades for reneging on twenty dollars in debts and stealing a box meant for James Emmons. When Horton proved the letter a hoax, Goulding's reputation plummeted further. "I tell you Ann," James Emmons wrote to his sister, "Ab has not got one friend in the company there is not one that will go to the hospital to see him. . . . If he ever comes back to the company they would if they could kick him clear home for they thinks that he is a disgrace to the company all of the boys in the hospital perfectly hates him but enough of that." Sometimes rifts between disgruntled comrades were healed. Nathaniel Brown became "some gritty" when his Company D tent mate, Eason Bull, left him to drive a brigade ammunition wagon. "I will tell you something I don't want you to tell of," Bull confided to his brother and sister-in-law. "There is one man from Yorkshire his name is Nat Brown, he is one dammed shit ass. I tell you this is the place to find out who your friend is, dont let no one see this letter." But Bull and Brown got over their difficulty and resumed sharing a tent. In February 1863, Brown was the one to inform Bull's family, with heartfelt sorrow, that Eason had died of disease.[9]

Camaraderie inspired the men to dub each other with nicknames. It is easy to understand why some of Barzilla Merrill's younger comrades called him "Uncle Merrill," why former sailor Clark Oyer was known as "Salty," and why Private Joseph B. Sherwin of Company I—who stood six feet, three and three-quarter inches tall and weighed well over two hundred pounds— was called "Babe." And reasonable guesses can be made as to why the men called officers Commodore Vedder "Yawpy Boy" and Philander Hubbard "Old Bright." But it is uncertain why Private Andrew Curtis of Company B was known as "Pod," Private Bradford Rowland of Company G was dubbed "Mouse Ear," and Private Thomas Murray of Company G was called "Ash-Cat." Murray was remembered by company comrades as a good soldier but a "mean little chap when drunk" who "would keep very dirty." His friends would rile the "Ash-Cat" by purring like a cat when he passed. Another notoriously unkempt soldier, Private Asahel Hollister of Company H, was known as "Beauregard" by his comrades. Hollister could not have been less like his namesake, the natty Confederate general Pierre Gustave Toutant Beauregard. The 154th's Beauregard typically looked like a tramp, with holes burnt in his pants and overcoat from sleeping too close to campfires. One nickname seems to have spread from an individual to his entire company. Captain Lewis Warner was called "Lummadoo" by the men. After the Battle of Chancellorsville, the men of other companies sang about Warner and Company C, "The Lummadoos, they lost their shoes, at Chancellorsville, the Rebs got the new shoes."[10]

At least one fraternal subgroup existed in the 154th New York: Freemasons. Lieutenant Colonel Henry C. Loomis and Sergeant Andrew M. Keller of Company D were Masons, and no doubt there were others. A comment made by Charles Abell regarding one of the regiment's prisoners of war might well have referred to Keller. "I should know better what to do if I were to enlist ever again," Abell wrote. "I should be a mason not by trade but by initiation I know of a man who belongs to the 154 that is in Richmond and he fares better for being one than those who do not have the honor to belong to that society." According to his nephew Charles Whitney, Keller reportedly enjoyed advantages extended by Confederate Masons while he was a prisoner of war at Richmond.[11]

Attrition whittled away the ranks of the regiment as disease, discharge, and death took their toll. Most men left the regiment for legitimate causes, such as illness or other disability, or assignment to detached duty. Some soldiers, however, sought to evade duty by shirking or by seeking a discharge through a feigned sickness or a self-inflicted injury. Others actively sought duties that would remove them from the front lines. The most desperate took the most reprehensible route out—desertion. Such cowardly behavior was an affront to esprit de corps. Shirkers, fakers, and deserters were thoroughly resented by the steadfast soldiers who stayed with the regiment, endured the inevitable hardships, and performed their duties faithfully.

Shirking began as soon as the 154th reached the front. A week after the regiment arrived in Virginia, George Taylor wrote, "They have a rule that no man shall be excused [from duty] unless he is excused by the surgeon at his call in the morning at 8:00. And each orderly Srg't. has to take his men from his co. and get them excused. You ought to see the line they form before his tent in the morning. There is no co. in the reg't. that can show as many men as his list in the morn." Taylor later identified some shirkers by name, including his tent mate. "Munroe Young has not been well," Taylor informed his wife, "and between us and ourselves, he is a confirmed shirk, does not want to do his part when he can. There are several of the kind in the company." One of them, according to Taylor, was Robert McKee, who was sent from the Stafford camp to a Washington hospital. "Our surgeon who has seen him several times has not much confidence in his illness but thinks he would be all right if he wanted to be," reported Taylor. "He [McKee] writes that he is sick of hospital life, that he did not enlist to spend his days in a hospital, that if he is not going to be fit for service, he wants to go home, and I guess in this is the great secret of his continued ill health." Taylor later identified a secondary but significant effect of shirking: the suspicion by surgeons of truly sick men. "In the Army there are so many cases of men 'Bumming' as we call it and playing off to get rid of duty that a Surgeon has to act as if all men were working on the same principle and the really sick are obliged to suffer the neglect caused by such proceedings."[12]

Thus the diagnostic abilities of Surgeon Henry Van Aernam and his two assistant surgeons, Dwight W. Day and Corydon Rugg, were tested in separating the truly sick or decrepit from the shirkers. This task had its occasional dangers—some shirkers became belligerent when exposed. When Private Cornelius Nye of Company G "played off" one day and was diagnosed as a shirker by Surgeon Van Aernam, Nye responded by kicking the doctor.[13]

Members of the 154th recognized that shirking was not limited to their regiment. As George Newcomb noted, "All new Regts have two classes in it which have to be sifted out one is a class of sneaks who pretend to be sick and get sent to the hospital and there buy a discharge The other is those . . . who were not able to stand the privations of a soldiers life and are discharged because they are good for nothing here." William Chittenden wrote, "As soon as orders to march come many are sick I presume it is so in other companies and regiments." As Newcomb suggested, regiments were better off when rid of their shirkers. Nevertheless, malingerers were resented for the extra work they caused dutiful soldiers. "There are many who try to slip out of all kinds of duty and that brings a double portion on some," Chittenden observed. Devoted soldiers also were contemptuous of the reported well-being of discharged shirkers. "We hear that those that have been discharged," John Griswold wrote, "get home fatter and healthier than they ever wer before."[14]

On the other hand, some believed that feigning sickness could become a self-fulfilling prophecy. In November 1862, William Charles reported that all of the Welsh boys were well except for Private William Williams. "Some of the boys say that he only pretends to be sick so as to save himself from duty," Charles wrote, "but he cannot play that game long, because his very pretensions of being sick will make him so." Considering the disease-ridden atmospheres of Civil War army hospitals, Charles's theory might well have been correct. In this particular case, Williams entered the hospital system and remained until he was discharged. But according to the last report Charles had of him, "Bill never looked better in his life. you see Bill knows just enough to have a good time of it all the way through." Williams was an artful and accomplished shirker.[15]

Feigning sickness was perhaps the most popular form of malingering, but reluctant soldiers found other ways to escape duties. Sheer laziness kept some soldiers idle—and their resentful comrades had to put in extra work as a result. "I am now lying in my tent covered with my blanket and overcoat for I am cold and shivering having got wet while getting breakfast and washing the dishes," William Chittenden wrote to his wife. "There are ten in our mess and Nat [Brown] Eason [Bull] & myself have to do the most of the work but we must bare it without complaining." Expressing the typical reluctance to have negative news spread back home, Chittenden added, "Do not mention it." After fabricating a sheet-iron stove to heat his tent, George Taylor noted, "We have a great deal of company by our fire all the time as about half of the men are too negligent to pay much attention to their comforts when they have to do it all by their own extertions but this cold snap is going to learn them a lesson." In addition to his expertise as a charlatan patient, William Williams was an accomplished all-around slacker, as William Charles reported:

> Bill Williams is so lazy that it is most impossible to get him to do anything at all. he has not done any camp duty to amount to any thing in a great while He says that he feels kind O weak and he cant do any thing. There is no use to say any thing to him for he says that he does not care for any thing or any body. And in fact I dont think that he

does He says if the Rebels would come he would let them take him prisoner for he thinks that the Rebels would let him go home He is chummy enough to get along any wheres. He went over to Stafford the other day, and stole a very nice towel out of some Officers tent. He said that he thought that the towel would do him as much good as any body else *Keep this to thyself.*[16]

Sometimes a reluctance to serve was more subtle. Private Daniel R. Read of Company G was remembered sarcastically in the postwar years by his company comrade Sergeant Clark E. "Salty" Oyer as "one of the brave ones," a windbag who flaunted an extensive vocabulary and stood atop a high pedestal of dignity. Read so often said he would like to carry the colors—a post of great honor and danger—that Captain Matthew Cheney finally arranged to have him join the regimental color guard. But once Read's wish was attained "he caved," according to Oyer, and left the color guard for the pioneer corps. Thereafter, the chagrined Read "did not show his nose in [the] Regt. hardly."[17]

Then there were the skulkers, soldiers who lagged behind at their own pace on the march or furtively sought the rear when bullets flew. During the great artillery barrage at Gettysburg on July 3, 1863, Private John Wheeler of Company D disappeared from the brigade hospital, where he was doing duty as a cook, and did not reappear until nightfall. Asked his whereabouts by Surgeon Henry Van Aernam, Wheeler replied that he had been taking a nap in some bushes. Van Aernam scoffed at the story and said if Wheeler could sleep through the recent tumult, he would not awake for Gabriel's trumpet on Judgment Day. Wheeler then revealed himself as a skulker with the impudent reply, "Say, Doctor! There is one man in the town of Humphrey that, if he should be killed, no one could fill his place and that is myself, and as long as my name is John Wheeler I intend to have my legs take care of my body."[18]

Some men who succumbed to fear in battle were saved from the ignominy of skulking by the intercession of fellow soldiers. At the Battle of Chattanooga, Private Howard Whitford of Company F, recovering from a sickness, lost his nerve when he came under fire and ran for the rear. He was caught, held, and calmed by his company comrade Corporal Theodore Loveless. Whitford regained his composure and was thereafter a steady soldier. During the same battle, Private William Brown Jr. of Company H was so overcome by fear that he could not load his musket. Colonel Patrick Henry Jones told the regimental surgeons to take Brown away and make use of him if they could. Brown subsequently did duty as an orderly to the surgeons and a nurse in the brigade hospital, and proved to be perfectly satisfactory in those roles.[19]

"Like all regiments," Clark Oyer recalled, "the 154th had its compliment of bummers who never got to the front but served on details or managed to keep to the rear." At any given time a large number of soldiers, like Daniel Read and John Wheeler and William Brown Jr., were detached from the regiment doing duty at the brigade, division, or corps levels as teamsters, pioneers, orderlies, saddlers, guards, stewards, clerks, blacksmiths, cooks, nurses, and in other occupations. Many of those men were quite happy to be serving in the rear echelon—hospitals; headquarters; quartermaster and commissary depots; ambulance, ordnance, and supply trains—and some no doubt sought such positions to avoid taking their place in the firing line. But many were randomly assigned to detached duty, and some were rightfully proud of the essential support services they provided. Furthermore, performing the duties of a brigade pioneer or a division hospital nurse could be as hazardous as serving in the front lines.[20]

Emory Sweetland spent most of his term of service as a nurse and steward in the regimental and division hospitals. He candidly listed his reasons for taking the hospital duty:

> In the first place I can not stand to make such marches & carry such loads as we have to carry in the ranks. . . . When we moove [we] have our packs carried for us & a hospital does not moove so often as a regiment does. . . . In the hospital we have enough to eat & of a better quality than we get in the Co. . . . It will be much more pleasant under a good tent beside a good fireplace than it would be standing out in the rain as we did while guarding the pontoon train the other night another reason is the 2 shillings pr day extra wages we get. This is quite an object with me.[21]

While admitting that life in the hospital was in many respects easier than life in the front lines, Sweetland nevertheless was unapologetic about the duty he performed: "My lot has been easier than most of the regt. I am quite healthy & I think I am thoroughly acclimated. I have learned to take care of myself & I think that I am in but little more danger than I was at home, & I have too the conciousness that I am in the path of duty. My concience approves of the act of enlisting I feel too that I have been of much use in alleviating the sufferings of the sick & wounded."[22]

Some men who sought to evade service took the drastic measure of self-mutilation in order to procure a discharge. Private Jackson Hoisington of Company F was the first known member of the regiment to shoot himself. The incident occurred on October 14, 1862, just twelve days after the 154th arrived in Virginia. Hoisington alleged he was stalking a red squirrel or a chipmunk—accounts vary—in the woods near Fairfax Court House when his gun discharged and the bullet perforated his left foot. It was an accident, Hoisington claimed, and some of his comrades believed him. But George Taylor wrote, "If he could sit in his rocking chair and rest his foot on his pillow in a chair"—in other words, if Hoisington could recuperate at home—"then he would not care much about the hurt." Hoisington never returned to duty with his company. He eventually received a discharge and returned to his home and rocker.[23]

In another case, Corporal Jerome Averill of Company K was on picket near Thoroughfare Gap, Virginia, on November 16, 1862, when he was shot through the right wrist. Averill claimed to have been hit by a bushwhacker, but Assistant Surgeon Corydon Rugg examined the wound and proclaimed no bushwhacker had made it. If Averill's wound was self-inflicted, it was more drastic then he would have wished. He was admitted to Harewood Hospital in Washington on November 19 and his arm was amputated above the elbow on December 23. Surgeons saved the shattered bones of Averill's forearm, and they are preserved today in the collection of the Armed Forces Institute of Pathology in Washington, D.C. (The collection also includes bone specimens from Oscar Wilber and Private Michael Walsh of Company I, both wounded at Chancellorsville.)[24]

Soldiers used axes as well as rifles to wound themselves. Private Henry Clark of Company D supposedly was sharpening tent stakes when he cut off two fingers. Surgeon Van Aernam asked him how he came to sever the fingers from his right (trigger) hand. Clark replied that he was left-handed. The doctor said he knew otherwise, and added sarcastically, "You will now make a good color bearer." Instead of receiving a discharge, Clark underwent a lengthy hospitalization and in March 1865 was transferred to the Veteran Reserve Corps, a unit for soldiers unable to do duty at the front but capable of performing support services. Clark's company mate, Private Samuel P. Bard, received a letter from his wife begging him to leave the service even if he had to cut off a finger to do it. Bard obediently left camp to split firewood and returned with a gash in his boot. When a comrade pulled off the boot, one of Bard's toes fell out. Two months later he was discharged from a Washington hospital.[25]

Not all self-inflicted wounds were intentional, and some men who accidentally hurt themselves were determined to remain on duty. Private Francis M. Riant of Company C shot himself in the hand during the Battle of Gettysburg, a wound that might have happened by accident in the heat of combat. Private William R. Nichols of the same company ran his bayonet through his foot on the morning of February 28, 1863, but he was captured at Chancellorsville a little more than two months later and mustered out with the 154th at the war's end. Shortly after Chancellorsville, Joel Bouton accidentally shot off one of his toes while on picket. But Bouton was still with the regiment several weeks later at Gettysburg, where he was killed. Corporal James P. Skiff wounded himself in February 1864 at Lookout Valley, Tennessee, but he too stuck with the regiment and was present at the muster-out. According to John Griswold, Skiff "accidentally discharged his gun by stumbling in the dark while on picket, the ball past through the ball of his left hand, making a severe flesh wound."[26]

Whether a man shot himself or feigned illness to acquire a discharge, he earned the enmity of his comrades who were determined to stay the course. Faithful soldiers voiced their disgust with shirkers. "Tell me what the brave boys that have got home have to say about the war," Alva Merrill requested of Ruba. "The most of us think they were home sick." Barzilla Merrill was even more pointed than his son in condemning shirkers. "I was just thinking what a warm attachment some seemed to have for their country and how soon they manage to get out [of the army] and back [home] and leave the rest here," he confided to Ruba. "It makes me disgusted to see men sing another tune so quick I was thinking about hearing a certain man say farewell Sunday school scholars fairwell Brothers fairwell sisters fairwell all." Safe at home after an ill-gotten discharge, the shirker represented a smug affront to regimental esprit de corps. As the steadfast Barzilla Merrill put it, "I think that I could not do justice to my own feelings to grunt around a while and leave my regiment here and go home with a discharge nor could I do justice to the town to which I belong. . . . I came with the regiment and I want to go with the regiment."[27]

There was one class of men that faithful soldiers despised even more than shirkers and skulkers: deserters. Forty-five members of the 154th New York were listed as deserters on the regimental muster-out rolls; almost as many more deserted or were absent without leave and returned to the regiment at some point during their service. Most of the desertions occurred during the first year of service, and almost half of the deserters were away from the regiment when they fled. Some soldiers openly voiced consideration of desertion; more soldiers condemned it. A deserter turned his back on the cause, his comrades, and his regiment. His act was the ultimate repudiation of esprit de corps.

After receiving their bounties and advance pay, four members of the 154th deserted before the regiment left Camp Brown in Jamestown. They were most likely "bounty jumpers"—men who would travel to a different area, assume a new identity, volunteer again, take the money and run, and repeat the process as often as they could. Only one of them, Private Charles Coon of Company A, was ever heard from again. "Young Coon was *treed* working in a cornfield in the west," Emory Sweetland joked in January 1864, after Coon was brought under guard to the regiment's camp in Lookout Valley. In a fairly typical punishment, Coon was tried by a court-martial, sentenced to hard labor on the public works, had thirty dollars pay withheld to cover the cost of his apprehension and transportation, and remained under arrest until August 1864. He served faithfully with his company thereafter until the muster-out.[28]

Desertions generally came in clusters after the regiment reached the front—a dozen or so during the early months at Fairfax Court House, a half-dozen during the march from Fairfax to Falmouth in December 1862, another half-dozen during the hard marches in Maryland before and after the Battle of Gettysburg. Often two or three company comrades deserted together. Some of the men fled hospitals in northern cities while being treated for an illness. More went absent without leave or deserted from the parole camp in Annapolis, Maryland, or the parole and convalescent camps in Alexandria, Virginia, after they had been captured in battle, imprisoned by the enemy, and released back to Union authority. Battlefield desertions were infrequent. One certain case involved Private Charles R. Brown of Company D, who threw down his gun and refused to fight during the Battle of Rocky Face Ridge. Brown lurked in the rear for two weeks before leaving for good.[29]

Two of the Welsh boys, Privates Richard Lewis and Benjamin D. Morgan of Company F, deserted with their company comrade, Private William A. Scott, in September 1863, during the lengthy railroad journey that delivered the regiment from Washington to the western theater, via Maryland, Virginia, West Virginia, Ohio, Indiana, Kentucky, Tennessee, and Alabama. The Welshmen's comrades condemned them in letters home. William Charles wrote, "[I] was very sorry to find that Dick Lewis & Ben Morgan had left the Regiment without leave. I trust that they will come back before they are Reported as *Deserters*." A few days later Charles declared, "It will be much better for those boys if they will return before they are reported as deserters I am ashamed of them any how and I never could believe that they would do such a thing. It was no harder for them than it was for others, in fact they *had no excuse at all*." Writing a month later, Private Lewis L. Jones indicated that the two were skulking around their homes in Freedom. "I supose that Ben Morgan [and] Dick Lewis do keep themselves pretty sly," Jones wrote. He continued, "I dont think that they can anjoy themselves very good at Home there after Diserting I think it will go pretty hard with them if they will be caught Diserting is a thing that I wont do let it come as it will." In January 1864 Charles wrote, "There is but little doubt but that Ben. Morgan & Dick Lewis have gone to Canada. I hope that shame if nothing else will for ever keep them from coming in that town again." Charles then pondered the impact of desertion on Lewis's wife: "I am very sorry for her, for she did all she could to encourage her husband to be a faithfull Soldier and I know that she is ten times as unhappy now than she was when Richard was in the army It would be much better for her to be a Widow at least so I think." What happened to Lewis is uncertain—he was mustered out in Elmira in May 1865—but Morgan did indeed flee to Canada, only to return under the terms of President Lincoln's March 1865 pardon proclamation.[30]

"I had know rong or eavle intention in comeing home," declared Stephen Green after he was apprehended at home while absent without leave from the Annapolis parole camp. "I never felt verry bad about it for I done no more than many other good Soldiers and honest men done." Green was correct; other members of the regiment were nonchalant about leaving Annapolis for an unapproved visit home. A soldier on parole could do no duty until exchanged, and so, the reasoning went, he was temporarily outside of army control. So thought Corporal Philo A. Markham and Private Leonard L. Hunt of Company B, who walked out of the Annapolis camp without permission on August 24, 1863, and kept walking until they reached their Cattaraugus County homes on September 5. Markham and Hunt returned to Annapolis without incident, unlike Green. But Green reported, "There is not one sent of charges againts me for arrest transportation &c and I have good reason to suppose that there will be none." He was correct—he went unpunished.[31]

"There is some that think a man should be shot for leaving Parole camp and [they believe that he] commited as large a crime as if he had Deserted from a picket post in front of the enemy," Green wrote, adding, "Sutch persons had better come here a short time and learn some thing." Other members of the regiment saw unauthorized departures from parole camp in a different light. "Some of my own Regiment I know are at home," wrote Charles Abell from the Alexandria convalescent camp, "but most of them are marked as *deserters* from Parole camp which in my estimation is no very enviable name in my humble opinion I would love most dearly to see home and friends [but] I do not want to run away."[32]

Men threatened to desert as they endured an inordinate wait for their first payment. "There is lots of boys that says [they] will desert when they get their pay," Eason Bull noted. Their motive was not always selfish. As Amos Humiston noted, "Thare is a grate menney men in this regament that say that if they cannot get their pay they will desert and go whare they can support there families." Other men voiced frustrations with army life in threats to desert. "I will not stay in this cussed army much longer," George Newcomb blustered in January 1863. "I shall not have any fighting to do this winter for it is so muddy our army cannot move. . . . I shall not stay in this army for this summer." Newcomb also cautioned his wife, "Do not let anyone see this Burn it as soon as you read it." But like many others, Newcomb stuck with the regiment.[33]

Occasionally a soldier expressed ambivalence regarding desertion. Referring to his brother, who had deserted from another New York regiment, William Chittenden wrote, "I can not recommend his way of getting discharged nor can I censure a person [for deserting] as strongly as before I came here." But a soldier was more likely to declare his flat-out opposition to absconding. "As for me I shall never go home if I have to desert to do so," declared Marcellus Darling. Soldiers boldly vowed not to let their families down by deserting. "Mother said she did not want me to desert," wrote Eason Bull. "Tell her as long as my name is Eason Bull I will fight before I desert." Emory Sweetland assured his wife, "I to with you detest a deserter. Your husband will never disgrace his wife and child in that way." Disgrace would tarnish more than a deserter's family, William Charles understood. In response to a false rumor that two Freedom men had fled from a Gettysburg hospital where they had been assigned to nurse the wounded, Charles wrote, "I hope they have not Deserted that would be a Disgrace not only to the Army but to the Regt. and to the town."[34]

A year later, Charles upbraided his wife when she made a remark about moving to Canada. "You seem to be some what discouraged that the war [has] continued so long," he wrote. "I too am discourage at times. But I shall never get so disheartened as even to wish to go to Canada. No let that be the Paradise of cowards Sneeks & traitors." Charles cautioned her, "Do not say any thing about Canada untill the war is ended then if you wish to go and become a subject to Johny Bull I shall have no objections you know that the wife of a Soldier should *not be a coward*."[35]

Canada's proximity to western New York made it a haven for deserters who returned to Cattaraugus and Chautauqua counties. When Susan Griswold notified her husband that William Scott was home on a furlough, John Griswold replied that Scott in fact had taken "French leave." In later comments to Susan, Griswold speculated about deserters at home and across the border, contemplated their severe punishment, but ultimately tempered his remarks with mercy:

How is it with your friends the Deserters, are they still lurking around, a part of the time lying in the woods for fear of the [Provost] Marshall & at all times ashamed to see the face of an honest & honorable man, or have they all gone to that bourn of refugees & niggers— Canada; one or two of them served up in the presence of the regiment might serve as a warning to others but the punishment to them [would be] too slight, Death by Musketry in the hands of true and Loyal men engaged in the defence of their Country, is to honorable, rather let them suffer through a long life the upbraidings of their own guilty concience & the execrations & contempt of their fellow men. However I hope that thare will be an opportunity offered by the government this winter for them to return to duty & that they will be wise enough to profit by it.[36]

Griswold was being sarcastic in referring to the deserters as Susan's friends. Some home folk no doubt rendered friendly aid to deserters; others were quick to assure soldiers of their refusal to help runaways. "I learned yesterday that there was a current report at Franklinville that I was implicated in assisting a Deserter," a civilian wrote to Henry Van Aernam. "I wish to say to you that it is false and I am very sorry that such a story should get in circulation. . . . I wish you would contradict any such report and think better of me than to take such measures against our Government."[37]

Sergeant Francis M. Bowen of Company I was recovering from a wound and an illness at a Savannah hospital in March 1865 when he had a chance encounter with a member of his company who had deserted during the Atlanta campaign. Like John Griswold, Bowen believed that a deserter deserved death, but he too moderated his judgment with mercy. "While in the street today," Bowen wrote, "I run across Chas. V. Depuy once a Serg't of my Co. but now a *deserter*. He has not been with the command since last May. Poor fellow. I pitty him; his just deserts is death. He is cowardly & tretcherous but I hope justice may fall with a downy hand for his is a weakness impossible for him to overcome." In the eyes of a devoted soldier, a deserter was innately flawed, and therefore deserving of compassion as well as condemnation.[38]

Using his canteen as a writing surface, Ambrose Arnold composed a letter to his wife from Lookout Valley in April 1864. "I am well as common . . . only a good deal lonesum," he wrote. "The boys are all out on Picket and it is verry lonely in Camp." Soldiers who were separated from their comrades by legitimate means—illness, wounds, capture, detached duty—expressed esprit de corps when they wrote of their loneliness, their displeasure at being away from the regiment, and their desire to return to its ranks. When they were able to rejoin their comrades and retie the broken bonds of esprit, they wrote with pleasure of their reunions.[39]

Doing duty as the regimental armorer, William Charles spent much of his time in the rear with the quartermaster when the 154th New York was on campaign. "It is very lonesome," he wrote on one such occasion. "I [would] much rather be with the boys. but you know that a Soldier can not have his own way, but I did feel some disapointment this morning when told that I *must not go* [to rejoin the regiment] for I had got my things all packed up and ready." Stationed miles away from the battlefield with the wagon train while fighting raged at Gettysburg, Charles voiced his anxiety for his comrades:

> I wanted to go to the front this morning to see if I could find how things were going on with our Regiment but the Quarter Master said that I could not stand it [having been unwell], and I must not think of it, so I must wait and hope for the best and pray to my heavenly father to Shield my comrades in these terrible days. How I should like to know how it is with the Freedom boys today. I am really afraid that I shall never see them on earth again. If I had been a little stronger I should certainly be with the boys in this Battle, for I do not consider my life any better than *other mens*.[40]

Hospitalized soldiers hungered for news from the regiment. "When you write," Henry Munger implored a home friend from a Baltimore hospital, "write what you know about my regiment for I halve not herd from them for over 3 months and I would like to here from them." Life in an Alexandria hospital was "a hard roe to hoe," declared Private Joseph H. Andrews of Company I. "I long to be at my Reg a gain." Recovering from his Chancellorsville wound at an Annapolis hospital, John Griswold dictated a letter to Susan. "I have herd nothing from the Comp since i last wrote," he stated. "Still i should like to hear from them as i think so much about them i feal it My Duty to bee with them as they are on the move but sircomstances wont permit it." When Private Mervin P. Barber of Company E was sent to the division hospital at Atlanta with a lame leg, he recorded regular visits to the regiment in his diary. Diarist Francis Bowen repeatedly expressed frustration with his lengthy hospital stay in Savannah, and an intense desire to rejoin the 154th. "I wish I was with my command. . . . But there is no getting to the front now. God speed the time when I can get out of Savannah. . . . There is no getting to the command now. I wish there was for I am tired of this place. . . . I will lite out of this [place] as soon as communication is opened to Sherman's army. . . . Time drags heavily this afternoon. In fact it does every day. I shall not remain here many days longer for I long to see my command."[41]

Soldiers at the Annapolis parole camp had the same longings. "I hope I will soon be sent back to the Regt," wrote Stephen Green from Annapolis. "It will seam like home to get back there again." "I do not know how soon I shall be exchanged," wrote Commodore Vedder, "but [I] hope soon, for I wish to return [to the regiment], so as to be near my wounded boys." Horace Smith wrote, "Are expecting to be sent to our Regt's everyday. the sooner the better to suit me." Five days later he added, "O! I wish I could be sent to the Regt but my time will come bye and bye." In the meantime, Smith contented himself exchanging visits with three comrades of the 154th who were doing detached duty at Annapolis.[42]

During the regiment's time at Alexandria in August and September 1863, members of the 154th swapped visits with regimental comrades in the nearby holding camps. "We are about 3 miles from parole and convalescent camp," John Griswold reported, "& some of the Boys are here most every day." Salmon Beardsley wrote, "To day I have been up to the paroll camp with Lieut [William] Chapman . . . and [we] have seen most of the parolled prisoners of our Regt had a real good visit it seemed like meeting friends at home after being so long away from them as we had stood side by side on the field [of Chancellorsville] where death was dealing destruction broadcast around and I had to describe the scenes of Gettysburg for them."[43]

Reunions with comrades were joyous occasions. On rejoining the 154th at Bridgeport, Alabama, in October 1863, after being hospitalized for his Gettysburg wound, James Quilliam declared, "It seems like ole times to be with the Redgement again." When Edgar Shannon recovered from his Chancellorsville wound and rejoined the regiment at Lookout Valley, he wrote, "I never was more cheerful than since I got back to the reg't never so full of fun, never so fat and never healthier." Mervin Barber and Corporal Thomas K. Bambrick, on duty with the brigade pioneer corps, sometimes visited their Company E mates as often as three times a day. "They are as ancious to come and see us when they have an opertunity as a twelve year old Boy would be to go home and see his parents," Stephen Green observed. Sometimes soldiers were happily reunited far from the regiment. William Charles was doing detached duty at a military depot in South Carolina in March 1865 when he reported, "In the afternoon to my great joy Wm E. Jones and Capt. [Harrison] Cheney came here and some other boys of our Regiment I was more than glad to see them, and to hear from home. . . . Wm has staid with me and will be here on the same duty as long as we remain here that will make it pleasant for us. . . . Had a long talk with Capt Cheney last night giving me a history of matters and things in Freedom."[44]

Sometimes reunions were bittersweet, as was the case when Private James Monroe Carpenter of Company K rejoined the 154th at Lookout Valley after a lengthy hospitalization for illness. Carpenter's return reminded his tent mate, Marcellus Darling, of the losses their company had endured—including Darling's brother, Delos, who had been captured at Gettysburg and was a prisoner of war. "Monroe is here now and it seems a little as it used to [be] before the battle of Chancellorsville," Darling wrote, "though our Co. is not only about one third as large now as then. If Deloss was here now all of our Bunk would be together once more." A few weeks later he wrote, "It seems like old times to have one of my mess mates with me again." But Darling was fated to be alone once more. Monroe Carpenter took sick during the Atlanta campaign and was sent back to a Chattanooga hospital, where he died on July 20, 1864. Delos Darling was eventually released from prison, but he succumbed to intermittent fever at the Annapolis parole camp on January 16, 1865. Marcellus Darling was the mess's only survivor.[45]

Shirkers, fakers, and deserters removed an unknown number of undesirables from the regiment. Many more soldiers—more than two hundred of them—were genuinely taken ill, wounded, or disabled, and came by their discharges honestly, honorably, and painfully. Approximately eighty were transferred to the Veteran Reserve Corps, where they continued to serve the cause in a limited capacity. Disease carried almost ninety men to their graves. And in battle after battle, the losses mounted. By the end of the war, the 154th New York's casualty count had reached roughly 70 killed and mortally wounded, 200 wounded, and 360 captured, of whom 60 died as prisoners of war. After each battle, the reduced ranks drew closer together, tightened by the bonds of esprit de corps. The little band of hardy survivors that Colonel Lewis Warner saluted at the regiment's discharge reflected with pride on their own endurance and achievements. At the same time, they held their absent comrades in reverent memory.

The 154th lost 240 men at Chancellorsville—about 40 percent of those engaged—and 207 at Gettysburg, 77 percent of the force that took part in the battle. Those horrific casualties, just two months apart, left the regiment a mere skeleton of its former robust self. The stunned survivors struggled to come to grips with the severe losses and to endure the crushing burden of grief. "Back again to our old camp," Henry Van Aernam reported, "fresh from the bloody field of Chancellorsville where we have left 2/5 of our Regiment (dead or prisoners) or brought them back with us wounded. We are a sorrowing and stricken band." A week later, Van Aernam buried sorrow for the losses under a layer of pride for the reputation the regiment earned in the fight. "Our ranks are thinned but our name is untarnished and whosoever of us may live to return once more to our family and friends can do so proudly and unblushingly!"[46]

In the ranks, the soldiers tried to cope with the heavy losses. "We have 11 [left] for duty in our company instead of 50 that we had before we left camp in the spring," Corporal George J. Mason of Company K wrote after Chancellorsville, "and I can assure you that it is rather lonesome. We have not heard anything from those that are missing. I presume we never shall." Mason's company comrade George Newcomb lamented, "All the boys that I used to associate with are gone what there fate is I cannot tell for we were driven from the field How many are killed I cannot tell A good many of them I fear were wounded and left out in the woods." A few days later Newcomb wrote, "It makes one feel lonesome to look at our little company."[47]

In Company E, Charles Anderson was the only one of five tent mates to escape Chancellorsville unharmed. Months later he described his feelings on returning to camp to messmate Stephen Green, who had been captured in the battle. Anderson offered Green a picture of a home violated by war, a picture Green then passed on to his wife:

Chas A. said he was verry lonely when he got back to Stafford last May he went in the tent we maid and found everything as we left it our

Bed, Seats & Cubbord with Pork, Bread &c and our dishes that we used while there. the cans that we had sent by the Dear ones at home, and all sutch things that we would get together and make in the few weeks we was there was there as we left them. when he was talking to me about [it] he said Steve you must know that I felt bad for I was the onley one to return to the tent out of the five.[48]

"You wished to know something of our Regiment," Newton Chaffee wrote to a friend after the Battle of Gettysburg. "They went into battle with nearly 300 men and only came out with about sixteen. . . . What is leaft of the Regiment is usualy well and in good cheer." Fortunately for the 154th, the eighteen initial survivors of the battle on July 1, 1863, were afterward augmented by stragglers and a lucky detachment of fifty men that had missed the fighting while on a reconnaissance. Consequently, George Mason was able to note, "There are but 75 of us left, but we are as good, what there is left of us, as ever we were." So few members of the regiment survived Gettysburg to leave testimony that their overall mood is difficult to assess. Chaffee and Mason indicated that morale was high in the 154th despite the regiment's severe losses—no doubt because Gettysburg was a clear-cut Union victory. But William Charles voiced the usual sadness. "Since that Battle I have felt very lonesome," he told his wife, "& if it was not for you & those two little ones I would rather die than not you see all the Welsh boys are gone every one of them and I am left alone."[49]

The news of Gettysburg fell hard on the regiment's absentees. At the Alexandria convalescent camp Stephen Welch noted, "Received a letter from [Corporal Dudley] Phelps, from the Regiment. It is badly cut up. They have about 60 left. Company 'C' numbers about 8." Colby Bryant, writing from the same camp, stated, "We have heard how our Regiment suffered at Gettysburg. It seems that many of our brave boys have fallen in defence of our beloved country, and we are all of us ready whenever exchanged, to again do battle in the same good cause." Edgar Shannon, at home in Cattaraugus County on furlough while recovering from his Chancellorsville wound, voiced the same determination on hearing the news of Gettysburg. "Our regiment is cut up awfully, I think I shall soon be with it again the boys are most all gone & I know it will be lonesome at first but there is my place."[50]

The next great bloodletting came during the Atlanta campaign. Slightly more than 300 officers and enlisted men were recorded as present on the regiment's April 30, 1864, muster rolls, but detached and extra duty men reduced the number actually in the ranks to about 240. The campaign opened on May 4. When it ended four months later, after several pitched battles and sometimes constant skirmishing, the 154th had suffered 110 casualties, a 46 percent loss rate. A number of sick also had been sent to the rear, reducing the total present when the regiment marched into Atlanta to about a hundred men. In reporting the losses, surviving members of the regiment mixed sadness with pride and determination, much as they had after Chancellorsville and Gettysburg. "We have now 140 guns," Lewis Warner wrote in May after the battles of Rocky Face Ridge and Resaca, "hardly enough to be called a regiment, but as good for our numbers as any in the army." "We have had about 75 men killed & wounded since we started out from Lookout Valley out of 200 men that we started with," Emory Sweetland reported in early June. "It is sad to think of." Later that month Marcellus Darling noted, "The Regiment is very small now but what there is of it is good ones." Early in July Darling wrote, "I am thankful to the all wise being that I have thus far been spared to relate the history of eight hard fought battles which I have been in. . . . We have lost a larger proportion than the rest of the Regiments or Corps in this Army." About the same time, Milon Griswold recorded that only eight men remained in Company F. Reporting on the campaign to a hometown newspaper, Griswold wrote, "We have only got about 100 guns in our regiment now; the 154th Regt. is but a mere shadow of what it was before we started for active service."[51]

Perspectives widened as survival lengthened. Emory Sweetland's brother, Private John Wesley Sweetland of Company B, was hospitalized early in the regiment's service and transferred to the Veteran Reserve Corps in February 1864. With the exception of several months when he was detached at Gettysburg to tend the wounded in the aftermath of the battle, Emory Sweetland remained at the front until the 154th's muster-out. Pondering the difference in January 1865, after the regiment had completed the March to the Sea in Savannah, Emory realized he had been blessed—although his good fortune had not come without cost: "I was just thinking that Wesley would be likely to go home from the war without seeing much more of the war, or of the world than he would have if he had stayed at home, whilst that I am likely to have the United States pretty well mapped over & to have visited all the principle citys in the Union also the great battle fields & seen all the great Generals in the army. some times I have seen a little more than I wanted for a short time."[52]

Out of the thousand-plus men who served in the 154th New York, eleven soldiers deserve special mention as extraordinary survivors. First Sergeant Henry Barbour and Musician James C. Helms of Company A, Corporal David Sherman Jr. of Company B, Corporal Charles Grossman of Company C, Private Charles Bookman of Company D, Private James Henry Cole and Corporal Rodolphus P. Edgerton of Company E, Private James H. Scott of Company F, Sergeant Samuel Hogg of Company H, and First Sergeant George J. Mason and Corporal Henry C. Gould of Company K were the only men of the regiment recorded as present for duty on every bimonthly muster roll from muster-in to muster-out. They did not survive unscathed— Barbour, Bookman, Hogg, and Mason were all slightly wounded in battle. But somehow the eleven managed to escape more serious wounds, debilitating disease or injury, capture by the enemy, and other hazards of camp and battlefield. They escaped the demoralization that led to shirking, absence without leave, and desertion. Gould and Hogg were temporarily absent from the regiment when they were assigned to the March 1864 detail that returned to Cattaraugus County to seek recruits—a plum job to reward their steadfast service. Others of the eleven might also have been absent for short periods of time between musters, but that in no way diminishes their accomplishment. Buoyed by esprit de corps, they stuck with the regiment throughout the war and proved to be its staunchest soldiers.[53]

CHAPTER 5

Enduring Hardships

More than three hundred soldiers stood beside the stalwart eleven at the muster-out and discharge of the 154th New York. They too were survivors, and in many respects the ordeals they had endured exceeded in hardship the travails of the eleven who had stuck with the regiment throughout its service. Among them were convalescents who had rejoined the 154th after lengthy hospitalizations for a variety of debilitating illnesses and dangerous wounds, and exchanged prisoners of war who had survived incredible sufferings under unbelievably squalid conditions while in Confederate hands.

Also in line at the muster-out were thirty-nine of the fifty-six recruits who had joined the regiment at Atlanta in October 1864. An inspection of the muster rolls reveals that only thirty of those recruits—little more than half of the original number—had withstood the rigors of army life and Sherman's campaigns to be present throughout their entire nine months of service. The others, like their veteran counterparts, had succumbed to illness, discharge, and capture. Five of them had surrendered to the ultimate enemy, death.

The single greatest factor in the development of esprit de corps among the soldiers of the 154th was their mutual struggle to endure a variety of physical and psychological hardships and to survive the lethal ordeal of battle. Together, the men were hardened by suffering, fired in the crucible of combat, and annealed in hospitals and prisons. Along the way, the shirkers and deserters and sick and disabled took their leave, unwilling or unable to stand the strain. "Who would not be a soldier?" the survivors asked in a sarcastic catchphrase. They strode onward, reconciled to their lot, virtually uncomplaining, resolved to meet and conquer the obstacles that army life, nature, and the enemy put in their way. They fought on for personal honor, for the Union cause, and for the good name of the 154th New York Volunteers.

"I often think that if I will get home that i will know how to enjoy it," James Quilliam wrote in October 1863, "after living so long more like an ani-

mal then like a man." In attempting to describe their hard lives, some soldiers could only compare themselves to animals. "We are turned out into the
lots or woods as the case may be like dum bruits," Barzilla Merrill wrote.
"We slep out in the rain like hogs," declared Private Harvey Earl of Company
H after a march. He added, "I was wet as a drounded rat." Oscar Wilber
informed his uncle, "If we could have youre barn to sleep in we would think
that we was well provided for We have to fair harder then youre cattle does."
Levi Bryant told his wife, "You hant no idea how a soldier is used worse than
a Brute Beest."[1]

The brutal physical life of the soldier was cause for frequent complaint
early in the regiment's service. On reaching the front, the men found their
food, clothing, and shelter to be adequate, albeit occasionally meager and
substandard. Shortly after arriving in Virginia, an anonymous member of
Company K complained that the men were "starved," and that their rations
consisted of "nothing but the raw material without any spicing." He added,
"Our meat we sometimes chain in order to keep it from running away," infested as it was with vermin. Sometimes rations were scarce during campaigns, and food shortages were common during the winter of 1863–1864 in
Lookout Valley. "We have not had quite enough to eat for the past week,"
William Charles noted on Christmas Day 1863. "Some of us are actually *suffering from hunger.*" But the shortage was an aberration; for most of the regiment's service, rations were abundant enough. "We have plenty to eat if we
had it cooked right or fixed up in any shape," James Monroe Carpenter
wrote a week after his Company K comrade had complained of starving. To
Carpenter, any culinary deficiency was understandable: "I guess I have not
the cook that I was used to have that is what the matter is I think."[2]

During times of plenty a soldier could claim, "I have anough to eat of
such as it is and not very bad nether," as James Quilliam did in February
1863. At that time rations included hardtack, salt pork and beef, beans, rice,
sugar, and coffee, augmented occasionally by potatoes, dried apples, molasses, tea, and whiskey. Although rations were plentiful, the men nevertheless
found them monotonous. "I have got so tired of eating hard bread and pork,"
John Porter wrote, "that I think if I had some money I would get something
different." Hardtack, the prime army staple, was the subject of much comment. "I can't eat hard tacks," Eason Bull declared. "My mouth is as sore as
[a] baby's." Alva Merrill sent a hardtack to his younger brother and in-

structed, "I want you should eat it and see if you could live on them without much of anything else and not half enough of them." Contrasting his sister's holiday meals to the kettle of bean soup he and his messmates were preparing, John Porter resorted to sarcasm. "What are your Christmas & New Years dinners to be compared with such a dinner as ours will be?" he asked. "How I do pity you poor folks at home You dont know what good living is. . . . I am afraid I shall get accustomed to good living so I shall hate to break off if I keep on eating Hardbread."[3]

A poor diet could weaken men and even make them sick. Poor water was perhaps even more hazardous. "We got some very good water at Washington yesterday," William Chittenden wrote on the regiment's first day in Virginia, "but when we got here last night we wer tired and verry thirsty and could get none as good as a Cattaraugus mud puddle." A few weeks later Barzilla Merrill linked bad water at Fairfax with an outbreak of diarrhea. "The water is poor here and there is quite a number in camp that is troubled with a back door trot and it runs some of them quite hard."[4]

Complaints about their uniforms were few and usually limited to headgear and footwear. "I do not like our caps," Emory Sweetland wrote. "The wet runns off from them into our necks & from their shape they are easily knocked of from our heads." In the opinion of Dwight Moore, "These caps are no better than a cabbage leaf." Sweetland described the socks issued to the men as "useless things." "I drawed two pair of socks some 3 weeks ago," he wrote in December 1862. "I wore large holes in both pairs the first time that I wore them." Two months later Newell Burch recorded in his diary, "Learned a new thing to day, viz, to change & wear the leg of a sock when the toe got worn out." Campaigning wore uniforms ragged; in camp, quartermasters were quick to issue new gear and clothing.[5]

More bothersome to the men was the scanty protection afforded by their small shelter tents. "The rain still pours down in torrents," John Griswold noted on an October day at Fairfax in 1862. "The boys are complaining grumbling swearing &c about their tents, and not without just cause for they are miserable things in cold or storm." The men bemoaned the peril such poor shelter presented to their health. "We have had some of as cold nights as I want to see whil I have to stay in these little nasty tents," Alva Merrill wrote from Fairfax. "Some nights when I go to bed I put on my overcoat and button it up and put on my night cap and then my cap and then turn my overcoat cape over my head then put a blanket over me and then when I wake up I am [still] shaking as if I had the ague." Also writing at Fairfax, Amos Humiston reported, "I took a hard cold and it settled on my lungs and that threw me into the camp feaver and having nothing to shelter me from the cold and storm but our shelter tents which are not as good as a last years birds nest it went hard with me." The regiment had moved to Falmouth when William Charles wrote, "When we came to this camp, we did not expect to stay but a day or two—but here we are yet, and the boys have not fixed their Tents very well and some of them [are] begining to suffer some from Sleeping on the ground. The Rheumatism or some thing else has taken hold of my left arm & made it quite lame." But the soldiers soon became quite adept at building comfortable winter huts, and acclimated to sleeping under their shelter tents in all kinds of weather.[6]

Fires for cooking and warmth burned almost constantly, draping a pall of smoke over the camps. "It smokes so here in camp," George Newcomb noted, "that my eyes are nearly smoked out of my head." "It affects my eyes very much," Barzilla Merrill wrote of the smoke, but the problem was alleviated somewhat when the men moved into winter huts. "I have received some inconvenience from camp smoke," Barzilla wrote, "but now they have mostly got chimneys and the smoke is not as bad."[7]

Much of their civilian life as farmers had been spent outdoors, but soldiering took living in nature to new levels. The weather was a frequent topic in their diaries and letters. Sweltering in heat and humidity, shivering in the cold, marching through viscous mud, buffeted by howling winds, soaked with rain and damp with snow and sleet, the men either broke down and fell sick, or acclimated and toughened. "The wether is severely cold here now," George Newcomb wrote at Fairfax in December 1862. "The inhabitants say it has not froze here so hard before in four years. . . . I was out on picket last night and had a cold time of it the wind blew hard and the snow would squeak under my feet as it does in [Cattaraugus County] some cold February morning. . . . I tell you soldiering is tough business [in] such wether I can look around camp and see groups of soldiers standing around camp fires burning one side and freezing the other." On a similar inclement morning the following month, Newell Burch recorded in his diary, "Rained all night and commenced snowing this morning and snowed and thawed all

day An awful day in camp Boys huddle around fires like calves in fence cor-
ners."[8]

Writing on a day of continual rain in Fairfax, James Emmons noted, "It
is [a] cold and very disagreeable time to be huddled up in small tents and so
much mud you have to take off your boots every time you come in." The
soldiers were amazed at the extent, depth, and stickiness of Virginia mud.
"Thare is plenty of mud and the mud is not like the mud in our country,"
Amos Humiston observed. "It is like glue." The 154th took part in the notorious Mud March of January 1863, when the Army of the Potomac bogged
down in a sea of mire to the taunts of the Confederates from the opposite
shore of the Rappahannock River. "You cant begin to imagine anything
about the mud," Alva Merrill stated to Ruba in describing the march. "Here
was a Canon stuck and there was a pontoon stuck and there a baggag wagon
and there a dead mule and here a tired out Soldier and so it went."[9]

Sometimes it seemed like nature conspired against the regiment. "If
there is any bad storm the 154 has to march or else go on picket," Alva Merrill declared. Other times, the men blamed their generals for the exposures
they suffered. Marching back to Lookout Valley after the relief of Knoxville
in December 1863, Lewis Warner noted, "Encamped in an open field in a
heavy rain, which however did not prevent the Gen Commanding from enjoying their Luxurious quarters, while the men less favored lay in the mud &
water, within ½ mile of good dry camping ground under shelter of a wood.
But such is war, particularly where the Head Quarters have no sympathy
with the Rank & file."[10]

As the soldiers were hardened by exposure to the elements, they developed a stoic attitude about the vagaries of the weather. "What tries the endurance of the men the most," John Griswold stated, "is lying on the ground
nights, especially during the winter season when the nights are cold and
damp." But in the same letter Griswold observed, "Thare is nothing verry
Pleasant or agreeable in soldiering, still it is no worse than I expected."
Eason Bull noted that after the Mud March slogged to a stop the foul
weather continued, but he remained undaunted under the onslaught of pre-
cipitation. "When we got back it rained so we pulled our tents over a pole
to keep dry. We had a hell [of a] rough concern that night. it began to snow
and blow and freeze, by thunder in Mars if I did not think of home that
night, I never did. . . . Well the next morning the snow was so deep on us

[we asked] who would not be a soldier? I will because I can't help it. It is fun." Barzilla Merrill wrote, "There is a great many exposures to bad weather connected with souldering I find but I stand it like a horse." During the retreat after Chancellorsville, Horace Smith recorded in his diary, "Rather wet night but we were so tired we could sleep any where that [we] could find a place to lay down. we slept first rate for all that we were covered with mud and wet clothes on the wet ground, ha!! Ha! this is soldiering in good earnest. 'let her Rip.' "[11]

One annoyance the soldiers never grew accustomed to was lice. Most of the men were infested with the vermin at some point during their service. George Newcomb's initiation came in May 1863, as he described to his wife:

> Well Ell I have been lousy for the first time since I have been in the army. . . . I found quite a number [of] fat greasy Sleek looking chaps on me It looked like a pity to kill such noble looking fellows But I mustered up the courage and after a considerable exertion I succeeded in laying them out with a good sized club I should judge by the amount of eggs or knits rather that they had deposited on my shirt that they had some good times and had been verry busy the short time they staid with me Boiling hot water will soon use them up and I think I have them subdued now.[12]

Lice afflicted the men no matter where they were. Describing the march from the vicinity of Knoxville to Lookout Valley, Milon Griswold wrote, "When we were on the march, we had to every time we stopped, take off our shirts and drawers and kill the lice, to keep them from carrying us off. We had no change of clothes for four weeks, and were lousy and dirty as hogs. Such is the beauty of soldiering." Emory Sweetland described the lice near Atlanta as "GREAT BIG lusty fellows regular gray backs. . . . Our boys are pestered most to death with the varmints for days & some time weeks they have to sleep on the ground & in their clothes with no chance of washing or changing them." Creatures other than lice also pestered the men in Georgia, Sweetland noted: "Bugs, flies, Wood ticks (or Ricks properly) Quicks [lizards], snakes, Jiggers & lice . . . are a perfect plague to us." But lice remained the most constant nuisance. "It is hard work to keep the Boddy-Lice of wash as often as you may," Levi Bryant observed. "I find some on me in spite of all I can do. But they cant live long on me for I wont Let them I rint my shirt some every day & that helps some." With his long arms, the stalwart soldier James Scott could pluck a louse off the back of his shirt; after getting the attention of his Company F comrades he would crush the insect with his teeth and throw it to the ground.[13]

Lice-ridden, stiff and damp after spending a rainy night in a shelter tent, eyes watering from the smoke of the fire he used to cook his breakfast of hardtack, salt pork, and coffee, the soldier shouldered his load for the march. As Ira Wood described the regiment's first tramp into Virginia, "The Drums beat . . . the old npsack rolls . . . the Captain says we must be redy In 5 minutes the Boys says What Shall we through a Way our lod is So heavy that we cant carry them." Toting his ponderous load, Sergeant Hugh N. Crosgrove of Company E declared, was "the hardest work that I ever don I had rather cradel all day than to march and cary the knapsack and gun and sixty rounds of Catrages and from three to five day's rations which makes about as big a load as a man wants to cary." John Dicher agreed. Marching "with napsack [cartridge] box & gun . . . is harder work than farming if there is aney [home folk] that grumble about their heavy taxes or think we do not earn our money & bounty let them carry my load through the wood I know it would draw the sweat if it did not [draw] the bounty." Levi Bryant wrote, "You take a load of forty or fifty pounds on your Back & then your gun that ways fourteen pounds & march all the time rain or shine up nights & all thiss & it is any thing But fun for me. I would far rather be home a holding my Nelly By the Stove to keep her warm."[14]

Emory Sweetland itemized the soldier's usual burden. "Our knapsacks, haversacks, & from 3–5 days rations, a canteen of watter, gun, gun weight 12 pounds & accouterments & 40 rounds of ammunition (which weighs 4 pounds), a tin plate knife & fork & spoon & a cup holding about one quart to steep coffee & a smaller one to drink it out of & an overcoat & one piece of tent six feet square made of heavy sail cloth make the load that the common soldier has to carry. it would make a decent load for a mule." "If you would like to know anything about a forced march," John Porter informed his sister, "just strap a bureau on your back take a meal-bag and fill it with provisions then tie two flat-irons on each foot in place of mud and start off on a double quick and you will have a faint idea of a soldiers life." Corporal Martin D. Bushnell of Company H joked about a solution to the load problem while in Lookout Valley. "I think I shall pop the question to some of these Tennessee Servant Ladies," he wrote. "I think I need one to do my cooking [and] washing and to carry my Knap Sack. I dont love to tote it."[15]

As they did with other unpleasant aspects of army life, the men became accustomed to their heavy loads. "I can lug round and carry luggage like a horse," Barzilla Merrill boasted. "I did not think that I could begin to stand what I have." Furthermore, they learned from experience what essentials they had to carry and jettisoned the rest, thereby lightening their loads. "The boys cary very small loads," Richard McCadden wrote during the march to Gettysburg. "Mine consists of one shelter tent rubber blanket one pair of socks portfolio and needle book and three days rations which all told weighs about 25 lbs and the gun and acutrements weighs about 16 lbs. and that is all I want to cary this warm weather."[16]

Reviewing the regiment's first five months in Virginia, Private Isaac N. Porter of Company E calculated, "We have marched 27 days and have not seen any good road yet. If you want to see bad roads just come down here in Dixie." Rutted roads, muddy roads, dusty roads, steep roads, endless roads—in the list of the hardships of a soldier's life, marching ranked high. Following one of the regiment's first long treks, the expedition to Thoroughfare Gap and back to Fairfax in November 1862, Lewis Warner noted, "Our recent marches, and consequent exposure and fatigue, tells somewhat upon our soldiers who are not yet inured to these hardships, and quite a number are unfit for duty." After the march from Fairfax to Falmouth in December 1862, Eason Bull wrote, "I marched 4 days on a hard tack a day. This hard feed on [top of] muddy roads and the ground to sleep on in the night. After a man lives in the army 6 months he just as soon die as not."[17]

The worst was yet to come. The march to Gettysburg, carried out in extreme heat during a drought, was particularly grueling. The first leg of the trip ended on June 17, 1863, when the 154th reached Goose Creek, near Leesburg, Virginia. Resting for a few days, the men wrote letters describing the tramp. "We left [Centerville, Virginia] yesterday morning and reached our present camp before night, doing the best marching we have ever done yet," Dwight Moore wrote. "We marched sixteen miles in four hours and twenty minutes, which I call pretty good traveling, considering we carry forty or fifty lbs." James Emmons informed his sister, "We have done a good deal of marching, very hard marches. . . . My feet was blistered so bad and was so very sore." William Charles wrote, "We have been on the go almost night and day since we started and of course we are or rather was very tired. We are suffering very much for the want of water. It is very dry here. . . . The weather is and has been very hot. The Boys suffered very much from sore feet but they are all getting better."[18]

Even the march to Gettysburg paled in comparison with the march to the relief of Knoxville and back after the Battle of Chattanooga. "The Regt. got back to day just before dark," William Charles wrote at Lookout Valley on December 17, 1863. "The boys are very tired indeed. many of them are without shoes and have been entirely barefoot for many days. it is to bad but it could not have been helped But I have not heard a single complaint the boys take all their Hard ships as a matter of course." Milon Griswold described the Knoxville campaign in a letter to a Chautauqua County newspaper:

> We saw some tough times on this march. We have marched about 250 miles, and the boys are hard up for shoes and boots. I have seen the boys march, when the ground was frozen hard, with nothing on their feet but some old rags wrapped round, and I have seen them march through the mud with nothing on their feet all day, and that looks tough, especially in the month of December. I have marched when my boots were so poor and feet so sore you could track me for miles from the blood that ran from the sores on my feet, and when I pulled my boots and pieces of socks off, the skin came off my feet with the socks.[19]

Hardships encountered in the epic marches with Sherman through Georgia and the Carolinas were often tempered by the plenty the men found along the way. "We had Some gay times & Some that were not so gay," Edgar Shannon wrote of the latter campaign. "Occasionaly [we were] in a Swamp ten miles long, I was going to say as many miles in depth, but I thought you might think I was lying, then again [we] had good roads Splendid foraging & lots to eat. Chickens & Turkeys until I got sick of it. fresh pork & sweet potatoes, jellies & all such luxuries, honey on every side." Emory Sweetland and Richard McCadden offered contrasting opinions of the difficulty of the Carolinas march. "We have passed through many swamps & as it has been quite rainy the roads have been verry bad," Sweetland reported. "I think that we corduroyed one half of the distance from the Savannah river & pontooned 7 rivers." According to McCadden, "It was an easy march for so long a one the roads were generaly good, we have a pontoon train with us and we can build a bridge across a river as large as the Allegany in half a day or less . . . and take it up in less than a quarter of the time. . . . So you can see we are not dependent on the country for bridges, and when ever the roads get muddy we codaroy the road with rails and make it almost as good as a plank road."[20]

The sheer drudgery of soldier life wore at the men. They wielded axes and shovels while doing fatigue duty like roadwork far more frequently than they fired their muskets in the battle line. "I . . . have done a great deal of hard work for the past three months more than I ever did at home in double that time," Thaddeus Reynolds wrote in February 1863. But in the same letter Reynolds noted, "I am perfectly well and hearty as a buck." He had gained nineteen pounds and was "very fleshy." John Langhans, on the other hand, favorably contrasted his tedious but light army duty at Atlanta to his former chores at home. "I suppose you have had cold fingers more than oneces digging those potatoes and husching Corn," he mentioned to his brother. "We dont do aney thing [like that here,] onley drill 3 times a day 1 hour at a time."[21]

On the march or in camp, the soldiers faced one aggravation that caused universal displeasure—the chronic lateness of their pay. In general, they showed remarkable resignation to the paymaster's tardiness. After three months in the field, in January 1863, the regiment had not yet been paid. "I expected that i would have my pay before now," James Quilliam wrote, "but I must wate tel they get redy." Amos Humiston wrote, "We . . . hope to get some pay before long. . . . I can not hurrey them up if I could I would rais the D with them the onley way is to take it cool." When the paymaster finally paid a visit, the men received only a partial payment. "Old Uncle Sam dont do as he agreed a bout paing the soldiers for you see that he is owing me three munts pay," Oscar Wilber wrote. "But I shant find no falt for I know that old Uncle Sam has got his hands full [and it is] moar then he can do to pay off the soldier but I guess he is a long winded old fellow slow and shure and so I guess that we shall git oure pay."[22]

Their patience was tried continually. In July 1864, while the men were camped near the Chattahoochee River in Georgia, they had six months' pay overdue. Major Lewis Warner described their plight in a letter to a Cattaraugus County newspaper:

Those soldiers who have families at home dependent upon their earnings for food and clothing are many of them troubled (while hazarding their lives for their homes) with visions of grim want entering and installing himself within their cottage homes, while the anxious mother gathers her little flock around her and invokes Heaven's aid, in this her day of trial. Small as is the soldier's pittance, many a heart would no doubt be made glad were the army paid at this time, and the men allowed to send home their six months' pay, less what is due sutlers, and what they keep for their necessary expenses here.[23]

The grueling physical life of the soldier was accompanied by tormenting psychological trials. Chief among them was separation from loved ones. Stephen Green stated the obvious: "Soldiering would not be as mutch dreaded as it is if it was not for the seperation of families & friends." As William Chittenden informed his wife, Mary, "If a man has a comfortable home with loved and tender ones by his side he little knows how great a sacrifice he is making by leaving them for a soldiers life nor are the hardships and dangers to which he is exposed the greatest sacrifice he has to make all this I could endure for my country without much complaint but [my] greatest trial is to be deprived of your society and the childrens." Cries from the hearts of husbands and fathers like William Charles were not unusual: "Ann do you ever kiss Tommy & Frances for me. When I see little ones about their size running about here [in Alexandria], it almost makes me cry right out, because I can not see my own But we must hope for the best, trusting that the time will soon come when the father can return from the scene of Bloodshed & Horror, to dwell in peace with his wife & little ones."[24]

In George Taylor's opinion, homesickness was a major cause of shirking. "We have many on the sick list," Taylor wrote, "whose only complaint is being away from home." Some men admitted to homesickness. "There is some Boys that is sick of it," Ira Wood recorded. "One told me that he would give 100 dollars to Bee at home But I told him that he must not feel So for he could not go home there is no way to get away." Other soldiers were determined to resist homesickness. "It is plesent wether here now," Harvey Earl wrote in the spring of 1863. "The birds sings just as sweet as they ever did in old Cattaraugus it makes me home sik but that will never do I will ceap up good curage and when this war is over I will come home and see my friends once more and never go to rambel agane." John Griswold declared, "It will not do for a soldier in the field especially in the winter to indulge too much in the thoughts of home and society and the comforts to be enjoyed thare for it only serves to make him dissatisfied with his lot which he cannot change." Griswold realized that the soldier faced a psychological battle: "His mind will at times go back to times past when enjoying the comforts of home and the pleasure of mingling in the society of friends and all that makes life pleasant; and then compare it with his condition in camp, he finds that contrast not very encouraging, but we are learning to take things as they come and not fret about that which we cannot controll."[25]

Some soldiers denied being homesick. "I can tell you I enjoy myself wright well," Richard McCadden declared to his sister, "and I can say what a good many cant [that] I have never been home sick or tired of Soldering." According to Private Martin Van Buren Champlin of Company C, a full belly kept his mind off home. "Some of the boys is home sick here but it hant me," he wrote. "If they will give me nough to eat I am O peachy." Homesickness seemed to abate as the war dragged on. Edgar Shannon boasted in November 1863, "I never was tougher in my life nor felt better. I have hardly thought of home lately." Private Esley Groat of Company G expressed a sarcastic indifference to news from home of local girls' weddings. "I guess they will all get married before my time is out," Groat wrote from Lookout Valley. "If they do what will the Soldiers do O dear what Shall I do Well I shant go and kill myself for there is a pretty good chance for the rebs to do it for me So I will rest content for the present." John Porter gave his denial of homesickness an interesting twist: "I am not homesick yet but if I *was* at *home* now *I should not be here at the same time*."[26]

Long periods of stasis in camp induced boredom. "If I were at home I could tell you some big stories about Soldiering but I have no news to write. . . . I am as bad as in a Jale [as there is] nothing going on, But I suppose I will have to write to let you know that I am still a live," Richard McCadden informed his sister from Stafford Court House. Inactivity made news for the home folk hard to come by. "I fear I shall not give you a very interesting letter," Dwight Moore informed his mother from the Stafford camp. "Nothing has occured since the battle [of Chancellorsville] to interupt the monotony of camp life, and no one but a soldier has any idea how dull such a life is, and it is hardly fair to expect anything but a dull letter." Writing from the

Lookout Valley winter camp, Private Orlando White of Company K observed, "Here in the 'Sunny South' where a soldier has not much to do at this time of year but lay in the sun and wilt, time lugs heavily." He added that the men were "eager to go to the 'front' where they can get a chance to try their 'shooting sticks' on the 'Johnneys.'" Edgar Shannon voiced a somewhat different opinion from the Lookout Valley camp. "This life even if [there is] nothing to do, is no life for a man to live," he declared. "I would rather be busy have something to do & live to some purpose besides shooting some miserable reb." The soldiers also found some aspects of active campaigning to be tedious. "A soldiers life is about the same thing over and over," George Newcomb wrote when the 154th made several movements up and down the banks of the Rappahannock River preliminary to the Mud March in January 1863. "It is march and countermarch." Dwight Moore summarized the often overwhelming boredom in a letter to his brother:

> Well I dont care how soon they wind this war up, for I am getting tired of a soldiers life and I am not the only one either that is. I am getting tired of having nothing to do I am getting too lazy to enjoy life, at least a soldiers life. I do not believe we shall be good for much to work when we get home. If we had anything to read we could get along better. but to have nothing to do all day but lounge around, I never got half so tired sawing as I do doing nothing. I did not know the meaning of 'ennui' until I came to Virginia.[27]

Uncertainty—endemic in the army—plagued the men. They were helplessly afflicted by a typically military myopia. As Richard McCadden put it, "All we know is to get in to the ranks and right dress sholder arms &c. &c." The soldiers generally had no inkling of the plans or objectives of their commanders. "I cant tell any a hed what I can do we are not our own men now," Barzilla Merrill wrote. "We may lay here some time yet and we may leave soon we are just as likely to go as stay and stay as go." Rumors ran rampant through the camps; most of them proved to be false. "We hear so many reports that we do not put much confidence in them," John Griswold observed. Movements were made or terminated for no apparent purpose. Beyond the spheres of their brigade, division, and corps, the men had little idea of the status of the rest of the army, let alone that of the enemy. If active campaigning put them incommunicado, they had no idea of current events at home or in the nation at large. "To be thus cut off from the world at a time when of all others one wants to know what is transpiring outside, when each day is developing anew what may decide the fate of a World, is to say the least anything but pleasant," Lewis Warner wrote during the march to Gettysburg.[28]

On June 4, 1863, William Charles recorded a typical occurrence: "We were awoke this morning very early by an orderly who came with an order for *us to be ready to march by Sunrise*!!! Well that was short notice to be sure we went to work at once to get breakfast and some to pack up, and before sunrise the Regiment was marching off!! But they did not go but a little ways for the order was countermanded and we came back to camp So here we are with every thing packed up ready to move at a moments notice. Such is a soldiers life."[29]

In a letter to his hometown newspaper, Newton Chaffee well summarized the uninformed soldier's lot as a pawn of the powers that be: "Truly it can be said that to-night the soldier knows not where he shall lay his head. He is like the wandering Arab who has no abiding place of his own. He knows not why he is placed here or there, but goes at the word of his commander as chess-men follow the wish of the player."[30]

The unrelenting passage of time induced war weariness in the soldiers. In a ubiquitous army tradition, Levi Bryant knew exactly how much time he had left to serve when he wrote in March 1865 from Goldsboro, North Carolina: "I have five months & 8 days Longer to work for Old Abe & then I am done for him & he haint got money enough to hire me an other year in the sirvices." More than a year earlier, Newton Chaffee voiced similar feelings from the 154th's camp at Lookout Valley:

When I look back and think how long we have been in the Army of the maney marches we have made of the verey many hardships & Exposuars we have encountered and come to think that our time is only about half out, I must admit it looks like a long time & dark, and that I get almost discuraged but I hope for the best. the Future only knows what it has in store for us. there is one thing I do know that is if I do live to searve my time out and get home I shall be a wiser and I hope a better man. I shall know anough not to enlist again. I would like to see the man who would dare to say come reinlist & be a Veteran for I am Veteran anough now to suit my fancy—but I must stop writing this for you will think I am discuraged now.[31]

William Charles was on detached duty in northern Georgia in June 1864 when trainloads of wounded from the Atlanta campaign passed by on their way to Tennessee hospitals. Struggling to express his feelings of sorrow, he finally gave up the attempt: "I feel so utterly lonely to night, that I hardly know what to do with my self. . . . Seeing so many pass by on the train to day, so badly wounded and suffering so terribly from the heat, no doubt has something to do with my present feelings. indeed I cannot help but feel sad when—but it will do no good to dwell upon the subject."[32]

Pondering the ultimate indecency of war, the soldiers voiced their dismay. "There is something about war that makes me feel mad all the time," Eason Bull noted. "I feel as though I would like to fight somebody and I don't care who it is." Private Landers Wright of Company A offered some blunt advice to a relative or friend. "Tell bil," he wrote, "that i would rather see him in the grave than to see him down here." Their intimate knowledge of war's hardships made their resilience all the more remarkable. The war crushed the bodies and spirits of many of them. Those who survived somehow managed to retain faith, determination, and hope.[33]

John Griswold proposed a maxim for a soldier's emotional survival: "The way that a soldier in the field can make his lot endurable is to take no thought of the past or future, let past seens be forgotten and tomorrow take care of itself and make the best of the passing moment and get what enjoyment he can out of surrounding circumstances." When he and the rest of the regiment were shipped to the west on the mammoth railroad journey in September 1863 after rather soft duty at Alexandria, Griswold followed his own advice. "It was rather a sore disappointment to us to leave Alexandria," he noted. "We wer flatering ourselves that we should stay there sometime but it does not seem our fortune to get an easy berth any length of time. . . . I begin to think the tender mercies of war are cruel but shall have to make the best of it for the time being."[34]

John Langhans ascribed to Griswold's philosophy. "You have been writing about the nice times you have had at the parteys and dances," he wrote to his brother, "but never mind I shall make all that up. maby I was laying in some mud hole about those times down in S.C. but that is all forgotten now." Martin Bushnell expressed an optimistic attitude in a letter to his parents written in June 1864 at the 154th's "Camp in the Wilderness, Ga." "We had a terrible rain yesterday," Bushnell wrote. "We were standing in line of battle all the time saying with a grin 'who would not be a soldier?' It is hard but all live in hopes of better times." Bushnell then switched from the collective to the personal voice. "You will please be as little concerned about me as possible. I trust that all will be well with me. My fate be what it may. My chance and situation is no worse than thousands of others. I have always felt I should survive this war the end of which cannot be very far distant." Bushnell's war ended three weeks later when he was shot in the ankle, a wound that cost him his leg and, eventually, his life.[35]

A certain callousness overcame the men as they were exposed to hardship after hardship. Horace Howlett was in a Philadelphia hospital when the Battle of Gettysburg was fought. In a letter to his sister he used black humor and sarcasm to comment on the wounded and his own situation. "Thare was a lot of woonded brough in from the frunt last night [but] nun that I new," he wrote. "Take a man with both arms off the Boys say they are going to put hooks on thare arms and make them cary water. . . . O Shit thare is no use of talking the war is a bout over and I shall have to come home and go to work wont that be to bad after playing of gentleman so long I am a frade it will soil my delicat hands." The soldiers had become hardened, although they generally avoided mentioning the transformation to their loved ones. Charles Abell was an exception. Writing to his home folk from Washington at the end of the war, he warned them, "I do not want you to expect a refined gentleman to step across your threshold for according to my idea I am very deficient and ought to put for the Backwoods as soon as convenient and if Ind[iana] is all backwoods I guess I shall have to *run there and go wild again*."[36]

Some of the men philosophized more than others. Barzilla Merrill was an introspective sort. He voiced his resilience and determination in a letter to his wife:

> Ruba there is two things that I have learned since I have been in the army one is a man can endure a great deal more fatigue than I thought he could and the other is he can get along with a great deal less of the comforts of life than I thought he could do. . . . Some of us will live

through it and go home and some will fall and sleep in Virginia without doubt I am in hopes to be favord with the privileg of a gain returning home but I want to see this trouble cleared up and removed first if I can.[37]

William Charles, like Barzilla Merrill, was free in expressing his feelings. In various letters, he outlined his thoughts on overcoming hardships:

A soldier must consider himself comfortable under all circumstances. If he is wet and hungry some times, 'that's nothing,' and if his wet blanket freezes to him while attempting to get a little sleep, why, he is nothing but a soldier, and must expect such things. If he complains of being sick or unwell, he is told to keep 'bumming,' for he may get a furlough some day. So, you see it isn't a soldier's place to complain, however disagreeable or painful his lot may be. . . . Indeed a Soldier must not think upon the horrors of war. if he does he soon becomes unfit for the duties of one. He must always look on the bright side, and hope for the best. . . . If we do not fare any worse than we have thus far we shall do well enough We as a Regiment have been very lucky indeed since we came from home And the blessing of our Heavenly Father will continue with us if we deserve it.[38]

After serving for a year, Marcellus Darling took stock of his experience. "To be sure I have seen some hard times," he wrote, "but I guess I could stand it two years longer. I did not think I could endure half as much when I enlisted but I find a man can endure a great deal when obliged to." Three-quarters of the way through another tough year, in the middle of the Atlanta campaign, Darling wrote, "I tell you Mother we [have] had rather tiresome times. . . . There was eight days that we were under fire and all of the sleep we got we had to sleep on our Arms and not much sleep at that but it takes hardships and fatigue to subdue this Rebellion and it is no worse for me to endure this than others that do. . . . I expect our work is not done yet and what I am going to do I had as soon do this Summer as next and have it done." On the second anniversary of his service he reflected again: "Our time is rolling away swiftly two years . . . has all ready passed and I can say truthfully that I never have seen the time since I enlisted that I regretted putting down my name. though we have seen hardships in the field it was unpleasanter at Jamestown on some accounts than any place I have been yet since then I did not know [then] what Soldiering was and was all of the time dreading it though anxious to leave there and find out the realities of Soldiering. I think I know now about what it is."[39]

"The health of our Regt is not verry good," George Newcomb reported in December 1862. "Out of one thousand strong when we left James town but 550 are left fit for duty the rest are sent to fill up the Hospitals." Four months later Newcomb noted, "The Sanitary Conditions of the Regt is good there being but a verry few sick at the present time Our Regt has been pretty well culled out and what is left are old peaches Eney new Regt has to go through the culling process before it will become a good and efficient Regt."[40]

All of the soldiers endured the physical and psychological hardships particular to army life. A sizable portion of them had the misfortune to fall prey to chronic diarrhea, dysentery, typhoid fever, pneumonia, smallpox, and a variety of other ailments ranging from measles to "inflammation of the brain" (meningitis). In the care of its sick, the regiment provided a large dose of comradely compassion in addition to the standard medical treatment. Esprit de corps prompted tent mates to become nurses and caregivers for their stricken friends. In the surrogate families of the messes, brother tended ailing brother.

When William Jones was laid low with dysentery in the spring of 1863, his comrade William Charles cared for him as best he could and sent reports home on his condition. "Billy Jones is not much better," Charles wrote on one occasion. "I do all I can for him but that is not much. But if he was my Brother I could not do any more for him." Sick with fever for two weeks, Amos Humiston reported, "I am very weak yet the boys have stuck to me like brothers if they had not I do not know whare I should have ben now." Some of the men had actual brothers to care for them when they fell ill. Emory Sweetland became sick at the 154th's first camp in Virginia and was nursed to health by the regiment's medical staff and his brother, John Wesley Sweetland. Less than a month later, Wesley Sweetland caught a cold standing guard overnight and soon developed a fever. Emory stayed by his brother's side, tending a fire to keep him warm and wiping his forehead with a wet towel. "I tell you it seems good to have a brother here," Emory wrote, "one to take an interest in ones welfare. of all places I was ever in camp is the poorest place that I have ever seen to be sick in." Edwin Osgood echoed Sweetland's comment about the dangers to health presented by camp life—as did many other of the men—when he worried about his brothers Stephen and William. "If one of them shoud be sick i shoud have them on my mind and it is the worst place that a man Can be sick in." When George Taylor received news that his brother, a member of the 112th New York, had died of typhoid fever, he voiced a regret. "I have always wished we had got John transferred to the 154th," Taylor wrote. "Still it might not have been any better for him except the satisfaction of being able to care for his wants and relieve him at many times from hardships which I could better endure than he. Then it would have been much satisfaction to me if I could have been with him during his sickness. I could have provided for a brother many comforts which strangers and particularly hospital nurses will never take it upon them to interest themselves about."[41]

Sick men dreaded to be sent away from the regiment to a military hospital at the division level or in a distant northern city. When Sergeant W. Devillo Forbush of Company F was sent to a hospital in Fairfax, coughing badly and unable to speak above a whisper, he sent negative word about his treatment to his company comrades. "God save me from being sick and having hospital care such as I have seen," George Taylor commented. "Those in Washington perhaps are not as bad, but Devillo says that the medical treatment [at Fairfax] is a damning one. Blisters then diarrhea powders next then cough powders & damning and so on." When Amos Humiston was laid low with chronic diarrhea, he initially was able to avoid being sent away from the regiment. "I did not go to the [division] hospital," he wrote, "for I had a good shanty and the boys said that they [would] rather do my work than to have me go." When he was finally sent to the division hospital, Humiston reported, "I am very cumfortable here it is onley a little ways from the regament and some of the boys are here every day to see me so that I do not get very lonesome."[42]

As Devillo Forbush indicated, sometimes hospital cures seemed as dangerous as the diseases they were meant to treat. Private Hiram Straight of Company C was admitted to Satterlee Hospital in Philadelphia on December 12, 1862, suffering from jaundice, chronic kidney inflammation, enlargement of the spleen, respiratory irregularity, and a hacking cough, all brought on by a severe attack of remittent fever. He had lost his appetite and was emaciated, fatigued, and mentally dull. To combat this severe case, the Satterlee doctors deployed an impressive pharmacological arsenal, dosing Straight with iodide of potassium, bicarbonate of potash, fluid extract of taraxacum, tincture of iodine, an anodyne expectorant mixture, liquor potassae, tincture of cannabis indica, extract of uva ursi taken in mint water, and cod-liver oil. During his treatment Straight coughed up bloodstained sputa, was frequently weak and nauseous, and complained of "flying pains through the body" in general and excruciating pain in his kidneys in particular. But slowly his condition improved, and by February 14, 1863, Straight had recovered and was sent to the 154th for duty.[43]

Sometimes soldiers in distant hospitals were fortunate enough to receive succor from regimental comrades. Suffering from a pulmonary ailment, Marion Plumb was admitted to Ward Eight of the Finley Hospital in Washington in November 1862. In letters to his wife he assured her that he was well taken care of, that "the other boys in our Company are getting along well," that it was doubtful whether he could return to the regiment for months, and that he might be discharged. In an undated letter, he shared some good news. Harland E. Locke, a musician in Plumb's Company D, had been admitted to Ward Eight. "He brought a large trunk full of provision and he shares it with me," Plumb wrote. "[He] takes just as good care of me as he does of his own Brother." Plumb died several days later, on November 24, 1862, comforted in his dying days by the ministrations of his company comrade.[44]

Sometimes several comrades were hospitalized together, to their mutual satisfaction and benefit. William Chittenden contracted a lung disease in November 1862. While still in camp he noted, "The boys are all verry kind to me Nat [Brown] in particular." After Chittenden was sent to Harewood Hospital in Washington, he kept a close watch on fellow patients from his Company D, including William Wellman and Private Dennis Snyder. "William Wellman is a verry sick man," Chittenden observed. "I think it is doubtful if he is ever better but if I get well enough to do it [I] shall take as good care of him as I can it is a hard place to be sick." Days later Chittenden reported, "I went up to ward B to see Denis Snyder and the other boys of the company this morning Denis is better and he said that he shall try to get a furlow and come home for awhile you can tell his folks if you see them."

Chittenden's letters from Harewood made frequent mentions of his interactions with Wellman and Snyder.[45]

Seldom did a soldier refuse to care for an ill companion, although Stephen Green voiced some reluctance when his comrade Private Perry Wheelock of Company E was hospitalized at Lookout Valley in January 1864. "I am one of three that takes care of him," Green wrote of Wheelock. "We do no other duty I had twice rather do duty in the company but I am willing to do what I can for any one that is sick." Green's understandable preference was to be with his healthy comrades in camp instead of with an ill comrade in a disease-ridden hospital. Most often, though, well men willingly attended their hospitalized comrades. "Mister [Colby] Bryant went to the Hospital to day and I went with him," Ira Wood wrote. "We Will take cair of him. . . . I Went and see the captain about him. . . . I went and don all I could for him."[46]

Many of the soldiers were both givers and beneficiaries of comradely care. Soon after arriving in Virginia, John Griswold was hit by "a violent attack of camp sickness." The men of Company F rushed to aid their lieutenant. "The night I was sick the boys took some hay from the teams belonging to our regiment," Griswold recorded, "and put [it] into our beds which made it very comfortable (I think the boys will take good care of me when necessary)." As Company F men began to fall ill a month later, Griswold made special efforts to do what he could for them. After five members of the company were left behind at Fairfax Court House when the regiment moved to Thoroughfare Gap in November 1862, Griswold made a special trip back to Fairfax to look after them. "I found the boys in an old house in a room upstairs with a fireplace in it, tolerable comfortable in warm weather," he wrote. "I got them into a more comfortable room in a building used as a hospital whare they could have better medical attendance." Griswold himself experienced another bout of bad health in Lookout Valley during the spring of 1864. Company F rallied around him again. "He is on the gain now and I think he is out of danger," Homer Ames notified Griswold's son. "He has had a hard sickness but he has had as good care as could be given a man here in this country [Private Marvin M.] Marve Skinner has taken care of him day times and then the boys have taken turns seting up with him nights."[47]

Surgeon Henry Van Aernam's jurisdiction expanded when he was appointed chief surgeon at the brigade and division levels, but he never ceased to work on behalf of the members of the 154th New York. Although only one example survives, it seems likely that Van Aernam answered and acted on many letters like that written by Almina Ball of the Cattaraugus County hamlet of Eddyville. Mrs. Ball, mother of Private Lucius D. Ball of Company G, had heard from one of her son's comrades that Lucius had been hospitalized near Atlanta in August 1864. She wrote to Surgeon Van Aernam:

> I can assure you that I feel grateful to you for the many former kindnesses to my son and feel as if to ask other favors of you would be too much yet if you can appreciate a Mother's affection for a son far away from home, deprived of the care and treatment necessary for one that is sick you will overlook it in me. I wish if it is consistent that you would aid Lucius in procuring a furlough or his discharge and let him come home at least long enough to regain his health. I feel as if no one can care for him as well as myself. From what his friend wrote I think if he is obliged to remain in that southern climate his stay on earth will be short. If you can do anything for him you will confer a favor for which I will be forever grateful.[48]

One can imagine what Surgeon Van Aernam thought regarding Mrs. Ball's comment about her son being deprived of necessary care and treatment. Perhaps he emphasized the opposite in his response. It seems likely that he did write back to Almina Ball. Earlier that year, Van Aernam had assured his wife that the bonds of esprit de corps insured a ready flow of information between the front and home about the health of the members of the 154th. "The friends of the boys from our vicinity can always understand their friends in the Regiment are well unless I write to the contrary," Van Aernam wrote. "We have been through so many trying scenes together that these boys who are left with us seem almost like a part of our household and should any of them be sick with whom you are acquainted I should certainly mention it in my letters to you."[49]

The tender compassion that comrade extended to comrade when illness struck was a natural manifestation of esprit de corps. The soldiers felt a solidarity forged by shared hardships. When one of their own was stricken, they were drawn by esprit to his side.

CHAPTER 6

On the Battlefield

While the 154th New York was camped at Falmouth in December 1862, after only two months in the service, Captain Simeon V. Pool's Company B was temporarily detached from the regiment to guard a battery. The artillerymen—veterans of several hard-fought battles—were complaining to the 154th men about the hardships of war when one of the Company B boys silenced them with the remark, "You fellows think you have had a hard time, but when you have been through what we have you will begin to know what war is." Captain Pool laughed so hard at that naive comment that tears came to his eyes.[1]

The soldiers of the 154th could—and did—brag about the many hardships they had endured. But all of those hardships would prove to be secondary to war's cruelest trial. In battle a soldier would face his severest test. In battle he would prove his individual courage or cowardice and his ability to perform under the most extreme pressure. In battle he and his comrades would reveal their mettle as a regiment to themselves, to their loved ones and others at home, to their brigade, division, and corps, to the rest of the army—and to the enemy. In battle the regiment's ultimate reputation would be formed. Esprit de corps would face its most formidable challenge in battle—and receive its greatest stimulus.

They anticipated their first fight from the moment they enlisted. As a musician, Thaddeus Reynolds knew that during combat his duty would be to carry the wounded from the battlefield. Nevertheless, before the 154th left Jamestown he armed himself heavily in anticipation of fighting. "When I get to Elmira I am going to buy me an army steel plated vest," Reynolds wrote. "I am armed with a sword and a brace of six shooters [and] with a dirk so that if there is any pluck In me at all I can defend my self without much danger." At Elmira the regiment received its arms, British-made Enfield rifled muskets, and they expressed satisfaction with the weapons. "I think our regiment could do good exicution if we were only drilled to the use of arms," George Newcomb wrote the day after the 154th arrived in Virginia, "for we are well armed with the Enfield rifles." Some of the men were anxious to fight whether drilled or not. About a week after arriving in Virginia an unidentified member of the regiment wrote, "I want to fight if we have gone so far I dont wish to be a soldier longer than is necessary I either want to fight or go home."[2]

Some of the green soldiers issued bloodthirsty threats. "I have not scalped a Rebel yet," John Porter informed his sister, "but as soon as I do I will send . . . a lock of his hair." Marcellus Darling made a similar promise to his family: "We are now after the Rebs & I hope we will get some of them. If I do so I will send you some of his hair." "I would like to have the name of shooting one rebel," declared Thaddeus Reynolds, who carried enough firepower to shoot a dozen. Alanson Crosby did not issue any murderous threats or promise any grisly souvenirs, but he voiced confidence in the valor of the regiment. "I think we shall have fighting to do soon," he wrote. "When it comes the 154th will do its duty."[3]

But months would pass—to the good fortune of the inexperienced soldiers—before the regiment would undergo its baptism of fire. In the meantime, Colonel Patrick Henry Jones used the passing weeks to mold the 154th as best he could into an efficient military machine. Writing from Camp John Manley in the spring of 1863, First Sergeant Alfred W. Benson of Company H noted, "The efficiency of the Regiment has been greatly promoted during our stay here notwithstanding the unfavorable weather that has prevailed— preventing much drilling. Col. Jones has been indefatigable in his exertions to place the Regiment on a good 'fighting basis,' and I presume the first band of rebels we meet, will testify that his exertions have not been wholly without effect." By that time, the test was soon to come.[4]

Some of the more contemplative soldiers refrained from violent threats and soberly pondered their prospects. Writing from Thoroughfare Gap in November 1862, William Charles expressed slight concern for the Confederate army, but an acute awareness of being in hostile territory. "We do not think but very little of the Rebels, and feel just as safe as if we were there [at home]," he wrote, "but there are those around us that would be glad to take the life of every one of us if they dare do it." In a letter to his son, Sergeant John W. Bagdero of Company K voiced patriotism while imagining the worst. "How soon I shall be called upon [to] go into a battle [is uncertain]," Badgero wrote, "and if I do [I] may never come out alive and if I do not you must remember that your Father died fighting for one of the best governments the sun ever shone upon." Badgero was fated to fall, but from disease rather than a bullet. In June 1863, as a second lieutenant of Company A, he died of fever.[5]

Ambrose Arnold struggled with the terrible prospect of battle after receiving a letter from home. His wife informed him that their young son had offered to change places with his father. Arnold responded with deep emotion:

> God bless him it brot the tear to my eye to read that tell him his Pa is proud of his brave boy and hopes he is as good as he is brave but as he cannot take Pas place here he must do the best he can at home till I come. . . . My Dear Wife I cannot fear the battle when such little ones as Denny Volluntere to go with me for his little form will keep off the leaden hail from his Father but I must stop for I am getting as babiesh as a child altho a warrior.[6]

Sadly, the leaden hail took Arnold from his family forever at the Battle of Rocky Face Ridge.

Some soldiers showed reluctance to engage in battle. "Mother i dont think that We shall be in a battle for a good Whill," Oscar Wilber wrote in November 1862. "It may be [that] We Never Shall have to fight i hope Not Eny how for My part i dont Want to fight." Wilber fought at Chancellorsville—and received a mortal wound. Following a review of the 154th and the rest of the Eleventh Army Corps in April 1863, Emory Sweetland contemplated an ominous future. "It was a painful thought connected with the pomp & pagentry of war," he reflected, "that in all probability before 6 months has passed away that probably fully one third of these men now in the flush & pride of manhood would either be under the sod or mangled." Sweetland was right, but his estimate of casualties was low as far as his own regiment was concerned.[7]

After seven months of inconsequential service in Virginia, the moment of truth for the 154th New York came at sunset on May 2, 1863, during the famous surprise attack of Confederate general Thomas J. "Stonewall" Jackson on the Eleventh Corps at the Battle of Chancellorsville. All day, the uneasy soldiers of the 154th had heard rumors and caught glimpses of a Confederate movement through the tangled forest of the Wilderness, headed toward the corps' exposed right flank. But corps commander Major General Oliver Otis Howard ignored repeated warnings and took no precautions to meet an attack from the west, the very direction from which Jackson planned to launch his assault. Consequently the Eleventh Corps was unprepared, ill-positioned, unsupported, and outnumbered three to one when Jackson unleashed his troops. The Union soldiers were lounging about, cooking their suppers and preparing for the night's sleep when the surrounding forest exploded with a thunderclap of musketry, the bloodcurdling keen of the rebel yell, and a terrified scattering of deer, rabbits, and quail fleeing the van of the Confederate host.

The 154th New York and the other three regiments of Colonel Adolphus Buschbeck's brigade were the most distant Eleventh Corps units from the initial point of Jackson's attack, so they had time to reposition themselves behind a shallow rifle pit stretching north and south across the Plank Road near Dowdall's Tavern. The 154th held the extreme left of the line, with the 73rd Pennsylvania, 27th Pennsylvania, and 29th New York extending the line to the right. The soldiers of the 154th watched with astonishment as two largely veteran divisions of the Eleventh Corps were shattered by Jackson's juggernaut, fleeing past and through Buschbeck's line in a mad jumble of panicked men, careening cannons and caissons, and galloping horses, mules, and cattle. On their heels, filling the clearings as far as could be seen through the thick smoke, came the Confederate hordes.

Colonel Patrick Jones ordered the 154th to open fire, and the regiment's volleys briefly stopped the Confederate onslaught in their immediate front. But the enemy heavily outnumbered and far outflanked the small Union force, and soon the 29th New York and 27th Pennsylvania, together with some rallied elements of the rest of the corps, fled the rifle pit and joined the rout. A portion of the 73rd Pennsylvania also gave way, but its left companies, seeing the 154th standing fast, continued to hold the line with the New Yorkers. Minutes later, Colonel Jones realized the Confederates had outflanked both ends of the line and the regiment's position was hopeless. As the highest ranking Eleventh Corps officer left on the field, he gave the order to retreat. The 154th now had an open field of about eight hundred feet to cross to reach the shelter of the woods. Under a murderous fire, many of the men fell making the attempt. When the survivors plunged into the gloomy forest, some ran helter-skelter into Confederate hands, while others managed to stay together and fall back about a mile to the nearest Union lines. When it was all over, the 154th New York had lost 240 out of 590 men engaged—the Union army's fourth highest regimental casualty count in the battle.[8]

Back at Camp John Manley after the failed campaign, the soldiers tried to summarize the Chancellorsville experience and put it into perspective. "We have seen the sturn realities of war and that is no trifling affair," Richard McCadden wrote. Some men felt they could never explain combat to the home folk. "You can have no idiea of the roar of battle," James Quilliam informed his wife, "but it is over now and i hope there will never be another such." Horace Smith wrote in his diary, "How little do the folks at home know of the miseries of war. may they never witness its horrors, as I have." "You spoke of the battle field," Marcellus Darling wrote to his home folk. "Any one dont know what it is till they have been there. you can think some thing of it but then you dont know any thing about it. to see the confustion and see men fall all around you and then the noise and continual roar of Cannon and musketry. . . . O I think a great many times how lucky I was [to survive]."[9]

In recording their reactions, several of the men used a popular euphemism for the experience of battle. "I had sen the elephant and lord god how he did rare and below god they scart me some," declared Corporal Truman Harkness of Company H. "Take it all round it was the worst time I ever got into," John Porter wrote. He continued, "Sometime ago I wrote about staying in Dixie till I had seen the Elephant I believe I have seen all I want to now. When they have another fight I think I will get excused." In a similar vein George Newcomb wrote, "Well I have been through one fight But I have no desire to go in to another I did think I would like to go into one to see how it went But I have been in and seen the Eliphant and had rather be excused from participating in another."[10]

Like Newcomb, many of the soldiers had no desire to repeat the experience. "I tell you I don't want to get into another such place," declared Private Charles H. Field of Company B in a typical comment. Harvey Earl wrote, "The balls cum round my head like hail stone and the men was afalling on all sides of me I hope I shant see another such a time it ant a very plesent place to be in." Even William Charles, who was stationed with the supply train during the battle, saw enough to wish to see no more. "I have seen enough of this war, and I pray that God in his mercy will not permitt me to see an *other Battle*," he wrote. "Three different times the Rebels threw their shells into our Supply Train One man was killed only a little ways from me, and a span of mules torn all to pieces, and an other [shell] went right over my head and struck in the road a little ways a head of me, but it *did not burst*. Such a time I have never seen and I hope never to see again." Thaddeus Reynolds, on the other hand, emerged from the ordeal rather unperturbed. "Please dont worry about me," he urged his family, "for I am just as likely to come home as I am to be killed I dont think of that at all I did not think of getting hurt while I was in the Battle I was looking out for some body else all the while." He added, however, "I feel very thankful to think that I should pass through that shower of bullets without being hurt."[11]

In describing the 154th's role in the battle, many of the men proudly stressed the regiment's heroism. "Our regt fought like tigers and were all cut to pieces. . . . I tell you we had a *hard* place in the fight. . . . Our regt was the last that retreated and the rebs wernt four rods from me when I left [the rifle pit]," Thomas Aldrich wrote. George Mason and Horace Smith used the same simile as Aldrich to describe the ferocious fighting of the 154th. "We were badly cut up," Mason wrote, "but the boys fought like tigers. I think if they had retreated sooner we should not have had so many prisoners." Smith repeated a rumor that the Confederates were inebriated when they made their charge. "Our Regt fought like tigers but the drunken Rebs flanked us on both sides, so we had to foot it for the woods. 2 minutes more and we would all [have] been prisoners." Smith promised that in the future, the Confederates "will find the 154th on hand every time." Henry Van Aernam contrasted the regiment's bravery with the poor conduct of the rest of the corps. "The 11th Army Corps shamefully fell back," he wrote, "—a few regiments fruitlessly trying to stay the panic and skedaddle, among them stands out conspicuously the heroic 154th. There is not a coward in the regiment— every man is a hero and possesses the fortitude of a veteran." A week later Van Aernam wrote, "All the officers and men in our Regiment did their whole duty and did it well too. . . . I am proud of the bravery, the heroism and the valor of the 154th!"[12]

"Nobly did the 154 respond to the call of duty, and bravely did she sustain the credit of old Cattaraugus," Lewis Warner wrote in his diary the night after the battle, anticipating the esteem the regiment would be granted by its home community. "Not a man flinched amid the most withering fire of Shell Grape Canister & Musket Balls," he continued, "while their deadly rifles made terrible havoc in the ranks of the advancing enemy. But numbers could not but prevail. Their ranks were filled as fast as they fell and they were fast turning our flanks. At last prudence became the better part of valor and our Colonel ordered a retreat." Only the overwhelming size of the enemy's force guaranteed his victory over the dauntless 154th.[13]

"The boys that are in the Company are feeling first rait now [as] to what they did" at Chancellorsville, Homer Ames asserted. Their retreat, after all, had been inevitable, and came only after a gallant stand. As Charles Field wrote, "We give them the best we had in the house untill they had flanked us on both sides then we had to fall back through a cross fire of grape and canister and shell & rifle balls." Dana Horton declared, "We was in a tight place with no Support So wee was compelled to fall back, though verry reluctantly no sane man or person could expect that our Regt. could hold a force of 50,000 Rebels for any considerable length of time." Horton greatly exaggerated the enemy's strength; Jackson attacked with about 21,500 men.[14]

The premature retreat of other regiments of its brigade, members of the 154th stressed, left them and a portion of the 73rd Pennsylvania to meet the attack alone. Thus the poor behavior of the veteran 29th New York and 27th Pennsylvania and some of the 73rd contrasted badly with the stubborn stand made by the untried 154th—reason for pride among the members of the regiment. "The 29th N.Y. . . . broke and run," noted Isaac Porter. "Next was the 27th Pa. who also shamefully retreated. the last line was composed of the 73rd Pa and 154th N.Y. two companies of the 73rd fell in with us and fought like tigers but the other eight companies followed the example of the 29th and 27th, so you will see that with the exception of a few men from the 73rd we the 154th was alone." "The 29th N.Y. of our Brigade ran like deer," Horace Smith wrote in his diary the night of the battle. Three days later he declared of the "cowardly 29th," "How I would like to give them a volley of musketry from our guns."[15]

In the aftermath of the battle, the soldiers of the 154th basked in the praise of their brigade commander, Colonel Buschbeck, and division commander, Brigadier General Adolph von Steinwehr. "Our Brigadier General Bushbeck said that we fought the best of any new Reg't he ever saw," James

Washburn proudly wrote. "The 11th Corps have got a bad name for running except for Bushbecks Brigade," John Porter noted. "Gen. Bushbeck said this Regt stood longer than they had ought to but we did not know when we were outflanked and supposed one Brigade could whip Jackson's whole Army." Thaddeus Reynolds boasted, "Brigadier Gen. Bushbeck thinks more of this Regt. now then any others in the brigade." Reynolds also recounted an exchange between Steinwehr and Lieutenant Colonel Henry Loomis of the 154th some two weeks after the battle. "Major Gen. A von Steinweigh rode up to our Lieut Col. yesterday while [we were] on drill and says he your Regt. is not large any more Col. Loomis answered no they got badly cut up in the engagement Well says the Gen. you did well boys and you have my best respects and highest gratifications." Such commendations confirmed and boosted pride in the regiment. The men also noted with approval how their veteran brigade comrades judged the battle's severity. George Newcomb wrote, "The old soldiers in our Brigade who were in the [Second] Bull Run fight said they never saw the shot fly so thick as it did there [at Chancellorsville] for a short time."[16]

Members of the 154th candidly confessed that they, too, like the rest of their brigade and corps, had eventually been routed. But they emphasized that they had stood as long as was humanly possible. "The rebs was so close on us that we had to run for our sweet lives," Homer Ames noted. George Newcomb wrote, "We stood our ground as well as we could until they flanked us and poured a cross fire into us Then let me tell you there was some tall skidadling grape shot and cannister flew amongst us like hail stones." Writing to his cousin Adrian Fay, who was serving in another New York State regiment, Charles Field stated, "You said you had been in six or seven battles and never run but once. Well Add I had to run the first one I went in to but I wunt any to blame for that." John Porter noted, "I had been told that the Rebs. would not fight, that we had but to show them fight and they would run but the running where I had a chance to see was all the other way."[17]

On a few rare occasions, members of the 154th admitted that not all of the regiment behaved heroically at Chancellorsville. "There was but one instance that I know of where any of our men really showed their backs from the first," George Taylor informed his wife. He added, "I will not call names, but when I see you, I will tell you all about it." According to William

Charles, "Some of the boys acted like men but others acted very shameful Some of the Captains in this Regiment Ran as fast as ever they could and left their men to take care of themselves." Charles condemned the actions of William Davis in particular. Noting that Davis had been listed among the wounded in newspaper casualty lists, Charles scoffed that he had merely received a tiny scratch in the face from a branch hitting him as he ran through the woods. "He heard that the Rebels were coming and *ran* as fast as his legs could carry him," Charles wrote, "and hundreds of others did the same thing and that is the reason that so many of our Boys are missing—they did not keep together but ran in all directions Many of them no doubt ran into the Rebel lines and of course was taken prisoners." Charles added, "Of course you will keep the contents of this letter to yourself as far as I have said any thing about *Bill Davis*."[18]

Three decades after Chancellorsville, a veteran of the 64th New York, Joseph Charlesworth, related an anecdote that illustrated how the prefight braggadocio of a soldier of the 154th had completely evaporated in the heat of battle. Months before the battle, Charlesworth had visited the 154th at Falmouth and conversed with a diminutive but bellicose member of Company G, who peppered the veteran with questions about battles and fighting and declared that he wished the 154th was going into battle that very day, that he was anxious to fight as soon as he could, and that the 154th was the best regiment to come out of western New York. Charlesworth next encountered the Company G man on the Chancellorsville battlefield. The hapless soldier was without his equipment and badly demoralized. "Where's your cap?" Charlesworth asked. "Lost it," came the reply. "Where's your gun?" "Lost it." "Cartridge box?" "Lost it." "Well, have you had fight enough?" Charlesworth asked. "Yes, I have," the Company G man responded, "and all I want is to get out of this and find my regiment!"[19]

While the frank and honest descriptions of Chancellorsville in letters from soldiers to their home folk remained private, largely sanitized accounts of the regiment's actions in the battle entered the public record. A week after the 154th's doomed stand at Dowdall's Tavern, the Soldier's Friend, John Manley, composed a letter to the *Cattaraugus Freeman* extolling the regiment's courage and contradicting the regiment's rout: "I have no letters direct from the 154th Regiment, but from eye witnesses I can say that they stood their ground, fighting against fearfully overwhelming odds, until *or-*

dered off, and then marching in good order! . . . This regiment has won laurels of enduring fame, and made a proud record amid the most adverse circumstances—a panic on the battle field. . . . With heroic devotion to the Union, they merit the plaudits of their kinsmen and friends on the far-off hills of Cattaraugus and Chautauqua!"[20]

Two weeks after it printed Manley's letter, the *Freeman* published another article praising the 154th. In the absence of other information, a reader of the tribute would never have known that the regiment had been shattered in one of the most famous routs of the war:

> The battle of Chancellorsville, Va., fought May 2d, 1863, will long be memorable to the people of Cattaraugus County. On its bloody field fell many of the noblest sons of Cattaraugus, combatting bravely for their country and her institutions. Others, in large numbers, there received wounds which will bear honorable evidence of their heroism through life; and there, too, the 154th Regiment N.Y. Volunteers, the representative Regiment of Cattaraugus, made a name for their steadiness in the shock of battle, courage and heroic conduct, of which they and their friends at home may justly be proud. The courage and chivalrous bearing of the 154th should be known to every citizen of the county, and kept in grateful remembrance by all loyal people.[21]

Colonel Patrick Jones was wounded and captured at Chancellorsville, so the task of writing the regiment's official report fell to Lieutenant Colonel Henry Loomis. Loomis's report, sent to the New York State adjutant general on May 19, was a fair and accurate representation of the 154th's role in the battle, although he did gloss over the chaotic retreat by merely stating, "We then retired, the heavy columns of the enemy being close upon us." Loomis closed his report with an effusive accolade to the regiment. "The command behaved with all the firmness and unflinching bravery peculiar to the American soldier," he wrote. "Many instances of personal and conspicuous gallantry came under my observation, but when all behaved as well I might do injustice by singling out any individual for specific commendation simply because he fought under my own eye and when his conduct became personally known to me."[22]

Colonel Buschbeck apparently did not write a report of his brigade's actions at Chancellorsville, but General Steinwehr submitted one for his division. Within two weeks after the battle, John Manley forwarded a copy of Steinwehr's report to the *Cattaraugus Freeman*. In a cover note Manley emphasized, "The lines in *italics* will show the gallant Steinwehr's judgment of the obstinate bravery of Col. Jones and the 154th boys. All honor to the Heroes!" Steinwehr's report, while it praised Buschbeck's brigade for "defending [its] position with great firmness and gallantry" and fighting "with great determination and courage," made no mention of its piecemeal retreat and ultimate rout. Steinwehr instead declared that Buschbeck "withdrew his small brigade, in perfect order, towards the woods, the enemy closely pressing on"—a very different picture than that painted by members of the 154th in their letters home. Henry Van Aernam, who also sent home a copy of Steinwehr's report, commented, "The real fact is the 27th [Pennsylvania] and 29th [New York] both skedaddled without showing fight and all the fighting that was done by his Division was done by the 73rd Pa. and our own Regiment. Both these Regiments are worthy of great praise—much more than they get in the report," which Van Aernam otherwise judged to be "truthful and sapient."[23]

Accompanying Colonel Loomis's report was a list of the 154th's many casualties. Alanson Crosby sent a duplicate list to the *Cattaraugus Freeman*. "By publishing the same," Crosby wrote, "you will, perhaps, relieve the friends of our brave boys from much anxious and painful suspense concerning them." He then was compelled to add some hyperbole. "Our casualties are very heavy, which cannot be wondered at considering the determined resistance our Regiment made to the overwhelming numbers of the enemy that were precipitated upon us. *Every man proved himself a hero!* When old soldiers, that have faced the storm of war on a hundred battle-fields, broke and fled from the terrible conflict, our noble fellows stood until surrounded on three sides, and then withdrew under a murderous storm of bullets and shells."[24]

A number of privately compiled casualty lists went out in addition to the official list. Men sent home detailed lists of the losses in their companies, so that families could notify other families of losses. Having abandoned the field, there was necessarily much doubt about the fate of those left behind. "I have only stated those that I knew were killed or wounded," George Newcomb wrote in sending a list of the thirty men Company K left on the battlefield (out of forty-six that went into the fight). "Probably [a] good many others were wounded and perhaps some killed but I think the most of them were taken prisoners." In a grim sense, the regiment's reputation was forged in its lengthy casualty list—the price it had paid in blood and loss for its steadfastness. "That they tried to do their duty," Henry Van Aernam wrote of the regiment, "their thinner ranks and melancholy losses will stand as a perpetual witness." Amos Humiston put it in simpler terms. "The 154 has gained a name," he wrote, "but at what a loss."[25]

Two months after the debacle at Chancellorsville, the 154th New York found itself in an eerily reminiscent situation at the Battle of Gettysburg. On the afternoon of July 1, 1863, its brigade—commanded by Colonel Charles R. Coster in the absence of Colonel Buschbeck—was rushed from a reserve position atop Cemetery Hill through the streets of Gettysburg to the village's northeastern outskirts to cover another precipitate retreat of the Eleventh Corps. On the way through town, the 73rd Pennsylvania was detached from the brigade and placed near the railroad depot. The 134th New York (which had replaced the 29th New York), 154th New York, and 27th Pennsylvania hurried out Stratton Street and filed into a brickyard, where they took position behind a post-and-rail fence. No sooner had they done so when two Confederate brigades—outnumbering the small Union force by more than three to one—assaulted the brickyard, their long lines overlapping both flanks of Coster's position. The 134th New York on the right was sent reeling in retreat after suffering heavy losses. Seeing its position in the center thus undermined, the 154th retreated to the left, toward the brickyard's gateway. On reaching Stratton Street, they found that the 27th Pennsylvania had already fled its position and the road was swarming with Confederate troops. A hand-to-hand melee erupted and a few members of the 154th managed to escape the enemy's clutches, but most of the regiment was surrounded and forced to surrender. As several of the men put it, they were "gobbled up" by the Confederates. After a chaotic race through Gettysburg's streets, only three officers and fifteen enlisted men returned to the safety of Cemetery Hill. Some forty stragglers eventually rejoined the regiment, augmented by another fifty men who luckily had been detached that morning to make a reconnaissance in Maryland. But the 154th lost 205 of the 265 soldiers who fought in the brickyard fight—at 77 percent, one of the highest regimental casualty rates suffered in the battle.[26]

With so few survivors, first-hand accounts of the regiment's fight were scarce. George Mason, one of the fifteen to reach Cemetery Hill after the 154th was crushed, offered his mother a terse description of the battle: "We have had a hard fight and our Regiment was most all taken prisoners. . . . The 134th Regiment was on our right and the enemy flanked them and cut off our retreat and the few that did get away were the best runners and the most exposed to danger." James Quilliam, who was wounded in the head and captured, reported to his uncle, "The redgement started back dubble quick i got up and went as fast as any of them but when we got to the road it was full of rebbels and they were comeing up behind us so there we had to stay and but few got away they made us lay down our guns and marched us of." The night after the fight Horace Smith recorded in his diary, "Many of our boys were wounded. the rest taken prisoners. I among the rest. I received a slight flesh wound in the leg just above the knee. . . . It was by poor Generalship that we were taken." In a letter written the day after the brick-yard fight, Thaddeus Reynolds, who had been on detached duty, described the decimation of the 154th. "Our Regt & the 134th N.Y. went into the field yesterday noon with about Eight or nine hundred men & come out last night with 80 in all they were completely surrounded and had to cut their way through I went to find some of them last night [but] could not. I saw Lieut Col [Dan] Allen and Major [Lewis] Warner and a Lieut [Byron A. Johnston] of Co I with one private I expect that all of the Olean boys were killed wounded & taken prisoners."[27]

Private letters to home folk were submitted to newspapers, to be shared with readers desperate for news of the regiment. "Three small Regiments of our Brigade . . . were attacked by two whole Brigades of the enemy, and soon, of course, were surrounded," wrote Alanson Crosby in a letter to his brother published in the *Cattaraugus Freeman*. "The men had no idea of giving themselves away, however, for they fought after being surrounded and a few escaped by cutting through. There was a general mixed fight for a long time by our boys and the rebels after they had closed in upon us." In a lengthy letter to a former officer of the regiment which found its way into the columns of the *Jamestown Journal,* Crosby adopted a florid tone to describe the 154th's brief stand: "Not a man flinched or gave an inch to the overwhelming force opposed to them. There they stood, firm as the Pyramids, fighting with the desperation of a forlorn hope, a murderous fire all the time raking them in front and flank." Assistant Surgeon Dwight Day's parents forwarded a letter to the *Arcade Enterprise,* and it was later reprinted in the *Cattaraugus Union.* "Our Regiment suffered terribly—there are only 17 men and 3 officers left of those engaged the first day. . . . Our boys were flanked on both sides and ordered to surrender. When the order came to fall back, the 27th Pa. complied very readily, but the 154th and 134th boys would not retreat, and fought until escape was impossible. Only 17 of our men escaped."[28]

In a letter written specifically for the *Gowanda Reporter,* Newton Chaffee puffed the 154th's courage in extravagant terms that were a clear expression of intense esprit de corps and ardent patriotism. "Our Regiment was in the battle of Gettysburg, which, no doubt, was the greatest battle ever fought by the army of the Potomac, and its effects are to be seen upon the ranks of our once noble regiment," Chaffee wrote. "No braver or truer men are to be found than in the 154th, and old Cattaraugus may well be proud of the men she sent forth, for none have been more faithful to their country in this time of her greatest need, in trying to sustain the beloved flag of our Union, which traitor hands are trying to tear down."[29]

Lieutenant Colonel Dan Allen, who commanded the 154th at Gettysburg, submitted his official report to the New York State adjutant general a couple of weeks after the battle. Allen related the sudden attack of the enemy, the regiment's retreat to the left, and the men's surprise at finding the 27th Pennsylvania gone and the Confederates in possession of the path of escape. "We were compelled to cut our way through them," Allen wrote, "and in doing so our losses were heavy." Allen closed his report by stating, "During the engagement both officers and men displayed great Gallantry and are entitled to the highest credit"—his only comment on the regiment's behavior. He appended a list of the casualties, but the sad tally never was published in Cattaraugus County newspapers. The many families who did not receive letters from their soldier loved ones after Gettysburg were left to agonize about their fate.[30]

A month after being transferred by rail to the western theater of the war, on October 28, 1863, the 154th New York and the rest of Buschbeck's brigade formed the vanguard of the Eleventh Corps in a drive from Bridgeport, Alabama, toward besieged Chattanooga, Tennessee. In the vicinity of a railroad junction at Wauhatchie, Tennessee, the brigade encountered enemy pickets, who gave way before the Union advance. Several miles beyond, Buschbeck's men came upon the 6th South Carolina atop a wooded knoll to the side of the road. Buschbeck ordered the 154th New York and the 73rd Pennsylvania to drive the Confederates from the hill, which they did with dispatch, sending the Rebels flying. The 154th New York suffered but one casualty in the fight. Hiram Straight, back with the regiment after his stay in Satterlee Hospital, had one of his fingers shot off.[31]

This seemingly inconsequential skirmish had one consequential result: after the twin disasters of Chancellorsville and Gettysburg, the 154th New York had at last driven the enemy, instead of the other way around. The soldiers' spirits soared after Wauhatchie. Part of their elation was owing to the fact that their march to Lookout Valley—and its attendant skirmish—had opened the famous "Cracker Line" and broken the siege of Chattanooga. That night Major Lewis Warner, who commanded the regiment in the fight, recorded in his diary, "Our boys are in good spirits and quite jubilant over their afternoons performance. This is the first time they have had a chance to make the Rebs run, and the way they made the woods ring with their cheers was really amusing."[32]

Their elation was evident in letters describing the action. "We was ordered into line of battle double quick and made a Charge on the Rebels and Drove them kiting in to their holes," James Baxter wrote. "Our Regt. and the 73 PA Don the whole of this we Drove one whole Brigade of Rebs," he exaggerated. Edgar Shannon provided Francelia Hunt with a dramatic account of the skirmish:

> A sharp firing broke out right ahead & five or six bullets came zip over our heads. . . . Our faces paled a little & lips closed for we expected a big fight but there was no run in us; every man was ready. . . . We skirmished about half a mile then were ordered to charge & the way the rebs got out of our way was fun. . . . Our faces were red enough when we stopped for we went nearly a mile on a dog trot with [our] heavy loads. We soon formed a junction with [the besieged Chattanooga] men. They cheered us & we them till this old valley fairly rung. I tell you if the old flag did not look good as they waved it & welcomed us to their aid & if they were not pleased I never saw men that were.[33]

Martin Bushnell described the Wauhatchie skirmish to a friend with palpable pride:

> The 73rd exchanged shots with them, that is their pickets, But to be sure of success the 154 must come in which they did with a right good will. We formed in line of battle & deploied a little and pushed on. Soon we were on double quick and at once dashed over the 73rd and at the same time commenced cheering & hurahing eagerly. We dashed acrost a field about 50 rods and there came to the foot of a steep hill covered with a thicket of bushes where the Rebs wer but we sent them to hunt their holes in the Mountain.[34]

In the subsequent Battle of Chattanooga the regiment played a minor role in a dramatic Union victory. Skirmishing on the morning of November 24, 1863, cost the 154th six men wounded. In their letters home several of the men described the regiment as lucky to have escaped such a large battle with so few casualties. "We were right in the midst of it for three days," Edgar Shannon wrote, "but were lucky enough to get out all right." Although many of the men had close calls—bullets penetrated Colonel Patrick Jones's boot and clipped a tuft of mane from his horse's neck—William Charles declared, "Our Regiment have been Very lucky this time." Buoyed by the victory, Richard McCadden enthused, "It is fun to fight the rebs here compared to Virginia. they do not fight half as hard. Our Regt was on the skirmish line during the three days fight and we made them run at every point although we were not generaly engaged." However, Milon Griswold offered a different view of the fight. "I tell you I thought of my parents and home when the cold lead was falling round me like hail," he wrote, "but God was with me, and saved me from the enemies missiles. . . . The 154th was lucky [for] once."[35]

Reminiscing in the postwar years, veterans of the 154th admitted they had skedaddled when firing first broke out along the skirmish line on the morning of November 24 and that Colonel Jones, highly displeased with their behavior, had ordered them to retake their former position. But when Jones wrote his official report of the Chattanooga battle a month after the fight, he praised the actions of the regiment. "The conduct of both officers and men of the command then engaged was highly commendable," Jones wrote. The colonel singled out for special tribute the "gallant conduct" of

Captain Harrison Cheney, who commanded the skirmish line that morning. "It was the fortune of Captain Cheney to be posted in the most exposed position of the line and he acquitted himself with utmost gallantry and cool decision," Jones wrote. It was the only special citation of one of the regiment's officers to be found in any of its after-action reports.[36]

The next fighting the 154th engaged in was unlike any that had come before. When the Atlanta campaign opened in May 1864, the regiment had been in the service for nineteen months and had fought in three battles and a skirmish. As General Sherman drove into the interior of Georgia, the 154th fought in significant battles at Rocky Face Ridge on May 8, Resaca on May 15, New Hope Church on May 25, Pine Knob on June 15 and 16, and Peach Tree Creek on July 20, with frequent skirmishing in the interim and afterward, during the subsequent siege of Atlanta. In all of the battles except Peach Tree Creek the Union forces were the attackers. On every occasion, the regiment was either repulsed or stymied. But each setback was followed by another movement to the south. The soldiers realized perfectly well that despite their reverses the campaign was being won. And although the campaign drained them physically with almost constant marching and fighting and steadily whittled away almost half of their number as casualties, the men's morale remained high throughout and pride in their regiment soared.[37]

In his diary entry recording the activities of the 154th at New Hope Church on May 25, Colby Bryant aptly described the tenor of the campaign as a whole:

> Near night we fall into line and march far to where the battle is raging. We are soon ordered in line of battle and on we go through brush and over logs until we soon come to the battlefield where the missiles of death are flying all around us—and still the battle rages in all its fury until it is dark when there is a lull and it begins to rain. We get orders to remain where we are and keep our ammunition and guns as dry as possible. We are so very warm when we first get quiet that soon most of us feel very chilly out in the cool rain and many of the boys get so chilled through that the next morning they shake as if they had the ague, but we have no reason to complain—the groans of the wounded around us remind us that they are the sufferers.[38]

"The boys are pretty well worn out [from] marching and fighting so long," Emory Sweetland wrote in early June, but the soldiers refused to capitulate to their fatigue. As the month neared its end Sweetland reported, "There is steady fighting on some part of the line all the time indeed one scarcely had a moments cesession of cannonade & musketry. . . . I am getting so used to the noise that I can sleep soundly whilst heavy fighting is going on near us." Major Lewis Warner, who commanded the 154th through much of the campaign, kept the Cattaraugus County home folk informed of the regiment's progress in a series of weekly letters to the *Olean Times*. Writing on July 1, Warner noted that the 154th's casualties for the campaign had exceeded one hundred, but the men's morale remained undiminished. The regiment had lost half of the force it had begun the campaign with, Warner observed:

> Few regiments can show a stronger record than this. It shows that where there was danger we were to be found. I think there is no regiment in the corps (I know of none in the division) that has been in the front line more than ours, or that has acquitted itself better. Our boys, notwithstanding their severe losses, are in the best of spirits, and enjoy the excitements of the picket line as well as ever they did squirrel shooting at home. They will sit for hours, peering from behind their tree, log, or rail pile, with their musket cocked and the finger upon the trigger, waiting patiently for some Johnny to expose his cranium.[39]

The following day Milon Griswold offered a view from the ranks. "We have had a tough time on this campagne I tell you," he wrote. "We have fought the rebs clear from Resaca to here. . . . We have driven the rebs over 100 miles since we started and for the past 20 miles we have fought over every foot of the ground." After the fall of Atlanta, Griswold indicated that the difficulties of the campaign were offset by its triumphant conclusion. "Well, we have at last succeeded in capturing the rebel stronghold 'Atlanta,' but it has been a hard road to travel," he wrote. "The saying is, 'Jordan is a hard road to travel,' but the road we have come to Atlanta is a harder one than Jordan, I believe, and there are more bullets whistling on the Atlanta road. We have seen some stormy times since we have started. . . . Now the old flag floats in triumph over Atlanta, where but a short time ago floated the ensign of treason and rebellion against a glorious Union." In a letter to his mother-in-law written about the same time, Sergeant Addison L. Scutt of Company C also stressed the grueling nature of the campaign. "This summer campaign I tell you granma it has been a hard one and one of a great many exposures and some hare breadth escapes I have been under the enemys fire for 125 days or more within the last 5 months and some days the bullets and shells flew pretty thick." Scutt proudly stated that "the 154th took a conspicuous part" in several battles, and "most allways took the lead."[40]

In a sense, the climactic moment of the campaign came for the 154th New York in the very first battle. As a diversionary gambit, the regiment's division was ordered to assault Dug Gap on Rocky Face Ridge, a looming mountain crowned with an immense palisade of jagged stone. As the 154th toiled up the mountainside, the Confederates atop the crest sent huge boulders and volleys of musketry crashing down the steep slope, but the men struggled on, paused for a moment to catch their breath beneath the rocky outcropping, and stormed the summit in a bayonet charge, planting their colors on the mountaintop—one of the few regiments to do so. The moment of glory was quickly dashed, however; the men who reached the crest were shot down or captured, the colors were rescued after a mad scramble, and the regiment fell back down the mountainside, having lost fifty-six men killed, wounded, or captured. It was a defeat, yet the 154th had carried out its assignment in a most praiseworthy manner, and the overall assault had achieved its purpose. The attack on Rocky Face Ridge would be remembered as a legendary moment in the history of the regiment, a shining example of esprit de corps.[41]

"The boys as usual fought nobly," Emory Sweetland wrote of the battle. Marcellus Darling boasted, "We were nearer to the top [of the mountain] than any other Regiment. . . . At one time our colors were within six feet of the Rebel pits. here the color bearer and one of the guard was shot dead and our men fell fast." Writing of Rocky Face Ridge in his regular letter to the *Olean Times,* Major Lewis Warner described how "our brave boys advanced (many of them never to return)," charging up the mountainside, cheering lustily as they clambered up the palisade; the refusal of the 27th Pennsylvania to advance as the line neared the summit, and the consequent danger to the 154th; the regiment's severe losses, including some who were injured by the tumbling boulders; and the rescue of the colors, with one man after another falling in the attempt to save the flag. Warner admitted the action was an "unsuccessful attack upon an almost impregnable position." But he proudly added, "The 154th was the only regiment which gained a footing upon the crest, and had they been properly supported, they would have maintained their position." Warner noted the regiment's bitterness toward the 27th Pennsylvania, which had skedaddled once again. "Our boys are in good spirits, although they feel that they have been again sacrificed by being joined with troops on whom no reliance can be placed."[42]

In addition to Major Warner's weekly letters to the *Times*, other word from the regiment reached the newspapers back home. Surgeon Henry Van Aernam sent casualty lists and an error-filled account of the rescue of the colors at Rocky Face Ridge to the *Cattaraugus Freeman*. Colonel Patrick Jones, who was injured at Rocky Face and assumed command of the brigade on his recovery, sent lists of the 154th's casualties in the fights at Pine Knob and Peach Tree Creek. He did so, he noted, "in order to relieve the minds of the friends of the Regiment of apprehension. After a fight, matters are reported worse than they really are. God knows it is bad enough as it is." The colonel noted with pride that the 154th New York had won the commendation of Generals Joseph Hooker, commander of the Twentieth Corps (formed by the consolidation of the Eleventh and Twelfth Corps in April 1864), and George H. Thomas, commander of the Army of the Cumberland, in which the Twentieth Corps served. "Hooker and Thomas speak of the command in the highest terms—the poor fellows deserve it," Jones wrote. "The 154th is doing its full share and getting its full compliment of glory. No one is jealous, however, since they deserve it so fairly."[43]

In their official reports of the Atlanta campaign, commanders of the 154th mixed the typical effusive praise of the regiment's gallant conduct with an unusual candor about its failures. Lieutenant Colonel Dan Allen described the climax of the Rocky Face Ridge fight, as the regiment assaulted the summit after its brief rest beneath the outcropping. "I immediately ordered a bayonet charge, which was executed with the greatest heroism, and our colors were planted for an instant upon the crest, but the superior strength of the enemy as regards position and numbers, both in front and on our right flank, rendered the greatest valor unavailing, and we were compelled to fall back with heavy loss," Allen wrote. He added, "I cannot too highly commend the bravery displayed by both officers and men."[44]

Major Lewis Warner admitted in his report of the campaign that the regiment had retreated at Resaca, but he cited mitigating circumstances. The regiment had been ordered to dig a road into a captured redoubt to remove some artillery during the night of May 15 when the enemy suddenly opened fire from a few yards away and sent the men running. "Our men, who [were] not expecting an attack, were somewhat surprised," Warner admitted. He added, however, "It was not cowardice which caused these men to thus abandon their position. They were moved to the front after dark, and could obtain but a limited view of the position, or that of the enemy, the whole hill being covered by a dense forest." Warner made no such excuses for the regiment's retreat at Peach Tree Creek, when it and much of Jones's brigade was sent reeling by a sudden surprise attack by a large Confederate force. "The first line at once gave way and fell back in confusion through our lines, to which their panic was communicated," Warner reported, "and the whole right of the line retreated to the foot of the hill." But Peach Tree Creek was no Chancellorsville. The 154th and the rest of Jones's brigade rallied and helped repulse the enemy attack with awful slaughter. The regiment had seven casualties.[45]

Decades after the war, Marcellus Darling recalled the nerve-wracking moments before a fight. "It was common for men going into battle to relieve the tension by jokes and quips and chaffing," he remembered. "Some never speak, but grimly set their teeth and go forward. Some swear—few and rarely. Some—many, doubtless—pray inwardly. I never saw or heard a man pray openly." As terrifying and terrible as it was, however, battle also had its seductive side. "I have been up with the boys all the forenoon listening to their stories and talking some myself about the late Battle," William Charles wrote a month after the Chattanooga fighting, as the men basked in warm memories of their recent victory. However, as James Quilliam noted a couple of weeks later, "I am not surprised that the boys thinks it is fun to drive the rebs but there is more fun in telling of it then in doing it and it is not quite so hard." To Henry Munger, a soldier had little choice but to be stoic: "A Soldier can stand most any thing but the led bulets but there is a good many that halve tried to stand them but halve found them most to much for them and have bin shot to the ground no more to remain in the army I never want to see any more fiting and I halve always said I had rather they would settle this war some other way if it could be done but I think that it has gon so far that it can not be settled very easy with out they fight it out."[46]

James Quilliam was driving the Rebels at Pine Knob when he was shot through both legs—wounds that proved to be mortal. Henry Munger fought it out until a bullet pierced his neck at Rocky Face Ridge.

CHAPTER 7

The Wounded, Captured, and Dead

With comradely compassion, soldiers instinctively extended a helping hand to the casualties of battle. Esprit de corps moved men to rescue wounded comrades from the battlefield, to visit and care for them in the hospital, and to notify loved ones of their condition. Esprit kept the regiment's captured soldiers together to look out for each other under the horrific conditions of southern prison camps. And when the spark of life flickered and faded, esprit drew soldiers to their dying comrades, to comfort them as best they could, to give them as decent a burial as possible, and to break the sad news and offer condolences, with gentle respect, to the departed's loved ones.

As the 154th New York fought in the shallow rifle pit near Dowdall's Tavern at Chancellorsville, a Confederate bullet struck Nathaniel Brown a glancing blow above his left eye, tearing away an inch-square piece of his skull and leaving a glob of lead stuck to the ragged bone. Brown collapsed at the feet of Sergeant Andrew Keller of his Company D, who turned him over, found no signs of life, and presumed him to be dead. Corporal Benjamin Franklin Phillips and Private Benjamin S. Bently nevertheless picked Brown up and carried him under fire to the rear, where he regained consciousness and even walked a bit with their help. That night a surgeon at the Eleventh Corps hospital—possibly Henry Van Aernam of the 154th—scraped away the lead, exfoliated some pieces of bone, and bandaged the wound. There was no apparent damage to the brain, the doctor noted, and he told Brown that he would come along all right with good care.

Brown was soon moved to Carver Hospital in Washington. When he left the Eleventh Corps hospital, he told his brother-in-law William Chittenden that he felt better and thought he would recover as soon as could be expected. In the meantime, as concern about him spread, news of Brown's condition went back and forth in letters between Cattaraugus County and the front. Brown wrote to Andrew Keller, asking him to write to his wife, Nancy Wheeler Brown. William Chittenden, waiting for a promised letter from Brown, asked his wife, Mary, whether her sister Nancy had news from

Nat. Mary replied, "Nancy has heard from Nat but once since he went to Washington I fear he is worse or dead, but O I hope not for her sake." Chittenden waited for news of his friend from Captain Harrison Cheney, who was expected to visit him in Washington, and vowed to find Brown himself if his own poor health improved.

Nat Brown was sent from Carver Hospital to DeCamp Hospital, on David's Island in New York City's harbor, and thence to a hospital at Lookout Mountain, Tennessee. He did not rejoin the 154th until shortly before the muster-out. For the rest of his life he was troubled by his wound. It discharged chronically, so he always wore a bandage around his forehead. He suffered from vertigo, spasms, and bouts of unconsciousness. His wife, children, or friends kept him constantly under watch, for fear he might suffer a fit and come to harm. The shadow of Chancellorsville loomed over Brown until his death in 1892.[1]

Two years after he helped to rescue Nat Brown, Benjamin Bently was involved in a similar effort. At the Battle of Pine Knob on June 15, 1864, as the 154th New York drove the Confederates about a mile through the woods to a strong line of entrenchments, Private Joseph R. Crowell of Company D was shot through his left lung and groin and fell near the enemy's breastworks. Bently tried to help him to the rear and was wounded slightly in his arm by a spent ball. Corporal Amos B. Weast then came to assist. He and Bently managed to carry Crowell to the shelter of a ledge of rocks; Weast's haversack and canteen were shot to pieces in the process. When darkness fell, Crowell was carried to the foot of the hill and examined by the surgeons, who observed blood frothing from the chest entry wound. They told Crowell he had but minutes to live. Crowell gasped that he couldn't die—he had to see his old mother again, he was her only boy. Crowell's prognosis proved to be the correct one. A couple of days later an ambulance conveyed him to the railroad. He was loaded onto a boxcar with other wounded and carried to Chattanooga. After hospitalizations there and in Nashville, he was discharged in Buffalo in July 1865. Crowell lived with his pain and scars until 1891, when he died in South Dakota.[2]

Nat Brown, Joe Crowell, and Ben Bently were just three of approximately 225 members of the 154th who were wounded in action during the regiment's service. Twenty-five of them died from their wounds. All but one of the 225 were struck by bullets or shell fragments. The sole exception, Addison Scutt, had his head sliced by a saber wielded by a mounted Confederate officer when Scutt refused a surrender demand during the melee at Gettysburg. The gravity of the wounds varied widely, from slight ones such as Bently's to grisly and dangerous mutilations. The severe or unusual nature of a score of the men's wounds earned them mention in the postwar compilation *The Medical and Surgical History of the War of the Rebellion*, including sixteen cases of limb amputations.[3]

"I have given both my blankets and one of my shirts to a poor wounded boy that had lost all he had in the fight," William Charles wrote after Chancellorsville. A soldier could rescue a wounded comrade from the battlefield, visit him in the hospital, share material goods with him, and communicate with his loved ones. But his fate ultimately rested with the army's medical department. The slightly wounded generally recovered quickly and returned to the ranks; the more grievously wounded typically were sent as soon as possible to hospitals in northern cities, to be cared for by strangers. In the interim, during their treatment by the regimental medical staff, the wounded were nursed by friendly hands.[4]

Tending the wounded extracted a heavy toll on the caregivers. Surgeon Henry Van Aernam never wrote about individual cases in letters to his wife and seldom referred to his medical duties at all. When he did, it was with sorrow. After Chancellorsville, Van Aernam wrote about his work on the night of May 2, attending "the poor fellows who had fallen in the fight" in a hollow in the woods. "Here the sight was sad and melancholy in the extreme—too sickening to tell," he wrote. "Suffice to say that more than 500 wounded in every way and place that man could endure and fire arms inflict—have applied to me for help." After his work at Gettysburg, Van Aernam could only say, "I have operated largely. My heart is sick contemplating the mutilations."[5]

As Van Aernam indicated, after large battles the hard-pressed surgeons had to tend many patients beyond those of their own regiment. A week after the 154th fought at Gettysburg, Assistant Surgeon Dwight Day wrote to his parents from Baltimore, where he had accompanied some six hundred wounded from the Eleventh Corps. There were sixteen hundred more wounded left in the corps hospital at Gettysburg, Day reported. He sent along particular news of one of them, a family friend from Day's home town of Freedom. Private Chauncey G. Pinney of Company D was shot in the chest at Gettysburg. The bullet injured his left lung, fractured a vertebra, damaged his spinal cord, and lodged in his side, whence it was extracted. "A portion of the lower tube of the left lung protrudes through the wound—he will probably die," Day reported. But the protrusion proved to be tissue and was burned away with caustic. Private Curtis S. Pinney, who had survived unharmed, cared for his brother at Gettysburg. Chauncey remained hospitalized in various locations until he was discharged at Elmira in July 1865. In the postwar years he suffered from neuralgia, permanent lameness, severe pain, dysfunctional eyesight, and prostrating fatigue—but he managed to live until 1921, surviving his unharmed brother by six years.[6]

During battle, the surgeons often found themselves in harm's way. At Gettysburg on July 3, Doctor Van Aernam recorded, the hospital came under heavy artillery fire. Reminiscing in the postwar years, veterans of the 154th recalled Assistant Surgeon Corydon Rugg as particularly courageous. By staying with the wounded during the fighting at Gettysburg, Rugg fell into the enemy's hands, irately refusing a Confederate officer's demand for his sword. During the Pine Knob fight Rugg was treating the wounded Private Thomas Mason of Company I under fire when Mason was hit a second time. Later in the campaign Colonel Patrick H. Jones reprimanded Rugg for taking too many risks and asked him why he was so far to the front. To look after the boys, Rugg replied. Jones ordered him to the rear, but Rugg was soon back near the front line.[7]

Assisting Rugg during the Atlanta campaign was Emory Sweetland, who spent most of his term of service as a nurse, orderly, and steward in the regimental, division, and corps hospitals. After Chancellorsville, Sweetland was with the detail that crossed the Rappahannock to retrieve the regiment's wounded from enemy hands and convey them to the Eleventh Corps hospital at Brooks Station. The wounded men had lain for ten days, exposed to the elements and largely unattended, although they were otherwise treated kindly by their Confederate captors. They "had not had much care and their wounds stank teribly," Sweetland noted. "It made me sick." Sweetland was detailed after Gettysburg at the Eleventh Corps hospital and later at the general hospital that was established there, distributing clothing and victuals, supervising the laundry, overseeing the nurses, and caring for patients of a ward. In a letter to his wife from the corps hospital, he described an event that had interrupted his writing:

It has been an hour since I stopped writing. The nurse cried out that a man was bleeding like a stuck hog. He had been wounded in the breast & was apparently doing well when some artery rotted off inside & the blood was spurting. Those around did not know what to do I put my thumb on the artery & stopped it, & the doctors are going to cut into him and take it up. Such things as this are of daily occurrance (it is the second one today) Some days I hold the legs or arms of 4 or 5 men to have them taken off.[8]

In another letter Sweetland outlined his tasks as an orderly to the regimental surgeons during the Atlanta campaign: "My duties now [are] to deal out what medicines are needed in our regt. & in time of battle to carry a box of instruments & bandages & do up wounds. we follow the regt. when they go into the fights & get behind some knowl or big tree & do up the boys wounds as soon as they are wounded & then they are taken back to a hospital. we are in some considerable danger & also have an exilent chance to see all that is going on, we being just farther enough in the rear to see to advantage."[9]

After every battle, Sweetland sent his wife a list of the wounded and the nature of their injuries, but he rarely exposed her to details of their sufferings. His letter relating the Battle of Pine Knob was an exception. He wrote about how Dennis Brand died, "praying God to forgive him & Telling us to tell his wife that he thought of her to the last"; how Corporal Augustus Rogers of Company A was killed trying to carry his dead company comrade Private Thomas Haffren from the field; and how Private Elias W. Kinyon of the same company had the bridge of his nose and his right eye shot away. "I think he will live," Sweetland accurately predicted of Kinyon. "He has been one of our best soldiers always in every fight. he is cheerful & confident of recovery. he will be discharged if he recovers Send word to his folks if you can." Sweetland buried Haffren, Rogers, and Brand, carving their names into headboards to mark their graves. He wanted Rogers's wife to be notified that "I saw him well burried & the spot marked," and that the items Rogers had in his pockets would be sent home by a company comrade.[10]

Almost thirty years after the battle, the events of Pine Knob remained seared in Sweetland's memory. He recalled with crystal clarity Elias Kinyon laying on a stretcher with "no semblance of a human face," probing Kinyon's wound with his finger, and telling him he had escaped death by an eighth of an inch. He remembered the poignant last words of Dennis Brand: "Oh God be merciful to me a sinner. I believe He will, I know He will. Tell Clarissa my last thoughts shall be of her." He remembered searching for the corpses of Rogers and Haffren in the gloomy nighttime woods, finding them in the blackness by the moonlight reflecting from their ghastly white faces.[11]

The carnage became so commonplace that some soldiers grew callous. As the regiment toiled up Rocky Face Ridge, Private Franklin Rector of Company B engaged in some habitual profane language, cursing and finding fault with the officers. His company comrade Thomas Aldrich superstitiously told Rector not to swear so much, or he would be hit. Rector replied that he did not care a goddamn, he would just as soon be hit as not. He had scarcely uttered the words when a bullet struck his upper right thigh and he tumbled backward down the slope. Aldrich broke into laughter, causing First Lieutenant Winfield S. Cameron to chide him for laughing at a wounded man. At the Battle of Pine Knob, when Private Nicholas Cook of Company G was shot in the jaw, his friend Clark Oyer said, "Nick, you've got hit at last." "Yes, by God," Cook replied, "and they've broke my hardtack machine too." During the siege of Savannah, Private Wellman P. Nichols of Company C was playing cards with some comrades when he was severely injured in his back by a shell fragment. "Here, take this man to the hospital and someone come and play his hand," one of the card players hollered. Nichols was carried off on a stretcher, a soldier picked up his cards, and the game resumed.[12]

Differences in seconds of time or inches of space could have considerably lengthened the 154th's casualty lists. Many of the men reported close calls. Addison Scutt's hardtack was destroyed when a bullet perforated his haversack at Peach Tree Creek. Amos Humiston was struck above the heart by a spent ball at Chancellorsville; the near miss "made me think of home," he wrote. After the Lookout Valley skirmish, Private William D. Harper of Company F recorded in his diary, "Had a ball shot through my overcoat." At Chancellorsville a bullet cut through a plug of tobacco in Clark Oyer's pants pocket and fell harmlessly into his boot. Men who were hit sometimes counted themselves fortunate that their wounds were not as bad as they could have been. A bullet that struck Private Thomas Regan of Company G in the chest at Rocky Face Ridge was slowed by a towel that he had folded inside his jacket pocket. Regan was severely wounded in the left lung, but his company mates believed the towel had saved his life. Homer Ames was shot at Pine Knob and a month later reported to his parents from a Chattanooga hospital, "My wound was a light flesh wound in the left arm. the ball went through my Haversack & through my tin cup & A piece of the cup went in my leg but it all was slight I think I was lucky [compared] to some of them for I did not loose any limbs."[13]

When James W. Phelps, a resident of the Cattaraugus County town of Great Valley, visited Gettysburg in the aftermath of the battle, he found eight severely wounded members of the 154th sharing a tent in the Eleventh Corps hospital. Five of the eight succumbed to their wounds. On his return home, Phelps provided the *Cattaraugus Freeman* with a note listing the regiment's dead and wounded. He also wrote to the loved ones of the men he had visited. In a letter to the father of Thaddeus Reynolds, Phelps described the teenager's last days. A shell fragment had torn away part of Thaddeus's hip and much of his left hand; lockjaw set in and young Reynolds was kept under the influence of chloroform to quiet his agony. During his awful demise, Phelps reported, Thaddeus was tenderly cared for by members of his regiment. Surgeon Dwight Day and nurse Richard H. Kerr, a corporal of Company D who was wounded himself, "did all that could be done for his comfort." Lying next to Thaddeus was John Bush, his right arm amputated, who "although *helpless* himself watched him & called attention to him when he required during the last two days especially." Private William A. Freeman of Thaddeus's Company I "was in frequently to see him & assist." Private Newell Butler of Company K gathered Thaddeus's effects to send home. With regimental comrades clustered around him, Thaddeus Reynolds slipped away. He died July 12, 1863.[14]

More than 150 members of the regiment (about three dozen of them wounded) were captured at the Battle of Chancellorsville. While the severely wounded were left behind on the battlefield and eventually returned to the Union forces, the other captives were marched to Richmond. There they spent a couple of days in the prison camp on Belle Island, in the James River opposite the city. After that brief confinement they were marched via Petersburg to City Point on the James, where they were paroled—pledging not to take up arms again until exchanged—and released to Union hands, boarding steamships for Annapolis. After about a week in the Annapolis parole camp they were conveyed by steamer to Alexandria, where they began an imprisonment of another sort, a stultifying months-long wait for their official exchange and the chance to return to the regiment.[15]

The 173 members of the 154th captured at Gettysburg were not so lucky. To a man they refused parole on the field, under the belief it was illegal and would not be recognized by the federal government. The prisoners were marched south through the Shenandoah Valley to Staunton, Virginia, where they were loaded onto freight cars and rode into Richmond. There the officers were confined in Libby Prison and the enlisted men were herded onto Belle Island. Some forty of them died in the coming months, victims of malnourishment verging on starvation, exposure to extremes of weather, an assortment of deadly diseases, an appalling lack of sanitation, rampant vermin, brutal behavior on the part of cruel Confederate guards and ruffian Union prisoners, and mind-numbing boredom—all of which brought the sufferers to the edge of inhumanity and induced a psychological helplessness and hopelessness that sometimes proved lethal. Beginning in February 1864, the surviving enlisted men were shipped by rail to Andersonville, Georgia, and confined in what became the most notorious Confederate prison camp. They were joined that summer by several regimental comrades captured during the Atlanta campaign. At Andersonville, the prisoners suffered horrors that even exceeded those of Belle Island. At least twenty members of the 154th died there, and when Sherman's penetration of Georgia caused most of the stockade's prisoners to be sent elsewhere, the survivors endured more suffering in prison camps at Millen, Savannah, and Blackshear, Georgia; Florence, South Carolina; and elsewhere.[16]

Through it all, members of the 154th New York stuck together as best they could. In their diaries and memoirs, surviving prisoners wrote of their attachment to regimental comrades in touching terms. Newell Burch was captured at Gettysburg with Corporal Eben S. Ely of Company E. "Ely & myself lived under the same blanket until Aug 22d 1864," Burch recalled. "He showed himself a man in battle & in camp [and] in prison by his great care of sick and hungry [men] and I am more indebted to him for life than any other man on earth." At Belle Island, Ely was detailed to ferry provisions from Richmond to the prison camp on a flatboat, for which he received an extra ration to share with Burch. In the city or aboard the boat, Ely surreptitiously bought pies, biscuits, tobacco, and other goods from black people or guards, which Burch in turn sold or traded in camp. It kept the two in cash and enabled them to participate in the prison's extensive black market. When they were sent from Belle Island to Georgia in February 1864, Burch noted, "I was very sick with lung fever and carried by comrade E. S. Ely in his arms to Andersonville a good share of the way." The two stayed together through the spring and summer of 1864 until August 22, when Ely helped Burch, prostrate with scurvy and a gangrenous arm, to the stockade's south gate to answer sick call. "Mr. Ely was a good nurse when I was sick and a good man to help any in need as far as he was able," Burch wrote. The two friends never saw each other again after that August day, although both survived their imprisonment and the war.[17]

Horace Smith and his Company D comrade Corporal Benjamin F. H. Andrews also were captured at Gettysburg. The day they began their journey to Richmond as prisoners, Smith recorded in his diary, "My chum Benny Andrews marched by my side all day. we are bound to stick together as long as possible." That autumn, Smith's diary entries at Belle Island told a sad story. October 11, 1863: "Ben is about sick today." October 25: "Ben is getting very weak from the Diarhea." October 29: "Poor Benny Andrews is growing weaker every day." October 30: "Ben is not able to go out doors without help." October 31: "Ben is growing worse very fast." November 1: "[Andrew] Keller and I took Ben Andrews out to hospital this morn. he was sent across the river to the city. he will probably be sent to our lines in a day or two, he is very weak, not able to stand up alone. poor fellow, I hope he will get around all right." Andrews never got around; he died in Richmond on January 27, 1864.[18]

Esprit de corps was harshly tested in the hellish atmosphere of the prison camps. Occasionally it collapsed when comradely compassion surrendered to selfishness. Thomas Aldrich cited one example in a memoir of prison life based on his wartime diary. An unidentified Andersonville tent mate of Privates Othnial Green and George W. Bailey of Company G refused to share rations and water or cook for them as they weakened with disease. He even scraped a line across the dirt floor of their shelter and pettily forbade them from leaving their space. Other members of the regiment, including Aldrich, did what they could for Green and Bailey—and bitterly cursed their hard-hearted tent mate—but their efforts were unavailing. Green died of dysentery on August 10, 1864; Bailey died of scurvy five days later. Such selfishness, however, was unusual. More representative was an act of Corporal Orange J. Abbey of Company H, who while suffering from acute diarrhea at Andersonville in June 1864 presented his tall boots to company comrade Corporal Leroy Litchfield. Abbey died on June 15. Litchfield survived and never forgot his friend's kind gesture.[19]

While the regiment received the occasional written report from the Soldier's Friend, John Manley, or first-hand accounts of life on Belle Island from exchanged and returned prisoners, little was known of the Andersonville captives until August 2, 1864, when Private Sidney Moore of Company D returned to the regiment. Moore had been captured at Rocky Face Ridge and held at Andersonville until July 2, when he became one of the few prisoners to successfully escape the place. He told an exciting story of hairbreadth escapes from pursuing men and bloodhounds and help received from friendly blacks. "He tells a tale of hardships endured that needs only one look at his face to convince one of the truth of what he asserts," Charles Abell wrote. Moore also brought news of the regiment's captives and their life in the stockade. "They were generally well," Surgeon Van Aernam reported Moore as saying, "though somewhat scorbutic and debilitated." Moore's news of the Andersonville prisoners was spread by Van Aernam in a letter published in the *Cattaraugus Freeman,* and in private letters from members of the regiment. "It must look sad and lonely to see so many widows weeds and hear of so many Orphans tears as there are," Charles Abell wrote, "But some hearts will rejoice when they hear of Sid Moores safety."[20]

When Atlanta fell, members of the 154th attempted to communicate with regimental comrades held at Andersonville. Among them was Marcellus Darling, who tried to contact his captive brother. "I wrote a letter to Deloss yesterday and sent it by a citizen that is going south through our lines," Darling wrote. "He said he would carry it right through and he thought sure Deloss would get it. . . . Most all of the Reg't. wrote that had any acquaintances there and the man promised to see the letters safe through." Whether the mail carrier fulfilled his promise or not went unrecorded.[21]

Soldiers with the regiment had two general reactions when they learned from paroled comrades of their prison ordeals. Some voiced relief and wonder that the prisoners had survived at all. William Charles received news in December 1864 that his fellow Welshman and friend William Jones was on his way home after his capture at Gettysburg and a lengthy imprisonment at

Belle Island and Andersonville. "I had almost given up [hope of] seeing him any more," Charles declared, "but I do hope now. It is a wonder though that he was enabled to keep soul and body together, when so many thousands of his fellows died all around him." Other soldiers expressed outrage at the sufferings and deaths of their imprisoned comrades. Lieutenant Colonel Lewis Warner, in notifying the father of Almon Gile of his son's death at Andersonville, commented bitterly, "His lot was with thousands of other brave and true men, to waste away life in southern prisons, victims of Rebell malevolence, and disregard of every claim of humanity. Had they drawn their prisoners up in line and at [a] signall deliberately shot them, the act would have been praiseworthy, and commendable compared with the deliberate murder by inches which our boys have undergone." Warner added, "But a small part of [the survivors] will ever fully recover from the effects of their imprisonment." At the war's end, Newton Chaffee posed a rhetorical question. "How much mercy would these Rebels show us if we was in their power," he asked. "They have proven how much mercy they will show by the worse than Barbarious treatment they have inflicted upon our Soldiers, while prisoners in their hands. the murdered bodies of our Brothers call to us from the lothsome dungeons of Libey and Andersonville for Revenge."[22]

Edward Jones, the poetic civilian brother of David Jones of the 154th, gave voice to the unified support of the prisoners by both soldiers and home folk in an undated poem titled "The Starving Prisoners in Richmond." Jones's verses quoted gallant Union soldiers dying in Richmond's dank and gloomy prisons, appealing to their comrades for vengeance and asking for the home folk's support. Jones's stout reply:

> Yes, Defenders of our Nation,
>   All your wants shall be supply'd,
> And your comrades they are ready,
>   To avenge the ones who've died
> Through neglect, and by starvation,
>   While in prison they have lain,
> Pining on the bed of anguish,
>   Groaning 'neath the captive's chain.[23]

Imprisonment scarred the survivors for the rest of their lives. Charles Whitney weighed 145 pounds when he was captured at Rocky Face Ridge.

After six months at Andersonville, Savannah, and Millen, he weighed only 85 pounds and his legs were blackened and twisted by scurvy. For decades after the war he was haunted by memories of the horrors of Andersonville. In nightmares he saw himself helping to load carts with the dead before his own lifeless body was tossed atop the pile.[24]

Perhaps Whitney exorcized some demons in 1914 when he returned to Andersonville with Robert J. Woodard, a former private of Company C and fellow prisoner. On April 29 the two represented the 154th Regiment at the dedication of New York State's Andersonville monument, located in the National Cemetery amid 13,000 tranquil green graves. State flags marked the headstones of 2,500 New York soldiers for the occasion. The men listened to long-winded speeches, marched to the old stockade and received commemorative medals, ate a meal, and returned to the cemetery for the unveiling and dedication of the monument and more orations. Then the veterans were given and hour or two "to ramble around here amid the graves of your comrades," and Whitney and Woodard were engulfed by memories.[25]

Esprit de corps offered the soldier a precious opportunity to extend to his dying comrade the solaces so eagerly sought by Americans of the Victorian age. At home, the deathbed was a sacred spot where the family circle closed around its loved one to offer comfort and reassurance and to witness a peaceful passing. At the front, dying soldiers looked to their surrogate family—their company and regimental comrades—to stand by them in the deathwatch, to bury them and mark their graves, and to send their effects and the fateful letter of notification and condolence to their loved ones. Esprit de corps insured that those melancholy duties would be fulfilled.[26]

Because they occurred outside of the regiment, the first three deaths of members of the 154th caused little comment in the ranks. During the bustle of the regiment's departure from Camp Brown at Jamestown on September 29, 1862, Private William Hale of Company H fell into a convulsive fit and was sent to the hospital, where he became unconscious and died two hours later. Hale's passing was described in a brief note from Surgeon Henry Van Aernam to the *Cattaraugus Freeman*. Two days later, with the regiment gone to Washington, Private William H. Reynolds of Company E succumbed in Jamestown to an unidentified disease. Resolutions of regret adopted by his company were distributed to Chautauqua County newspapers, but no other comment on his death has been found. The first death in Virginia occurred on October 17 when Private Evander Evans of Company C died of "typhoid pneumonia" at the Prince Street Hospital in Alexandria. Evans left a wife and three children in his Cattaraugus County home town of Portville. While his death no doubt was mentioned in letters and diaries of his townsmen and company mates, no such references have yet been located.[27]

In contrast, the first death in camp caused widespread comment in letters and diaries of soldiers throughout the regiment. Private John L. Myers of Company D had been sick for a few days with dysentery but seemed to be getting better until early in the morning of October 20, 1862. About 3 A.M. his tent mates, his brother Private Edmond Myers and Horace Smith, were awakened by John's harsh breathing. Unable to rouse him, they called the surgeon, who had him removed to Captain Harrison Cheney's tent. About twelve hours later Myers died of congestion of the brain.

A discussion ensued in Company D as to whether to send the body home. It was decided not to, William Chittenden reported, because "the corpse would not look natural and it would be impossible to do so in every case." The company would, however, take up a collection for Myers's widow and two young children residing in Machias, Cattaraugus County. The following afternoon the regiment attended its first military funeral. Chaplain Henry Lowing based his sermon on Romans 8:18: "For I reckon that the sufferings of this present time are not worthy to be compared with the glory which shall be revealed in us."[28]

William Chittenden informed his family of Myers's death. "I will again pencil a few broken centences to the ones so near to me but it is under more painful circumstances than heretofore," he began. "We are called to mourn the loss of a comrad from our company." Chittenden then offered a detailed account of Myers's last hours. The fact that the deceased left a wife and two children, Chittenden told Mary, "will enable you to know how to sympathize with the mourners." He was particularly touched by the grief of Edmond Myers. "They seemed to think of each other with brotherly love, always marching togather & sleeping togather & [Edmond] will feel deeply the loss of his Brother." Myers's death, Chittenden concluded, "shows most conclusively that whether in Camp or the Battle field death is the most certain & yet the most uncertain of all events."[29]

"I saw him about ten minutes before he died and How I Did pitty him,"

Ira Wood wrote of Myers. He added, "Death has Began its labors in our rankes [Who] Will Bee the next one the lord only noes." In a letter intended for newspaper publication, Alanson Crosby couched a formal tribute to the deceased in more stately language:

> One brave heart has been buried beneath the soil of Virginia which has caused a melancholy gloom to settle over our camp. . . . In his death we have lost one of the best soldiers in the regiment. He leaves a small family to mourn his loss, but it will be a consolation to them to know that he died in so noble a cause, and received the kind minis-trations of a brother in his last moments. We buried him in a quiet spot by the side of other heroic martyrs who have laid their lives upon the altar of their country, and gone to their reward. A rude tablet marks the place where he sleeps in the quiet grave yard.[30]

Never again did a single soldier's passing cause such extensive commen-tary—death became too commonplace. "The state of V[irgini]a is but little less than one vast Grave yard," Charles Abell declared a year after the regi-ment reached the front. By the end of the war, 232 members of the 154th had died. The rituals of deathwatch, burial, and notification of loved ones continued to be carried out faithfully, but individual deaths were seldom mentioned beyond the deceased's immediate circle of comrades.[31]

Writing a letter of notification and condolence to a dead soldier's loved ones was a solemn duty. Most often, the melancholy task fell to the company commander or another officer, but home folk also heard from enlisted men, hospital personnel, and visitors to the front, as circumstances dictated. Writ-ing to the loved ones of dead soldiers, comrades attempted to narrow the distance between a deathbed at the front and a family at home. They de-scribed in great detail the deceased's last hours, carefully detailing the na-ture of mortal wounds and sparing no particulars of pain and suffering. They told how they had cared for the dying and relayed messages and statements from dying soldiers to their loved ones, even reporting the absence of mes-sages. They offered loved ones praise of the deceased's good character and tendered to the bereaved the solace of religious consolation. Formalizing their respects, they composed and presented resolutions to the families of departed soldiers and made their eulogies public in the columns of home-town newspapers. Comrades attempted to have the deceased's remains embalmed and sent home; failing that, they did their best to insure a decent burial and a well-marked grave. They sent the dead soldier's personal effects to his loved ones. They also took care of the business required by military regulations, handling matters of wages, ration allotments, sutler's accounts, clothing allowances, receipts for effects, bounties, and final statements of departed soldiers.

Letters regarding Private William Henry Sprague of Company E encompassed many of the elements of a deathwatch and its aftermath. Sprague died on March 2, 1863, two days before his twentieth birthday, at the division hospital at Stafford Court House. The young man had kept his parents in Ripley, Chautauqua County, informed of his well-being in a series of letters that began soon after he left home and ended abruptly on February 20, 1863. Two days later, Henry fell ill. His company comrades "did not take any harm about him at first," according to Private Truman A. St. John, but on February 23, Sprague's condition worsened. "He was the sickest boy I ever saw," St. John wrote. "He was crasy as a loon." Sprague was admitted to the regimental hospital that evening. Three of his comrades cared for him through the night. On February 25, St. John wrote to Sprague's parents and notified them that their son had been rediagnosed with inflammation of the bowels, adding that a doctor predicted recovery. By March 1, however, St. John wrote that "Henry is a great deal worse." He had been transferred to the division hospital, where he had been rediagnosed with inflammation of the brain and was laying insensible, unaware of his surroundings and unable to recognize his comrades. St. John and Private James F. Bacon "watched the poor fellow in his sleep," having been summoned to his bedside. "I have not heard Henry say any thing about you, nor any of his friends since he has been sick," St. John informed Sprague's father. He closed his letter "hopeing that poor Henry will be better by morning." But the next morning, Corporal William Kendall finished the sheet begun by St. John the previous day:

> I am sorry and sorry to Half to turn on this side [of the page] to Inform you that your Dear Son Henry is Dead he Dide Last Night [The] Poor Boy has Left us out of all trubels I Beleave he hadent his senceses He Had a good many friends here we miss Him Verry much Poor fellow I Hope he has gon to a Beter Place than this which he has no Doubt we have started his Remains to the Landing to Bea sent Home

to you and a man with him But we Dont Know wether he will get threw or not as he has no Pass from the General If He Dont he will Have to bea Burried hear and if he is we will send you a nother Line oh this unholy ware it's a Disgrace on all of Gods Good People.

Later that day, Joseph Fay, Company E's captain, sent the elder Sprague official notice of his son's death and enclosed resolutions of regret from the company:

It is with deep regret that I am called upon to write you the particulars with regard to your son Perhaps as you have already been informed he was taken very sudenly ill one week ago today Feb 23d with inflama-tion of the Bowels terminating on the Brain. He did not have his senses but very little of the time during his sickness. . . . I made every effort to have him Embalmed and sent to your care, but could not I had his remains taken to Brooks Station near the Rail Road so that you can get his remains if you think proper The *Sacred Spot* will be marked plainly with the Name of the Co Regt. &c I believe all has been done that could be under the circumstances in which we are placed I will enclose a copy of Resolutions passed by his company which I fully endorse.

Truman St. John later described the unsuccessful effort to have Henry's remains sent home:

Your request was to have his boddy sent home. we was very ancious at the first period of his death to forward his boddy to you, and this Co did raise the money to send him home, and tried to get a pass for a man to go to Washington with the boddy but did not get the pass, and could not get one. his boddy was taken to the Station. but at last we had to bury *him there*. he had a good rough board coffin, and was laid out in his military suit he was buried in a good place and we put a board up at the head of his grave with his name and co. and regt *on it*. it would be impossible for us to send his boddy home now, unless you come or send some one for it, and it would cost a great deal to take him now he has been dead so long I should therefore advise you to let him rest where he now lies near brooks Station Va. We would all be very glad to have him sent to you for we all know how you must feel to have your Son buried so far from you. but he was buried in *peace,* and it was a striking blow to this Company to have him taken from our *midste.* but he has gone I hope & trust to that land where war is never known and trouble is never brought uppon us. I Truman as an individual deeply sympathize with you in your affliction, and hope that he who is higher than *earth* will sustain you in this hour of trial.[32]

Simpler but no less poignant was the letter Nathaniel Brown sent to the brother of his tent mate Eason Bull, who died on February 19, 1863, at the regimental hospital near Stafford Court House.

It is with a trembling hand and an aching heart that I address you with a silent pen. I have lost a bunk mate and a friend. Your dear brother, Eason, is dead. He died yesterday about noon. He was taken a few days ago with the bowel complaint, then the typhoid fever set in which was the cause of his death. He was out of his head the last few hours but the night before he died, he called out for [his infant nephew] little Willey. He had as good care as could be had. I was with him when he breathed his last. His remains are on a little hill at the edge of a pine grove. There is a little pine at the head of his grave. It is about one mile from Stafford's Courthouse on what is called the old Wheeler farm. He has had a good buriel [compared] to what most of the poor soldiers have.[33]

William Charles described a typical military funeral. "After the body is put in the grave and a little dirt droped upon the coffin, the guard fires two volleys over the grave that is *twelve shots,* then the chaplain if there is one to be found gives out a hymn, reads, prays &c. and the poor soldier is left *all alone* in his narrow house of clay." All in all, Charles thought, "A military funeral is grand impressive and very solemn when conducted properly. But here in 'the field' many a soldier bids farewell to all things earthly and is thrown into the grave without as much as a board under or over him." Survivors did the best they could to see that deceased comrades were decently buried, but they often were hampered by inadequate means. According to family legend, a hollowed log served as Eason Bull's casket. When Private Adelbert Rolf of Company K was buried on April 9, 1863, the day after he died of typhoid fever at the division hospital, Barzilla Merrill noted the deceased was "put in as desent a coffin as the circumstances would permit." Some men were buried in more formal settings. "I have been this afternoon to see about the setting of Austin [Munger's] grave stone," John Griswold wrote in September 1863 from Alexandria. "The yard is to be a permanent one & fitted up in nice style." Today it is the Alexandria National Cemetery. Emory Sweetland visited a cemetery near Atlanta in which the regiment's division had its own graveyard, surrounded by a white picket fence plundered from a local home. Neat rows of inscribed headboards on sodded ground ornamented with rose bushes and evergreens surrounded a marble monument listing all of the battles in which the dead had fallen. Sweetland noted that the grave of Sergeant Thomas S. Willis of Company H, who was mortally wounded at Rocky Face Ridge, was about five rods from the monument. When the Welsh boys of Company F learned that their comrade Samuel Williams had died at home in Freedom while on furlough following his release from imprisonment, they offered to purchase a flag to mark his grave.[34]

Although Company D decided not to ship the remains of John Myers home and Company E was unsuccessful in its attempt to do the same with Henry Sprague, the corpses of some soldiers were sent to Cattaraugus and Chautauqua counties for burial. After Private Martin Yelsey died of disease at the regimental hospital in March 1863, members of his Company H subscribed two dollars apiece to express his remains to his home town of Randolph, Cattaraugus County. In another case from the same company, Wilber Moore was sick for two weeks at Alexandria in September 1863 before he began failing rapidly. On the night of September 24, Moore sent for his company comrade, Corporal James M. Gallagher, who hurried to the division hospital. Gallagher described the scene to Moore's mother:

> I immediately went to see him, & found him very weak & pale. I saw that he was dieing. He was perfectly sensible, and told me that he was going to die. He told me to send him home, to his mother. This I promised to do. He then told me to take hold of his hand which I did. He said no more, but died, in about a half an hour. He died very easyly; without a strugle. I then saw his body taken care of, and to day it has been embalmed & to morrow will go by express to Steamburg

Station. If you wish to take the corpse from the coffin that it is in, you can do so with safety.

Gallagher expected to be reimbursed by Mrs. Moore; he enclosed with his letter receipts for the embalming ($25), express shipment to Steamburg ($25), and a telegram ($3.50). Company H would have covered the costs, Gallagher indicated, had it been able to do so. "If the company was large," he explained, "I would not ask you to return this bill. but there is very few men in the company, and there wages is small." Emeline Moore presumably received her son's remains, but Wilber's burial place is unknown.[35]

With high prices prohibiting the soldiers from shipping all of their dead comrades home, it fell to relatives to retrieve the remains of their loved ones if they so desired—and could stand the expense. When Private Theodore F. Hall of Company E died of typhoid fever in a Washington hospital in January 1863, his father accompanied his remains to Chautauqua County and young Hall was laid to rest in his home town of Portland. The brother of Private Edward Shults of Company K arrived at Odd-Fellows Hospital in Washington just in time to witness Edward die in delirium on February 15, 1863. Shults's corpse—presumably accompanied by his brother—was shipped to Ellicottville and interred in the village's Jefferson Street Cemetery. "A large concourse of our citizens accompanied the remains to their last resting place," the *Cattaraugus Freeman* reported. "Edward was universally loved and respected by all who knew him." Sometimes a loved one traveled to the front to mark a soldier's grave, as was the case when a relative of Corporal Amos F. Keyes of Company C visited Virginia two weeks after Keyes died of typhoid fever on December 26, 1862.[36]

Loved ones also gathered the remains of battle casualties. After Private John Mearns of Company D was wounded and captured at Chancellorsville and his leg was amputated, his brother traveled to Virginia to care for him. John pleaded, "Oh! take me home George, when I die." With the aid of Surgeons Henry Van Aernam and Dwight Day, George Mearns fulfilled his brother's request, and John was buried in his home town of Freedom. "A large concourse met at the [Mearns] house to look once more upon his cheek now cold and pale, and weep with parents, brothers and sisters that wept," a eulogist wrote. "He was buried at home away from the place where his blood stained Virginia soil, and he will be remembered for his bold purpose to go when his country called him. For his bravery in the battle field, and his lingering sufferings while in rebel hands." In October 1863, James Wilson traveled from Chautauqua County to Gettysburg to search for the body of his son-in-law, Corporal Byron A. Wiggins of Company F, who had been seen to fall on the battlefield. But Wilson experienced difficulty because Wiggins was not buried in one of several thousand marked graves. After a lengthy search, Wilson finally found Wiggins's grave by a fence overgrown with bushes in an out-of-the-way place—quite likely in the vicinity of the brickyard where the 154th had fought. Wiggins's remains were conveyed to the Chautauqua County town of Hanover and buried in a cemetery there, with a local militia company according full honors. The corpse of another Chautauqua soldier, Private Oscar M. Taylor of Company E, was removed by his brother from the prison camp on Belle Island to his home town of Portland, a rare occurrence.[37]

During and after the war, the remains of tens of thousands of Union soldiers were retrieved from their battlefield, camp, prison, and hospital graves and reinterred in newly established national cemeteries. Among them were dozens of members of the 154th New York, who rest today in national cemeteries in Washington, D.C.; Andersonville and Marietta, Georgia; Annapolis and Baltimore, Maryland; Gettysburg, Pennsylvania; Chattanooga and Nashville, Tennessee; and Alexandria, Fredericksburg, and Richmond, Virginia. Many of their graves are identified. But the dead from Belle Island prison and the battlefields of Chancellorsville and Dug Gap, who were buried anonymously in mass graves by the Confederates, repose today under headstones inscribed "Unknown."

In March 1863 a regimental order established a council of administration consisting of three officers to convene at headquarters "to administer upon and dispose of the effects" of Privates Fernando C. Jaquay of Company A, Bethuel R. Harvey of Company B, and William Henry Sprague, who had recently died within days of each other. Such a formal disposition of a dead soldier's personal effects was apparently rare. More often, one of the deceased's comrades would take care of the matter. Thus, when Corporal Hugh Erwin of Company F died of fever at the corps hospital at Acworth, Georgia, in June 1864, his effects were secured by Homer Ames and recorded by William Harper: "Two wallets, one silk handkerchief, one Gents fingerring, one house wife with some articals in it such as Sissors thread needles &c Also three dollars in green backs and a three cent peace and a six cent." Sergeant Charles H. Brown of the same company died of congestive intermittent fever at the division hospital during the March to the Sea. When the 154th reached Savannah, Private Edson D. Ames (Homer's brother) sent Brown's effects home in a cigar box. Another member of Company F, Lewis Jones, was shot in the wrist and hip at Rocky Face Ridge and hospitalized in Nashville, where gangrene infected his wound and killed him. His comrade Sergeant John M. Irvin, in the same hospital with a wound from Rocky Face, sent Jones's father the sad news and enclosed two receipts to sign for his effects, on the return of which they would be forwarded to him—standard practice in the hospitals. Irvin also sent the elder Jones a memento: "I have taken off a lock of his hair and I will send it to you for I know that friends often desire sutch." On one occasion, a member of the regiment was thwarted in his effort to obtain a comrade's effects. Lieutenant Winfield Cameron, wounded in the thigh at Chancellorsville, was carried to Dowdall's Tavern, where he found the regimental adjutant, Samuel Noyes, shot through the abdomen and shoulder and coughing up blood. Noyes asked Cameron to send his wife his watch and pocketbook and to tell her he wanted to see her. A few minutes after Noyes died in Cameron's arms, a Confederate surgeon took the watch and pocketbook and refused to return them.[38]

Although a variety of men sent letters of notification and condolence, the duty formally fell to the commander of the deceased's company. So it was that Captain Alfred Benson took the first opportunity he had to send a letter to a father in Lyndon, Cattaraugus County, describing a shocking accident during the March to the Sea:

> A painful duty devolves upon me, and while I deplore the sad event I trust that Heaven may give you fortitude to hear the sorrowful news. Your son Jesse D. Campbell is no more. He accidentally shot himself while on the march about two miles north of Springfield in this state [Georgia].
>
> He had gone a little in advance of the Regt. to get some potatos in a field by the road-side and was accompanied by Sergt Allen Williams and [Corporal] Oziah F. Adams of his co. They were sitting by the side of the road waiting for the Regt. when Campbell whose gun was lean-

ing against the fence reached out to draw it toward him when the hammer caught upon the ground or in some weeds, and the load was discharged in his right breast killing him instantly. He was buried there by his comrades. This was on the 7th of Dec.

Thus perished one of the noblest and bravest of soldiers, and a virtuous and ever faithful Christian. The moral purity of his character and his ever kind and genial disposition had endeared him to all his comrades in arms, and we mourn the departed as a brother, and will ever cherish his memory as one of the bravest and truest of the many who have fallen in this bitter contest.

May the Good Angels, in mercy sustain you and all the family of our late comrade, to whom the summons "to come up higher" has come, and been obeyed.[39]

Benson's letter followed the conventions of the formal notification and condolence letter in offering praise of the deceased's character and relating the esteem in which he was held by his comrades. James Gallagher did likewise in his letter to the mother of Wilber Moore:

Mrs. Moore, concerning the character and private conduct of your son I might indeed say much, and everything to his praise and credit. He was always a noble boy with a true manly soul. Kind and generous and affectionate. Strictly moral & upright in all his dealings. He was highly beloved and respected by all. He drew around him warm friends, and good associates. And his memory shall ever remain as a brilliant jewel at the bottom of every heart in his company. You may well feel proud of your son, & know that his memory is cherished here in the army where his noble & brave deeds have become familiar to all who knew him.[40]

Sometimes an officer faltered and could not find the words to notify a loved one of their loss. Such was the case when Private Isaiah S. Washburn of Company C died at the corps hospital in December 1863. Washburn's townsman, Quartermaster Timothy Allen, could not compose a satisfactory letter and turned to William Charles for help. Charles described the circumstances:

The other day one of our Boys died his Wife and 4 children are living in Hinsdale where the Q.M. lives. So it became his duty to write to her the sad intelligence of her husbands death So he did write but some how or an other he could not finish the letter to suit him. So he wanted me to finish it for him so I took his pen and wrote the following words. He that doeth all things well hath deprived you of your husband and your little ones are fatherless but mourn not as our having no hopes for that same Being hath promised to be a protector to the widow and a Father to the fatherless. Besides your husband died for a noble cause Battling for his *country Freedom* and the dearest *rights of man*.[41]

Other writers were considerably less eloquent than Alfred Benson, James Gallagher, and William Charles. When Private David Moore of Company H died on May 20, 1863, of wounds received at Chancellorsville, his nephew Dwight Moore conveyed the news in stark terms. "I regret to inform you that Uncle David is dead," Dwight informed his mother. "He died at the Hospital about 2 miles from here. he was shot through the right lung. He was taken prisoner by the rebs and paroled, but they did not do anything for him, and it was twelve days before he had his wound dressed. Probably he would have lived if he could have had the right care."[42]

The most formal language was used in obituaries and eulogies meant for publication in the press. An occasional enlisted man was awarded such a tribute, but they were given most effusively for officers. After Chancellorsville the *Cattaraugus Freeman* received conflicting reports concerning the fate of Adjutant Samuel Noyes until a telegram from Addison Rice confirmed his death—"He fell at the post of duty, while bravely cheering and urging on his men." A week later the paper published testimonials and resolutions promulgated by the regiment (as did the rival *Cattaraugus Union*) and ran a lengthy tribute to the slain officer. "The loss of Adjutant Noyes," the *Freeman* editorialized, "was a severe blow to the Regiment. Few if any of the officers enjoyed the confidence of the Regiment more than he, and the loss of none would have cast a deeper gloom over the Camp, when they became satisfied that he was dead. Kind, generous and brave, in life, they admired him as a friend, a patriot and a soldier, and in death they mourn him with a soldier's sorrow." In memory of Noyes, the officers of the regiment wore mourning badges on their left sleeves for thirty days.[43]

The publicity accorded the death of Adjutant Noyes was exceeded by that for captain and former adjutant Alanson Crosby, who died at a Nashville hospital in July 1864 after his mortal wounding at Pine Knob. As soon as the news reached Ellicottville the *Cattaraugus Freeman* published an article extolling "a young man of much promise, of fine culture, excellent abilities and pleasing address." When the village's bar met and adopted resolutions "expressive of our esteem for the deceased and sorrow at his death," they were printed in the paper. The arrival of Crosby's remains in Ellicottville and his funeral in Franklinville were reported. More tributes followed. An anonymous writer from Connecticut sent the *Freeman* a lengthy and florid tribute, in which he lamented, "Dead—dead,—Another of our best and bravest gone to heap the hetacomb to the foul demon Slavery!" A letter from Commodore Vedder to Crosby's brother found its way into print. Vedder described a final visit with Crosby. "Com., I cannot live, I am going to die," Vedder reported the young man saying in a low tone, his eyes lifted heavenward. "I believe my country is right, and I deem it glorious to die in her cause." Summarizing the impact of Crosby's death on the regiment, Vedder wrote, "From the heart of Georgia a voice of sadness comes, and wherever a member of the 154th New York is found, there is unmingled woe." Major Lewis Warner, in his regular letter to the *Olean Times,* confirmed the sentiment: "The announcement of [Crosby's] death, coming unexpectedly as it did, has cast a gloom over the regiment with which he has so long been connected, to the members of which he had become endeared by his many excellent qualities, as a soldier, companion and friend. I feel that I can say for his late companions in arms, that they sympathize with his family and friends at home in their bereavement, and would add this testimony as to the worth of the departed, while they drop a tear over his grave."[44]

Formal too were the resolutions of respect for the deceased written by comrades and sent to families and the press at home. The preamble and resolutions adopted by Company E on the passing of Private Eleazer Swetland, who died at the brigade hospital in Lookout Valley in March 1864, were typical:

WHEREAS, He who directs all human affairs, has removed brother Eleazer Swetland from our midst, therefore

Resolved, That in the death of Eleazer Swetland, this company has lost one of its most faithful members, a true-hearted gentleman, a sincere patriot, and one who was beloved by us all.

Resolved, That we extend our warmest sympathy to the friends and relatives of the deceased, and especially to his youthful widow, so suddenly called upon to mourn the loss of an affectionate husband, and that we sincerely hope she may be consoled by our Heavenly Father in this severe affliction.

Resolved, That a copy of these resolutions be furnished to his worthy brother [First Sergeant George Swetland], one of our number, also to the family of the deceased, and that a copy be also forwarded to the Westfield *Republican,* Fredonia *Advertiser,* Fredonia *Censor* and Mayville *Sentinel,* respectively, for publication.[45]

"If you see it published in the papers that [I] am dade," James Quilliam informed his wife, "you need not believe it." Quilliam cited the case of Corporal John Wilson of Company E, who was reported as dead of wounds received at Chancellorsville in the *Fredonia Censor* of May 13, 1863—an error the paper retracted the following week. (Wilson survived his wound, only to be shot a second time in the Atlanta campaign.) False reports of death were unusual, but they did occur. Private William Cone of Company I was reported killed at Chancellorsville, his funeral sermon was preached in his home town of Salamanca, and his wife made application for his bounty money and back pay. "Luckily, however, she was in no hurry to marry again," the *Cattaraugus Freeman* commented in December 1863, "for a few weeks ago her husband came home all right, having only been wounded and a prisoner in Rebel hands." A similar case involved Private Robert M. Grinard of Company C, who was also reported killed at Chancellorsville. His wife and family mourned his loss, a lawyer procured his back pay and bounty and secured a pension, and after two years of grief his family became reconciled to his death. But in August 1865 Grinard returned home. "It is said his wife was about to be married again," the *Cattaraugus Union* reported, "and Mr. Grinard seems to have arrived none too soon. He claims to have been a prisoner for more than two years."[46]

Death knit home and the front in mutual dread and grief. "I will try and be patient in regard to your absence," Mary Chittenden informed William Chittenden, "for when I think how many hearts are almost broken for their loved ones who they can never behold again I try to feel thankful that God has spared your life thus far and at his throne of grace [I] plead for your return." After Ambrose Arnold was killed at Rocky Face Ridge, William Charles requested of his wife, "Be sure to do all in your power to console & comfort the Wife & family of my friend & comrade Ambrose Arnold." Soldiers' loved ones needed no such urging. Ruba Merrill attended church on February 1, 1863, to hear a sermon preached in memory of her husband's and son's comrade, Private William H. Seeker of Company K, who had died of typhoid fever in a Washington hospital the previous November. No doubt Mrs. Merrill offered consolation to the deceased's young widow, Runette Randall Seeker, about seven months pregnant with the couple's only child. And Mrs. Seeker in turn must have offered her sincere sympathy to Ruba when Barzilla and Alva Merrill were killed months later at Chancellorsville.[47]

Sometimes a family augmented the photograph, the bundle of letters, or the little grouping of personal effects of their deceased loved one with a commercially produced commemorative lithograph, to be hung in a place of honor in the parlor. The widow of Corporal Gardner D. Walker of Company F, who was captured at Gettysburg and died as a prisoner of war in Richmond, purchased one from the Army and Navy Record Company of Harrisburg, Pennsylvania, and presented it to their two children. In the monochrome lithograph Walker's war record was surrounded by illustrations of President Lincoln, naval and land battle scenes, soldiers and sailors, and an eagle, flag, and shield. After Corporal Seymour Sikes of Company C died of wounds received at Chancellorsville, his family purchased a hand-tinted lithograph titled "The Soldier's Grave," published by the famous New York City firm of Currier & Ives. It depicted a black-clad woman leaning against an elaborate, patriotic-motif tombstone beneath a weeping willow. Upon the tombstone was printed "In Memory of . . . who died at . . . a brave and gallant soldier and a true patriot," and the Sikes family filled in the blanks to memorialize their departed soldier.[48]

Sometimes soldiers depended on the home folk for news of their comrades. A letter from his wife informed William Charles of the death of his fellow Welshman, Lewis Jones, who had been mortally wounded at Rocky Face Ridge. Charles responded with an outburst of emotion:

Poor Boy, how sorry I am that I could not have been with him little did I think when I last saw him, as I bathed his wounded hand that it would be the *last act* that I would ever be permitted to do for him. God only knows how I *loved that boy,* and he alone knoweth the grief that fills my breast at the thought that I shall never see him again on earth. I will pray & hope to meet him in that world where no Rebels can come to hurt him I would very willingly risk my life to save his and he would do the same for me. will you be so kind as to let me know the particulars of his death if you can, then I will let you know more of his life as a Soldier. He was a good soldier in every sense of the word and it will do my heart good to write [and] talk about him.[49]

The deaths of regimental comrades remained lodged in the memories of veterans decades after the war ended. They recalled a macabre incident that happened one night during the Atlanta campaign. As Alanson Crosby walked the line shaking men awake to build breastworks, one soldier did not respond. Crosby, thinking he was "playing off," gave him a vigorous shaking. "Hit him ag'in, he's Irish!" some of the men shouted. Crosby grasped the man by his shoulder, turned him over, and discovered he was dead. Members of Company F remembered Private Albert Bemis raising himself up from the shelter of the rifle pit at Chancellorsville, saying he wanted to see the sons of bitches come—and promptly taking a shot to the head and pitching over onto his face, dead. Several men recollected the scene of June 28, 1864, near Kennesaw Mountain, Georgia, when Private Devillo D. McBride of Company E started back from the breastworks to cook some bacon for his supper and was hit in the neck by a stray bullet that severed his jugular vein and sent blood spewing for yards. One man was haunted by the image of the fallen McBride's face, turned toward him and fixing him with a lifeless stare.[50]

Loved ones and soldiers alike were moved to compose verse to best express their sorrow over the dead. When news of the death of Barzilla and Alva Merrill reached Dayton, Betsey Phelps Howlett, the mother of Alva's tent mate Horace Howlett, commemorated her fallen friends in a poem:

> They sleep afar from their cherished home,
> No flowery wreathe can we place on their tomb.
> But angels stand centry around their remains,
> They will safely arise with the sanctified slain.

> Oh! could we but kneel on the cold sod there,
> And bathe it with tears and breathe one prayer.
> Twould be a sad pleasure to treasure the scene,
> In future days its memory to glean.[51]

When Private Anson N. Park of Company B died of disease at Lookout Valley in March 1864 and his body was shipped home for burial, his comrade David Jones reflected sadly on the loss in verse, and expressed a mournful esprit de corps:

> Another home is smitten,
> For another grave is made;
> And hearts again are riven,
> Mourning for the dead.
>
> Again a father bends his head,
> A loving sister wipes her eye;
> A brother goes with solemn tread,
> Alas! the dead is nigh!
>
> They had prayed for his welfare,
> Ever hoping for his safe return;
> But he is now beyond their prayers,
> Oh! why for Anson mourn.
>
> Here in camp we miss him to,
> And now an empty place is seen;
> We always miss the brave and true,
> Always such has Anson been.
>
> Oh! many brave boys have fell,
> Of the hundred and fifty fourth;
> And few will be left to tell,
> Of the fallen in the south.[52]

CHAPTER 8

In Camp and Beyond

The soldier's life was not always clouded by the storms of hardship, battle, and death. Months at a time were spent in camp during the winters of 1862–1863 and 1863–1864, and even the hyperkinetic General Sherman allowed his army occasional periods of rest during his campaigns of 1864–1865. The regimental camp itself became an expression of esprit de corps. The activities the soldiers engaged in to amuse themselves in camp deepened their camaraderie. But not every aspect of camp life was all-inclusive. The practice of religion drew some men together, but distanced them from their skeptical comrades. Differing perspectives of morality pushed men apart instead of pulling them together.

Looking beyond the regimental camp, the soldiers of the 154th New York sometimes did not like what they saw. Ethnic prejudice prevented the 154th from developing close relationships with the other regiments of its brigade during the early part of its service. Alienated from those natural allies, the men when possible turned elsewhere for outside companionship. Most often, they turned to soldiers from home who were serving in other regiments throughout the army. But the 154th was not entirely without pride in its brigade, division, and corps, and esprit for those larger organizations increased as time passed and affiliations changed. At the same time, the men found themselves drawn to certain of their generals and repelled by others.

For almost three years the soldiers lived among the people of the South. Away from the battlefield, they met their Confederate enemy in largely friendly fraternization. They also had extensive encounters with the two civilian populations of the South: the whites and the blacks. Attitudes toward the whites varied from unconcern to pity, while encounters with civilians ranged from friendly to deadly. Although the regiment had its abolitionists, many of the men were hostile to African Americans. But as time passed and blacks became a common sight in camp, negative attitudes toward them lessened. Blacks even became recognized as unofficial members of the regiment—but esprit de corps only went so far in bridging the racial divide.

From the beginning of their service, the soldiers took pride in their regimental camps, much as they did in their houses and villages back home. An example was provided by a Philadelphia engraver named Louis N. Rosenthal, who produced a series of gilt-bordered prints in 1862 depicting various regimental camps in the Washington area. Among them was an image of the 154th's Camp Seward—named after Secretary of State William H. Seward, the former New York State governor and U.S. senator—on Arlington Heights, the regiment's first camp in Virginia. In the foreground of the print members of the regiment were depicted standing guard and clustered in small groups, conversing and pointing out new sights. Behind them were their tents, arranged in neat rows along company streets. In the background loomed a barren hill, crowned by a fort. In a week's time, the enterprising Rosenthal somehow managed to obtain a drawing of the camp, convert it into an engraving, publish a run in two formats—as a hand-tinted print and as stationery—and peddle them to members of the regiment. Sending them home to loved ones, some of the men made notes on the prints, identifying Fort Richardson, marking their company street, putting an X on their tent, and the like. Already homesick after only a week at the front, sixteen-year-old Devillo Wheeler sent his father a copy, on the back of which he inscribed, "Old Allegany is the place for me."[1]

While living in tents, the men did what they could to make themselves more comfortable. After moving from Arlington Heights to Fairfax Court House, they dismantled the brickwork of a nearby mansion to construct fireplaces and chimneys for the regimental hospital and headquarters tents. "It was really surprising to see the assiduity and industry of the boys when they went into that house," Surgeon Henry Van Aernam noted. "We were a summer encampment and in two days there was a good brick chimney to the hospital and to nearly all the large tents. In approaching [the camp] we look like a village." But tents were generally deplored as poor shelter by the men, especially early in their service and in bad weather. A view expressed by Edgar Shannon on a warm day in April 1865 at Goldsboro, North Carolina, could only have been made late in the war. "I am now seated in my tented home, in the sunny South . . . with the sides thrown up so as to make it cool and comfortable," he wrote. "We lay on our gay little beds of Pine poles & boughs, enjoying the prospects & our laziness." By 1865, the men had become used to living in tents.[2]

It was in winter camp, when their tents served as roofs for log huts, that the soldiers found the most comfort. The first huts built by the 154th went up in January 1863 at the regiment's camp near Falmouth. Soon after their completion, George Newcomb wrote, "We have got good comfortable quarters and enjoy ourselves verry well We have got a bully good fire place in our tent We have plenty of room to sit arround the fire and read tell stories and write to our friends at home." With tongue in cheek, Amos Humiston wrote, "We have made us a sort of log hut that rivles all modern architecture we have laid it up four logs high and coverd it with our tent cloth for a roof we sleep in one end [and] have a fire place in the other and a kitchen in the seenter. . . . It is better than it was when we lived out doore." Wishing she could see the new camp, Barzilla Merrill told wife Ruba that "yankey wit" could fix things up despite little to work with.[3]

But good things certainly did not last for the soldiers, and on returning to the Falmouth vicinity after the Mud March, they had to construct a new camp. Henry Van Aernam described his new quarters as "an aristocratic log shanty covered with the 'fly' from Hospital Tent. It has all the modern improvements available in camp." In describing his hut, James Emmons presented a picture of domestic contentment and proprietary pride:

> We have a log hous four feet high from the ground to the eaves and 7 by 10 feet with canvas for the roof and the gabel ends nailed up with bords and a tiptop fireplace with a shelf over it for our pipes and tobacco and pack of uckers they all say we have the best hous on the ground of eny in our company it is very cold out dores but we do not mind it when we are in our hous we have plenty of visitors today there is one of them [who] fetched in some butter and we are eating hard tacks and butter so you see that we are just living high.[4]

But the day after Emmons described his snug little home, he had to abandon it when the regiment received orders to move to the vicinity of Stafford Court House. There, on a dry, sandy ridge covered with tall, straight pines, the men built a camp that surpassed their previous efforts. The 154th arrived at the site on the evening of February 6, and Alfred Benson noted, "Long before dawn on the following morning hundreds of these [pines] came crashing to the earth; and by noon of that day many a comfortable log hut was ready for its tenants. The sturdy woodsmen of the 154th had not forgotten how to wield the axe, however expert they might have become with the musket. The wilderness disappeared like magic, and soon wore the aspect of a frontier village." George Newcomb described the "log city" as "a queer looking town." Boasting of the 154th's prowess in constructing the camp, Barzilla Merrill wrote, "The Cat[taraugus] Regiment is the greatest regiment to nock things together that you ever saw."[5]

When a winter camp of oak slab huts went up in Lookout Valley, Tennessee, in December 1863, James Quilliam declared, "We have better shanties here then we ever had be fore." The regiment's quarters, Newton Chaffee bragged, were "as good as can be made in the Army." "We have put up *Splendid* winter *quarters*," William Charles wrote. "Goodness it would do you all sorts of good to behold *our city*. Our houses are far and more comfortable [than] the houses of the people that have lived here all the days of their lives!! It may be difficult for you to believe that but it is true never the less." Charles was so proud of his shanty that he included a drawing of it in a letter. But the men knew their handiwork was doomed to be temporary. "You think we would hate to leave our quarters after we have them fixed comfortable," Corporal Marshall A. Perkins of Company B wrote from Lookout Valley. "Well it is rather perplexing but we are something like Bees. when a part of their work is torn down they will build again. so it is with us. we have fixed comfortable quarters four times but then this is all *Military* as the boys say."[6]

Once the soldiers had erected a comfortable winter camp, they took pride in decorating it and keeping it clean. Rows of cedar, holly, and other evergreens were embedded along both sides of company streets, and at the head of each street two tall cedars were bent and tied to form an arch, from which was hung the company letter fashioned from entwined boughs. Charles Abell thought the evergreen decorations at the Stafford camp "would grace a rich mans front yard." He judged the Lookout Valley camp's trimmings as even "a great deal nicer" than the previous year's, and boasted, "Co. E they say has the nicest street in the Brigade." Company streets, James Emmons observed, were kept "as clean as eny floor we are not allowed to chop our wood in front of our shantes." "Every thing is slick around us," Lyman Wilber wrote from Lookout Valley. "Wee keep our streats swep so it looks veary nice." The men perhaps displayed some bias when they judged their neatly swept and ornamented camps to be superior to those of other regiments. Emmons bragged that the 154th's Stafford camp "is the nicest camp that I ever saw and attacks a great deal of attention by the passers by." Milon Griswold wrote of the Lookout Valley camp, "We have got the nicest camp in the brigade."[7]

The naming of a regimental camp was powerfully symbolic of esprit de corps. The living and the dead, members of the regiment and outsiders, all were honored as camp namesakes. The 154th's camp near Fairfax Court House in November 1862 was named after their new colonel, Patrick Henry Jones. Camp John Manley near Stafford Court House was named in gratitude for the support of the civilian Soldier's Friend. That camp had to be abandoned when the regiment returned to it after Chancellorsville; its outskirts were littered with dead horses and mules and the offal of slaughtered cattle. To escape the unhealthful atmosphere and sickening stench, Lieutenant Colonel Loomis and Surgeon Van Aernam located a new campsite in the nearby woods. The new camp was named on May 30, 1863, in memory of the slain adjutant, Samuel Noyes, "to commemorate his gallant conduct in the battle of Chancellorsville." The following day Chaplain Henry Lowing preached a sermon at Camp Noyes in memory of all the members of the regiment killed at Chancellorsville. A regimental order in December 1863 named the 154th's Lookout Valley camp in honor of Lieutenant Isaac Jenkins, who had been captured at Gettysburg and died at Libby Prison, tied to the floor in a fevered delirium. During the siege of Atlanta, the 154th commemorated a martyr from outside its ranks by naming its camp in memory of a captain of the 73rd Pennsylvania who had been mortally wounded at Pine Knob.[8]

Gazing at his neatly constructed, gaily trimmed and tidy camp, a source of pride that acquired symbolic luster in being named after a hero of his unit, a soldier of the 154th was witnessing tangible evidence of regimental esprit de corps.

To while away the long hours in camp, the soldiers turned to a variety of pastimes. As they shared amusements, their camaraderie strengthened. Music was a favorite. Newell Burch noted that Company E formed a good chorus at Camp Brown in Jamestown, with First Lieutenant Isaac Jenkins as tenor, Second Lieutenant Orlando W. Avery as bass, and "the boys in general for suprano." "The boys are singing about camp this evening and it sounds like [a] camp meeting," Barzilla Merrill wrote at Camp John Manley. "They seem to enjoy themselves well." There were some good fiddlers in the regiment, and many of the men enjoyed dancing to their music. Colonel Jones noticed that the dancers never seemed to get footsore and said he should detail the fiddlers to play for the boys on the march to keep their feet in good shape.[9]

Baseball was the men's preferred sport. After a game in the spring of 1863, Barzilla Merrill was pleased to note that he "could play a bout as well as ever." At Lookout Valley in April 1864 Homer Ames noted, "We are having quite an excitement here at Ball play." When the 154th lost a game to the 33rd Massachusetts by a 1–0 score, Colonel Jones bet $200 that his regiment would win a rematch, but marching orders apparently canceled the second contest. Other recreations the men enjoyed included playing cards and checkers, pitching quoits, fishing, wrestling, whittling, swimming, and snowball fights.[10]

The soldiers sought humor wherever they could find it, and they seemed to have a particular predilection for practical jokes. They laughed at the antics of cutups like Andrew "Pod" Curtis, who kept the barracks at Jamestown in an uproar by bleating like a lamb after taps, and who rejoined Company B after the Chancellorsville fight minus his musket and equipments and swore to his captain that a cannonball had smashed the gun in his hands and passed around his body, cutting the straps of his accoutrements. They enjoyed teasing soldiers like Private Edmund F. Tracey of Company G, a large, stout, simple-minded fellow, by telling him that he had to stand in front of a smaller soldier in the ranks because he could stop two bullets to the slighter man's one. Tracey had a habit of entering a comrade's tent and helping himself to the fullest pipe of tobacco he could find, until he lit a specially prepared pipe on one such occasion and was shocked by an explosion that singed off his eyebrows.[11]

Horseplay seems to have been indiscriminate and not particularly malicious. Men put flat stones over the chimneys of winter huts to smoke out the inhabitants, assaulted comrades with squirt guns, cut the seat out of the pants of diarrhea sufferers, and attached Chaplain Lowing's shirt to the top of a flagpole. Sleepers were often the butts of practical jokes. One man, drunk and sound asleep, was shorn of his carefully cultivated and curled mustache by razor-wielding comrades. At Camp John Manley, conspirators placed logs on either side of the sleeping Truman Blowers, covered him with brush, and startled him awake by yelling, "Officer of the day!" At Lookout Valley, friends of Corporal Marvin D. Root of Company G somehow managed to fasten him tightly to the ground while he slept.[12]

Esprit de corps allowed for good-natured joshing, but some pranks had a distinct edge to them. Delegates of the United States Christian Commission, a soldiers' relief agency with a primarily religious mission, once distributed pocket testaments to the regiment. Scoffers in Company G did not want to keep or carry the little books, so they surreptitiously packed them in Marvin Root's knapsack. Root worked up a sweat under his extra load on the subsequent march, and was dubbed by his comrades "the Colporteur." When the Christian Commission distributed housewives and stationery imprinted with its letterhead, the same skeptics scorned the sewing kits as "pauper bags," and only used the writing paper after cutting the "pauper mark" from it. More maliciously, irreligious members of the regiment squirted mule urine on the attendees at prayer meetings in Chaplain Henry Lowing's large wall tent, and broke up one such gathering by dropping cartridges down the chimney into the fire. The resulting explosions scattered the worshipers and burned holes in Lowing's tent.[13]

Suffering abusive behavior at the hands of comrades was a cross for Christian soldiers to bear. Surrounded by "contaminating influences," Emory Sweetland stated, "I am trying to be a Christian here in camp. I find it rather hard sometimes." Oscar Wilber informed his uncle, "I wish I was a good Christian I try to live like one but you know that there is every thing to lead a man a stray." Ignoring the taunts and tricks of their nonbelieving comrades, seeking to avoid the usual lurking temptations, the devout clung to and were sustained by their faith.[14]

"Those soldiers that love to read their Bibles are the men that can be depended upon every where," William Charles declared. "They are true on the Battlefield and always faithful on guard." But how many members of the regiment were men of faith? Nine of the nineteen soldiers of the 154th New York for whom more than twenty letters survive were obviously pious; that random sample would indicate that slightly less than half of the regiment was religious. The devout had their own war to win—to keep their faith and be able to express it in a sometimes antagonistic atmosphere. Religion consequently brought devout men together, but set them apart from their skeptical comrades—and thus was an impediment to esprit de corps.[15]

The religious members of the regiment were overwhelmingly Protestant. There were approximately eighty-five churches in Cattaraugus County in 1862; six were Roman Catholic parishes, the rest were Protestant congregations. The Methodist Episcopal church held greatest sway, followed by the Baptists, with smaller numbers of Presbyterian, Congregational, Universalist, Lutheran, and variant churches. The religious men of the 154th New York presumably were divided by similar denominational ratios.[16]

Religion offered great consolation to the God-fearing. After a prayer meeting in his lieutenant's tent early in the regiment's service, Charles Abell declared, "It was good for me to wait upon God for I felt that he was with me to bless me and protect me." Following a prayer meeting at Falmouth in January 1863, William Charles wrote, "O what a comfort it is to have the same sin forgiving God to go to as we did at home Dear Friends We know that you pray for us, and we try to pray for you— O what a blessing it is to have a God that can hear our prayers no matter how distant we are from one an other." Writing a short time later, Emory Sweetland declared to his wife, "I endeavor to put my trust in the god of battles for I know if it is his will I might be in a hundred battles & receive no harm if it is his will that I should lay my life down in the defense of my country his grace can be sufficient for both you & me. but I trust that through his goodness we both shall be spared to meet again on earth." In their comments, Abell, Charles, and Sweetland touched on three matters of importance to the regiment's religious men: how faith enabled them to endure; their reliance on the prayers of their families; and the opportunity for them to band together in worship.[17]

"This world is so full of iniquity, and especially here," Francis Strickland wrote from camp after the Chancellorsville battle, "that I sometimes become almost discouraged and feel like giving up and was it not for the confidence I have that God will eventually bring it out right, I should completely despair." Faith helped buoy spirits under assault by the upheaval of the war and the sinfulness of the men's surroundings. "I rejoice that I have the Love of Christ in my heart," Philo Markham informed his sister from Lookout Valley in January 1864. "It is worth every thing here in my present circumstances." Faith helped men simply to survive. "It is the kind protecting hand of a merciful Providence who has . . . directed my steps and given me health & strength to endure the life of a soldier as long as I have," Charles Abell wrote at Camp John Manley. He continued, "To him I would ascribe the praise & ask him still to guide & Protect me." Emory Sweetland wrote in June 1863 that God had "preserved me through all the dangers that I have been called to pass through. I have truly found religion to be good for me here." Almost a year to the day later, on a Sunday during the Atlanta campaign, Sweetland wished he could attend a service. "I truly feel the need of having my spiritual strength renewed," he wrote, "that I might be better fitted for the trials that I have to encounter here in the army."[18]

Facing spiritual decay and mortal danger, the men pleaded for the prayers of their families. "You say in your letter that you pray for me," Charles Abell wrote to his "Dear Dear Mother" during the regiment's first month in Virginia. "God Bless You my dear Mother. . . . I believe your prayers are answered for I feel that I am under the protection of (our heavenly father) and that he will bring me back again to my home." That same month Ira Wood instructed his wife, "Now Hester Ann Wood Dont forget me at the sane of grace you can pray in faith that I may come home and see you again the lord Will hear you if you ask him rite He will bring me home to Clasp you again in mi armes." As if to forestall any objections, he added, "I Dont Want you should think Hard of me for asking you to pray for me if anny body Wantes the prares of Christians people it is the Soldiers [to] keep him from Dangers." Two weeks later Wood reiterated his plea to Hester Ann, tears falling from his eyes as he wrote: "It is your prares that Sustains me in Virginna altho many Hundreds [of miles] a part. . . . I no when you pray I feel the Influence of it on my poor Hart When I think of the time When you go to retire I think you are on your nees [praying] for me. . . . Now you must keep up good Courag your prares Will bring me home to you again I no it Will the lord is [merciful] & he keeps me from all harm and if I put my trust in him I shall Bee all Wright." The devout Woods were reunited in 1864 when Ira was discharged.[19]

William Charles believed that his wife's prayers had helped to shield him from harm at Chancellorsville. "My Dear Wife how wonderfully good our Heavenly father has been to us," he wrote after the battle. "Your prayers *have been answered* For to night you are not a widdow and our little ones *are not fatherless.*" During the fighting shot and shell had burst in every direction, men had fallen by his side and all around him, but he was unharmed. "Why I should be spaired when so many fell is a mystery to me," Charles admitted, but he made certain to request, "You will continue to pray for me, and have faith that some day, we shall meet again."[20]

Devout soldiers cherished the opportunity to worship together. During the regiment's first year, services were held on a semi-regular basis by Chaplain Henry Lowing, former pastor of a Congregational church in Napoli, Cattaraugus County. The soldiers found services in the field quite a change from attending church at home. "I must tell about the meeting House," Barzilla Merrill wrote after Lowing's first service at the front, at Fairfax on Sunday, October 19, 1862. "We formed a square in two ranks or in other words two men thick with one side left out on a spot of clean grass on a side hill and [Lowing] stood in the open space and preached to us that is the way that we do business all in the open air." Stephen Green compared a Sunday service conducted by Lowing in Virginia, with officers and men sitting on the ground coatless and in some cases barefoot, to a church meeting at home, with "Ladies looking around to see who had got a new Bonnet or any Clothing (*new* style)," and concluded that the soldiers were more attentive and better able to concentrate without such distractions.[21]

"We have a sermon once in a while by Bro Lowing & also once & in a while a prayer meeting," Emory Sweetland noted at Falmouth in January 1863, but he added, "It seems to me as though every thing was against us it either storms blows or is to cold, or we have to march every time we are to have a meeting." At Camp John Manley, where Sweetland shared the chaplain's wall tent, the good work went well. Lowing held nightly prayer meetings in addition to Sunday services. Several members of the 154th were converted. A regimental Christian association was formed, and its membership elected officers. But some of the men, including religious men, were put off by Lowing. "Our Chaplain is not very well liked by the boys—in fact, he is not the man for the place he occupies," William Charles wrote after a sparsely attended service. "I dont fancy him verry much and I dont think that he is doing much for the reg," Barzilla Merrill wrote about Lowing. "I guess that he is a good man but he is to distant for that place that is he ant familare enough." Nevertheless, when Lowing resigned in December 1863 citing ill health, the commissioned officers passed and published resolutions extolling his service to the regiment and praising him for having "ever labored to elevate the moral tone and character of this command" and being "uniformly zealous, consistent and patriotic."[22]

Never again did organized religion attain its former prominence in the regiment. Cut adrift by Lowing's departure, the regiment's faithful conducted their own prayer meetings and attended services held by the Christian Commission at Lookout Valley, where that organization established an Eleventh Corps station consisting of a chapel, delegates' quarters, and a library outfitted with a writing table and a supply of weekly newspapers. There, members of the 154th attended prayer meetings and Sunday school, often in the company of their corps commander, the pious General Oliver Otis Howard, who James Quilliam described as "one of the best Sunday school teachers I ever had." After attending a prayer meeting at the station, Charles Abell noted, "Though there were but few present yet there were enough to claim the Blessing. To day some of our boys have gone over to hear them Preach."[23]

Not until October 1864 did the regiment receive a new chaplain to replace Henry Lowing. The Reverend William W. Norton, minister of the Congregational church in Otto, Cattaraugus County, joined the 154th at Atlanta and remained on duty until the muster-out. "I think he will be well liked and prove to be a valuable addition to our Regimental Staff," wrote Major Lewis Warner. Norton assumed his duties with enthusiasm. "If I should be spared as I hope," he wrote on joining the regiment, "I shall ever after have to rejoice in the part I shall have been permitted to take in [putting down] this rebellion." But Norton held just a handful of Sunday services for the regiment during his tenure, preferring to concentrate his efforts among hospitalized soldiers; writing letters for them, distributing stationery and tracts to them, and conducting their funeral services.[24]

Throughout the regiment's existence, religious soldiers bemoaned the infrequency of organized services. "O you cannot tell how lonesome it is and how sad it makes one feel with out having any meeting at all," William Charles wrote to his wife on Thanksgiving Day 1862. "I was sorry to hear that you had got so wicked as to play cards on the sabath," James Emmons chided his sister in February 1863, "but we soldiers pass a good many by so [doing.] there is no Sunday in the army." "It is a long time now since I have heard a sermon or a prayer," William Charles wrote after the resignation of

Chaplain Lowing and before the advent of Christian Commission services at Lookout Valley. "It seems that I would give most any thing if I could only go to a prayer meeting where men pray in ernest and with faith." "Since I left Lookout Valley I have not heard but one sermon preached," Charles Abell wrote during the Atlanta campaign, "and how long it will be before I hear another I do not know." Ten days later Emory Sweetland noted sadly, "We have no meetings of any kind now & there is nothing to promote any groth in Christianity." For soldiers of faith, apathy was yet another enemy to overcome.[25]

If the practice of religion was not a unifying force in the regiment, neither was individual behavior. "We are good companions and we could get [along] anywhere," George Taylor observed, "but at the same time there is much going on in camp that is not intended to improve the morals nor the manners or the mind." To Taylor and other men, the army was a morally corrosive environment. "I mean to avoid as much as possible all that which I would avoid at home," Taylor vowed, "and cultivate a familiarity with what little good there is to be found in camp." "There are some whose manners and morals are daily on the decline," Edgar Shannon lamented at Camp Jones. He continued, "This place seems adapted to make a man coarse & rough." William Charles agreed: "Many a man does that here that he would be utterly ashamed to do at home and excuses himself by saying that others do it or that it is customary in the Army to do it. But that is no excuse for them. It is worse than no excuse at all." The army was "a good place to study human nature," Barzilla Merrill thought. "I see some men that are men in mind and body and a great many that are only men in body," Merrill wrote, "and a well develop mind looks better to me than it ever did before." Emory Sweetland declared, "This war is corrupting the morals of a majority of the Soldiers." A few weeks later he observed, "The society is not at all congenial to me We are away from the refining influence of women, home & Christian society & many of the boys throw of all restraint & plunge into almost all kinds of wickedness." Sweetland added, however, "Some of the boys I can not see as being in the army has any effect on moraly."[26]

Certain soldiers refused to acknowledge widespread moral turpitude. "You carssioned me to guard against evil habits," James Emmons wrote to his sister, "but i donot see any to be led into that is followed at eny rate in our company the soldiers is not as reakliss the majority of them as the people think they are In our company you could not hear as much cursing as you would in the same number of them if they were at home." Playing euchre for fun was the worst habit in the ranks, Emmons declared, "and i do not call that [a] very bad one, it helps pass away many lonsom hours." Edgar Shannon went so far as to proclaim the soldier morally superior to the civilian. "A soldier is generally what they would call at home rough," Shannon wrote. "He does not plaster over his actions as smooth as some of those at home, but at heart he is apt to be the better of the two; what he says you may depend on; folks at home are terribly concerned about their boys in the army. They would do well to look a little more to the morals of those at home."[27]

Shortly before the war ended, Francis Bowen wrote in his diary, "The evils of intemperence should be oftener pointed out to the soldiers. Intemperance is ruining and killing more men than the bullets. What a loathsome, *miserable* & wicked habit." During the first two months of the regiment's service, liquor was scarce—at least among the enlisted men. Ira Wood was surprised to see a company comrade drunk one morning in November 1862. "How he got it I dont know," Wood wrote, "But the poor Soldiers cant get a drop the oficers keep it to run to when they want it." But a month later Emory Sweetland noted, "Lately our regiment has commenced to draw whiskey rations, each soldier having a gill delt out to him once pr day this will create a taste for liquor in the men & I fear lead many to a Soldiers drunkards grave." By January 1863, the men drew whiskey rations once a week. Sweetland recorded "some half a dozen that do not touch it in our Co." More than seventy men were present for duty in Company B at the time, so the teetotalers were a distinct minority. Some men avoided drinking because of the inferior quality of "commissary," as the regularly rationed whiskey was sometimes called. "We draw Whiskey quite often," John Porter wrote in April 1863, "but luckily for me it is so bad that I cant drink it so I sell it or give it away There is no danger of my learning to drink in the Army if they keep such poor whiskey to deal out as they have done."[28]

For the most part, however, the men were quite willing to imbibe as much alcohol as they could get their hands on—no matter how they got their hands on it. When members of Company B were assigned to guard commissary stores, including some barrels of whiskey, in an old stone mill at Thoroughfare Gap, they drove nails into the tops of the barrels, tipped them, and filled their canteens and several large kettles with whiskey. At Fairfax Court House, the sutler of a Wisconsin regiment refused to sell any of his large stock of lager beer to members of the 154th. Under cover of night, three 154th men crept up a hillside to the Wisconsin camp, cut a hole in the sutler's tent, and rolled several kegs down the slope to their camp. Drinking did not diminish as the war dragged on. "It is a general time of getting drunk in the Regt.," Martin Bushnell observed at Lookout Valley in March 1864. From Savannah in January 1865, Emory Sweetland wrote, "There are but verry few in our regt. that do not get tight about as often as they can get liquor, & I scarcely know anyone that does not smoke or chew tobacco & generally both. It is sad to think of so many fine brave young men being ruined for life. I think if fathers & mothers knew the temptations & dangers that their sons were exposed to that they would earnestly pray for the return of peace."[29]

Gambling was another of the temptations and dangers of soldier life. "When the rest of the boys are of in some tent playing cards I improve the time in reading my testament and in prair to god for my family," Levi Bryant assured his wife. Thaddeus Reynolds insisted to his family, "I do not play cards and have not since I came into the service." But Bryant and Reynolds appear to have been in the minority. "Ball-playing and card-playing as much today as any other," Stephen Welch recorded on an idle day in camp. After the regiment received its first pay, in January 1863, Corporal Alexander Bird of Company G noted in his diary, "The boys play poker tonight and the green backs change owners pretty fast some few get rich many get poor." Bird considered the gambling "poor practice when well followed." Efforts to prevent gambling were futile. At the Falmouth camp, Captain Matthew Cheney banned card playing for money in Company G, ordering the men to use beans instead of cash. But they ignored the captain and continued to play for money, hiding it in their blankets when he made an appearance. And gambling was not restricted to card games. "All quiet in the military line but a great day for sporting running horses," Joshua Pettit noted in April 1865 at Goldsboro, North Carolina. "One bet of two hundred on a ride and several other races."[30]

Widespread use of profane language disturbed proper men. "One thing sure," Barzilla Merrill promised Ruba, "I have no disposition to join in the wickedness that is going on around me. . . . There is card playing swaring and in fact all kinds of obscene talk going on every day." Ira Wood informed his wife, "The Curses and Swearing it is a nuff to make the Blood run cold in my vains." Emory Sweetland lamented, "Many are led into a system of petty thieving, Lying, telling obscene Stories & singing obscene songs." Theft appears to have been quite common. "Men who at home were considered honest men," Sweetland noted, "many of them soon have a taking way with them, soon are bragging how slick they stole such an article from the sutler, commissary or some half Union farmer near camp." Alva Merrill declared to his mother, Ruba, "I tell you it is astonishing to see folks steal here folks that would not do it at home no more than nothing in the world." He cited an example. "Pa got about 2 lbs of sugar . . . and in the middle of the night one of his tent mates stole part of it I will not call any names but it was one from our own town." But a month later, Alva expressed some ambiguity on the subject. "Mother you cant begin to think what a hard place for morals it is here," he informed Ruba. "When I first got here I was perfectly astonished at it but I tell you when you have lived without bread for 2 or three days you would get something if you could I hope I shall not get to be a very big thief."[31]

At first, foraging and looting from southerners were deplored as immoral by a segment of the men. "It is . . . an expensive and destructive business in which our country is engaged," William Chittenden declared after reaching the front. "Thousands of well to do citizens will be made penniless [and] promising young men will have their morals ruined for it is a school where vicious seeds are sown with a lavish hand." When the regiment first foraged on a wide scale, during the movement to Thoroughfare Gap, some of the men were regretful. "I am very sorry to be oblige to say that some of our boys act very shameful. . . . Some of the boys steal and Dystroy every thing they come to, which I think is very wicked and enough to make Rebels of any one," William Charles wrote. During the same campaign, William Chittenden wrote, "I feel disgusted as we march along to see the reckless disposition for plunder showed forth by our officers and men and the officers are the most to blame. . . . To day as soon as we stopped some of the men wer on the hunt and soon came in with turkeys hens sheep and pigs also aples and other eatables [meant] for the sustenance of old men women & helpless children it seems wicked to see I have not taken any thing yet nor do I wish to."[32]

As time passed, however, the soldiers distinguished between foraging food and looting personal items, and their attitudes toward the former loosened. Major Lewis Warner noted after a Georgia foraging expedition, "So clean is the work done that I much doubt whether a forlorn hope of catterpillars can winter where our Army has foraged. Without doubt much suffering will [result] among the poor people who inhabit this section, but who has not suffered from this terrible war?" Foraging became a necessity during Sherman's incommunicado campaigns, and the men became expert at it. Looting, on the other hand, was still perceived as criminal by upright men. Levi Bryant wrote during the Carolinas campaign, "I never had face enough on me to go into a house & step up to a young girl & demand her rings or [threaten to] Blow out her Brains. & I thank God for the hart I have it is not so hard as some I find. When I can Stoop to Rob the wimin of their Little keepsakes I must have my hart hardend & case hardend first."[33]

Unfortunately, not all of the members of the regiment were as conscientious as Bryant. William Chittenden cited a case that occurred during the Thoroughfare Gap campaign which he judged "a disgrace even to the savage." Several members of the 154th were plundering a home when one of them robbed a young woman of her finger rings and earrings and a photograph, "and then offered her Father $ .50 for liberties with her person." Chittenden admonished his wife, "Do not mention it it [is] no credit to the Regt that man is as deserving of death as the meanest rebel." In response, Mary Chittenden wrote, "I think you have some very mean men in your Regiment to serve a young lady in that way It seems as though I could almost shoot such a man he is certainly deserving of death."[34]

Almost entirely, the soldiers eschewed making explicit sexual references in their letters. On rare occasions the veil was lifted, as when Joel Bouton used double entendres to describe an army "drill" to a friend: "We have a peculiar drill to go through when we meet a female down here. It is this. Present arms—close (clothes) up,—lie down,—draw rammer,—ram cartridge. There is one time and two motions to each command but the last when the recruit makes as many motions as he has a mind to. Yo can guess how each command is exicuted. Such is military." Emory Sweetland deplored the licentiousness prevalent in the army in a letter to his wife from

Savannah in January 1865: "You would be verry much shocked if you knew how much demoralized (in regard to morals) that 9 tenths of the soldiers have become. The lower class (both black & white in the south) seem to be totally ignorant of the meaning of the word 'Virtue' & both officers and men appear to have cast off all the restraints of home & indulge their passions to the fullest extent. Many of the officers keep Quadroons for private use. I will tell you all about it when I get home so I will say no more about it now."[35]

Differing moral standards were a matter of contention among the men, and consequently an impediment to esprit de corps. Governed by his own conscience—or lack thereof—each individual soldier sought like-minded companions to associate with. But in the end, he had to stand in line with men whose behavior he either deplored or scorned. In the intimate surroundings of the regiment, a live-and-let-live attitude probably served a man best, no matter what his moral persuasions.

Beyond their regimental camp, Civil War soldiers entered a obligatory association with the other regiments of their brigade, division, and corps. Those connections generally resulted in friendships, rivalries, or indifference. But an unusual situation early in the 154th New York's service led to another result: prejudice. The regiment was an ethnic outsider in its brigade, which resulted in friction with the other regiments. The same was true at the division and corps level. Their own intolerance pulled the men of the 154th together, and consequently contributed to their regimental esprit de corps. But the arrangement was detrimental to the 154th's brigade, division, and corps esprit.

It happened by chance, when the regiment was randomly assigned to the 1st Brigade, 2nd Division, Eleventh Corps on its arrival at the front. The brigade was commanded by Colonel Adolphus Buschbeck, the division by Brigadier General Adolph von Steinwehr, and the corps by Major General Franz Sigel. As the names of those officers indicate, a large portion of the Eleventh Corps—fifteen of its twenty-eight infantry regiments—was composed primarily of German Americans. In this the Eleventh was distinctive; no other corps of the Army of the Potomac had such a high representation of a single minority ethnic group. The other regiments in Buschbeck's brigade were the German American 29th New York and 27th Pennsylvania, and the 73rd Pennsylvania, in which many English, Irish, and native-born American soldiers augmented a largely German core. The men of the 154th New York found themselves in a decidedly Teutonic atmosphere.

On joining the Eleventh Corps, some members of the regiment initially voiced satisfaction with Sigel and their place in his command. "We have as yet no reason to complain of the disposition that has been made of us," Lewis Warner wrote from Fairfax; "indeed we are all highly gratified and thank our lucky stars that, to use the Dutchman's phrase, we are to fight 'mit Sigel.'" But soon complaints were heard about their forced association with the Germans, commonly called *Dutchmen* by the native-born Americans in a corruption of the word *deutsch*. When Newell Burch was detailed to serve as an orderly to General Steinwehr, he complained, "Have my share of business, but dont like so much dutch." Writing a letter to the *Cattaraugus Freeman*, Alanson Crosby heard a member of the regiment sing an impromptu song: "O, I'd better staid at home with the gal I love so much, than be traveling round the Country with these dam Dutch."[36]

The German element was dismayed when Sigel was replaced as Eleventh Corps commander by Major General Oliver Otis Howard in April 1863, and members of the 154th New York tended to agree with Edgar Shannon's assessment of the change: "I believe I'd rather have Sigel." A month to the day after Howard took command of the corps, it was shattered by Stonewall Jackson's attack at Chancellorsville—owing in no small part to Howard's negligence. In the aftermath of the battle the Eleventh Corps was made the scapegoat for the Union defeat, and faultfinding broke out within the corps itself. Some members of the 154th castigated the Germans for running away during the battle. "Just now it is a reproach for a man to belong to the 11th Army Corps and the Dutch part of it did behave like slinks in the fight on the 2nd inst.," Henry Van Aernam wrote. Private Allen L. Robbins stated in a letter to the *Gowanda Reporter*, "We as a corps are demoralized, and a disgrace to the army of the Potomac, or at least we are said to be. I, for one, don't relish the name, but I am forced to bear it being one of that body." Robbins asserted that the 154th and some Irish companies of the 73rd Pennsylvania "held the ground till every dutch 'sour krout' had retreated to the woods or fallen in the attempt. For my part, I have no confidence in the fighting qualities of the Dutch." Other members of the regiment faulted General Howard for the disaster. "The criminal negligence of Gen. Howard was the cause of our defeat," Dwight Moore stated flatly. Stephen Welch declared, "I shall never believe that there was anyone to blame at the Battle of Chancellorsville for the stampede, except the General of the Corps." Even Allen Robbins, who criticized the Germans for running, agreed that Howard was culpable: "I am quite sure there was a great lack of generalship in the battle of Chancellorsville on the 2nd inst., and circumstances point strongly to Gen. Howard as one of the delinquents on that (to us) unfortunate day." Robbins added, "Curse such stupidity!"[37]

Not until the Eleventh Corps was merged in April 1864 with the Twelfth to form the Twentieth Corps and its brigade was largely rid of German regiments and officers was the 154th free of interorganizational ethnic tensions. In the meantime, the men sought companionship not among the regiments of its own brigade, but in the camps of regiments containing fellow Cattaraugus and Chautauqua County men. When the 154th camped near Falmouth in December 1862, the men discovered to their pleasure that the 37th, 44th, and 64th New York infantry regiments, all of them containing friends from home in Cattaraugus County, were quartered nearby. A flurry of visits between the several regiments ensued. "The boys from the 64th are over here every day or two," Emory Sweetland noted. A member of the 64th New York wrote, "I was over to the 154th Regt yesterday I saw . . . lots of the Randolph and Coldspring boys that I was acquainted with." The 64th's surgeon recorded, "I met Dr Rugg of the 154th today and a considerable number of others at their Regt which now lies within ½ mile afar." "I was over to the 64th the other day and what a 'visit' I did have," Edgar Shannon stated. He continued, "Oh, I just enjoyed it [and it] done as much good as to have went home." Newton Chaffee wrote about visits with the 64th for the *Gowanda Reporter,* describing how it was "a sad sight to see so few left of that once proud Regiment," and extolling their bravery. "They have our thanks for the call they made us," Chaffee wrote, "and we hope the time will soon come when we shall meet again at home, with peace reigning over our now distracted country."[38]

Such visits for the most part ceased when the 154th moved away from Falmouth to its Stafford camp. "The sixty forth lays 10 miles from us and it is quite of a hard mater to get there when we pleas," Private Alansing Wyant of Company B wrote after the move. "I presume I shant go there again to see them." In the future, encounters with soldiers from home were few. The men met acquaintances when they crossed paths with the 6th and 9th New

York Cavalry regiments during the Gettysburg campaign, and they greeted their old friends from Jamestown's Camp Brown in March 1865 when they rendezvoused with the 112th New York at Goldsboro, North Carolina. And every now and then a serendipitous meeting occurred. In one instance a member of a Wisconsin regiment, a former resident of Cattaraugus County, was visiting the 154th's camp at Chattanooga to see old friends when the battle commenced. He went into the fight with the 154th and did good service, and Colonel Patrick Jones provided him with an alibi when he was arrested as a deserter from his regiment.[39]

"Generals are as plenty here as wood churchs at home," Emory Sweetland observed at Camp John Manley in April 1863. For the most part, the men were initially unimpressed with the army's highest-ranking officers, judging them to be avaricious and self-serving. "All our Generals care about is to get good salarys and then carouse and drink and live on fat things," George Newcomb declared. "Our head officers in our Brigade are drunk most of the time." Generals, according to Barzilla Merrill, "dont seem to think of the govornment or the good of the souldiers they think of the large pay and they seem to be jealous of each other they all seem to want to be the largest toad in the puddle consequnly when one makes a move another will try and take off his head." The soldiers made surprisingly few comments about the generals who commanded the armies. They referred more often, however, to the commanders of their brigade, division, and corps, and their esprit de corps for those larger organizations was reflected in their comments about those generals, the symbolic embodiments of their commands.[40]

Owing largely to its anomalous situation as a primarily native-born American regiment in a German American brigade, in a corps that was generally perceived by the rest of the army as composed of foreigners, the 154th New York expressed little esprit de corps for those organizations—especially after the Eleventh Corps was disgraced at Chancellorsville. The men nonetheless were proud of the praiseworthy reputation that Adolphus Buschbeck's brigade gained at Chancellorsville, although they insisted that it was owing chiefly to the actions of their own regiment and a portion of the 73rd Pennsylvania. They admired Colonel Buschbeck. "He is the finest dutch man that I ever saw," Thaddeus Reynolds declared. "He is not afraid to speak to a private and he thinks more of some of the privates then he does of one half of

[the] shoulder straps." Their lukewarm assessment of General Howard when he took command of the Eleventh Corps chilled considerably after the Chancellorsville disaster. Cheering for Howard ceased after the battle, and one officer of the 154th had the temerity to refuse to shake the general's hand after a review of the regiment. Howard's sole support in the regiment came from the religious men, who appreciated the general's deep faith.[41]

Only after the successful fighting in Lookout Valley and Chattanooga did the men express pride in wearing the crescent badge of the Eleventh Corps. But they voiced little regret when the Eleventh and Twelfth Corps merged, Howard departed, and Major General Joseph Hooker took command of the newly formed Twentieth Corps, which dropped the crescent badge and kept the Twelfth's star. "The 11th Corps accepts the change in their status without a single regret—Knowing as we do that our new Commander in a military point of view is every way superior to Gen. Howard," Henry Van Aernam wrote. "In fact, as a 'fighting' man to lead a single corps in battle, I think 'Old Joe' has no superior in the army." Van Aernam added, however, "Still it is a sad thing to see an organization with all its Sad & pleasing association of nearly two years so cruelly be [swept] away and the old 'Crescent' go down to rise no more!"[42]

No other corps commander captured the loyalty of the 154th New York as did Joseph Hooker. After observing the general ride through the 154th's camp "in his usual affable mood," astride his white charger and accompanied by a single aide, Lewis Warner commented, "He is one of the most military looking men on horseback I ever saw and on his power full Horse of almost snowy whiteness He looks every inch the General." Emory Sweetland wrote, "I have seen all of the Generals in the army that are of any note but Hooker is the King of soldiers in appearance. Tall, straight, well proportioned, his smoothly shaven face always in every time of danger wearing a smile & no matter how hot the fire he will ride up to see how matters progress." To Sweetland, Hooker was "my Beau Ideal of a Soldier." To James Quilliam, Hooker was simply "one of the bravest and best fighten men in the army."[43]

The regiment's association with Hooker extended back to the Army of the Potomac, which the general commanded at Chancellorsville, and the Tennessee campaigns, during which Hooker led the Eleventh and Twelfth Corps. At winter camp in Lookout Valley, Richard McCadden noted, "Gen

Hooker wished our Regt to camp near his Head Quarters." When the move was made, James Quilliam reported, "It is suposed that our buisnes now will be to take cair of old fighting Joe he of course wants a few guards to selute him and take care of priseners when nesesary but he do not put on half the stile that some Colonels do." "Our camp is now near Genl. Hookers head quarters," Martin Bushnell wrote. "Joseph and Col. Jones are pretty good friends and I dont know but what he wants us all for staff & body guard. Joseph knows that we are about as good as they make." "Hooker's affection for the Regiment was always the source of greatest pleasure to us indeed I may say of pride," Colonel Jones recalled in the postwar years, and at Look-out Valley the general "was in daily connection with us all a mark of af-fection which we greatly appreciated and in which we cordially reciprocated—you bet."[44]

The regiment's bonds to Hooker grew tighter during the Atlanta cam-paign. Together, Hooker and his Twentieth Corps compiled a combat record of which the men were proud. "The rebs have great fear of Hooker & the *Star Corps*," Emory Sweetland boasted late in June 1864. A few weeks later he wrote, "Our corps has made itself a name here of which we may well be proud." Still later Sweetland declared, "Our Corps has borne the brunt of the fighting thus far. . . . We are the only corps in the whole army that have never been repulsed. We have carved ourselves a name in history & have the respect of the whole Army." Milon Griswold measured the corps' achieve-ment in blood. "The army has lost 15,000 men on this campaign," he noti-fied the *Fredonia Censor*, "and the 20th Corps has lost 7,000; so you can see whether the 20th Corps has seen any fighting or not." The three-corps Army of the Cumberland, to which the Twentieth Corps belonged, reported 19,452 casualties during the Atlanta campaign, of which the most, 7,417, were in the Twentieth Corps. Griswold's figures were a bit off, but his point holds—the Twentieth suffered the highest losses of any of Sherman's seven infantry corps.[45]

In July 1864 the 154th New York received a jolt when General Sherman (who despised Hooker) gave a major promotion to Howard (who Hooker outranked and loathed) rather than to "Fighting Joe," who resigned in a fit of pique. The soldiers of the 154th lamented Hooker's departure. "Gen. Hooker has left us and we all miss him much," George Mason wrote. "I wish he could have stayed with us, they all liked him so much. He was a good

Commander and very careful of his men." "We had a general with us whom you could depend upon," Milon Griswold asserted, "and he would not ask his men to go where he would not go. This man is General Hooker. He was well liked by the whole corps, and we disliked to part with him. He was a man who would never let his men go hungry as long as he could get anything."[46]

Pride in the regiment's 2nd Division, called the "White Star Division" after its badge, accompanied pride in the Twentieth Corps. "Our Div . . . is so small," Marcellus Darling wrote from Atlanta at the termination of the campaign. "The white star have done some fighting since the fourth of May last." Emory Sweetland noted the cost of the division's valor. "Our Div . . . had on leaving Lookout Valley 5700 men . . . & now have 2700." William James was inspired to compose an poem celebrating the accomplishments of the division. It began:

> The White Star Division the star of the west
> The heroes of Sherman forever be blessed
> May the badge of the Regiment Division and Corps
> Be heralded abroad from mountain to shore.[47]

The men never idolized their division commander, Brigadier General John W. Geary, as they did Hooker. An immense man, Geary was feared as a strict disciplinarian who was not above kicking and otherwise maltreating his men. Nevertheless, the regiment felt a moment of pride when Geary presented his division and each of its three brigades with new flags in April 1865 at Goldsboro. "He made a very nice speech to the Div when he presented them to us," Richard McCadden wrote, and a veteran of the 154th recalled that Geary brought the men to tears when he acknowledged how roughly he had treated them, but noted he had never refused to accompany them into battle, and they had always won laurels in their fights.[48]

Only one other general gained a level of respect from the men of the regiment similar to that accorded Hooker—Fighting Joe's nemesis, Sherman. The tremendous success of Sherman's campaigns made him (and them) unconquerable in their eyes, and they appreciated his common touch during personal encounters. Years after the war, veterans of the 154th recalled joking with the general about skimpy rations during the siege of Savannah, and chatting with him under fire on the skirmish line at New Hope Church.

"This army knows nothing but victory when General Sherman is at the head of it," Milon Griswold declared after the fall of Atlanta. He continued, "He has outgeneralled every opposing leader he has encountered yet." About the same time Emory Sweetland wrote, "I will risk W. T. Sherman with the best General that the rebs have." And when Sherman brought his army to Goldsboro after his great marches through Georgia and the Carolinas, Sweetland announced, "The reb Gens. in the west are no match for old Sherman. He is probably the best Gen. that the war has brot forth."[49]

Despite its desperate encounters with the enemy on the battlefield, whenever the regiment came face to face with Confederate soldiers during times of quiet, fraternization ensued. The first opportunity occurred in December 1862 when the 154th camped about a mile and a half up the Rappahannock River from Falmouth, Virginia. An Alabama brigade was stationed on the opposite shore and the two sides quickly established contact. Conversations were shouted across the water and before long men from both sides were hopping across the large rocks clogging the river to visit the foe. "Our boys and the Rebs talk to each other across the river & go across & drink coffee & swap papers &c.," Emory Sweetland wrote. An extensive trade developed, with the Alabamians offering tobacco for the New Yorkers' coffee. Officers ordered a halt to the crossings, but the men ignored the ban. When sterner orders prohibited any communication whatsoever across the river, the men resorted to pantomime—sometimes pretending to throw their muskets or cartridge boxes into the water—and painting messages on the rocks.[50]

Discontent with the war and a desire for peace were frequent topics of conversation between the enemies. "They said they was sick of the war and wanted to go home as bad as we did," Devillo Wheeler wrote after a meeting with some Alabamians. "Some of them throwed down their arms and come over and give themselves up." In Barzilla Merrill's opinion, if it was not for the "big toads"—the political leadership of North and South—"we and the . . . Reb souldiers would not quarrel or fight much." The men marveled at their peaceful coexistence with the Confederates. "It seems singular to me to be in sight and hearing of the Rebs here & [have] no fighting going on," Emory Sweetland wrote. "All is apparently as quiet and peaceable as in a time of peace. From the door of my tent where I am writing I can see the Rebel pickets on the other side of the river walking back and forth."[51]

Similar situations ensued when the 154th faced the enemy across the Rappahannock at Kelly's Ford in April 1863 and Georgia's Chattahoochee River in July 1864. Treading the riverbank one night at Kelly's Ford, Private William H. H. Campbell of Company A heard a call from the opposite shore and looked up to see a Confederate. "He asked me if our boys shot pickets," Campbell wrote. "I told him no, and asked him to what regiment he belonged. He replied, the 2nd North Carolina [Cavalry], and added that he was sick of the war and thought it ought to close. We parted," Campbell noted, "wishing each other well." "The pickets are along the water's edge," Major Lewis Warner wrote at the Chattahoochee, "and they are on very good terms, and quite a traffic has sprung up in the articles of coffee and tobacco." Warner reported that Confederate officers had ineffectively tried to ban the communication, "no doubt fearful of the effect on their men. There are no such fears entertained with regard to our boys." Warner also noted that the enemies would often bid each other to "take care" as they closed their meetings.[52]

The 154th's prisoners of war had little good to say about the treatment they received from Confederate guards at Belle Island and Andersonville. To a man, however, they reported considerate treatment by the frontline Confederate soldiers who guarded them immediately after their capture. After his wounding and capture at Chancellorsville, Colby Bryant observed in his diary, "Our men are as well cared for [as] the circumstances of the enemy, who have as many and more of their own wounded than they can well tend to, will admit. I find there are many kind hearted, good men in the Southern army, who for their kindness to me now while I am helpless in their hands have won my esteem and gratitude." As Newell Burch was being escorted to the rear after his capture at Gettysburg, a Confederate handed him a basket of cherries and said, "Here, Yank, you will need these before I shall." Burch never forgot the kind act. "Well," he wrote years later, "that was about the only chance I got at southern hospitality for nearly two years I was boarding with them." Gettysburg captive Horace Smith wrote of his guards, "They are a hard looking set of beings," but he admitted, "They treat us as well as they can, especially the privates." Officers also reported kind treatment at the enemy's hands. When Colonel Patrick Jones returned to camp on parole after his Chancellorsville wounding and capture, he told William Charles that the enemy had "treated him very kindly and took first rate care of him."[53]

The members of the 154th left western New York blustering about killing rebels and filling Confederate graves, but meeting the enemy in person changed their perspective. They still strove to defeat the enemy army, but they no longer felt hostility toward the Southern soldier as an individual.

Throughout the regiment's thirty-two months of service in the South, the soldiers commented on the devastation the war had visited on the countryside and its inhabitants. Members of the regiment quickly became active participants in sowing that devastation—within two months of entering Virginia they burned the village of Haymarket and became adept foragers—and while some of the men felt that white Southern civilians had it coming for instigating the war, others pitied the victims of the destruction.

"I have . . . seen considerable of the desolation and Ruin that accompanies War," George Taylor wrote within weeks of the regiment's arrival in Virginia. "There are but 2 or 3 whole families living in Fairfax and not a single house but bears the marks of violence." Describing the countryside around Thoroughfare Gap to his sister-in-law, Eason Bull wrote, "It was thickly settled before the war broke out but now there is not a house once in 10 miles. Great nice houses [have been] torn and burnt down. There is once in a while a old man and woman and niggers [that] lives [here,] but they might as well die." After robbing a civilian of "all he has got," Bull noted, the soldiers would "damn him because he has not got more. It is to bad but I tell you their honey goes good after all." When the men stripped a house near Falmouth of its doors, windows, and other wood for their campfires, First Lieutenant Marshall O. Bond of Company D observed, "It looked Rather hard, but the Boys say they had no business To live in Virginia if they did not want Everything tore to pieces." Devastation reached fierce extremes during Sherman's marches. After listing the bounties the men had foraged during the Carolinas campaign, Edgar Shannon noted, "But if we lived well Some one else must Suffer. I tell you that Some of the people in North & South Carolinas must Suffer. I have seen families who in times of peace could look over their thousands of acres & count their gold by thousands, who after our army passed through had not a mouthful to eat, or a quilt to cover them. I have pitied them, but such things are the result of war, & I think they will hesitate next time ere they urge a rebellion."[54]

Some of the more thoughtful men contrasted the devastated South with their own peaceful homes in the North. "I think that we would not verry well like to have our home and property served in this kind of way," Barzilla Merrill commented to Ruba after describing the ravaged Virginia country-side. Responding to his wife's wish that he was home, James Quilliam wrote, "Think how much better it is for us to come here and defiind our homes than it would be to stay at home and let them come and distroy every thing that we have. . . . I am thankful tha our house hath not been burnd by an envading enemy as i have known and you left to loock out for your self." William Charles presented a hypothetical case to his wife.

> How do you suppose the people of Freedom would feel if three or four thousand Rebels would come up that way and steel every Horse & cow & sheep in the town & *compel* the young men to go & help drive them off!! And how do you suppose you would feel to see 50 or a 100 rough looking men with guns & swords & large knives coming into the house, & helping themselves to whatever they liked & after going into the cellar & drinking what milk they wanted & spilling the rest, & destroying what Butter they did not want to take with them and after that going to the Barn & shooting all the chickens & hens &c, and maybe set fire to the Barn . . . [and] drive all the cows, the horses & sheep & hogs into the road!! And that would be the last you would see of them!! That would be pretty hard would it not, but such scenes as that takes place very often only a great deal worse.[55]

Many of the men commented on the beleaguered Southern civilians' de-votion to the Confederacy. Residents near Thoroughfare Gap provided exam-ples. "We are now in a country without the semblance of claim of a particle of loyalty in it," Henry Van Aernam wrote. He continued, "Everybody here are thoroughly and earnestly rebellious." Lewis Warner noted, "They profess the strongest faith in Southern courage and exhaustless resource, and be-lieve that the South can never be whipped into submission." Alanson Crosby met a lawyer who "told me frankly he was for resistance to the last. With a great deal of enthusiasm he remarked that the South had already gained her independence, and that hope of reconstruction was dead."[56]

Many of the civilians the men encountered were women. As Marcellus Darling wrote, "I have marched in Va enough to see who is left there. I have never seen only one man in or near the lines that I should think was fit for army service there is not a young or middle aged man to be seen in Va." But the women were not hesitant to express their views to the Northerners. On the contrary, as Horace Smith noted at Kelly's Ford, "The secesh women wish the Yankees all dead." "Most of the inhabitants in this vicinity are secessionists," George Newcomb observed at Camp Jones. "Although the men folks keep quiet the women do not spare any pains to let it out." As the war progressed and the Southerners' situation grew more dire, the men could not help but voice a grudging admiration for the loyalty of Confederate women and their contributions to their cause. "Thousands & thousands of women that never did any work in their lives before this war, are working from daylight untill dark, either *spinning weaving* or hoeing corn in the field," William Charles noted during the Atlanta campaign. "All of the clothes of the Rebel soldiers are made *at Home,* the cotton is growed at *Home* it is carded at *Home* and spun at *Home* and woven at *Home* and made up at *Home* and it is no wonder that the rebel soldiers fight so well for their Homes & are willing to die rather than *to give up* their Homes to those that *they believe to be their Enemies.*"[57]

The soldiers relished encounters with Southerners loyal to the Union. In general they were rarely met, but during two campaigns—the marches through western Maryland before and after Gettysburg, and the march through eastern Tennessee to the relief of Knoxville—Unionists were found in plenty. "The inhabitants along the road greet us kindly," Emory Sweetland wrote during the march through Maryland. "A good many ladies gave us milk & bread & pies & requested us to kill a reb for them." This was a most welcome change from their encounters with staunchly secessionist women in Virginia. "We have been used for the last 6 months to having *wimin* look sourly at us," Sweetland noted. "But here all is changed. lovely women smile upon us, waive their handkerchiefs at us and stand by the side of the road with pints of milk to give us to drink & tell us to fight for them & protect them." During the Tennessee march, Unionists were met in village after village. Colby Bryant recorded in his diary the reception the regiment met in Athens. "When we marched through the village with our banners waving unfolded and keeping step to the martial music, we were welcomed by women waving handkerchiefs and in one or two instances our flags, which had evidently been kept secreted since the war [began]. Most all seemed pleased at the sight of a Union army."[58]

There was one species of Southerners the men dreaded to meet: guerrillas, or, as they were commonly known, bushwhackers. "There are a considerable many guerillas around here," Dwight Moore noted at Edwards Ferry, Virginia, "and several soldiers have lost their lives by going to far from camp. They have a woman under arrest at headquarters for shooting two soldiers this morning, or at least they think she shot them. they were found dead at her door. Two more were found with their throats cut in the woods." On the return from Gettysburg, the regiment marched through Middleburg, Virginia, which Major Lewis Warner described in his diary as "about as purely a cecesh hole as I had ever seen." Warner continued, "The woods are infested with Bushwhackers rendering it very unsafe to go outside on Picket Yesterday a train of Waggons went out for forage and are reported captured not more than 1 ½ miles from camp These Gurrillas are under the renowned [Colonel John S.] Mosby whose name spreads terror among the union Soldiers or citizens." Despite several close calls, none of the men with the regiment ever fell prey to bushwhackers. But one soldier away from the regimental home was not so lucky. While he was stationed at Fort Rosecrans in Murfreesboro, Tennessee, Private Patrick Griffin of Company I ventured outside the picket line on October 2, 1864, and was killed by a gang of guerrillas.[59]

Union soldiers' stomachs often drove them to encounters with Southern civilians. Seeking to augment their monotonous and sometimes scanty rations, the men knocked on farmhouse and cottage doors in search of food. Their letters and diaries contain numerous passages like one written by Andrew Blood at Thoroughfare Gap: "I went to a farmers and got what light wheat bread and milk that I wanted for breakfast and it cost me seventeen cents." He added, "This was a grand treat I assure you." The men had other friendly encounters with Southern civilians, particularly with young women. Alfred Benson "visited with some Tenn ladies" at Lookout Valley and called on an Atlanta family that included some "fine girls." "Some young ladies called in the evening," Alexander Bird recorded at Savannah, "and we had some fine singing." Charles Abell made pleasant visits to a Savannah family, which, he wrote, made him feel "more at home than any other spot I have seen since I left that *dear Roof*. . . . I can go there and spend an evening in a nice social chat to much more advantage to me than spending my time and money at these museums and Theatres."[60]

Many of the men were struck by the poverty they saw in the South, particularly in the mountainous regions of northern Alabama and Georgia and eastern Tennessee. Emory Sweetland commented on the "miserable log cabins . . . we so often see here in the South." William Charles met a justice of the peace in the Tennessee mountains living in "a *very old log hut.*" The man was ninety year old, "covered with Rags and no shoes or any thing on his feet." When the regiment arrived at Bridgeport, Alabama, Charles opined, "I have but a very poor oppinion of this State & the state of Tennessee the country . . . is very poor indeed and the people look as if they *never had half enough* to eat."[61]

Observing "miserable log houses" and "rich but poorly cultivated" soil in the area around Chattanooga, John Griswold wrote, "Everything denotes a want of that thriftiness and enterprise to be seen in the free states." Other soldiers also remarked on the backwardness of the South when compared to the North. "The Virginia folks are some time behind so far as the customs are conserned," Barzilla Merrill thought. Stephen Green judged the country around Kelly's Ford to be the finest he had seen in Virginia, but still found it lacking. "With the industry and enterprise of the Northern people," he commented, "it would be the nicest in the U.S." Some of the men attributed the South's backwardness to a specific cause. "The institution of Slavery has proved the utter ruin of the whites of the south," William Charles asserted. "I did not used to believe all the stories told about the slave holders but now I know them to be true and the truth not half told. It is impossible to believe unless you *can see with your own eyes.*" Charles had long believed "that slavery did the white man more harm than the black," but until his experience in Dixie, "I never could believe that the white people of the South had become half so much degraded as they have."[62]

Throughout its sojourn in the South, the regiment encountered African Americans. The black population in Cattaraugus and Chautauqua counties was tiny, so for most of the men the war provided their first interactions with black people. At first sight, some members of the regiment viewed them as nothing more than part of the exotic landscape of the South. Describing the area around Fairfax Court House, Edgar Shannon wrote, "No fences, no crops, & no nothing but a few grinning blacks & worse looking whites." Eason Bull described the same countryside. "The timber," Bull informed his brother, "is oak, red cedar, pine, chestnut, walnut, shell, and grape, and log cabins and niggers, and lots of ground to sleep on." (The shell and grape Bull referred to were artillery projectiles.)[63]

Personal encounters soon gave the men a closer look at African Americans. Many of them came away with an intense dislike of blacks. "I have nothing to do with them," Samuel Williams wrote, "nor i dont like the looks of them." George Newcomb assured his wife, "I would not leave you again for the whole South niggers thrown [in]." Some believed that blacks were treated better than soldiers, and deeply resented it. "I am well now and tuff and like it first rate the soljour part but the d–m niggers they take me down," Landers Wright informed his mother. "They seem to think more of a nigger then they do of a white man." Levi Bryant described North Carolina "nigars" as "grait fat lazy fools" and declared, "I was quite an abulitionist when I came into the army but I have got over it now, for it is first a nigar then a mual & then a soldier & the soldier is used worse than any of them."[64]

Some soldiers resented blacks as the putative cause of the war, and rejected emancipation as a war aim. As Harvey Earl wrote, in a comment echoed by other members of the regiment, "I have seen anuf of this niger war." Isaac Porter declared, "I hope the President will go ahead and put down the rebellion but let the mighty nigger alone." Barzilla Merrill wondered if President Lincoln was ahead of public opinion in issuing the Emancipation Proclamation and noted that it put the army in a rebellious mood. "When the nigger as they call him [is] mentioned they say that they will throw down their arms and there is a large class of this stripe in the army."[65]

In a bitter passage in a letter to his wife, George Newcomb catalogued the racists' various gripes with blacks:

A nigger fares here better than a common soldier On one of our marches a sick soldier went up to the baggage wagon and asked the driver if he could carry his knapsack no he said it was strictly forbidden by the officers on top of his load lay a great fat greasy nigger riding along at his ease and the poor fellow had to trudge along afoot with his knapsack on his back and let the stinking nigger ride I would like to see those northern Abilishionists . . . who are so eager to carry on this war down here with a knapsack on their backs wading through the mud over their shoes and laying on the cold frozen ground instead of staying home and crying out push ahead and not go into winter quarters but free the cussed nigger.[66]

At the other end of the spectrum were soldiers sympathetic to African Americans and supportive of emancipation. "We have grate reason to be thankfull that we air made the honered instraments in gods hands of removing the curse of slavery from our land," James Quilliam wrote. William Charles put his sympathy for African Americans to practical use by teaching black children to read and write. Supported by the Freedman's Aid Society, he provided books to his students and conducted day and night classes. "You have never seen any black children have you?" Charles wrote to his young son. "Well they learn as quick as white children and they are so glad that a white man is willing to teach them. Many of them have no *shoes* to put on their feet but for all that, they come no matter how cold it is because they wish so much to learn their books."[67]

According to abolitionist soldiers, both blacks and whites had been debased by slavery. Henry Van Aernam declared, "The institutions of the south have blotted out the moral sensibilities of the people," citing an aristocratic Virginian woman he met who bemoaned the loss of her black field hands and "breeding women," swore Abraham Lincoln was wholly or partly black, and vowed that "the South *never* would submit to being ruled by a nigger!" Wrote Van Aernam, "Here we have positive proofs that the curse of God visits all that come in contact with this atrocious institution."[68]

Early in the 154th's service, the soldiers learned they could count on the friendly and helpful support of blacks. In slave quarters the men met with a warm reception and offers of food, if any was to be had. "A *negro* woman gave me some rice and molasses to day," William Charles wrote when the 154th arrived in Virginia, "and I can assure you that I was very thankfull for it." African Americans were particularly helpful during foraging expeditions. "Our officers foraged a good deal for the teams," James Quilliam noted of the regiment's stay at Kelly's Ford, "and the negroes would tell them where to find their corn and anything they wanted the [white] folks about there hid everything." When the regiment looted the elderly Kelly's rich farm at the ford, Quilliam reported, "The old man looked very sour but the negers seemed to enjoy it very much." Horace Smith confiscated bacon, preserves, pickles, flour, molasses, milk, and a bottle of gin at Kelly's Ford. Smith noted, "The niggers told us where to find everything."[69]

Polarizing racial views seemed to moderate as the war went on, the men became more familiar with blacks and their plight, and African American troops were added to the Union army—a move that met with universal approval in the regiment. "I am glad they have concluded to put the negroes in," wrote Private Asher Bliss Jr. of Company I. "They are just as able to fight as whites & if they will *not* they certainly do not value freedom much. It seems to be established *so far* that they will fight." After the massacre of black soldiers by Confederates at Fort Pillow, Tennessee, in April 1864, Horace Howlett exclaimed, "Let them talk about the Niggers not fighting they fight good and I had rather they would fight then fight myself." Observing black soldiers at Savannah, Francis Bowen wrote, "They are fine looking soldiers. Neat, tidy & soldierly bearing. I must say that the colored regiments now in this city . . . are superior to our white vols. in drill & discipline."[70]

The U.S. Colored Troops were commanded by white officers. Enlisted men of the 154th were offered a chance in April 1864 to take an examination and enter a special school in Philadelphia to obtain a commission in a black regiment. Several of the men mulled the possibility. William Charles, a particular friend to blacks, was encouraged by Colonel Jones to apply, but could not make up his mind. "There are a good many reasons why I should go," he reflected, "and there are some why I should not go. . . . Sometimes I feel as if it were *God's will* that I should go and if I was shure of that course I would go." Charles eventually decided to stay with the 154th. So did Edgar Shannon. "I would go in if I had not got a commission here," he wrote, "but I am glad I have one here. I [would] rather be here than in a black Regiment by all odds." Private Ariel H. Wellman of Company B felt differently. He was the only member of the regiment to take the examination, attend the school, and receive a commission as an officer of black soldiers, serving as first lieutenant and captain with the 42nd U.S. Colored Infantry in Alabama and Tennessee from August 1864 until January 1866.[71]

By the time of Sherman's campaigns, the men had come to accept black freedom and a black presence in the regiment. Large contingents of newly freed slaves flocked to the regiment in Georgia and the Carolinas and marched with the white soldiers as laborers and servants. "Probably 10,000 slaves had escaped with our army & are now employed in every capacity," Emory Sweet-land wrote near Savannah toward the end of the March to the Sea. Many of the blacks ignored lies they had been told about the terrifying Yankees. "The rebs had told the darkies we would kill them all," John Langhans wrote in North Carolina, "but they were all glad to see us they stood in crowds of 10 to 30 all along the road." The soldiers greeted them sympathetically. "They are Suffering for food and clothes," Edgar Shannon noted. "They have ever been friendly to us & our cause. it is our duty to help them."[72]

Former slaves became adjunct members of the 154th, but the soldiers continued to use derogatory racist terms in referring to their black comrades. "There has been six in our family," Edgar Shannon wrote of the Carolinas campaign, naming four white comrades "& the Nigger." "The boys are lively and merry around the regiment tonight," Francis Bowen wrote during the occupation of Savannah. "The boys are dancing and the darkies are jigging & patting & singing." Beyond the mess and camp, blacks even took on some of the duties and dangers of soldiers. They stood armed guard for foraging parties and were wounded in action at the side of the white men during the siege of Savannah and the Carolinas campaign. Still, they remained "niggers." "One shell burst in the Regt," Alexander Bird noted in his diary during the Savannah siege, "severely wounding one of the niggers and slightly wounding a few of the men."[73]

The soldiers' black companions went unnamed in their wartime writings. But in postwar reminiscences, the names of certain "niggers" and "darkies" were readily recalled. Members of Company D remembered employing a black cook named Rube, an outstanding wrestler who won them hundreds of dollars in bets when pitted against opponents from other regiments. Others remembered Richmond, who marched with Private John S. Belknap of Company G as his servant. Another Richmond, servant of Captain Alfred Benson, was recalled by members of Company D as an expert boxer and wrestler. Benson's Richmond stayed with the regiment all the way to its discharge at Elmira, where he was "dressed to fits & proud," and perhaps was in the audience when Colonel Lewis Warner delivered his farewell address.[74]

During the March to the Sea, members of the 154th devised a facetious ceremony to muster black men into their ranks. The prospective candidate was asked if he was willing to be a member of the regiment. If he replied affirmatively, he was told to remove his boots, hat, and jacket, and enter a "machine"—a blanket or tarpaulin gripped by a ring of soldiers. After a vigorous tossing, the dizzy initiate was lowered to the ground and proclaimed a member in good standing of the 154th New York, entitled to all rights and privileges. The racial chasm was never totally bridged, but esprit de corps acknowledged the black presence in the white regimental family.[75]

CHAPTER 9

Shoulder Straps and Courts-Martial

An able, efficient, and respected officer corps was essential to regimental esprit de corps. The field and staff officers and company-grade line officers held the critical responsibilities of training, disciplining, and leading the enlisted men—and inspiring them by example in combat. They also faced the challenge of upholding those responsibilities while earning the respect of their charges—a task made difficult because of the potentially adversarial nature of the two-tiered caste system of officers and enlisted men. A commission and a pair of shoulder straps brought a man power, privilege, and prestige. An officer received substantially higher wages (although he paid his own clothing and food expenses), occupied a larger tent, ate meals cooked by servants, had whiskey when he wanted it, gave orders and assigned duties to his underlings, and could tender his resignation if he chose to do so. Those perquisites of office created a gulf between enlisted men and their leaders. Officers could widen that gulf and damage esprit de corps by abusing their authority and lording it over their men, or they could bridge the gulf and foster esprit by displaying a friendly and fatherly regard for their boys while still maintaining the rights of rank.

Ambitious men, both officers and enlisted men, sought higher rank, and rivalries for office could be detrimental to esprit de corps. As in other volunteer regiments, political tugs-of-war played a role in the selection of officers in the 154th New York. George Taylor bluntly asserted, "The officers of our own regiment and, I may as well say, in our company are in their positions as a result of party favoritism." "There was a great deal of politics to the square yard of the 154th N.Y. Vols.," Captain Matthew Cheney recalled in the postwar years, "and especially around Dr. [Henry] Van Aernam's Head Quarters." Advancement usually required a knowledge of political as well as military tactics.[1]

Attrition in the officer corps was constant. As officers resigned or became casualties of disease or battle, replacements were generally recommended by the regiment's commander, who ideally had the best knowledge of qualified candidates. By the end of its service, a fighting regiment like the 154th New York typically had a largely different set of officers in place than the ones that accompanied it to the front. The 154th was mustered in at Jamestown with a full complement of thirty-eight officers, and almost fifty more men were commissioned during the regiment's service. Only twenty-five officers were mustered out at the end of the 154th's service. Sixteen of them had proven their leadership abilities in the ranks, generally as noncommissioned officers, before their promotions. Only one officer—Second Lieutenant Warren Onan of Company C—held the same position throughout the regiment's entire service, and he spent most of it on detached duty as commander of the brigade ambulance corps. During three years of war, the regiment was purged of incompetent, cowardly, drunken, or imperious officers. Promoted in their place were men so attuned to the enlisted men in temperament that they drew scant mention in the men's letters. Attrition, promotion, and esprit de corps molded a regiment with an ideal balance between its leaders and its led.

Enlisted men resented officers for several reasons. "It takes a rough wicked man to get office here as a general rule," Barzilla Merrill wrote from Camp John Manley in April 1863. He sensed that some prominent Cattaraugus County men seemed more interested in getting good berths as officers for themselves and their cronies than they did in having the war end. The thought that officers could wish the war prolonged for their own advancement and gain made enlisted men bitter. "I wish every offaser had thare little 13 dollars a month and had to cary a Napsack and eat with us," Horace Howlett wrote. He continued, "Then they would not want to keep the thing [going] eny longer then posable." Enlisted men scorned the resentments of officers bypassed for promotion. "If they cannot go forward as fast as they like or as fast as they are entitled to they are like a sulky mule," George Taylor wrote; "they don't want to draw at all." Enlisted men mocked officers' pretensions. Alexander Bird, who began his service as a corporal in Company G, was promoted to sergeant and sergeant-major and finally mustered in as first lieutenant of Company F in 1864. Bird had "got on the Sholder Straps," Levi Bryant wrote, "so you can guess how Big he is." When Corporal Eugene M. Shaw of Company F was promoted to assistant surgeon of the 89th New York Infantry, his company mate George Taylor wrote, "He is a great man since he got his shoulder straps on. The boys . . . who have seen him say he put on considerable Strut airs." Voicing distaste for officers in general, Francis Bowen referred to "the many misfortunes & ill treatments which the private must submit to, while if he were at home he would buy and sell his superiors in [the] military four times and keep them. And I would not feel honored with the company of many of them in civil life."[2]

Other enlisted men had a more favorable opinion of their superiors. "The officers treat me with respect," Emory Sweetland wrote. "I can get favors from them more readily than most of the Co. & they never call on me to do extra duty such as getting wood for them & building their quarters &c as they do of most of the Co." When Alanson Crosby was promoted to regimental adjutant, the *Cattaraugus Freeman* reported, the members of his former Company D, sorry that he was leaving them, "arrested him for desertion, tried him by a court-martial, convicted and sentenced him to be shot! He was subsequently pardoned, after being very gravely lectured upon the enormity of his offence!" Private Morris Keim of Company I, who encountered many officers of different regiments while serving as a clerk for the brigade assistant adjutant general, declared after the war, "The officers of our regt were without exception kind, pleasant & did not consider themselves above a private or Sergt. like many others I had occasion to notice."[3]

Keim's hindsight was selective. Like other regiments, the 154th New York had its share of disliked and inferior officers and only gradually rid itself of them in a weeding-out process. "Let them all go," George Newcomb exclaimed during a wave of officers' resignations. "I dont care if all of them go resign if we can get better ones." John Porter also bid the resigners good riddance—"Most of them are a pack of drunken Rowdies." But Porter resented the ease with which officers left the service. "I know of a 'goodly' number of privates that would Resign," he wrote, "but for 'Circumstances beyond their control.'"[4]

The politics of command in the 154th New York dated from August 1862, when lawyer and politician Addison Rice was appointed colonel of the yet-to-be-formed regiment by Governor Edwin Morgan. Rice never received a commission and accepted the command with the understanding that after organizing the regiment and delivering it to the front, he would be relieved by an experienced officer. This arrangement was much to the benefit of the

154th, as Rice's only military experience was in the prewar militia. Rice's stalwart work in raising and organizing the regiment earned him the support of the men. "Our boys all desire to have Hon. A. G. Rice to lead them," a volunteer wrote before Rice's colonelcy was announced. "They have the utmost confidence in him, and would prefer him for Col., to any that have yet been spoken of." Two weeks before the regiment was mustered in, Richard McCadden wrote, "Every body here 'and the rest of mankind,' are in favor of Col. Rice, as our leader, believing he is made of the material whose order would be 'come boys!'" Another volunteer at Camp Brown declared Rice to be as fine a soldier as he was an attorney. "The Military Toga sits upon his shoulders, and he honors it as well as he does that of the advocate. With that the people will be satisfied." When Rice prepared to leave the regiment in October 1862 after delivering it to Virginia, as per the agreement, Alanson Crosby wrote, "He has done well in getting the regiment organized and into the field, and the men regret that he could not remain with them permanently." At the same time, however, Charles Abell observed, "Col Rice is about played out."[5]

During the interregnum between Rice's colonelcy and the arrival of his successor, command of the regiment devolved on Lieutenant Colonel Henry Loomis. Loomis was a veteran soldier when he received his commission in the 154th and thus brought valuable military experience to the regiment. He had served from 1861 as a first lieutenant in the 64th New York and had been wounded at the Battle of Fair Oaks, Virginia. Loomis was a great favorite with the men, who called him "Uncle Henry." "The Leutenant kernel . . . is liked by every boy in the redgment," Alansing Wyant stated. Loomis "is one of the best men in the whole army," Charles Abell declared. "He is with us all the time and acts like one of us he does not have that proud overbearing way that some have but is kind [and] quite a Boy you might say." After the Battle of Chancellorsville, Loomis let it be known that he was considering resigning. "If he does we loose all," James Washburn wrote. "I hope that he will stay with us as long as we have to stay." But Loomis indeed tendered his resignation on June 1, 1863, indicating a desire "to take service in the Artillery arm of the service."[6]

"We are sad, for Lieut. Col. Loomis has resigned and is going home," an unidentified member of the regiment reported the following day in a letter to the *Gowanda Reporter*. "We all of us love and respect him. He has so far been steadily with us, caring for us as a father, and his departure from us is a sad event to the Reg't. He will be cherished long in our memories." Loomis never served as intended in the artillery. Instead, he returned to the 154th a year after his resignation in a most surprising capacity, given his former prominence as an officer. "He is sutler in our Regt now," Horace Smith noted in July 1864, adding, "He is the 'same old Coon.'" From the distinction of the lieutenant colonelcy, Loomis had stooped to the disreputable post of sutler, selling beer, tobacco, and sundries to the men he had once commanded.[7]

As previously arranged, Rice's successor as colonel of the regiment was another veteran soldier, Patrick Henry Jones. Not coincidentally, Jones was also Rice's former law partner. (It is noteworthy that two other future officers of the 154th—Dan Allen and Alanson Crosby—had been associated with the firm of Rice and Jones in the prewar years.) A native of Ireland, Jones had experienced the proverbial luck of the Irish when he went to war with the first two organized companies from Cattaraugus County and they were assigned to the 37th New York, a regiment whose other companies were composed of Irish militiamen from New York City. Jones, aided no doubt by his ethnicity, steadily rose from second lieutenant to first lieutenant and adjutant to major of the "Irish Rifles," earning along the way the commendation of his colonel for his conduct at the Fair Oaks battle, and the recommendation and commission as Rice's successor as colonel of the 154th.[8]

Colonel Jones joined the regiment for duty on November 19, 1862, and immediately began to shape the regiment's officer corps to military standards. He instituted an officers' school in the regiment, instructing them in the science of drilling and gathering them at his headquarters every weekday evening for recitations in tactics. Because all of the original officers' commissions bore the same date, Jones determined their ranking by lottery—an exercise that ultimately proved meaningless, as future promotions were based solely on the colonel's recommendations, and Jones ignored seniority as a criterion. For every vacancy among the officer corps—from second lieutenant to lieutenant colonel—Jones made recommendations to the New York State adjutant general, even to the extent of offering "un-official suggestions" while he was a paroled prisoner of war and barred by oath from partaking in official business. In addition to testing candidates' knowledge of tactics and the general duties of officers, Jones judged them on their deportment, gentlemanly bearing, and regularity of habits in camp. And he witnessed their conduct under fire at Chancellorsville, at Chattanooga, and during the Atlanta campaign. Without fail, his recommendations resulted in commissions. Like their predecessors, newly commissioned officers attended nightly tactical recitations and weekly recitations in brigade and corps evolutions at the colonel's headquarters to improve their efficiency. Thus Jones molded an officer corps to his satisfaction.[9]

"Our Col is a rough wooden kind of man [with] no refinement," Barzilla Merrill wrote, but his was a rare negative opinion of Jones. "Colonel Jones is with us," Alanson Crosby wrote in December 1862, "and universally liked by officers and men." "We have the best Cournal that ever was in the filde," Truman Harkness wrote after Jones was wounded and captured at Chancellorsville. "We miss him a considerable [amount]," James Washburn wrote after Jones left for the North to recuperate from his wound and await his exchange. Washburn added, "He was a fine little fellow he was an Irish[man] but he was smart." John Manley put the bond forged between Jones ("the dauntless, Christian soldier . . . no braver or magnanimous man lives") and Loomis and their regiment at Chancellorsville in sentimental terms in a letter to the *Cattaraugus Freeman.* "I know of the pride of Col. Jones in his command, his faith in his men, and of their good discipline," Manley wrote; "of the faith of the men in their Colonel and Lieut. Col.—tried veterans of many battle-fields—amounting as near to affection as men are capable; and when the terrible ordeal came, Commanders and Soldiers were not found faithless, but true to each other." Heeding the words of the Soldier's Friend, home folk were assured of the devotion of the colonel to their soldiers, and vice versa.[10]

Jones returned to the regiment just in time to participate in the Chattanooga battle, and "it was verry fortunate for us that he was with us," Stephen Green wrote. "He is a noble officer and knowes his buisness and cares for his men." Early in 1864 Emory Sweetland noted, "Col. Jones is verry popular in the regt." That year Jones was injured at Rocky Face Ridge in a tumble from the crags. After his recuperation he assumed command of the 2nd Brigade, 2nd Division, Twentieth Corps in June 1864 and led it during the remainder of the Atlanta campaign. Before embarking on the March to the Sea, members of the 154th decided to present the colonel with a fine gift to demonstrate their esteem. A subscription of some $600 was raised in the regiment to buy a set of horse equipments, with a specially engraved presentation escutcheon affixed to the saddle's pommel, and sutler Henry Loomis went north to make the purchase.[11]

After commanding the 2nd Brigade during the march to Savannah, Jones received word of his promotion to brigadier general, to rank from December 6, 1864 (although he was not commissioned as such until April 18, 1865). A clearly ambitious man, Jones had applied for the promotion himself, submitting a summary of his military history to Lorenzo Thomas, the adjutant general of the army in Washington. The advance in rank had also been recommended at various times by Jones's political ally Congressman Reuben Fenton, Governor Edwin Morgan, and Generals Howard, Hooker, and Sherman. The 154th naturally rejoiced on learning of Jones's promotion; one of their own would wear the star of a brigadier general. "Bully for 'Pat'!" exulted Francis Bowen on receiving the news. Newspapers in Cattaraugus and Chautauqua counties also heralded the news. Under the headline "Deserved Promotion," the *Cattaraugus Freeman* commended the "able and brave commander of the gallant 154th New York." "He has earned this mark of distinction by long service and meritorious conduct, and we most heartily congratulate him upon his good fortune.— General, we salute you!" Having "faithfully stood with his regiment in maintenance of the old flag through nearly three years of hard and constant campaigning," Jones "has secured a deserved recognition of his services in promotion to a Brigadier Generalship," stated the *Fredonia Censor*.[12]

On Jones's recommendation, Captains Dan Allen of Company B and Lewis Warner of Company C were each in turn promoted to major and then lieutenant colonel of the 154th New York. Allen commanded the 154th at Gettysburg and during part of the Atlanta campaign before he was discharged on account of illness; Warner took charge of the regiment during the Atlanta campaign and led it for the remainder of the war. One of the few comments recorded by the men about Allen indicates a certain ineptness. Relating an incident at the Stafford camp in March 1863, George Taylor noted that Allen "went out with us on Battalion Drill yesterday and got so befuddled he could not do anything, so we drilled or skedaddled about for half an hour then came back to camp." When a sutler set up shop in Major Allen's tent a few months later, Lewis Warner remarked, "Dont know which is the greatest nuisance, Maj or Hucksters." Warner stated the case for his own military competence in a letter to General Howard written five months after the 154th's discharge. "So far as attention to duty is concerned," Warner wrote, "I think I can say what but few Volunteer Officers can, with equal truth declare, that during the three years I was in the service, I was never absent a day from my Regt, except when in Winter Quarters. Although, for the larger part of the time, I held no higher rank than Major, yet I was in command of the Regt for nearly one half of my entire term of service, and I do not think the reputation of the Regt suffered thereby." The veterans of the 154th agreed with that assessment. "Warner was a brave man and *always* on hand for duty," Matthew Cheney recalled in the postwar years.[13]

As the companies arrived at Camp Brown in Jamestown in the summer of 1862, they elected their captains and first and second lieutenants, generally voting for the men who had led the recruiting drive in their communities. Some of those men proved to be better recruiters than officers, and when that realization set in, they submitted their resignations—redounding to the regiment's benefit. Most of them cited poor health, some no doubt legitimately. Second Lieutenant Henry W. Myers of Company F, sent sick to a hospital in Georgetown, D.C., soon after the 154th reached the front, earned the dubious distinction of being the first officer of the regiment to receive his discharge. It was dated October 31, 1862, a scant month and a few days after Myers's muster-in. In tendering his resignation, a sick officer typically submitted a surgeon's certificate of disability together with a signed statement, such as that given by Philander Hubbard on New Year's Day 1863: "Owing to the present state of my health, I fear I can be of little benefit to the service while I aggravate the disease with which I am afflicted by the exposure and hardship incident to the service." The range of reasons for resigning was wide. First Lieutenant John R. Burdick of Company G cited the failing health of his wife, "confined to her room by that fell destroyer Consumption," leaving his two small children "without a protector." Second Lieutenant Orlando W. Avery of Company E listed three reasons for submitting his resignation: family matters required his personal attention, his poor health had left him unable to do duty nearly a quarter of the time after the regiment reached the front, and—perhaps most telling—"I have reason to believe that my company are dissatisfied with me."[14]

The purge was wide-ranging. By the time the 154th fought at Chancellorsville, seven months after reaching Virginia, thirteen of the original thirty-eight officers had left the service, including five of the ten original captains. Captain Baker Leonard Saxton of Company A, an Ellicottville blacksmith, submitted his resignation the same day Colonel Jones recommended Dan Allen to be major, "Feeling myself injured by the recommendation of an officer of junior rank to my own, and entertaining a firm conviction that as ranking Captain . . . my right to the Majorship . . . is paramount to that of any other Captain." Jones endorsed the resignation with a candid note stating that he had recommended Allen for the promotion "without regard to seniority" and had "endeavored to do what in my opinion was for the interest of the Regiment and the Service." Word of Saxton's resignation was greeted with approval by members of his company. "I have heard some of the best news I have heard since I crossed the Potomac," Andrew Blood wrote. "Our Capt has [sent] in his resignation to day." Ira Wood was hospitalized in Washington when he heard the news. "They tell me Saxton has resined and gon home," he wrote. "If so the boys will be glad for that many hate him." (Saxton's December 3 resignation was not granted; he resubmitted it on March 3, 1863, citing family and business matters, and this time it was accepted. After receiving a commission in the 179th New York, First Lieutenant Saxton was killed in action on July 30, 1864, at the Battle of the Crater at Petersburg, Virginia.)[15]

In Company H, Captain John Nelson initially got along well with his men. "We all think a great deal of the Captain," John Porter wrote shortly after the regiment arrived in Virginia, "especially as he thinks a good deal of his men." But three months later, Porter's opinion had changed. "I dont like our Captain as well as I did and the rest of the company are Ditto," he wrote. "He is too cross and overbearing but I get along with him first rate." In February 1863 Nelson entered a Washington hospital, and rumors about him swept the regiment. "Capt. Nelson undertook to go home on a sick leave but when he got to Washington they could not find any thing the matter with him," Thaddeus Reynolds wrote. He added, "He is detained there for the space of thirty days and has got to pay his own board which is a good joke." George Taylor reported that Nelson "was discharged from the hospital and ordered to report to the regiment, [but] instead of doing so, it is said, he procured a suit of civilian clothes and went home." Soon after his return to the 154th, in March 1863, Nelson submitted his resignation, citing important business matters that needed his attention. Colonel Jones informed the army's paymaster general that Nelson owed three enlisted men of his company a total of seventy dollars, and requested that the amount be deposited with a paymaster when Nelson applied for his pay. In a letter to the *Cattaraugus Freeman*, Alfred Benson voiced support for Nelson, despite the captain's troubles. "We trust the cause which compelled his resignation—so much against his inclinations—may be obviated, so that although the Regiment lose his services—the country will not. At all events," Benson added, "we believe his patriotism and well known fighting qualities will not admit of his long remaining a civilian. Success to 'Capt. Jack' we say." John Porter made a more succinct comment on Nelson's departure: "We are all glad the 'old Mule' has left."[16]

When Captain Henry Hugaboom of Company K resigned on account of his health, declaring he could not stand the privations of camp life, some of his men were skeptical. "The Boys in our Company bought a sword and presented [it] to him last fall," George Newcomb recalled. "He made a short speech and said that he would stand by them untill it was wore up to the hilt Some seem to think that he was afraid there would be a chance to use it before long and he resigned on that account." In Newcomb's opinion, Hugaboom was a "perfect dead head. There is no fire in him he sits around like a stout bottle." The loss of Hugaboom turned out to be Company K's gain when Arthur Hotchkiss was commissioned captain and assigned to the command. "He appears to be a first rate fellow," Newcomb wrote of Hotchkiss, "and has made [things more] military about him in one hour than Captain Hugaboom had in a month." Six months later George Mason declared that Hotchkiss "is as fine a man as ever trod in boots and we all like him."[17]

Captain Thomas Donnelly of Company F was a drinking man, capable of consuming an entire canteen of whiskey (three pints) as a day's work, who did nothing to discourage alcoholic conviviality among his men. One day in February 1863 at the Falmouth camp, Donnelly doled out extra whiskey on top of the men's daily one gill ration. "There is some tolerable tight ones this evening," George Taylor recorded. "We came near 4 or 5 fights." About a month later, Taylor—then the company's first sergeant—blamed his lack of a promotion on Donnelly. "I am not in his favor," Taylor wrote. "I cannot condescend to flatter and crawl around any such Tinker Whiffet as he is. If we had an Honorable Captain, I should have been a Lieut since Jan 1st." According to Taylor, "I could today pass a better examination than Donnelly if he was obliged to depend on what he knows of military matters." Donnelly was at that time at home on a furlough, "in great glory probably, telling great stories and drinking much Whiskey with his friends," Taylor wrote. "We are getting along without him quite well." Not long after returning to the front, Donnelly resigned and returned home for good. "The boys of Company F are glad of it," William Charles reported. Before Donnelly left the regiment's camp near Kelly's Ford on the Rappahannock, the wagoner of Company D, Milton P. Burdick, borrowed some wax and nitric acid from Surgeon Van Aernam, and surreptitiously engraved an inscription onto Donnelly's sword, commending him for displaying heroic valor in resigning.[18]

Donnelly did not openly admit he had resigned on his return to Chautauqua County. "He tells some he has got a furlow of 4 months," Susan Griswold wrote. "He thought the summer climate would not agree with him but we do not believe he has got a furlow but [instead has] rezined." George Taylor asked his wife, "How do you like our Ex-Captain? Should you not think it a great loss to a Company to spare so great and good a commander as he is. If Ed Brown has the tavern yet, he must be acquainted with considerable of Tom's whiskey money."[19]

Thomas Donnelly was not the only officer of the regiment troubled by alcohol. As George Newcomb wrote the following passage, his handwriting got sloppier as he got drunker, and finally he abruptly stopped, to resume his letter the following day: "Well Ell I feel well now for our new [Second] Lieutenant [Salmon Beardsley] has just come in with a canteen of whiskey to wet his office And here comes our First Lieutenant [William Chapman] with another canteen so you see old woman we have got good officers in our company Our Lieu both are bully good fellows. . . . You must excuse me now for our officers are in here now calling all the men in here to take something to drink Well Wife if there is any officers in our Regt that I like it is our Lieutenants."[20] Whiskey was a major factor in the undoing of Henry Martin, who rose from private of Company I to captain of Company C. Martin was distinguished as the only member of the regiment who had attended the U.S. Military Academy at West Point (entering but not graduating with the Class of 1857). His alcoholic shenanigans became legendary in the regiment: he toasted his men with schnapps at every halt during a march; he was arrested after paying an inebriated call on the teetotaling General Howard; he declared that he had gotten "high enough" when he received his commission as captain, to the men's amusement at his choice of words; and he repeatedly tendered his resignation when he got particularly drunk. When Martin's formal resignation was accepted in August 1864, Major Lewis Warner wrote, "Glad he is going for he has long hung like a dead weight upon the regt demoralizing both Officers & men, both by his conversation and brutish habit."[21]

A situation that developed in Company F after Thomas Donnelly's departure hinted at the jealousies that could consume officers and mar esprit de corps. John Griswold noted that there were "plenty of Cattaraugus asperants" for all vacant offices, including the captaincy of the Chautauqua company. But ambitious Cattaraugus men notwithstanding, Griswold—as first lieutenant, the customary inheritor of the post—received the recommendation and commission as captain. Griswold was the type of officer who was not above carrying a sick soldier's musket and knapsack on a march. The company appreciated his paternal care, and early on had demonstrated its fondness for him by presenting him with a sword. "Lieut Griswold was thought every thing of by the Company and he was a good Commander as I want over me," Homer Ames wrote after Griswold was wounded and captured at Chancellorsville and First Lieutenant Dana Horton assumed command of Company F. "He done justice to them all and they all liked him well and they feel bad not to see him in comand of the Company but I am in hopes that he will come out all wright yet." After Griswold returned and resumed command, his nephew Milon Griswold wrote to the *Fredonia Censor*, "Our Captain . . . is worthy of the office he holds; and is loved and respected by all under his command. There is not a man in the Company but would do anything for him in their power. We are all right when he is with us. He would do anything in his power for us, and he is just the man for us. We will stand by him to the last."[22]

Available evidence indicates that John Griswold and Dana Horton enjoyed a friendly and respectful relationship. But some Company F men harbored negative feelings toward Horton and accused him of plotting against Griswold. According to Milon Griswold, "The boys in the company feel nice to think they have got the captain back again lieutenant Horton tried his best to get him thrown out of the service so he could get in [as] captain but he did not make it out quite." As for Horton, "The boys dont like him verry well," Milon wrote. "There is to much style about him for a soldier but the captain has got command of us again and we are all right now." The *Fredonia Censor* criticized Horton when it declared that Griswold "filled a high and responsible position in the 154th that could not be filled by his subordinate, which would prove apparent if we could have been within hearing distance and heard the very air echo and re-echo again with the loud huzzas that went up from every member of his company with but one single exception, on the return of their beloved Captain." Horton eventually succeeded Griswold as captain of Company F. He led the company at Gettysburg, where he was wounded, in the Tennessee campaigns, and in the Atlanta campaign up to New Hope Church, where he was wounded again. But he apparently never won the men's devotion. "Capt. D. P. Horton has resined," Sergeant Milton D. Scott reported in October 1864, two months after Horton was discharged. "Who cares for that," Scott added. "I dont for one."[23]

Not all of the original captains of the 154th were scamps like Jack Nelson and Tom Donnelly. Captains Dan Allen, Lewis Warner, and Harrison Cheney all received promotions, and Joseph Fay of Company E and Matthew Cheney of Company G both were admired and did good service. Fay "is a very nice man and well liked by all who know him," George Taylor observed. After Fay was captured at Gettysburg, Stephen Green wrote, "You cannot think how mutch he is missed by the co several times every day I hear some one here say I wish the Capt would come back and all of the rest of the absent ones. not onley in his company but all of the men in the Regt. speak greatly in his favor." In the postwar years, a veteran of Company G remembered Matthew Cheney as "brave, able, a martinet, [and a] very strict disciplinarian," and added that the "boys gave him an anonymous hint not to get in the way of their muskets in a fight." But his company realized the value of Cheney's unbending discipline. "He is the best officer in the whole line," Richard McCadden wrote of Cheney in February 1863. "The field officers are not much ahead of him. Our Co. is the best drilled in the Regt and it is called so by the field officers they can dust their garters you may bet." And Company G proved that proficiency on the drill field translated into steadiness on the battlefield. "When our Regt retreated it got scattered," McCadden wrote of Chancellorsville, "but our co kept together with the exceptions of three or four Our Capt was very cool in the action. Our Co remained on the field and all of the rest of the Regt was gon." Stragglers from other companies rallied to Cheney and his men, and together they fought with other units the following day before rejoining the 154th. Unfortunately, a wound received at Gettysburg removed Cheney from the regiment.[24]

Some officers who resigned relatively early in the regiment's service nevertheless retained the affection of their men. First Lieutenant Marshall O. Bond of Company D resigned in March 1863 to return to his home in Franklinville. "Our Boys . . . wanted to shake hands with me & bid me good by," Bond recorded in his diary prior to his departure. "So I went & bought A box of Cigars & passed them Around, & as they took my hand & bade me good by it made me think of the time that we had when we all left Franklinville."[25]

Two incidents involving regimental field and staff officers demonstrated the power of esprit de corps. One was precipitated when Edgar Shannon, former sergeant of Company B, was mustered in as first lieutenant and quartermaster in March 1864, much to the aggravation of Quartermaster Sergeant Newton "Dell" Chaffee, who had coveted and politicked for the post. "The beauty of this thing," Chaffee griped to a friend, "[is that] I have to do his work and learn him. and you know in the Army we have no right to say our soal is our own." Chaffee blamed his predicament on a lack of political influence. "It is well known that I am from the wrong part of our County," he wrote. But Marcellus Darling reported that Chaffee had pulled all the political strings he could, to no avail. Darling, who knew both men well, heartily approved of Shannon's elevation over Chaffee. "I am glad to see Edgar come up," Darling wrote, "and the best thing is he is put in over Dell Chaffee, who has been working his best and all of his friends at home also, to get him promoted. it appears that there is some [who] think there was no one come from Leon only Dell Chaffee and that he is the only one of importance from there. if he had never had any better chance than common Leon boys he would have been a Doehead in fact he does not lack much of it now." Shannon—who had expected Chaffee to receive the post and had written, "I hope he will get it"—did what he could to assuage his townsman's hurt feelings. But in describing the situation to his girlfriend, Shannon could not help but express some giddy pride in his new role as an officer:

I am now fairly situated in my new position & everything is going on swimmingly. . . . Del is with me & we have some gay times, play chess & keep something going most of the time. he felt hurt to think that I was put over him when he knew more about the business than I did but then it was no more than natural. I shall soon understand it as well as he does, may be better. the Col. did not want him Qm. because he thought he did not have go ahead enough to him. It is a wonder to me that he did not get it for all the influential men of Cattaraugus were to work for him. . . . It seems however that it made no difference. [I] have got a smart horse & most [of] a new set a clothes. have got the straps on my coat. wouldn't you like to see them on a greeny like me. I tell you they look grand. I'll get my profile taken when I get my whole suit & give you the nicest one.[26]

Any antagonism Chaffee felt toward Shannon melted away as the two worked together during the Atlanta campaign, and after the city's fall, Shannon, Chaffee, and Marcellus Darling lived together in friendship and comfort in an abandoned house, reading newspapers and novels, playing cards, and enjoying meals prepared by Shannon's waiter. Chaffee and Shannon, their differences behind them, shared a four-poster bed so immense that "when Del get to the outside I cannot find him," Shannon reported. "[I] have to hallo to keep up a conversation." Esprit de corps had smoothed the ruffled feelings.[27]

The resignation in November 1862 of the regiment's original major, Samuel G. Love, initiated a challenge to esprit in the 154th New York. Colonel Jones wrote to the New York State adjutant general recommending Dan Allen for the vacancy, assigned Allen to the rank, and placed him on duty as such. While Jones and the rest of the regiment waited for Allen's routine promotion to be approved, they received a great surprise when a stranger, Jacob H. Ten Eyck, scion of a blue-blooded Albany family and former captain of the 3rd New York Infantry, arrived in camp bearing a commission as major of the 154th. There was nothing the stunned regiment could do to prevent Ten Eyck from being mustered in at his new rank.

Within days of his arrival at Falmouth, Ten Eyck was handed a letter signed by every officer on duty with the regiment. In polite but firm language, the letter requested that Ten Eyck resign his commission for three reasons. First, Ten Eyck was a total stranger to the regiment, assigned in disregard of "a just right to select our own officers." Second, Dan Allen had been recommended for the post through proper channels and assigned to its duty, as had officers to other grades as a result, "and we believe them all fully competent and worthy of filling these positions." Third, the filling of vacancies from outside the regiment was "destructive of harmonious action, and that incentive to emulation among the officers and men of the command which is of such vital importance. If men are to look outside of their Regt. for promotion and among politicians instead of within and among soldiers, the incentive to discipline and duty are gone." Colonel Jones added a blunt endorsement to the letter, condemning Ten Eyck's political patrons for an act "dishonorable to them and highly injurious to the service," and strongly suggesting that Ten Eyck accede to the officers' request "before other and more effective means are resorted to."

Ten Eyck was no fool, and eight days after his muster-in, he submitted his resignation to Colonel Jones, "for the reason that it is not agreeable to the officers that I remain with the regiment." Shortly thereafter, Dan Allen received his commission and was mustered in as major, and all was well in the regimental world.[28]

In the coming months, four other outsiders were commissioned as officers of the 154th. Two were never mustered. One was mustered strictly as a courtesy to General Adolph von Steinwehr, so he could join the general's staff as a topographical engineer. The final outsider, a former army medical cadet named George H. Bosley, joined the regiment as assistant surgeon at Savannah in January 1865 and served with the 154th to the close of the war, performing a vital service well and consequently being accepted as a comrade.[29]

A primary task of commissioned officers was the enforcement of discipline, including supervising the sanitary and health conditions of the men, insuring adherence to military rules and regulations, and issuing punishments when necessary. Action at the company level and by regimental courts-martial adjudicated cases of lesser infractions; more serious offenses were tried by general courts-martial at the brigade or division levels. Regiments were inspected on a regular basis and rated as to the quality of their discipline (in addition to their instruction, military appearance, arms, accoutrements, and clothing). "Good leadership meant effective discipline, and effective discipline usually spelled high morale," Bell Irvin Wiley wrote in his landmark study of Union soldiers. For a regiment to enjoy good esprit de corps, its officers had to be firm but fair enforcers of discipline.[30]

An incident that occurred at Camp Brown in Jamestown on the night of September 27, 1862, demonstrated that the officers of the 154th New York had their work cut out for them in disciplining the regiment. Some fifteen or twenty prisoners, confined to the camp guardhouse for running the guard, raised a ruckus that culminated in a mass breakout and the burning of the guardhouse to ashes. "I suppose they had a gay time," the innocent Ira Wood wrote during the brief tightening of discipline in the aftermath of the riot, "But we have got to suffer for it. . . . I think it is hard to suffer for the conduct of others but it is so." Breaches of discipline by some, the regiment learned, could have an effect on all.[31]

Never again did such anarchy sweep the regiment. On the many successive bimonthly muster rolls, inspection officers almost always rated discipline in the various companies as good, with occasional ratings of fair or excellent. But despite the overall satisfactory quality of the regiment's discipline, a host of men were arrested during the regiment's service for a variety of infractions, ranging from the minor—having candles lit after taps—to the most serious—desertion. An early disciplinary crackdown occurred during the movement to Thoroughfare Gap in November 1862, when roll was called hourly for several days in a row to prevent plundering. Absentees were punished by carrying a fence rail for eight hours, or standing guard for twelve-hour shifts wearing a knapsack loaded with stone and toting a musket on each shoulder. Several men were arrested for unauthorized foraging during the regiment's stay at Kelly's Ford in April 1863. They were tried by drum-head court-martial. As punishment, the noncommissioned officers were reduced to the ranks, and all of the guilty parties were docked one month's pay. Private Albert E. Hall of Company C was also sentenced to wear a board across his back painted with the word "Marauder."[32]

Insubordination was a common offense. A prime example was offered by Corporal Horatio E. Andrews of Company D. Watching his comrades build a corduroy road in the Virginia mud, Andrews stood half-drunk with his hands in his pockets. A staff officer ordered him to grab hold of a log and help move it. "Maybe you don't know whom you are talking to," Andrews haughtily replied as he thrust his hands deeper into his pockets for emphasis. "I am Corporal Andrews of the 154th New York Volunteers!" Such impertinence brought a range of responses. When Andrew Blood spoke "a little saucy" to Captain Leonard Saxton, he was placed under arrest for two days and released after a talk with Saxton. Private Benjamin Michle of Company G found himself at the other end of the punishment scale. Captain Matthew Cheney caught Michle asleep at his picket post one night and took his musket from him. The following morning, Michle made some impudent remarks to Cheney in the presence of the company, and the captain immediately had him bucked and gagged on the spot. While sitting on the ground, Michle's hands were tied at the wrists and pulled over his bent knees, a stick or musket barrel was inserted between his arms and legs, rendering him immobile, a bayonet or stick was tied in his mouth, and he was left to suffer for his insolence.[33]

Most penalties for insubordination fell somewhere between those two extremes of leniency and harsh physical punishment. First Sergeant William Clark of Company B was reduced to private for insubordination and neglect of duty, with a consequent drastic reduction in his pay, but nevertheless received subsequent promotions back to first sergeant and then to adjutant and captain. When Private Wallace Cole of Company I was ordered to turn out for fatigue duty by Sergeant Alonzo A. Casler of Company A, Cole responded by exclaiming, "By God, I will not until I get some hardtack." A regimental court-martial composed of three officers, finding Cole guilty of disobedience of orders and conduct prejudicial to good order and military discipline, sentenced him to half pay for four months and stopped his whiskey ration for a month.[34]

Occasionally an insubordinate soldier found himself hauled before a general court-martial. Joseph Cullen was chopping a log in the camp of the 29th New York near Stafford Court House when a lieutenant of that regiment ordered him to stop or face arrest. "I don't care for your arrest," Cullen belligerently replied. "I shit on your arrest." The lieutenant summoned the guard, and when Cullen swung his ax at them, he was forcibly subdued. He gave an alias when arrested, but his true identity was soon ascertained. Found guilty by a court-martial a month later, Cullen was condemned to three months of hard labor under the charge of a regimental guard, and kept in solitary confinement on bread and water for the first and last five days of his sentence.[35]

Asahel "Beauregard" Hollister was found asleep at his picket post at

Bridgeport, Alabama, in October 1863. When he was awakened by the corporal of the guard, Hollister announced that he would be damned if he got up until he was ready. At Hollister's general court-martial, Lieutenant Winfield Cameron testified in his behalf, alleging that the defendant was of below average intelligence, unable to understand his duties as a soldier, and "almost incapable of distinguishing between right and wrong." "When he first came out," Cameron stated, "his company officers punished him at different times for neglect of duty and insolence, but finally gave him up as hopeless, and allowed him to say and do pretty much what he pleased. From my acquaintance with him I believe him to be what is called half witted." The court found Hollister guilty of sleeping on post and disobedience of orders, but decided he was "not possessed of sufficient mental capacity to render him criminally responsible for his acts," and recommended that he be discharged. But "Beauregard" returned to duty and was with the regiment at its muster-out.[36]

Lieutenant Colonel Lewis Warner apparently had an ability to pacify rambunctious soldiers. When news reached the regiment in North Carolina in April 1865 of the fall of Richmond, Company D's cook, Oziah Adams, responded to the glad tidings by getting drunk and raising a ruckus, whooping loudly, throwing tin plates, and attracting a crowd of the boys. Ordered to quiet down by Captain Alfred Benson, Adams approached the officer as if to whisper to him, but instead shouted as loud as he could into Benson's ear. The angry captain stalked off, vowing to have Colonel Warner attend to Adams. Soon Warner slipped unnoticed into Adams's audience. After watching his tomfoolery for a while the colonel said, "Adams, you seem to be making a good deal of muss." "I guess not," Adams saucily replied. "I think you are," Warner responded, "and if you don't attend to your business I'll attend to you." Adams leaned back, folded his arms, and said to the crowd, "Well, if that old Colonel isn't a hard nut I'll be damned." Warner laughed and walked away, leaving a subdued Adams behind.[37]

Squabbles between soldiers were settled in a quiet way at the company level. When Barzilla Merrill had his tent mate Bornt Shelmadine arrested and tried for making an apparently slanderous "false statement," the court convened by Company K released Shelmadine "with a charge to be verry careful what he said after this." The incident apparently did not diminish the two's friendship. When members of Company D accused Sergeant George G.

Hopkins of Company G of stealing firewood at Savannah in January 1865, a jury composed of members of Company I tried the case. They found the defendant guilty as charged, and presiding judge Francis Bowen sentenced Hopkins to three tossings in a blanket.[38]

Officers were not immune to disciplinary difficulties. While in command of a picket outpost in Lookout Valley in March 1864, First Lieutenant Clinton L. Barnhart of Company E left the position to visit a private dwelling and get dinner. Barnhart pled guilty to a charge of neglect of duty in a general court-martial, and was sentenced to a reprimand by Colonel Jones. Captain Harrison Cheney was tried by a military commission in Washington in September 1863 on a charge of absence without leave. Cheney testified that after his capture at Gettysburg he escaped from the Confederates and reached the Union lines "out of money, nearly naked and not well," so he returned home to recuperate. After finally hearing from the regiment, he returned to the front without a pass or a surgeon's certificate. The commission decided he should be dismissed from the service, and the sentence was approved by General Howard and Secretary of War Edwin M. Stanton. Only through the intercession of Colonel Jones, who pleaded Cheney's case directly to Stanton, was Cheney's dismissal revoked.[39]

Stephen Green was one of several members of the 154th who went absent without leave from the parole camp at Annapolis to return home for a brief visit. After he was arrested and returned to the regiment, Green scoffed at the idea that he would be punished. "In order to punish or take pay from me they have to Court martial me and I no that will never be done," he wrote. "The Officers Commanding the Company or Regiment would as soon think of giveing me a furlow for two years or during the war." Green was right; he was never punished for his transgression. Other members of the regiment charged with absence without leave were not so fortunate, and were tried by general courts-martial. Privates Martin Hall, William Merrell, and Wellman Nichols of Company C were so charged, tried, and found guilty. The three received typical sentences: to forfeit pay and allowances due during their absence, and pay expenses incurred in their arrest and return to the regiment. Merrell was also ordered to perform two hours of knapsack drill daily for three weeks.[40]

The harshest penalties were meted out to convicted deserters. Although desertion was a capital offense, only a small percentage of Union army deserters were put to death, and none from the 154th New York met that fate. More typical was the punishment given to Hiram and Spencer Kelly, brothers and privates of Company H, who deserted together in Maryland on July 9, 1863, during the return march from Gettysburg. The two were apprehended by a provost marshal, returned to the regiment at an expense of $33.75 each, and kept under guard at the 154th's camp in Lookout Valley. At a general court-martial in January 1864, the brothers pleaded guilty to the charge of desertion. They were sentenced to forfeit all pay and allowances due during their absence, to pay the expense of their arrest and return to the regiment, and to be confined at hard labor, with ball and chain, for the remainder of their terms of enlistment—Hiram at half-pay and Spencer without pay. Spencer Kelly was also charged with "misbehavior before the enemy," specifically "shamefully abandoning his Company and Regiment" at the Battle of Gettysburg, but was found not guilty of that charge. Ordered to a military prison at Nashville, the Kellys instead were put to work under the supervision of the brigade provost marshal.

Something then went awry and the brothers were brought before another court-martial on the same desertion charges in November 1864; their plea for dismissal because of the previous trial was denied because no record of the first court-martial was located. Found guilty for the second time, the Kellys received the same sentence as before, with an additional penalty: they would serve an extra five months and ten days—the amount of time they were gone from the regiment—after the expiration of their original term of enlistment.

For the rest of the war, Hiram and Spencer Kelly toiled for the brigade provost marshal, barred from the regiment for their misdeed. Two days before the 154th was mustered out, they were transferred to another regiment to complete their sentence. The brothers had shown scorn for esprit de corps by deserting. Banishment from the regiment was their ultimate lot.[41]

CHAPTER 10

Morale and Regimental Pride

The term esprit de corps is sometimes used as a synonym for morale. But while esprit de corps specifically refers to the spirit of loyalty and pride among the members of a group, morale generally signifies the psychological state of an individual or group in reaction to current states of affairs. Esprit reflected Civil War soldiers' devotion to their regiments. Morale reflected their assessments of military, political, and home front matters. In essence, morale measured the confidence bred of well-being and victory, and it rose and fell in reaction to changing situations. Soldiers who were adequately fed, clad, and sheltered, serving in regiments under efficient officers and tight discipline as part of an undefeated army, generally enjoyed good morale. Their counterparts, poorly provisioned or equipped, drifting under lax discipline and inept officers, faltering after battlefield setbacks, suffered from poor morale. Although by definition different factors of soldier life, morale and esprit de corps often intersected. While esprit could remain intact during periods of low morale and defeat, it naturally strengthened during times of high morale and military success. The confident regiment was much more likely to be a proud regiment—and a victorious regiment.

As in other regiments of North and South, morale ebbed and flowed in the 154th New York in response to events. Some of the men had a confident—even cocky—attitude as they embarked on their great adventure. "We are all well & expect to leave for Dixie and then the rebels will catch H–l," Private William H. Keyes of Company C wrote from Camp Brown in Jamestown before the regiment departed for the front. "I have been led to say in my own mind Who wouldn't be a soldier?" Andrew Blood wrote during the train trip to Washington, responding to the cheers of crowds along the route. John Griswold noted during the journey, "Myself and the rest of the boys are all well and in good spirits." But he also noted warring emotions among the boys of Company F. "In moments of relaxation from conversation or other amusements," Griswold wrote, "a shade of sadness could be seen overshadowing the countenance a sure indication that the thoughts of home and loved ones wer crowding on the mind to be banished onely by new scenes constantly attracting our attention and exciting admiration."[1]

Impressed by the vast Federal martial array surrounding Camp Seward, Barzilla Merrill predicted the demise of the Confederacy. "I think as near as I can judge from what I can see the Cesesh is sick and wont live many months," he wrote. "I think there is men enough to berry the creature out right and have his funeral preached." Some of the men seemed lighthearted about their new venture. "We lead as happy lives as possible," Charles Abell wrote. For his part, Eason Bull declared, "I [am] no more afraid of the rebels than I am of a bear or that wolf out in Michigan. . . . This soldering aint so bad after all." But to other men, concerns multiplied on reaching the front. "The boys . . . are in tolerably good spirits," John Griswold wrote, "but most of them think that if they wer out of this they could not be caught again but they will probably get used to it and like it better by & by." In the opinion of George Newcomb, "If our Rulers would let the Soldiers old and new decide this contest they would settle it up without any more fighting." After getting a look at war-torn veteran regiments during a review at Fairfax Court House, Lewis Warner pondered, "How long ere the 154th Regiment will be reduced to the same condition? Of the 950 men who left Cattaraugus will not more than one in four be on hand to answer to their names when we are mustered out of the service, and will I be among that number? These were questions which came up for solution in my mind as we marched past these war stained veterans."[2]

Eason Bull's confidence remained undiminished when the regiment marched to Thoroughfare Gap. "I am tough as a bull," he bragged. "I can whip the whole South alright." But other soldiers voiced doubts as they penetrated deeper into Virginia. "The people at home all wish that the war would close," James Emmons wrote, "but I can tell you they do not wish so half as much as the soldiers dose they think that they have seen enough of it all of them the new troops as well as the old ones."[3]

Morale plummeted when the regiment reached the dispirited Army of the Potomac at Falmouth in the aftermath of the disastrous Fredericksburg defeat. The despondency weighing on the rest of the army spread through the 154th like a damp fog. "Military matters look dark for the present," Henry Van Aernam wrote in an understatement, "—and success if at all in the distant future." Emory Sweetland observed, "The army are verry much discouraged by the recent events. the feeling in the army is verry strongly in favor of making a compromise with the rebs & having peace in some way." George Newcomb concurred: "All of the old soldiers are disheartened and tired of this war and it is so with the new troops," he wrote. "All are home sick and would be glad to get home Another such defeat as we had here I believe our men would throw down their arms and go home." Amos Humiston noted that a visiting hometown veteran soldier "curses this war with the rest of us we do not like the way things are managed we are ready to fight when it will amount to some thing but the battle at this place had done a great deal to cool the patriotism of the troops as a general thing."[4]

Emory Sweetland likewise noted, "There is a verry strong & rapidly increasing feeling in the army in favor of peace. you at home know but little about this feeling or the strength of it. I hear many curses about this war every day by Officers & men." Yet Sweetland attempted to keep his own morale high, knowing that the consequences of poor individual morale could be dire. "My faith is still strong that I shall live to come home to my family," he wrote. "I do not allow myself to have the dumps I find from what I have seen if a man realy gets the dumps he stands a pretty good chance of dying."[5]

Barzilla Merrill engaged in some solemn introspection in a lengthy letter to his wife, Ruba, written on New Year's Day 1863: "I love my country and its govornment and I feel like weeping over the deplorable condition that we as a nation are in this present new years morning. . . . Unless God by his almighty power interposes we are lost lost as a nation I never was more disappointed in my life than I was when I came down here and see how this thing [is] run so far. . . . The souldiers are becoming discouraged and dishartened I have heard men that have been in all through the service say that they were sick and discouraged and that they did not never want to go in another battle."[6]

And yet, in another passage written the same day, Merrill stated the regiment was determined to persevere, despite the poor morale. "There is one thing that I beleave our regiment as far as I know are agreed in," he wrote, "that is to see the war close so that they can go home but we have got on the harnes and we are going to keep it on until we see the thing through and no whining."[7]

When Joseph Hooker took command of the Army of the Potomac in January 1863 and administered reforms ranging from rations of fresh-baked bread to the granting of furloughs, morale rebounded throughout the army. Writing in retrospect of Hooker's tenure, Henry Van Aernam noted, "While in command of the army he very much improved the discipline and *morale* of the army and very essentially improved the 'outer man' and conditions of the soldiers generally." "The army is in the best health & spirits that I have ever seen it," Emory Sweetland stated less than a month into Hooker's regime. He continued, "The general opinion here is that we shall end the war this spring." "There seems to be a better feeling in the army than there was right after the [Fredericksburg] battle," Barzilla Merrill reported, citing "not so much falt finding among the souldiers." James Quilliam likewise noted the general optimism. "I think that there is a better prospect of the war being closed this sumer than ever," he wrote, "and there is a general expectation amung the army that they will be to home nex wenter."[8]

Spirits in the 154th reflected those of the army as a whole. Richard McCadden wrote that the regiment had been depleted by almost half since it left Jamestown, "but what is left is of the right stripe and as tough as an ox." According to Alanson Crosby, "The Regiment is rapidly becoming proficient in drill and discipline, and if any fighting is to be done, the boys would be happy to participate. There has not existed so cheerful a spirit among them since we came down here as now exists. You may depend on it, they will reflect credit and honor to the Counties that sent them here if they have an opportunity." Alfred Benson also indicated that the regiment was ready— even eager—to face combat. "Here [in Camp John Manley] we have spent the most agreeable part of our soldier life: yet we do not regret to leave it, for we believe that the coming campaign will witness the final act in the ghastly drama of Secession, and although we do not claim to be inordinately blood-thirsty, we all feel a keen desire to be 'in at the death.' Yes, we believe the days of the Rebellion are 'few and full of trouble.' "[9]

Writing from Camp John Manley, Thomas Aldrich voiced a similar determination and bravado, fueled by high morale: "I dont care much where we go if it only helps the government to put down this cursed rebellion I would not give a snap to get out of this untill our country is once more united in the bonds of piece and brotherly love I came down here to protect the government in this her time of peril and I mean to stand by her to the last if fall she must I go with her but I do not prophisy any such result I think this springs campaign will settle the question we have them on all sides and if we do not succeed it will not be the fault of the brave soldiers but their leaders."[10]

Of course, high spirits were easily maintained in a safe and comfortable winter camp. As Alansing Wyant wrote, "Times is good hear plenty to do & enough to do it the mashene seems to run about as it has. . . . The folks is all well here [and having] pleanty of fun." George Newcomb summed up the prevailing mood as April 1863 opened. "Everything remains quiet here," he wrote. "The Boys are all feeling well and seem to enjoy themselves first rate We have been here in camp two months the longest we have staid in one camp We have had easy times here lived well and are growing fat and lazy I should hardly know how to go to work on a farm now I think I would have to get rid of some of my hard tack fat before I could do much hard labor."[11]

Then came the disaster at Chancellorsville. As he watched retreating troops fill the roads and fields on their way to the Rappahannock fords after the battle, Horace Smith declared, "A more disheartened set of fellows I never saw, all because we were ordered to retreat. it is thought by most of the troops that we could [have] held our position easily. this retreat has a very bad effect on the army." After returning to Camp John Manley, Henry Van Aernam recalled the moment he realized the army was retreating across the river. "I never felt so depressed in my life as I did when that unwelcome conclusion was forced on me. . . . Nearly four weeks ago we left this camp with high hopes of a successful campaign—and here we are again not having suffered defeat—yet certainly not successful." He added, "I have lived a sad and eventful age in that short time which I pray I may never experience again."[12]

The army-wide depression over the retreat was accentuated in the regiment by its severe losses in the battle. "Our old camp looks like a deserted village," Horace Smith observed. "Almost half the boys that left here with us 4 weeks ago do not return with us. many of them I fear lay on that bloody field yet unburied. God only knows where the rest are. . . . There is not tents and blankets enough to cover 1/4 [of] the shanties where we have had many a good time with each other, these are the fortunes of war." Considering the losses, Homer Ames expressed a grimly pragmatic outlook. "The boys all feel downhearted to see so menny of our comrades gone," he wrote, "but we have to look on the best side and hope for the best for it may be our turn next."[13]

The spirit of the soldiers was resilient, however, and when rumors of a northward Confederate thrust circulated early in June 1863, morale rose once again. "I have no idea what is up now, but it may be the rebs are putting their threats of an offensive movement on their part into execution," wrote Dwight Moore. "If so we shall probably have some work to do for a short time. but if they think Hookers army is so weak and demoralized he will not be able to offer them much resistance, they are grandly mistaken as they will find out when they attempt to cross the Rappahannock." While uncertainty reigned regarding the enemy's movements, the usual anxiety was felt. "The agony of the suspense and the suppressed excitement in such a time as this is really more painful and trying than the storm of the battlefields," Henry Van Aernam complained. When the regiment reached Maryland in its race after the Confederates, however, Alansing Wyant eagerly anticipated a decisive battle. "I have once [more] set my foot on free soil & things have changed so fast that I am quite anxious to see the war goe on," he wrote. "Perhaps they will be a little fight in a few days we are bound to make the rebs hunt there holes or do wors . . . so we can get through with this wicked war."[14]

When the Confederates escaped unmolested across the Potomac River after their defeat at the Battle of Gettysburg, Surgeon Van Aernam described the regiment's bitter disappointment: "When we were chasing the rebs, the boys, although barefooted and ragged and half fed, were cheerful on their forced marches, but today they feel chagrined and humbugged. They are silent and morose and what little they say is damning the foolishness and shortsightedness of the officers. They are right for they have endured everything, braved everything for the sake of success, and success bountiful and lasting was within their grasp—but lost by the imbecility of commandry. Our army is an anomaly—it is an army of Lions commanded by jackasses!"[15]

The decimating losses suffered at Gettysburg cast gloom over the survivors. "Our Regt made a small show," Stephen Green wrote after a dress parade in August 1863. "If our Capt had went out last winter with as few men [as survive] he would have ben ashamed of his company." "There are now 151 in our Regiment, officers and men all told," Surgeon Van Aernam wrote from Alexandria the following month. "They are encamped on the river bank just above the city and they are really quite well situated and I hope they may remain here for sometime as they need rest after the terrible ordeal they have passed through." The men found their duty escorting conscripts from Alexandria to the front to be somewhat disagreeable, but as George Mason noted, "It is not as hard as being out front." Furthermore, the men enjoyed camping in large, conical Sibley tents, and relished considerable freedom in Alexandria. "This is the best camp we were ever in," Mason declared. "We have the largest tent and all of our company is in one tent, only 8 men. We have lots of fun. In the town we go where we please, that is, we wear a badge on our hat that passes us anywhere—our regiment and the 134[th New York]."[16]

The Alexandria interlude ended with the regiment's transfer by rail to the west. Opinions were divided regarding the move. "It was a rather sore disappointment to us to leave Alexandria," John Griswold wrote. "We wer flatering ourselves that we should stay thare sometime but it does not seem to [be] our fortune to get an easy berth any length of time." Richard McCadden, on the other hand, described the transfer as "a change which I think the boys are all well pleased with." The week-long railroad trip was uncomfortable and tiring, but the men enjoyed the support they received from patriotic citizens along the route. After the successful drive from Bridgeport to Lookout Valley to open the Cracker Line, McCadden reported, "We are having verry good times here now and what is better it begins to look as if the war was on its last legs for I hardly think they can hold out much longer." Morale continued to climb after the triumph at Chattanooga. "Our record since [coming] here is a proud one," Henry Van Aernam declared. As 1864 dawned, morale was high and expectations for the coming campaign season were optimistic. Surgeon Van Aernam spoke for the veteran soldiers: "These men know what *war* is from a terrible experience—they know the toil and weariness of long marches, the cold and hunger and hardships of eventful campaigns—the heart aches of the loved ones at home and the blood and terrors of the battlefield—yet they will endure all and brave all for the cause of the Government and they *will* succeed. One more campaign and the war is over—for they [the Confederates] are now driven to their last extremity— the soldiers all see it—and all want to be in at the 'death,' and all I think who remain till June will be!"[17]

Voices from the ranks echoed the surgeon's comments. "I am feeling well [and] do not get homesick a bit but [am] very anxious to have the war end," Philo Markham wrote. He continued, "I am full of hope and believe the rebelion will yeald still I can stay the whole three years rather than to come home till the war is ended that is I want to see the end of the war worse than I want to come home." Meanwhile, life in winter camp at Lookout Valley afforded contentment. "We have erected comfortable Quarters and get plenty of rations and of course practice high and aristocratic living," Martin Bushnell declared to a friend. "We are very refined in Stile and manners as it is of course necessary for Soldiers to be. I hope that my brief description of our living will not make you envy me my comfort." He added, "I am thinking that I shall be very rusty if I live to get home in regard to literary matters, but I guess I will know how to *Shoulder Arms* & *right-face*. Well all right, my duty is here and let it be performed here."[18]

Some of the soldiers dreaded the upcoming spring campaign. "Soldiering goes very well with me & I with that while we are in camp & have plenty to eat," Charles Allen recorded. "But when it comes to marching and fighting, I had rather be counted out." Emory Sweetland wrote, "I some times grow almost heart sick when I think of the great battles that are soon to take place & of the thousands of widows & orphans that will be made God bless the right & subdue our enemies."[19]

Overlooking such misgivings, Richard McCadden proclaimed, "The boys are all feeling fine & gay," when orders were received to embark on the road to Atlanta. As the grueling campaign progressed, Major Lewis Warner reported on the men's morale in his dispatches to the *Olean Times*. "Our men have been for six days constantly under fire, and the want of sleep is telling upon their health," he wrote on June 1. "Their spirits are, however, good, and they are ready for what may occur." On June 21, Warner sent another update: "This campaign has been a trying one to the physical powers of the men. We have now had seven weeks of constant marching, digging, bushwhacking and some fair fighting, with an accompaniment of heat, dust, rain and mud, especially the two last. . . . Our progress, though sure, is slow, and it may be many weeks ere the spires of Atlanta will glisten before our eager gaze. But be the time long or short, we are bound to win in the end. Our boys are in the best of spirits and sanguine of success."[20]

Pursuing the retreating Confederates deeper into Georgia bolstered the soldiers' morale. "We are as well as could be expected," Colonel Patrick Jones reported to the *Cattaraugus Freeman* on June 24; "don't complain since we are drubbing them up, and driving them splendidly as we move on." Describing yet another pursuit of the enemy on July 3, Major Warner wrote, "Our boys were in the best of spirits, and all eager to be in the advance guard. Whenever or wherever there is a chance to bag game the 154th needs no urging." Four days after the Battle of Peach Tree Creek, on July 24, Surgeon Van Aernam observed, "Our folks are confident of success—considering the fall of Atlanta only a question of *time*." During the siege of the city, Charles Abell recognized an anniversary. "It is 2 years tomorrow since I first enlisted to serve my country," he wrote on August 21. "I would not give my wages for the experience I have had and some of it will be of great value to me when I return home."[21]

When Atlanta fell, Emory Sweetland conveyed the soldiers' elation in a letter home. "Hurrah! Atlanta is ours at last," he wrote. "The Glorious old Star Corps had the honor of taking the citty at last & my Division was the first (by about 15 minutes) to raise the flag in this, the commercial capitol of the Confederacy. . . . As we marched in our regt. sang the song Down with the traitors & up with the stars & the band played Yankee Doodle." Morale remained high during Sherman's epic marches through Georgia and the Carolinas. During the rest at Savannah between the two campaigns, Private Almon Deforest Reed of Company G declared, "If we have as good a time on this [upcoming march] As we Did on the other I Shall be Satisfied."[22]

The regiment was in North Carolina when the war ended. Edgar Shannon recorded the reaction when tidings arrived of the fall of Richmond. "When we got the news we . . . formed into a line of fight right around General [Patrick] Jones and gave three cheers for the unity & then three for Gen. Jones, three for the old army of the Potomac to which we used to belong then we all went home, & some felt so well they got drunk." Anticipating the end of the regiment's three-year term of service, Shannon added, "*Six months more & the old one hundred & fifty fourth will come home & then I bet Cattaraugus Co. will be a live place for a while.*" But the exultation of victory was tempered by knowledge of its cost. As Emory Sweetland put it, "There has been a long night of deaths & desolation to our beloved country which (Thanks be to our Heavenly Father) is now rapidly giving away & the war worn & weary soldiers can now see the dawning of peace & better days."[23]

At Camp John Manley during the late winter and early spring of 1863, members of the regiment discovered that the German soldiers of their brigade had a shortage of coffee, of which they were extremely fond, and a surplus of hardtack, which they did not particularly care for. The situation was the opposite in the 154th. An extensive trade soon developed, with the 154th boys trading their extra coffee for the coveted hardtack. Everything was on the up and up until some unscrupulous members of the regiment hatched a plan to get the best of the bargain. They saved their used coffee grounds, carefully dried and bagged them, and traded them to the Germans for good hardtack. On tasting the resulting weak brew, the Germans quickly saw through the ruse. "They immediately named us the 'hardtacks,'" Charles McKay later recalled. "When we passed their camp either singly or in a body they would turn out and yell, 'Hardtacks!' as loud as their lungs would allow." In response, the 154th boys would shout, "Coffee!"[24]

There were variations in the banter between the western New Yorkers and the Germans. "The 154 Regt is called the hard tack regt and we named the 73 [Pennsylvania] Regt [the] Whiskey Regt," Martin Champlin wrote. According to George Newcomb, the name-calling had an edge of ethnic prejudice to it. "The Dutch Regts in our Brigade call our Regt the hard tack Regt and we call them the sour crout Regiments," Newcomb wrote. "They are all dutch in our Brigade except our Regt and they do not like us verry well We can hardly get any water to use but what some Dutchman has washed his ass in it."[25]

The regiment had gained a name for itself, facetious though it was, and the Hardtack moniker stuck for the rest of the war and beyond. "I have always suspected that they [the Germans] applied this title to us as a sort of reproach," McKay mused, "thereby intimating that we were in some way hard customers." In fact, the army-wide reputation of the ubiquitous cracker was one of toughness. Writing to his parents, George Taylor described hardtack as "a little softer than cast iron. It is in fact ship biscuit; you know how hard they are." Dwight Moore informed his mother, "Each of us take a cup of coffee and break our biscuit into it (for you know they have to be soaked before they can be eaten by any one who has not the strength of an elephant in their jaws.)" George Newcomb complained, "I have lost another one of my teeth the last double tooth on my under jaw so it is hard work for me to eat their damed hard tacks." Rock-hard and unyielding, a hardtack was not a bad metaphor for a soldier. But soldiers, like hardtack, could be broken. Doing duty with the corps wagon train after the Battle of Peach Tree Creek, Charles Abell wrote, "One of the Regt who is with me here just reports another of the old Hardtack regt sent to his final account by the cursed rebels."[26]

A rakish regimental nickname, a sure manifestation of esprit de corps, was one of many expressions of regimental pride. The soldiers relished bragging about the Hardtack Regiment's accomplishments. After a review of their division by General Hooker near Stafford Court House in February 1863, members of the 154th proudly described the occasion. "Our officers told us that we done the best that day that we ever did and I think so my self for we had good music [to march to] and we were pleased to see our commander," James Washburn wrote. He continued, "It was as fine a time as we have had since we came in Old Virginia." James Emmons noted, "Our regt was the first on the field and the general told our Col that we don as well in our movements as the Old regts did."

Marching in review lost its luster with repetition, but the regiment's final parade was the most glorious of all. John Langhans described the march of Sherman's army through the avenues of Washington in the Grand Review of May 24, 1865. "It was a grate time," he informed his brother. "I wish you could have seen us that day, there were a good maney people in the city. the sidewalks, trees and housetops on the street through which we marched were crowded full, the people gave us a hearty wellcome as we past through the street, such spatting of hands such waveing of handkerchifs and such cheering as they made I never heard before the Ladies had prepared all kinds of flours which they gave to us as we past them."[27]

Music was a constant presence in the army. The 154th New York never had a band, but the company buglers, fifers, and drummers were organized into a regimental drum corps, whose camp duty calls regulated the soldiers' daily lives. After some initial musical stumbling—on first hearing them, Colonel Jones ordered the musicians to practice for two hours every morning—the drum corps coalesced, and the musicians eventually expressed pride in their accomplishments. "The Drum Corps is commanded by [Principal Musicians] Orville Bishop and Silas W. Bunce, and numbers 12 members," wrote drummer Orlando White from the 154th's winter camp in Lookout

Valley in March 1864. "It is the best one in the 11th Corps, and has been complimented by Gen. Howard several times."[28]

Regimental pride was evident from the beginning. No sooner had the 154th arrived in Virginia than the soldiers were sending home letters written on custom stationery featuring a woodcut of the U.S. Capitol and a printed heading, "Headquarters 154th Reg't N. York Vols., Col. A. G. Rice, Company." During the 154th's first month in Virginia, Thomas Aldrich was confident enough to declare, "We have got as good a regt as old New York ever turned out." The importance of maintaining their reputation was evident in an exchange that occurred after the movement to Thoroughfare Gap. On receiving reports that some of the Eleventh Corps had retreated in disorder during the withdrawal from the gap, the *Cattaraugus Union* editorialized, "We hope it was not the Cattaraugus Regiment, for we know there were some as brave boys in that regiment as ever went south." In a letter to the rival *Cattaraugus Freeman*, Alanson Crosby was quick to dispel the rumor and defend the 154th's honor. "I see by the *Union* that some body thinks our division fell back from Thoroughfare Gap in disorder," he wrote. "Such is not the fact. We were not on the retreat by any means, and certainly had no motive to hurry. We marched back in first rate order. This Regiment has not felt a *panic* yet, and until greater danger approaches than anything yet seen you may safely depend it will not."[29]

Great danger overwhelmed the regiment at Chancellorsville and Gettysburg; in both battles the enemy swept the 154th from the field. But the Hardtacks were proud of their actions in both fights. Their desperate stands at Chancellorsville and Gettysburg, the soldiers believed, had proved they were worthy sons of Cattaraugus and Chautauqua counties. "I can say that no Regiment has ever done better fighting then they did since the war commenced," Newton Chaffee averred to a friend after Gettysburg, "and Cattaraugus may well be proud of such men, for no truer or Braver men ever left their homes, friends, Wives, Fathers, and Mothers and all they hold dear to them, to sacrafise their lives and intrests to help maintain the integraty of that dear old Flag which our Fathers left us." Reflecting on the 154th's role in opening the Cracker Line and the subsequent Chattanooga fighting, Martin Bushnell declared to a friend, "You of course know that we did a big thing not only for our selves, but our Countrys glorious cause." During the first weeks of 1864, Emory Sweetland considered the regiment's reputation:

"Tough hardy veterans our boys have a good name in the corps," he wrote. "No regt. has a better name in the corps." The home folk could be proud of the regiment, Sweetland continued, "Cattaraugus has never had occasion to blush for the 154th. it has always done its duty." Writing to a friend on the eve of the Atlanta campaign, Homer Ames simply summarized regimental esprit de corps by datelining his letter from the "Camp of the Gallant 154th."[30]

Just before the 154th New York left Jamestown for the front, a local judge, the Honorable Richard P. Marvin, presented the regiment with a stand of colors on behalf of Governor Edwin Morgan. On receiving the flags, the *Cattaraugus Freeman* reported, Colonel Addison Rice responded to Marvin's eloquent and patriotic speech with "a few brief but pithy remarks." Rice offered thanks for the present "and promised, on behalf of the Regiment, that the colors should never be stained with dishonor, or sullied by defeat." This was a most solemn and sincere pledge.[31]

The colors—the U.S. flag and the regimental New York State flag—were the most potent symbols of the regiment itself, as well as of the cause it fought for. "Their display," wrote historian Frederick P. Todd, "was steeped in tradition to the point where the color, in a sense, was the regiment." On parades in camp and marches through the countryside, the flags waved in the breeze; when not in use they were carefully furled and protected in waterproof covers. On the battlefield, the two color bearers and their accompanying color guard were attached to the right center company of the line, designated the color company. Their's was a post of great honor and danger. Enemy fire would concentrate on the brightly colored flags, each more than six by six feet square. The flags would spearhead the regimental line as it surged to the attack, and serve as a rallying point during retreats. To prevent the humiliation of losing these precious emblems, the color bearers and color guard would sacrifice their lives.[32]

Chosen by Colonel Rice to carry the national flag as the regiment's first color bearer was a veteran of previous service with the 37th New York, Corporal Lewis Bishop of Company C. Who initially bore the state standard is unknown. A week after Colonel Patrick Jones took command of the regiment, seven corporals and a private were assigned to daily duty as the color guard. In April 1863, Bishop was promoted to sergeant and received a furlough to his home town of Allegany, where he was married before returning to the front. Not long after his return, Bishop met his first battlefield test as color sergeant at Chancellorsville. "When the enemy appeared, Col. Jones ordered the colors to be raised," the *Cattaraugus Freeman* reported. "Louis Bishop, of Company C, the color-bearer, stood up unprotected and waved the flag in the face of the enemy through the whole engagement, and brought it safely from the field; but that battle-flag tells the story of Louis' heroism. Twenty bullets passed through its folds, and three more struck the flag-staff, one between his hands, and yet, strange to say, that man, more exposed than any other, was unhurt."[33]

Bishop's seemingly miraculous escape from harm caused much comment by survivors of the battle, although reports varied on the number of bullet-holes in the flag. "There were 25 ball holes thrugh our flag and the man that carried it was not hurt," James Quilliam reported. "Thare was 24 holes through our flag and one between the flag and the felows hand that carried it on the staff," wrote Richard McCadden. "Our National Flag received 23 shots," Lewis Warner recorded. On learning of Bishop's Chancellorsville deed in the columns of the *Freeman*, Congressman Reuben Fenton sent the sergeant a token of his respect. "I read with admiration of your brave conduct in bearing the Flag of our country proudly through the contest and from the field of carnage in honorable triumph," Fenton wrote. "I offer you herewith the Silver Badge of your Corps, as a slight acknowledgment of your gallantry on that occasion."[34]

In the mad scramble to escape the brickyard during the Gettysburg fight, Sergeant Lewis Bishop and Corporal Albert Mericle of Company H—who was carrying the state banner—both fell wounded, and the entire color guard became casualties. Both of Bishop's legs were shattered; Mericle was shot through the bowels. Second Lieutenant James W. Bird of Company B picked up the fallen state flag and carried it safely from the field. Coming across a stand of colors lying on the ground and believing them to be the 154th's, Captain Matthew Cheney picked them up and continued his retreat to Cemetery Hill, receiving a wound as he did so. According to Cheney, they turned out to be the flags of the 134th New York, although a member of that regiment reportedly saved their regimental banner by ripping it from its staff and concealing it on his person during a brief period of captivity. The national colors of the 154th New York, according to a postwar account of the incident, were said to have been rescued by a member of the 134th New York.[35]

But what happened to the 154th's national banner at Gettysburg is uncertain. Evidence indicates that it was lost in the confusion of the retreat. "The colors, both State and National, were captured," Assistant Surgeon Dwight Day asserted from Baltimore a week after the battle, but his report was based on hearsay and incorrect; James Bird had indeed rescued the regiment's state flag. However, George Mason wrote eleven days after the fight, "We lost our Colors but [brought] out our State flag and the Colors of the 134th Regiment so that saves our bacon." In the postwar years, veterans of the regiment also reported the national flag was lost at Gettysburg, but Lieutenant Colonel Dan Allen made no mention of the colors in his official report. Stranger yet, the Confederates who drove the 154th from the brickyard made no mention of capturing any colors in their reports of the battle, as was customary. And aside from the postwar account mentioned above, which alluded that the flag was rescued by a member of the 134th New York, other sketches of the 154th's history failed to mention the colors at Gettysburg. Perhaps that neglect was an attempt to hide the shame of losing the colors, however inevitable their loss was under the circumstances.[36]

While uncertainty lingers regarding what happened to the regiment's national flag, the fate of color bearers Bishop and Mericle is well documented. After the Confederate retreat, ambulance train commander Warren Onan conveyed Bishop to the Eleventh Corps hospital, where his shattered left leg was amputated. Several visitors saw Bishop and Mericle in the tent they shared with other members of the regiment. When placed on the operating table, Mericle recognized James Bird, who was assigned to duty at the hospital, as the man who had saved his flag. Bird cared for Mericle during his last days, which ended on July 10, 1863. Two weeks later, a visiting Lutheran pastor reported, "I was for some time with Louis Bishop. . . . He was the bold soldier who would not give up his flag when one of his legs was shot off. He stuck to his flag until he was wounded in the other leg." On July 26, as the patients sweltered in the heat and swarms of flies buzzed in the hospital tents, nurse Emory Sweetland wrote, "Louis Bishop our color Serg' is dying to day. he is a noble brave man." But the courageous Bishop fought death for a few more days before surrendering on July 31.[37]

Replacing Lewis Bishop as color bearer was his older brother, Corporal

George Bishop of Company C, who was promoted to sergeant the day Lewis died. George Bishop carried the flag without incident in the Lookout Valley and Chattanooga fighting. At the Lookout Valley winter camp in January 1864, news reached the regiment that Cattaraugus County was planning to replace the shot-torn colors with a new stand. "We have been informed that the Board of Supervisors of our County have raised funds to present our Regiment a stand of colors and the chairman of the committee having the matter in charge . . . has written down the names of the battles we have been engaged in so to have their names inscribed on the banner," Surgeon Van Aernam reported. Asked by Colonel Jones to verify the list of battles, General Howard responded, "Colonel, I take pleasure to state that your Regiment participated with gallantry in the Battles of Chancellorsville, Gettysburg, Lookout Valley and Chattanooga." During the same period, Emory Sweetland wrote, "We are soon to receive a flag from our own county." But if the new colors arrived before the commencement of the spring campaign, it went unrecorded.[38]

In the first battle of the 1864 campaign, at Dug Gap on Rocky Face Ridge, Lieutenant Colonel Dan Allen ordered a bayonet charge when the 154th reached the palisades. He simultaneously ordered George Bishop to plant the colors on the mountaintop. Bishop clambered to the summit, jabbed the flagstaff into the ground, and was shot through the head and instantly killed. Several members of the regiment were shot or captured in attempting to rescue the flag. Finally, Corporal Allen Williams reached it and carried it away unscathed. Bishop's body was not recovered. He left a widow and three young children in Allegany. His courage—and that of the other soldiers who strove to rescue the banner—was widely heralded. "This is heroism of the truest and purest character," the *Olean Advertiser* commented in a report of the incident, which was reprinted in the *Cattaraugus Freeman*. "Is this incident of this terrible war paralleled anywhere?" the writer added. "We think not." Describing how George Bishop had followed his brother Lewis as color bearer and martyr, Marcellus Darling wrote, "They were both brave and good Soldiers as ever volunteered and we all mourn their loss."[39]

Allen Williams was promoted to sergeant on the Rocky Face Ridge battlefield, and carried the flag safely for the rest of the war. Six days after the Grand Review, on May 30, 1865, Governor Reuben Fenton of New York visited the 154th's camp near Bladensburg, Maryland, to present the regiment with a new stand of colors. Brigadier General Patrick Jones's entire brigade was drawn up in formation to witness the ceremony. The silk flags, made by Tiffany and Company of New York City at a cost of $325, were the gift of Cattaraugus County. The U.S. banner had the regimental designation embroidered on the central red stripe; the state flag was hand-painted on both sides with the state seal and motto, a spread-winged eagle, and Revolutionary War battle scenes, with the 154th's battles and campaigns inscribed in gold leaf.[40]

Members of the Hardtack Regiment wrote proudly of the presentation ceremony and the new banners. "Verry fine day," Alexander Bird noted in his diary. "Had two flags presented to us had the honor of shaking hands with the Govenor the whole Brig was out they are verry fine flags." Wrote Richard McCadden, "We have been presented with two splendid new flags one National color or battle flag the stars and stripes the other a State flag they are very nice. the State flag has engraved on it in gold letters a part of the battles in which our Regt was engaged." Color Sergeant Allen Williams received the new national flag. The state flag was entrusted to young Sergeant Charles McKay. Years later McKay wrote, "I can say in all truth that the proudest moment of my life was when, by direction of Col. Warner, I stepped out before the regimental line and received the flag as the Sergeant who was to carry it."[41]

A century later, the flag Sergeant McKay so proudly bore met a sad fate. For years the 154th's flags, together with many others from New York regiments, were displayed in glass cases in the state capitol in Albany. In the 1960s, the Hardtack Regiment's state flag was loaned for a display, and a vandal ripped away its lower right corner. A patch of plain blue silk was attached to replace the stolen piece, but the flag had been irreparably damaged.

Emblazoned in gold on the new regimental flag, the names of the 154th New York's battles and campaigns summarized a record of almost three years of hard service. As an emblem, the flag was priceless. But the mere names of campaigns and battles could only allude to the regiment's entire service. Soon the colors would be furled for the last time, to be turned over to the state for their protection. The survivors would return to their homes, and their recent experiences would recede into memory. But those experiences, the veterans knew, should not be allowed to fade away. Esprit de corps demanded that the regiment's story be recorded for posterity, so that its deeds would not be forgotten. That process had already begun while the war still raged.

Military requirements provided the means for at least a partial documentation of the regiment's service. Official reports of battles and campaigns by commanding officers insured that a record of those actions would be preserved. Voluminous routine paperwork generated by the officers detailed the minutiae of the regiment, although much of it disappeared during the war, including a substantial amount of books, papers, and muster rolls lost (perhaps intentionally) while crossing the Tennessee River in the autumn of 1863. Other historical material relating to the regiment was actively solicited by the New York State Bureau of Military Statistics, which had been established by Governor Edwin Morgan in December 1862. The following April the legislature had passed and Governor Horatio Seymour had signed a bill appropriating funds for the bureau.[42]

Even before the legislative sanction, Colonel Jones received a letter from Governor Seymour detailing the mandate of the bureau. "Everything will be done to preserve to the future the most perfect account attainable of the patriotism and splendid bravery of the New York Volunteers," Seymour declared. The bureau sought to obtain and preserve a history of every volunteer regiment, a biography of every commissioned officer, an account of every noncommissioned officer and private, and a diary or chronology of a regiment's activities. In addition, the governor noted, a room had been assigned in Albany for the deposit of regimental flags, trophies, and other war relics.[43]

The 154th had an extra incentive to cooperate with the Bureau of Military Statistics. From 1863 to 1868, the bureau's assistant chief was William Hotchkiss, the father of Captain Arthur Hotchkiss of Company K and Corporal Ephriam H. Hotchkiss of Company C, who died of chronic diarrhea as a prisoner of war at Richmond after his capture at Gettysburg. Items submitted by the regiment to the bureau included the regimental colors, an outline history composed by Colonel Warner, a "rebel letter taken from the depot at Columbia, S.C., by Capt. [Winfield] Cameron, Feb. 18, 1865," photographic portraits, and individual questionnaires. Whether members of the 154th sent any other material to the bureau is unknown, for much of its once-vast collection has unfortunately been lost over the decades.[44]

Beyond the official documentation of the regiment, the Hardtacks sought to perpetuate the memory of their deeds. They were well aware of the historical value of their letters and diaries. "I think my letters should you receive them all will post you in the part taken by our Regiment during the late eventful campaign," Henry Van Aernam wrote to his wife after the Chattanooga and Knoxville campaigns. He added, "But I do not know just what I have written, as the letters were sent away just as chance offered and some of them were written by the light of a camp fire after a weary days march!" Alva Merrill wrote to his mother, Ruba, in April 1863, "I have kept a dayly memorandum since I came in to Va and at the end of this month I will send it home I dont supose it will be worth much to you but may be it will be a pleasure to me when I get home to look it over." Alva's diary apparently never reached home; he must have carried it to Chancellorsville. As other soldiers completed their diaries and sent them home, new ones arrived at the front to be filled in over the coming year. "I received my Diary last Saturday night," James Washburn informed his parents. "I think it is a fine one but it cost altogether to much. I have got it all drawn off and I am going to send my old one home today or tomorrow." "Commenced re writing my diary to send it to 'Mary,'" Emory Sweetland wrote on March 30, 1865, at Goldsboro, North Carolina. For the next two days he transcribed the contents of his diary covering the Carolinas campaign onto writing paper to send home—a fortunate occurrence, since the transcription survives while the original diary has been lost. In a cover note accompanying a diary he sent home from a camp at the Chattahoochee River in Georgia in August 1864, William Harper reflected on his experience and summarized the motivation of the diarist:

> This is a memorandum of my life and campaigns while [performing] two years service in the United States [army] of which I have been absant 5 nights in the time when not on duty. I have been with the Regt in every battle except one of which I was sick. I have not had a mark on my flesh as yet from the effects of powder or ball Although I have had them gow through my clothes and knapsack. I have been very lucky and thank God for it Please keep this until I return home with care for if I niver return keep it to remember the writer Please send me another Book as near like this as possible and some pens.[45]

Harper was mustered out with the regiment and lived until 1905; his descendants have preserved his diaries ever since.

The soldiers knew the value of other sources in the telling of their story. About to rejoin the regiment after a stay in a Washington hospital, Private Charles H. Taylor of Company C urged his father to track the 154th's movements in newspapers. "My Regiment is camped near Stafford Courthouse or was when I heard from them last so you can tell very near where I am," he wrote. "If you see any papers you must look for the first Brigade second division 11th Corps Major General Sigel commanding." (Unfortunately, newspapers never informed the senior Taylor of his son's capture at Gettysburg and subsequent death from chronic diarrhea at Andersonville prison.) Other soldiers urged their loved ones to chart the regiment's movements on maps. "If you have not got a map of the seat of war I want you to get one," Alva Merrill instructed Ruba, "& I will write all of our marches so that you can see where we go."[46]

The men sent pictures of their surroundings to their loved ones. Some were commercially produced, like the Rosenthal engraving of Camp Seward. Others were their own artwork, or that of friends. "I have made a scetch of this camp," Stephen Green wrote on the reverse of a bird's-eye view of an unidentified bivouac. "It is not in verry good shape but will give you something of an idea of the shape of the camp." Green augmented his carefully drawn sketch with informative notations: "This space between our tents and Oficers is about five rods [We] do the cooking there. . . . This is front where we have collor line for Dress Perade. . . . The tent marked with four dots is ours." On the inside pages of a January 1864 letter from the Lookout Valley camp, William Charles made a detailed pencil sketch of the tent-roofed regimental ordnance office, with smoke curling from its barrel chimney.[47]

The picturesque countryside around Chattanooga was a popular subject. William Charles's descendants have preserved an unsigned pencil sketch depicting Lookout Mountain looming over the site of the regiment's valley camp. Henry Van Aernam sent a similar drawing home. "Inclosed please find a view of our Camp and surroundings," he wrote. "This view represents about a mile distance up the Lookout Valley occupied by the camps of the Regiments making our Brigade. My friend Dr. [J. E.] Trexler, 73d Pa. Vol. has done pretty fair justice to the residence of the chivalry." (Trexler's drawing of the brigade's Lookout Valley camp was later reproduced as a woodcut in the popular periodical *Frank Leslie's Illustrated Newspaper.*) James Quilliam also sent a picture home from Tennessee, together with a promise he was unable to keep because of his mortal wounding. "I have bought a large picture of chatonuga and the battle field for Unkle," he wrote. "It cost 2 dollars it shoes Lookout Mountain and Misianary ridge. . . . Tell Unkle that I will make a fraim for it when I get home it probabely will be there in a few weeks."[48]

Artistic products to commemorate a soldier's service were available during the war. When ill health forced Captain John Griswold to resign his commission and return home, he purchased a colorful reminder of his service with Company F. His "Martin's Soldier's Record" was a chromolithograph published by Samuel W. Martin of Madison, Wisconsin, in 1864. A large, spread-winged eagle, clutching in its talons a tattered Confederate flag and a serpent representing the rebellion, surmounted a panoply of patriotic imagery: bust portraits of George Washington, Andrew Jackson, and Abraham Lincoln; Mount Vernon and Washington's tomb; a row of tents overlooking land and naval battle scenes; and flag-wrapped Corinthian columns topped by Miss Liberty and a Union sailor, both bearing the Star Spangled Banner. Onto this ornate but standard background was custom printed a list of the 154th's field and staff officers and a complete roster of Company F, including comments about individual soldiers and a list of the company's engagements, with blank spaces for memoranda.[49]

Some soldiers made special efforts to record the regiment's history. After Stephen Green rejoined the 154th following his capture at Chancellorsville and stay in parole camp, he took pains to ascertain and record the activities of the regiment during his absence, and forwarded the summary to his wife. He explained:

> On this sheat is a brief sketch of the marche &c of this Reg't from the Chancelorville fight to the time I joined the Reg't again. as I had notes in my Diary and letters of all the movements &c of the Regt while I was with them I thought I would get this I will get there march and movement from the time I left [the] Reg. at Alexandria and went to parole camp to the time I joined them here in Lookout Valley then I will have all of the dates and movements of the Reg. or you will have.[50]

Stephen expected Ann Eliza Jane Green to assist him in compiling a history of the 154th New York. He sent her instructions in December 1862, after two months in the field:

> I want to keep the movements of this Reg. &c I shal send you my Diary Jan 1, 1863 I want you to send me one like it send it so it will get here Jan. 1. . . . There is one thing I ment to have rote to you about before but I never could think of it when I was riteing to you. that is to take that old Day Book . . . and make a Scrap Book of it and all of the news you can get from the papers &c concerning this regiment keep in it, and as mutch more as you like it will make a good Scrap Book.[51]

Historically conscious soldiers like Stephen Green and Private George Eugene Graves of Company D could rightfully be called the first historians of the regiment. Graves, who at various times during his service did duty as a bugler and a clerk to Surgeon Van Aernam, surveyed some of the regiment's battlefields after the fighting stopped, mapped the positions of the 154th and other regiments and batteries, and recorded the date, number of casualties, weather, distances between landmarks, and so on. Graves apparently compiled his surveys for his own amusement and satisfaction, with no intention of organizing them into a formal history. But it seems quite likely that he studied them during moments of introspection or exposition in the postwar years, for as a biographical sketch noted in 1899, a year before he died, "Comrade Graves, although an old gentleman, is still active and bright and takes great pleasure in relating the scenes of his early manhood, when he went forth to fight in a glorious cause."[52]

By that time, as the century was about to turn, Comrade Eugene Graves and his fellow veterans expected to have the 154th New York's deeds recorded and published as a full-length history book, the ultimate expression of regimental pride. How they were disappointed forms a bizarre and sad ending to the story of esprit de corps among the regiment's veterans in the postwar years.

More than fifty men lied about their ages to enlist in the 154th New York, including sixty-six-year-old Private Barney McAvoy of Company G, who dyed his hair to disguise his years. *Courtesy of the National Archives (RG 94, Entry 544).*

At least fifty-eight pairs or trios of brothers served in the regiment, among them Private Francis M. Bowen of Company I (center) and Private Moses Bowen Jr. of Company B (attributed to be at left), pictured with an unidentified comrade. *Courtesy of the Katy Heyning Collection at the U.S. Army Military History Institute, Carlisle Barracks, Pennsylvania.*

A half-century after they enlisted, Francis Bowen (left) and Moses Bowen (center) posed at a family reunion with their brother Cyrus H. Bowen, a veteran of the 50th New York Engineers, surrounded by the martial trappings of flag and drums. *Courtesy of the Ronald D. Bowen Collection at the U.S. Army Military History Institute.*

Eight pairs of fathers and sons served in the regiment. Asa and Calvin Brainard of Arkwright, Chautauqua County, served together in Company F, Asa as a sergeant and Calvin as a private. *Courtesy of the Sandra Chase Collection at the U.S. Army Military History Institute.*

Members of the regiment were largely of the same ethnic background—British—and virtually all white. The few known exceptions included three mulattoes and one Indian, Private Jacob Winney (or Winnie) of Company K, a Mohawk. *Courtesy of the Arnold
"Barney" Waterman Collection at the U.S. Army Military History Institute.*

Sergeant Major Alexander Bird, posing with his wife, Melissa Ada (Hyde) Bird, reveals regimental pride as he tilts his hat toward the camera to display the blurred number 154 on its crown. *Author's collection.*

Mrs. Celia A. (Stevens) Bailey accompanied her husband, Private Levi D. Bailey of Company A, from her Carrollton, Cattaraugus County, home to the front. In this postwar picture they sit in front of their son and an unidentified woman. *Courtesy of the Maureen McClune Collection at the U.S. Army Military History Institute.*

A soldier's death transformed his photograph into a sacred relic. When First Sergeant Ambrose F. Arnold of Company D was killed at the battle of Dug Gap, a nephew or niece inscribed the mount of his tintype. *Courtesy of the Robert L. Butikas Collection at the U.S. Army Military History Institute.*

After Corporal Seymour Sikes of Company C was mortally wounded at Chancellorsville, his bereaved family purchased and personalized this Currier & Ives lithograph to commemorate their loved one. *Author's collection.*

No one represented the home front's support of the regiment better than John Manley of Little Valley, Cattaraugus County, a government clerk in Washington who well earned his designation as the "Soldier's Friend." *Franklin Ellis, editor,* History of Cattaraugus County, New York *(Philadelphia: L. H. Everts, 1879), 280.*

In five instances, outsiders were commissioned as officers in the 154th—a challenge to esprit de corps. Only George H. Bosley, who joined the regiment as assistant surgeon in 1865, won the acceptance of his comrades. *Author's collection.*

Only two of the ten original captains were mustered out with the regiment at the war's end, among them Lewis D. Warner of Company C, who had been promoted to major and then lieutenant colonel. *Courtesy of the New York State Military Museum and Veterans Research Center, Latham, New York.*

Captain Byron A. Johnston of Company F, First Lieutenant Alexander Bird of the same company, and Corporal Thomas R. Aldrich of Company B (pictured left to right) were influential in regimental veterans' activities. *Author's collection.*

ATTENTION, 154th N.Y.V.

The survivors of the 154th N. Y. V. will celebrate the 26th anniversary of their organization by holding an

ENCAMPMENT
AT ELLICOTTVILLE, N. Y.,
Aug. 30th and 31st, 1888.

All members of the Regiment are earnestly requested to be present as nothing will be left undone that will add to their comfort or enjoyment.

ADDRESS OF WELCOME BY
HON. A. D. SCOTT, OF ELLICOTTVILLE.

Response by Maj. W. S. Cameron, of Jamestown.

Oration by Judge A. W. Benson, of Kansas.

Comrades are requested to prepare whatever they choose for the instruction and amusement of the comrades. Plenty of Tents will be furnished. Comrades in Catt. Co. are expected to fill their haversacks and prepare to camp out in Army style. The Q. M. Dep't will be in charge of Capt. B. A. Johnston and Comrade H. E. Bolles, who will furnish your meals to all at reasonable prices.

The committee on monument at Gettysburg will report and arrangements be made to erect the same.

Programme of Exercises will be announced from the Grand Stand each morning.

T. R. Aldrich, President.
Alex Bird, Secretary.

The August 1888 encampment of veterans of the 154th in Ellicottville, Cattaraugus County, became the first in a string of annual reunions that ran for more than a quarter-century. *Courtesy of the Scott Hilts Collection at the U.S. Army Military History Institute.*

Gettysburg was a magnet for veterans of the 154th New York, who pose at their monument at Coster Avenue on an unknown date. *Author's collection.*

E. D. Northrup—attorney, eccentric, and self-appointed historian of the 154th New York—in his cluttered Ellicottville law office in November 1911. By then, Northrup had failed to publish his book and the veterans of the regiment were dying off rapidly. *Courtesy of the Ellicottville (N.Y.) Historical Society.*

PART THREE

Veteran Ties

CHAPTER 11

E. D. Northrup and the Betrayal of Esprit de Corps

For the rest of their lives, until they were stooped and gray and wobbling over canes, Union veterans remained the Boys in Blue. As the years passed, they made excursions to their old battlefields, marched in parades and raised monuments in home towns to honor martyred soldiers, and gathered on a regular basis as members of various veterans' organizations, not the least of which was their regimental association. Esprit de corps was too strong to die at the muster-out of Civil War regiments. The bonds formed during years of hardship, toil, and danger were too tight to untie. An old soldier's regimental affiliation remained as important to him as it had during the war. With the passing decades, many regimental associations saw to it that their unit's exploits were recorded for posterity in published histories. Like the veterans of other regiments, former members of the 154th New York proudly recalled their service, and they too expected to commemorate their deeds in a book. Sadly for them, their hopes were dashed.

Little has been written about Civil War veterans. Historians of the war's common soldiers have typically ended their studies at Appomattox Court House and Bennett's House. Gerald Linderman and Earl Hess, however, have both investigated the veteranhood of Union soldiers. Linderman postulated what he called a "hibernation" after the war, for a period of approximately fifteen years, during which veterans and the public were generally content to put the war and its painful memories behind them. Then followed what Linderman termed a "revival" of interest in the war, beginning circa 1880. Linderman pointed to the flood of Civil War literature that poured from the presses at that time, including hundreds of regimental histories and the popular series of articles in *Century Magazine* which doubled that periodical's circulation and were later published as the four-volume set *Battles and Leaders of the Civil War*. Linderman also cited membership in the chief Union veterans' organization, the Grand Army of the Republic, which skyrocketed during the revival period, reaching almost a half-million members. Hess agreed with Linderman's time line, and described ways in which Union veterans participated in the revival, including writing their memoirs and visiting battlefields. Evidence regarding the 154th New York shows that its veterans adhered to the pattern of hibernation and revival outlined by Linderman and Hess—for the most part.[1]

Civil War soldiers participated in group commemorative efforts before the war ended, and members of the 154th New York were no exception. On September 16, 1864, a Great Valley hotel was the site of a convention of Cattaraugus County soldiers and veterans. Their purpose was to form a Cattaraugus Soldiers' Union. One of the objects of the organization, the *Cattaraugus Freeman* reported, was "to preserve the names and services of our Soldiers— those who have fallen as well as the living—their Companies, Regiments, and the Actions in which engaged." The group also planned to insure solidarity among veterans, aid indigent veterans, and care for soldiers' widows and orphans.[2]

Officers of the 154th New York played an instrumental role in establishing a Cattaraugus County branch of a national group, the United Service Society, in October 1865. The society's objectives were similar in nature to those of the Cattaraugus Soldiers' Union. Captain Winfield Cameron of the 154th was the first president of the Cattaraugus branch, and seven of the eleven members of the organization's board of control were veterans of the Hardtack Regiment.[3]

The Cattaraugus Soldiers' Union and the county branch of the United Service Society apparently were short-lived, victims perhaps of the hibernation. After their founding, references to them disappeared from the columns of local newspapers. A similar fate met the fledgling Grand Army of the Republic (GAR), founded in 1866 to pursue similar objectives as the two earlier societies. Destined to become the greatest Union veterans' organization both in numbers and power, the GAR experienced a long and slow growth during the hibernation. GAR posts were established during the order's early years in the Cattaraugus County towns of Olean and Allegany—the latter post was commanded by Warren Onan of the 154th—but they both failed. During the revival, however, more than twenty GAR posts were founded and flourished in Cattaraugus County, and a like number in Chautauqua. Veterans of the 154th were members of many of them.[4]

A noteworthy commemorative practice of the GAR was in naming local posts, usually to honor martyred soldiers from the post's particular town. GAR posts were named after nine members of the 154th New York; only a handful of New York State regiments had more soldier post namesakes. All but one of the posts with Hardtack Regiment namesakes were located in Cattaraugus County. The town of Dayton's post was named after Barzilla Merrill, killed at Chancellorsville. Ellicottville's post honored Samuel Noyes, also a Chancellorsville fatality. Although it was very unusual—and against GAR regulations—the post in North Collins, Erie County, was also named after Noyes, whose family came from there—which reportedly led to some confusion between the two posts. So, when the 154th's beloved surgeon, Henry Van Aernam, died in 1894, Ellicottville's post took his name. Franklinville's post honored Alanson Crosby, mortally wounded during the Atlanta campaign. The post in Limestone was named for Corporal George W. Baker of Company A, who was captured at Chancellorsville. The Machias post memorialized Private George W. Phillips of Company I; he was captured at Chancellorsville and wounded in the Atlanta campaign. The post in Onoville commemorated First Sergeant Henry F. Whipple of Company H, who was captured at Gettysburg and died as a prisoner of war at Andersonville. Steamburg's post was named in honor of Corporal James Randolph of Company A, mortally wounded at Rocky Face Ridge. The post at West Salamanca took the name of Captain Benjamin Casler, who was wounded at Chancellorsville, captured at Gettysburg, and endured an imprisonment of long duration.[5]

A brief sketch of Ellicottville's post depicts the rise, heyday, and gradual decline of a typical GAR post. Samuel C. Noyes Post, No. 232, was organized in October 1881 with about fifteen charter members. Among them were eight veteran Hardtacks, including Thomas Aldrich, Alexander Bird, and Byron A. Johnston, who formed a triumvirate of leadership in post and regimental affairs. Most prominent of all was Aldrich, who had been thrice wounded at Chancellorsville, captured at Rocky Face Ridge, and imprisoned at Andersonville and elsewhere. Bird had risen from corporal in Company G to first lieutenant of Company F during the war, and was injured at Rocky Face along the way. Johnston, a veteran of the 37th New York, had entered the 154th as first sergeant of Company A and been mustered out as captain of Company F.

At a meeting in 1885, Alex Bird presented the post with a "large and beautiful photograph" of its namesake, the martyred Noyes. "This life-like picture will be highly prized by the members of the post," the *Ellicottville News* commented, "and, no doubt, will be handed down for many generations as a valued relict of the war." But unfortunately the Noyes portrait and the rest of Post 232's archives were destroyed in 1969, when fire swept the old Cattaraugus County court house, site of the post's meeting room. (The building has since been beautifully restored.)[6]

At its peak, in the 1890s, Post 232 counted more than forty members, approximately half of them veterans of the 154th. They met monthly, elected officers annually, sent delegates to New York State department encampments, and sometimes attended national encampments. Occasionally they sponsored fund-raising events open to the public, like a local dramatic club's performance of a melodrama set during the war, or hosted a special observance, such as a memorial service for the deceased general and president Ulysses S. Grant. But the post's major effort was arranging and overseeing the annual observance of Memorial Day (or Decoration Day), the most important rite performed by the GAR. Every May 30, Post 232 typically met at its post rooms, marched in a body to a local church to attend a service, and led a band and a procession of townspeople up a steep slope to Sunset Hill Cemetery, where the veterans supervised schoolchildren in decorating soldiers' graves with flowers.

When the years of the twentieth century began to pass, the post's membership dwindled as death stalked the veterans. "A few years and the Grand Army of the Republic departs forever," the *Ellicottville Post* editorialized before Memorial Day of 1920; "we can see it in the fastly diminishing ranks in our little village; let these years be theirs. Let processions be magnificent and the fading blue their chief adornment." Two years later, commander Alex Bird announced that Post 232 was conducting its last Memorial Day ceremony; in the future it would be performed by the World War I veterans of Ellicottville's American Legion post. On that day in May 1922, the aged veterans were transported up the hill to the cemetery in automobiles. "It was a heart-rending scene to the handful of patriotic citizens who were present Tuesday to witness these veterans of the Civil War honor their fallen comrades," reported the *Post*. Finally, in December 1924, four of the six surviving members met and voted to surrender their charter, and Post 232 ceased to exist.[7]

During the revival, Cattaraugus GAR posts were instrumental in erecting soldiers' monuments throughout the county. Typically a statue of a soldier at parade rest atop an appropriately inscribed pedestal was placed in a local cemetery and dedicated with extravagant patriotic flourishes on Memorial Day. Post 232 was instrumental in erecting the first monument in Cattaraugus County, dedicated in Ellicottville's Sunset Hill Cemetery in 1883. About five hundred veterans attended the ceremony, and all were treated to a dinner prepared by the women of the town. Other monuments rose and were dedicated in the towns of East Randolph (1889), Salamanca (1899), Allegany (1904), Randolph (1906), Franklinville (1906), Portville (1909), and Leon (1911).

The ceremonial unveiling and dedication of the East Randolph monument was typical. A large crowd of citizens, including numerous veterans and "politicians unnumbered and ubiquitous," with bands, fire companies, and thirteen girls representing the thirteen original states, paraded to the cemetery. The village was gaily decorated for the day with loops of evergreen, arches spanning the streets, flowers and flags on porch columns, and hundreds of yards of star-spangled muslin stretching in every direction. As part of the Leon monument dedication, the elderly survivors of Company K held a Memorial Day reunion at the church where many of them had enlisted almost a half-century before. Marcellus Darling delivered the dedicatory address, and as his widow noted a few years later, "Though this was a great tax on him, it was a great joy to him." Ellicottville's monument no longer exists, having surrendered to time and the elements. All the others still stand sentinel over the soldier dead.[8]

As the years passed and the Boys in Blue were laid to rest under the gaze of the cemetery statues, Sons of Veterans groups were organized "to keep green the memories of our fathers and their sacrifices to maintain the Union, and to promote their interests and welfare as opportunity may offer or necessity may demand." When the idea for a camp in Ellicottville first surfaced, the *Ellicottville News* affirmed, "It is a good idea. The ranks of the old veterans are becoming much depleted. Soon there will be too few to carry out the usual exercises of honoring our fallen brave. Who can more properly take their places than their sons, loyal to their memory?" At least three Cattaraugus County Sons of Veterans camps were named to honor officers of the 154th New York. Ellicottville's camp, organized in 1902, commemorated General Patrick Jones. Eleven of its twenty-five charter members were sons of veterans of the 154th; Byron Johnston was appointed to muster the camp on behalf of the GAR. Portville's camp was named after Colonel Lewis Warner of that town, who was described in a historical sketch as "a leading representative war hero of Cattaraugus county." Franklinville's camp honored Surgeon Henry Van Aernam.[9]

Members of the 154th New York played a lesser role in the second largest Union veterans' organization, the Military Order of the Loyal Legion of the United States (MOLLUS), a group restricted to former Union officers and, at a different classification, their firstborn sons. Although founded in 1865, MOLLUS, like the GAR, did not flourish until the revival, when its membership burgeoned despite criticism by nonmembers of its officers-only policy. Only four former officers of the 154th joined MOLLUS: Salmon Beardsley, Winfield Cameron, Henry Loomis, and Jacob Ten Eyck—the outsider major who only served with the regiment for eight days. Colonel (and later brigadier general) Patrick Henry Jones was elected a member of MOLLUS in April 1866, but for an unknown reason his election was voided.[10]

When a national organization called the Ex-Union Prisoners of War Association was formed during the revival, a Cattaraugus County chapter was chartered in 1887. Considering the high number of Hardtacks who were captured at Gettysburg and elsewhere, it is no surprise that eight of the ten charter members—and all of the first officers of the organization, including president Tom Aldrich—were veterans of the 154th. "All ex-prisoners of war in the county are requested to join with us as soon as convenient," Aldrich announced on the group's formation. The former prisoners held monthly meetings in GAR Post 232's headquarters. "The men that were in those *Hell holes* with me . . . are a little nearer and dearer to me than any other people in the world," Aldrich wrote of his association comrades.[11]

Although the GAR and other veterans' organizations did not peak until the revival, former soldiers were not entirely quiescent during the hibernation. As early as the Fourth of July 1865, just weeks after the Hardtacks had returned home, members of the regiment reunited. Plans for the Independence Day celebration in Westfield included a reunion of the 112th New York and the Chautauqua County companies of the 154th. As the *Westfield Republican* put it, "This cannot fail to be gratifying to the many brave boys who have periled their lives together for the Union and the Government . . .

and it will afford the citizens an opportunity to mingle with these war-worn heroes, and welcome them back, and testify their respect for such gallantry and patriotism." An estimated eight hundred to a thousand citizens turned out for that year's Fourth of July celebration in East Ashford, Cattaraugus County. In addition to prayers, speeches, a reading of the Declaration of Independence, and a free dinner, the audience enjoyed a display of military maneuvers by veterans and an account of his recent service by the Reverend Nathan F. Langmade, late private, Company D, 154th New York.[12]

In November 1865, veterans of the 154th had an opportunity to demonstrate their political solidarity and reverence for their former commander by voting for General Patrick H. Jones, the Republican candidate for clerk of the New York State Court of Appeals. In voicing its support for Jones's candidacy, the *Cattaraugus Freeman* declared, "The soldiers of Cattaraugus cannot but appreciate this compliment to them, and with the aid of the masses who appreciate not only his services in the field, but his high personal standing as a citizen, will rally to his support with a zeal and energy that shall tell in the canvass of the estimation in which he is held at home." Jones won the election; in subsequent years he was appointed to several governmental posts, including postmaster of New York City by President Grant. Other former officers of the 154th—like hundreds of veteran Union and Confederate officers—parlayed their military careers into political posts, including Harrison Cheney, Edgar Shannon, and Dana Horton, New York State assemblymen; Commodore Vedder, New York State senator; Matthew Cheney, Nebraska state senator; Henry Van Aernam, U.S. congressman and President Grant's first commissioner of pensions; and Alfred Benson, mayor, judge, state legislator, and U.S. senator from Kansas. On learning of Benson's appointment as senator, Cattaraugus County veterans of the 154th wrote him a joint letter of congratulations, to which Benson offered profuse thanks. "I have received a good many letters from members of the regiment in different parts of the United States," Benson wrote, "and I assure you these letters have been very [gratifying] to me, and I appreciate them more than I can express."[13]

Veterans of the 154th New York formed their first formal commemorative organizations the year the war closed. In October 1865, members of Company E reunited in Chautauqua County to form a "Reorganized Union" of the company. The purpose of the group was to hold annual reunions every

October, to invite fellow veterans to their gatherings, and to attend the funeral of any member in a body. Company E's reunions ran for at least four years; the minutes of their gatherings are preserved by a descendant of Charles Abell, the group's secretary. Early reunions of Companies B and K of the 154th are also documented.[14]

In response to a call by Colonel Lewis Warner, the 154th New York held a reunion in the town of Randolph, Cattaraugus County, in September 1869. They invited all other veterans from the county—specifically those of the 64th New York—to attend. By the following year, the event had expanded and was billed as a reunion of soldiers of Cattaraugus and Chautauqua counties. But then, apparently, the hibernation took effect, because nine years passed before the next large reunion of area soldiers. In 1879, a group calling itself the Cattaraugus County Veterans' Association held its first annual reunion. This proved to be a long-lasting organization; it held reunions well into the twentieth century, and eventually absorbed the various regimental associations that were active in the county as attrition depleted them. The association occasionally took part in special events, such as the Cattaraugus County Centennial Celebration, held in Salamanca in 1908. Commodore Vedder, as president of the day, oversaw a historical parade that included Civil War veterans riding in carriages and floats featuring tableaux of wartime scenes—among them a veteran of the 154th plucking a chicken before a campfire—and a depiction of peace showing Union and Confederate soldiers together clasping the Stars and Stripes while little girls scattered flowers to the crowd.[15]

The Cattaraugus County Veterans' Association's lasting monument is the Cattaraugus County Memorial and Historical Building, which stands in the county seat of Little Valley. Plans for the building were endorsed at a reunion of the association in 1909. The cornerstone was laid in 1911, and in 1914 the finished building was dedicated to the memory of the county's soldiers and sailors of the War of the Rebellion. More than two hundred veterans attended the dedication ceremony, including many of the 154th Regiment, which held its reunion in conjunction with the event. In a proud moment, the old soldiers formed a semicircle to pose for a panoramic photograph in front of the new building, a half century after their service in the war.[16]

No discussion of Union Civil War veterans would be complete without mention of the pension system. During and immediately after the war, pensions were available to wounded and disabled veterans and the widows, orphans, and dependent parents of deceased soldiers. Lobbying by the GAR for so-called service pensions, to augment war-induced disability pensions, led to a congressional act of 1890 that stipulated that pensions could be granted to any veteran suffering from disability, regardless of its origin, at $144 per year. Soon the government was paying more than $60 million a year in pensions to Union veterans; by 1907 more than $1 billion had been dispersed, and the GAR continued to lobby for liberalization of the pension laws, sometimes successfully.[17]

Hundreds of veterans of the 154th benefitted from the government's largess, and they helped each other obtain pensions by offering advice, providing affidavits, and witnessing documents. Shepherd N. Thomas, a former corporal of Company A, wrote to an Illinois Hardtack veteran who was seeking a pension, "My advice is for you to send your statement & affidavit to *Alex Bird* or By Johnson all made out just as you want it," and the "Comrads at Ellicottville will copy it off & sign it & send it to you." Tom Aldrich pursued a brief career as a pension agent, helping veterans secure their stipend. "It is a good thing for the boys that Tom lives in these parts," the *Ellicottville News* commented. The regiment's former medical staff was particularly in demand to provide testimony on behalf of pension seekers. Affidavits by doctors Van Aernam, Day, and Rugg made their way into the pension files of numerous veteran Hardtacks. Veterans were not above exaggerating their ailments, or recalling with crystal clarity the precise origin of some malady in long-ago wartime. General Patrick Jones, for example, provided an affidavit to support James Baxter's pension claim. Jones declared that Baxter took sick with smallpox during the Carolinas campaign in February 1865—at a time when Jones himself was at home on sick leave.[18]

Local newspapers occasionally carried a brief item announcing a veteran's pension increase. But one pensioner of the 154th, Francis Patterson, former private of Company G, made major headlines as the central figure in one of the most notorious cases of fraud to emerge from the Civil War pension system. Two decades after the war ended, "Blind Patterson" was wandering the streets of Elmira, an alcoholic beggar, deserted by his wife and son and befriended only by his shepherd dog. He claimed to have lost his eyesight during the war. Elmirans disliked Patterson but considered him a hopeless case and pitied him. Once a resident bought him a hand-organ to assist him in his begging. The very day Patterson received the present, he drunkenly smashed it to pieces.

Agents repeatedly applied for a pension for Blind Patterson, to no avail. Time after time, a desertion charge caused his case to be rejected. But after receiving numerous affidavits on his behalf, the charge of desertion was dropped and Patterson was awarded one of the largest pension claims ever allowed: $72 per month and $13,000 in arrears. Elmira was stunned to learn her notorious blind beggar was suddenly rich. But Patterson promptly raised suspicions when he skipped town, accompanied by his wife—who had returned to him on learning of his good fortune. The blind man cashed several thousand dollars worth of pension checks before he was tracked down in Pennsylvania. By then his case was known to be a fraud, masterminded by his pension agents. His former regimental comrade Wilkes Miller confessed that he had been paid to provide false affidavits in Patterson's case, $100 apiece, with a promise of $1,000 in cash. Former captain Edward Porter of the 154th was also charged with providing a false affidavit to bolster Patterson's claim. Although $11,000 of the payment was retrieved, it all wound up in lawyers' pockets; the government never recovered a cent.[19]

Central to the postwar commemoration of the 154th New York was its regimental association, which was formed in 1887 with Tom Aldrich as president. The following year, the 154th held the first of a lengthy series of annual reunions. At that 1888 gathering in Ellicottville, the veterans voted unanimously to include Companies I and H of the 37th New York—the first companies raised in Cattaraugus County after the fall of Fort Sumter—as part of their association. Alfred Benson journeyed from Kansas to Cattaraugus County to deliver the main address to his old comrades. Benson's oration—poetic, moving, magnificent—revealed how esprit de corps still linked the veterans' hearts to their regiment. And it described the poignancy felt by the men as their ranks dwindled. "Oh! my comrades," Benson exclaimed, "—we are only the rear guard, and the stragglers." Pointing heavenward, he cried, "Yonder is the regiment!" More than a hundred veteran Hardtacks listened intently as Benson set the scene, a quarter-century after they fought together in the war:

We meet among the hills, dotted over with homes, where old photographs sent from the front are guarded as richest treasures. There are faded blouses, with blood stains upon them—and battered swords upon the walls, and musty muskets in the corner. The children with wide open eyes, are told of a father—or shall I say grandfather—time whirls on so—who fought with Hooker at Resaca, or marched with Sherman to the Sea. Of a brother who was borne down in the red tide at Chancellorsville, or swept from the awful ridges at Gettysburg. O, what a time for busy memories. . . . God bless the children, and the grandchildren, and may they never forget the story of the 154th in which their fathers served. . . . Yes we are growing old. We hail each other [as] boys today, but we are the boys of 30 years ago. . . . In this reunion time we cannot fail to remember the faces that faded from our mortal sight at Chancellorsville, at Gettysburg, in Tennessee, in Georgia and the Carolinas. And in the midst of this festival in the green hills at home, drop a tear for those our comrades who during and since the war have gone into the last camp. . . . Men of the old iron bound, storm tried and death swept 154th N.Y.—May your last days be your best. May you together with those who have crossed the flood muster again on the farther shore a thousand strong! Every man at his post. Hail and farewell![20]

Year after year, veterans of the 154th and Companies I and H of the 37th met in different towns in Cattaraugus County, most often in Salamanca, a rail hub easy to reach from all directions. Reunion events typically included picnic dinners, speeches, band music, prayers, more speeches, songs, elections of officers, still more speeches, and evening campfires, during which the veterans took turns swapping reminiscent yarns. These regimental reunions lasted until about 1915, when they seem to have been subsumed by the Cattaraugus County Veterans' Association. Attrition had taken its toll. "We have a reunion of the 154th Every year & generally get 40 or 50 . . . of the old Regiment together," Shepherd Thomas wrote in 1913, "but the number keeps growing smaller."[21]

Owing to circumstances, certain of the reunions were special events. The tenth annual was held in conjunction with the national encampment of the GAR in Buffalo in August 1897. "This without doubt will be the best and

largest reunion of the association since its organization," Tom Aldrich announced. "The comrades from the West and all over the country will be in
Buffalo on this occasion. The comrades of Cattaraugus and Chautauqua
counties are earnestly requested to be present. . . . Let us all get together
and have an old time talk." More than a hundred veteran Hardtacks gathered
in Buffalo, some of them from as far away as Michigan, Wisconsin, and Minnesota. They joined thousands of other GAR men in parades through densely
crowded streets under elaborate decorative arches, omnipresent flags and
bunting, and newfangled electrical displays. They welcomed a visit by President William McKinley, himself a veteran. Another noteworthy reunion was
the eighteenth annual, held in Jamestown in 1905, the only time the regimental association met in Chautauqua County. The 112th New York held its
reunion at the same time, and together the men of the two regiments remi-
nisced about leaving Camp Brown for the war more than forty years before.[22]

In 1888, the year of the regimental association's first reunion, veterans of
the 154th formed a committee to work with the New York State Monuments
Commission for the Battlefields of Gettysburg and Chattanooga in the place-
ment and erection of a monument to the regiment at Gettysburg. A party of
veterans and friends journeyed to Gettysburg to dedicate the 154th's monument on the anniversary of the battle in 1890, enjoying cut-rate excursion
fares offered by the railroad. In services conducted by Tom Aldrich, the ladies of the party sang "America" and "Rock of Ages," Colonel Dan Allen recounted the regiment's role in the battle, Colonel Lewis Warner made a few
remarks, and James S. Whipple, son of the martyred Henry Whipple, gave
the main address. A prominent lawyer and politician from Salamanca, Whipple was a frequent speaker at reunions of his late father's regiment. "It was
a solemn and interesting occasion," Whipple later wrote of the Gettysburg
event. "Standing there upon the spot where our soldiers fought twenty-seven
years ago, every heart beat faster and all eyes grew moist as our thoughts
went back to that memorable day." After the ceremony, the veterans and
their friends posed for photographs. The monument, marking the position
of the regiment's fight on July 1, 1863, is on present-day Coster Avenue, the
smallest parcel of the Gettysburg National Military Park, located off North
Stratton Street in the borough.[23]

The Gettysburg battlefield proved to be a perennial magnet for Civil War
veterans, and the Hardtacks were no exception. Whether or not they had

fought in the battle, they could not resist the field's allure. Veterans of the 154th traveled there in 1888 for the twenty-fifth anniversary of the battle, and in 1893 to dedicate the New York State monument in the National Cemetery. Colonel Warner led the men of his old brigade in the ceremonial parade on the latter occasion. Members of the 154th were on hand in 1902 for the dedication of the equestrian monument of General Henry W. Slocum, their former commander of the Army of Georgia during Sherman's epic marches. A group made the trip in 1913 to celebrate the fiftieth anniversary of the battle. Many Confederate veterans also were in attendance, and Alex Bird reported, "The feelings between Johnny Reb and Yank were of the very best." Every visit by the Hardtacks to Gettysburg of course included a pilgrimage to the 154th's monument, and often a photograph was taken for posterity. Charles Whitney brought one such picture to the office of the *Ellicottville News* in 1892. "Many familiar faces could be seen, in the little group of survivors who were placed in front of the monument when the photo was taken," the *News* commented, noting that most of the veterans pictured had "suffered the horrors of Libby and Andersonville prisons."[24]

Groups of veterans of the 154th also visited their other battlefields. A party of thirty Hardtacks went to Chattanooga in 1910 for the dedication of New York State's Peace Monument on Lookout Mountain. Following the ceremony they made a side trip into Georgia to visit their old battlefield at Dug Gap on Rocky Face Ridge. The New Yorkers were pleased and impressed to receive a friendly reception from the citizens and Confederate veterans they encountered. Reconciliation between veterans of North and South seemed to be complete. "Just down from Lookout Mt. after dedication of this Monument," John Langhans notified his daughter on a picture postcard. "It was a fine day, had a large crowd were mixed up some with the Johnie Reb." After the trip to Rocky Face Ridge, Langhans sent another postcard. "Just came from the old battlefield," he wrote, "and the People of Dalton met us with Autos and hacks and took us over the City." Among the Georgian reception committee were several staunch old Confederate soldiers, who "received the Northern veterans as friends and exchanged hearty handshakes," a Dalton newspaper reported.[25]

Individual veterans also trekked to their old battlefields. Shepherd Thomas found it convenient to visit the Chattanooga area battle sites—his married daughter resided with her family on a Missionary Ridge farm. On a visit to Chancellorsville, where he had been shot through the left lung and left for dead, Alfred Benson found the exact spot where he had fallen, and retraced the route over which he had crawled to a spring and an old barn which served as a hospital. Benson also took part in a fiftieth anniversary re-enactment of the Grand Review in Washington in 1915. "The fact that he was able to participate in the 'second review' caused Judge Benson a great deal of satisfaction," a biographer noted. A flood of memories swept over the veterans on their return journeys south. Alex Bird wrote up a trip he made in 1908 with his brother James to Chancellorsville and Gettysburg for his local newspaper. "We readily recognized the different points on the field," Bird wrote of Chancellorsville. "We had kept together during the two days' battle, and the scenes we saw at that time were so indelibly graven on our memories that it seemed as if it were but yesterday." One can only imagine the thoughts of Charles Whitney and Robert Woodard when they attended the dedication of the New York State monument at Andersonville in 1914. Fifty years had passed since the two had suffered in the infamous prison, but as they stood to represent the score of Hardtacks who died there—and the dozens more who suffered there—haunting memories must have consumed them.[26]

"I have a few relicks that I prize very highly," Charles Field wrote in 1893. Veterans preserved all sorts of relics of their war days: bayonets and bibles, cartridge boxes and corps badges, muskets and military manuals, swords and shoulder straps. No doubt these objects held tremendous sentimental value to the old soldiers. John Adam Smith, a former corporal of Company K, passed on to his son a prized keepsake—a briar root pipe he had carved during his imprisonment at Belle Island, Andersonville, and Charleston and Columbia, South Carolina, complete with an inscription and depictions of a palmetto tree and a pair of handcuffs. On his release from a long imprisonment, Captain Benjamin Casler returned home with a bag made from the bootleg of a deceased Union cavalry officer. It contained some drawings of prison scenes made by a comrade and a set of ornate bone implements Casler had carved to while away the endless hours. Some veterans donated personal relics to their GAR posts. For many years, the battered tin cup Tom Aldrich had carried throughout his imprisonment at Andersonville, Savannah, Millen, Blackshear, Florence, and Wilmington was displayed in Post 232's rooms in Ellicottville. The bloodied blouse Alfred Benson was wearing when he was shot at Chancellorsville hung on the wall of his GAR post in Kansas.[27]

The postwar years added regimental reunion ribbons, GAR badges, and relics gathered during trips to the South to the veterans' material bounty. During a trip to his Tennessee and Georgia battlefields in 1880, Alex Bird cut a hickory walking stick from Rocky Face Ridge and topped it with a grapeshot that he picked up at Resaca. Canes were popular presentation pieces. In 1882 veterans of the 154th presented a gold-headed cane carved from Georgia pine from the Andersonville stockade to their comrade William Hawkins, former private of Company B, who had survived a lengthy imprisonment. Portville's GAR post presented a gold-headed cane to Colonel Lewis Warner in 1893. An unidentified veteran of the regiment presented Alfred Benson with a cane whittled with an ax and jackknife, "In the use of which the *Hard-Tack Regiment* were so much *noted!*" A passage in the accompanying letter, written by the donor's son or daughter, defined postwar regimental esprit de corps. "When you look on this token, The Giver would have you remember the years of fire and storm of Battle through which you & He have passed, and which has left marks & memories on your hearts. . . . Memories which as the years Roll by, only bind more Strongly the Bond of Sympathy & regard for those with whom you Stood Shoulder to Shoulder amid the Storm of Battle."[28]

Some veterans chose commercially available products to commemorate their service. Mervin Barber, for example, bought a large lithographic depiction of the "Easel-Shaped Monument" with his service record carefully inscribed on a central panel. Proceeds from sales of the lithograph presumably were intended to fund the construction of the monument itself—an ornate and allegorical artistic monstrosity that was never built, and most likely was just a come-on to get veterans to purchase the lithograph and an accompanying book. In addition to graphic works like Barber's lithograph, subscription histories provided a veteran with means to preserve his war record. Around the turn of the century, Barber was one of more than ninety veterans of the 154th New York who subscribed to purchase a two-volume book titled *Presidents, Soldiers, Statesmen*. Each subscriber provided information for a biographical sketch to be included in the work, with strong emphasis on his military service. The first volume contained a standard history of the United States; the second volume was filled with "sketches of the officers and of the rank and file that fought and won the battles of the war," together with brief histories of the regiments raised in the subscription area and accounts of local GAR posts. More than sixty veterans of the 154th similarly subscribed to and submitted autobiographical sketches to a massive volume with the ponderous title *Historical Gazetteer and Biographical Memorial of Cattaraugus County, New York.*[29]

Veterans also contributed personal sketches and additional material to other histories of their counties and towns. Newton Chaffee included a thumbnail history of the 154th and a roster of soldiers in "The Part Taken by Gowanda and the Immediate Vicinity in the War of the Rebellion," his chapter of that town's 1898 history. A more complete historical sketch of the 154th, much of it drawn from Colonel Warner's diaries, appeared in a Cattaraugus County history published in 1879. In addition to Warner, the editor listed seven former officers of the 154th and the Soldiers' Friend, John Manley, among his contributors. Biographical sketches of a half-dozen officers were included in the book, accompanied by lithographed or engraved portraits.[30]

Veterans published accounts of their service on their own initiative. Alex Bird contributed an article describing "My First Experience Under Fire" at Chancellorsville to a hometown newspaper in 1894. During the fiftieth anniversary of Sherman's March to the Sea in 1914, Bird's wartime diary of the march was published in four weekly newspaper installments. Other veterans self-published autobiographical booklets. The "Sketch of The Life & Army Service of P. A. Markham" was largely given over to the war; all but three paragraphs of the twelve-page pamphlet were devoted to Markham's career with the 154th New York. Marcellus Darling likewise emphasized his army life in a booklet titled *Events and Comments of My Life.* Twelve of its nineteen pages detailed his service, and a wartime portrait and a drawing of a winter hut were used as illustrations. The published memoir of Asa Brainard was an exception to the rule of lengthy military accounts. Only a brief paragraph of Brainard's sixteen-page booklet mentioned his service with the 154th; the rest of his narrative described other events of a long and adventurous life.[31]

Charles McKay was the most ambitious Hardtack veteran to publish his memoirs. He and regimental comrades Emory Sweetland and John Dawley were among hundreds of Union veterans who contributed reminiscences to the *National Tribune,* the journal of the GAR. McKay also composed a lengthy memoir of his service which was published in a *National Tribune* compilation book and later ran serially in the *Ellicottville Post*. For forty years he had studied the war, McKay wrote, traveling more than ten thousand miles at an expense of more than $1,000 to revisit the scenes of his service. In his summary, McKay presented a prime expression of postwar esprit de corps:

> Cattaraugus County may well feel a pride in her sons that represented her in the 154th. The regiment was always at the post of duty and did manfully every duty assigned to it. Many of its exploits were brilliant. . . . It is a history of which its friends may well be proud. I do not pretend that I have written a full history of its service, nor have I done the subject justice so far as I have gone. There were many brave and worthy officers and men that I should have been glad to mention personally. But I have written without access to the regimental rolls, and much of my story is from memory, which, after a quarter of a century, would scarcely be expected to retain more than the salient points. . . . And now, old comrades and friends, farewell. If this memory of the old "Hardtack Regiment" shall afford you one iota of the pleasure in perusal that it has your old comrade in preparation, I shall be amply prepaid. It has indeed been a labor of love.[32]

While he worked on his memoir of army life, McKay also sought official recognition for a wartime act he performed with the help of Stephen Welch. After the regiment was driven from the palisades at the Battle of Rocky Face Ridge, McKay and Welch were asked by Major Warner to rescue Corporal George W. Greek of Company C, who was lying wounded in both legs between the lines. Under fire of the enemy the two reached Greek, rolled him onto a piece of tent or a blanket, and carried him to safety. In 1893, McKay applied through a senator to the War Department for the Medal of Honor for himself and Welch, supporting his request with an affidavit from an eyewitness company comrade. The application was approved, and in 1894 the two veterans received medals by registered mail. McKay and Welch thus became the only Hardtacks to be awarded the Medal of Honor.[33]

Some veterans of the regiment wrote up their war experiences not for publication, but for presentation as speeches, or as a personal record to hand down in their families. They often used their wartime diaries, embellished by recollection, as the basis of their memoirs. Tom Aldrich read such an account of his prison experiences to an audience at Ellicottville. "I have not told the half," he asserted of his Andersonville reminiscences, "and defy anyone that was there to tell or write the half of the suffering and privation that was undergone by the prisoners confined there." Expanding on his diary, Newell Burch jotted down the names of his five tent mates and noted, "Yes the names I [can] even remember to night after twenty one years and over." Emory Sweetland prepared a speech to his GAR post describing President Lincoln's Gettysburg Address, which he witnessed while nursing the wounded after the battle. The thirtieth anniversary of Chancellorsville inspired John Wellman to compose an epic poem describing the 154th's role in the battle, dedicated to his comrade and friend Alfred Benson. On May 2, 1893, Judge Benson and a few other veterans gathered at Wellman's home in Lawrence, Kansas, and the poet debuted his piece. It was a work, Wellman realized, motivated by esprit de corps. "I dont think any one would care for my story or poem except for members of the Regiment," he commented. "It is simply telling in rhyme some of the experiences of the Regiment, they are all true and would be remembered by all the Boys."[34]

Probably the strongest expression of a Civil War regimental veteran association's esprit de corps was the publication of a regimental history. Roughly sixty of New York State's 190 infantry regiments were chronicled in full-length histories published in the postwar decades, many of them during the revival. Those sixty or so regiments had two things in common. First, they were fighting regiments—regiments that had seen battle during active service at the front and compiled lengthy lists of casualties, not regiments that spent the war as garrison troops or in military backwaters and sustained relatively few losses. Consequently, they were regiments that had an eventful story to preserve—regiments like the 154th New York. Second, their veterans possessed enough postwar esprit de corps (and financial resources) to see the time-consuming, painstaking, and costly process of writing and publishing a history through to completion.[35]

Most regimental histories were written by an individual veteran or a committee of veterans appointed by the regimental association. In prefaces to the books, the authors explained that the works were instigated by the desire and urging of veterans to have their regimental story told. Their goal was to create a full, true, and impartial record of their regiment's exploits for posterity, particularly for the veterans' descendants and future historians. They also sought to inform the general public of the sacrifices they had made on the country's behalf, and thereby steer proper recognition to patriotic service selflessly performed. They wrote to correct errors that had cropped up in previous accounts. And they wrote for the pleasure of regimental comrades who sought to relive the bygone days of their army life—an articulation of esprit de corps.

The authors denied any literary pretensions and promised simple, unvarnished narratives. They realized their books would be of interest to but a few, but of intense interest to those few. They catalogued their research methods—collecting official records from the federal War Department and state archives, culling correspondence from wartime newspapers, poring over comrades' wartime letters and diaries, requesting them to fill out questionnaires. They expressed profuse thanks to comrades who offered assistance. They requested the reader's indulgence, realizing that errors were inevitable. Sometimes they indicated they had been reluctant to undertake a task of such magnitude. They bemoaned difficulties in locating source material, in the long, weary hours of work, in the impossibility of providing a complete history, one that would include every anecdote of every individual soldier. They looked upon their assignment as a labor of love.[36]

The 154th New York was supposed to have had a regimental history published during the revival. The fate of that effort forms a strange and ultimately sad story. Unfortunately for the Hardtacks, their history was not produced in the typical fashion, by a veteran or committee of veterans of the regiment. Instead, the 154th's history was initiated, researched, and written by an outsider. The project was out of the veterans' hands. All they could do was offer their support, trust in the author's sincerity, and hope for his success.

In 1878, nine years before the 154th's regimental association was formed, an Ellicottville lawyer named Edwin Dwight Northrup issued a printed flyer to the veterans. It announced his intention to write a history of the regiment and called on the men to assist him by providing written records and reminiscences of their service. "Aided by you," the flyer stated, "it will be a personal history of your regiment, replete with incidents, anecdotes, and events no general history of the war could give you, and it will also be a faithful record of priceless value to yourselves and your posterity." Northrup had the same aspirations as other regimental historians. He understood the importance of the work he was undertaking. He stated—truthfully, according to available evidence—that he had "no desire or expectation of any pecuniary profit out of the matter."[37]

Who was this self-appointed historian of the 154th? It seems likely that the veterans would not have chosen E. D. Northrup (as he preferred to call himself) as their regimental historian for many reasons. The most active veterans were generally rock-ribbed conservative Republicans—wags said the acronym GAR stood for "Generally All Republicans." Northrup was a Democrat who, as the years passed, drifted sharply toward socialism and engaged in frequent correspondence with Eugene V. Debs. He was an atheist who professed a bitter hatred of organized religion and its leaders, the Roman Catholic papacy and priesthood in particular, and bragged that the first of his seven children was the only to be baptized. He supported women's rights and suffrage, and corresponded with birth-control advocate Margaret Sanger. It was said he was a prohibitionist—although his diaries reveal numerous instances when he forswore drinking ever again. He subscribed to magazines promoting vegetarianism and other outré causes. Untroubled by criticism of his radical opinions, he was always bold in expressing himself, and showed no lack of self-confidence. "I was born a single horse, equal to a double-team," he boasted.

In addition to his infatuation with various isms of his day, Northrup had other peculiarities that seemed contrary to the beliefs and standards of veterans of the 154th. Although he bragged about a distant familial relationship to Ulysses S. Grant, Northrup perversely named his firstborn child, a son, Robert E. Lee Northrup. One can only imagine what the veterans of the Hardtack Regiment thought about that. The senior Northrup had an affection for the South, born during a trip made with Alex Bird in 1880 to visit the 154th's Tennessee and Georgia battlefields. Greatly impressed by Georgia, Northrup organized annual excursions to the state and encouraged Cattaraugus County residents (including some veterans of the 154th) to immigrate there. He corresponded with Georgia governor and former Confederate general John B. Gordon regarding his colonization schemes. He purchased a farm in Greensboro, Georgia (a few miles east of Madison, which the 154th had tramped through on the March to the Sea), and moved his family there for several years. He named his seventh and last child Georgia, after the former Confederate state where she was born.

In Ellicottville, Northrup liked to wake in the wee hours before dawn and toil while the rest of the village slept. He was a workaholic who routinely put in fourteen-hour-plus days and generally slept for less than five hours a night. As he walked the village streets, he picked up litter and filed it away in annotated envelopes. He refused to name his fifth child, preferring to let the boy choose his own name (Charley) when he grew up. For more than a quarter-century he wore only blue clothing, finally breaking the string with the purchase of a linen suit in 1900. In the new century, his daily diary entries began to include lengthy, detailed, and increasingly obsessive observations of Ellicottville's meteorology. Not all of his peculiarities were benign, however. A periodic squabble with a townsman, Joseph O'Donnell, gradually escalated into violence. On a summer day in 1881, Northrup was twice attacked by O'Donnell, at a store and at a hotel. During the second assault, he shot his antagonist dead. Deputy Sheriff Tom Aldrich conducted Northrup to jail in Little Valley, where he eventually was acquitted of murder in the second degree on a plea of self-defense.

But for all of his eccentricities, what made Northrup most unlikely to be the 154th's historian was that he had not served with the regiment. In fact, although he was of age—he was born in 1839—he had not served in the war at all. Instead, Northrup had been drafted in 1864, but had managed to escape serving. Surely the veterans of the 154th knew Northrup had been one of the stay-at-homes, and certainly they did not overlook that lapse.

Nevertheless, Northrup received the cooperation of many veterans of the 154th in his work, including an important trio of his townsmen—Tom Aldrich, Alex Bird, and Byron Johnston. "I have already received considerable encouragement and assistance from a number of the soldiers of the 154th regiment," he stated in his 1878 flyer, "and I assure you that no pains on my part will be spared to make the work complete in every respect." In immediate responses to the flyer, Northrup received pledges of support from General Jones, Colonels Rice and Warner, and other officers of the regiment. "Let me ashure you," Newton Chaffee wrote, "1st that I do sincearly hope for the prosperity of your undertaking, & shall feel a deep interest in the work, and will endeavor to do all I can to aid you, and hope that each member of the Regiment will contribute something of interest to the work."

Chaffee added, "I have got Two or Three War Widows who have promised me the particulars of their Husbands deaths."[38]

With esprit de corps excited by the promise of a regimental history, the veterans of the 154th apparently overlooked Northrup's peccadilloes. Over two decades he engaged in a wide correspondence with the former soldiers, met with them and recorded their reminiscences, copied their diaries by hand, accompanied them on visits to their old battlefields, and attended their reunions, at one of which—the sixth annual, in 1893—he was unanimously elected an honorary member of the regimental association. He visited Albany to search through records there and received preferential treatment from the state adjutant general, coincidentally his wife's cousin. He sent inquiries to numerous government officials, including the superintendents of national cemeteries, to determine the burial sites of 154th men. He found a valuable helper in Eliasaph D. Godfrey, a former private of Company C who was a clerk in the Pension Office, who answered periodic questions and provided Northrup with the names and addresses of more than five hundred surviving veterans of the regiment.

As he continued his research, Northrup worked sporadically on the writing of his history, with occasional intense bursts of concentrated labor. Every so often, local newspapers carried reports of his progress on the book, and estimates of its size grew from five hundred to more than a thousand pages. But the project seemed interminable. "To-day I commence my *final* work on My History of The One Hundred and Fifty Fourth Regiment N.Y. Vols.," Northrup recorded in his diary on June 7, 1888. On June 17, 1893, he wrote, "Special attention to Hist. of 154th N.Y.V. now." And on June 20, 1895: "I am 'clearing the decks' for finishing my history of the 154th N.Y. Vols." Still, the work went on.[39]

In 1896, Tom Aldrich asked Northrup to submit a brief account of the 154th's history to the New York Monuments Commission for the Battlefields of Gettysburg and Chattanooga. The resulting piece was included in the commission's massive three-volume work, commonly called *New York at Gettysburg*, which contains photographs of the state's regimental and battery monuments on that battlefield, accounts of their dedication ceremonies, and capsule unit histories. Northrup was displeased with some slight changes the editors made to his essay, but he nevertheless bragged that only he could have written it. "My Historical Sketch of the Regt., was, as published, *cen-*

sored somewhat, and not improved thereby," he wrote to Matthew Cheney. He added, "I was *able* to give it as no other living (or dead) person ever *was,* or *will be* able to give it." The author might have had trouble finishing his manuscript, but he did not suffer from a lack of vanity.[40]

While Northrup labored on his book, the veterans cheered him on. "I am awfully glad you are making such a grand success of our Regimental history," Clark "Salty" Oyer informed Northrup from California. "You know we all think our dear old Regiment *The Regt* for there was Regiments and Regiments but ours like Auld Lang Sine [was] the grandest of them all." From Chicago Earl Z. Bacon, a former corporal of Company E, wrote, "I feel as though a great wrong had been done the 154th Regt by Historians in not giving them the credit they deserved in both [the] Chancellorsville & Gettysburg Battles." Former captain Simeon Pool informed Northrup, "I am very glad you have taken hold of the enterprise in earnest, as it bespeaks for the work an assurance of being first-class in all respects, and I have no doubt will be truer, and superior to anything yet written about our boys (Cattaraugus boys) who so honorably, so valiantly served their country." Veterans' family members also voiced their support. "I have often wondered," wrote the widow of Byron Wiggins (who was killed at Gettysburg), "why a history of that Regt. which done so much service in the war was not written."[41]

As the years passed, a note of urgency crept into communications to Northrup from veterans and their relatives. William Jones, who had shared his diary of prison life with Northrup, wrote in 1893, "Hoping that you will be able to get your book done verry soon for I feel verry anxious to read it." Five months later Jones wrote, "I have not heard anything of you lately and I feel anxious to know how you are getting along with the History of 154." "When your book is completed & published, I want a copy," wrote a son of Andersonville victim Henry Whipple from Illinois in 1891. He continued, "Don't forget me. Let me know its price and the money will be forthcoming." Eliasaph Godfrey admonished Northrup in 1896, "You want to get that book on the move, or there will be but very few left to read it."[42]

Finally, in 1897, Northrup printed and distributed a flyer announcing that "preliminary terms" for the publication of his history had been made with the Courier Company of Buffalo, a large printing firm. With typical braggadocio, Northrup described his forthcoming book as "the best and most complete regimental history ever written, or that ever will be written . . .

containing 900 to 1200 double-column pages . . . with maps and illustrations." He added, "It is not a mere stereotype regimental history, but, as well a history of the events in which the members of the Regiment were engaged, and in which they made a proud record that should be made enduring. All this I was compelled to write to rescue the true record and honors of the Regiment from misapprehension and oblivion." Northrup urged the veterans of the 154th to subscribe to purchase the book as well as they fought in the war, and listed the price: "$4 in cloth; $5 in what is styled half leather; and $6 in full leather."[43]

But for an attorney, Northrup had done a most unlawyerlike thing. He had issued his flyer before finalizing his arrangements with the Courier Company, which caused the deal to unravel. "We very much regret that the circulars were printed and sent out without our knowledge," a company official informed Northrup, "as it would have been better to have completed some arrangements before mailing them. We dislike very much to appear as a party in this arrangement until something more definite has been decided upon." Whereupon the egocentric and stubborn Northrup promptly cut ties to his potential publisher. As he put it, "I modestly concluded, in my own mind, to let the Currier Company do its business its own way; and, as usual, proceeded to do my own business my own way." His only remaining contact with the company was a request that refunds be sent to the few veterans who had subscribed to the book before the deal fell through.[44]

Northrup made two more futile attempts to have the book published. Immediately after the collapse of the Courier Company arrangement he wrote to the large New York City publishing house of D. Appleton and Company, but quickly discontinued negotiations on receiving an estimate of more than $2,000 to publish a thousand copies of the book, half to be paid in advance. After the turn of the century Northrup claimed that his son Charley, publisher of the *Ellicottville Post* and a job printer, would put out the book in serial form, but nothing ever came of it. Northrup also rebuffed an offer from Commodore Vedder—whom he despised as a Republican politician and wealthy capitalist—to help finance the book, provided Northrup allow a committee of three veterans to read and if necessary revise the manuscript. Those terms were of course entirely unacceptable to the arrogant author.

Meanwhile, Northrup continued to insist to veterans of the 154th that he would succeed in publishing his history. "My said History is done and *well* done—the best, by far, ever written," he assured Matthew Cheney in 1903. "It only awaits my getting able to stand the expense of publication, about $4000." But Northrup's diaries reveal that he lost interest in the project after the Courier Company fiasco, and his subsequent correspondence with members of the regiment dwindled to almost nothing. Only a few veterans— notably Charles Whitney and Salty Oyer—continued to write to Northrup. They never gave up hope he would publish his book. "Some of the old Boys ask me when Mr. Northrup will get out the Regt'l History," Whitney informed Northrup in 1904, but the wait had become pathetic. In 1905 Northrup notified Whitney that he planned to publish the history in an edition of three thousand, "& it ought to be 10,000 for a book for such merit." Never doubting Northrup's word, Whitney responded, "I do hope you will have a large sale of the history when it is issued as I know that it will [be] one of the best Regimental history ever gotten-up." Northrup continued to bluster, but his monumental history was never published.[45]

In 1917 a fire swept the brick block containing Northrup's law office; he said his losses were serious, but did not enumerate them. "I hope you did not lose all," Charles Whitney wrote to him, "you had such a pile of papers and books and the history of the 154th with so many years of hard work. It was a pity that it could not have been published." Two years later, on January 25, 1919, E. D. Northrup died. "One of the most interesting, the most forceful figures in Cattaraugus County," his obituary declared in an understatement; it summarized his life in considerable detail, but made no mention of his work as historian of the 154th Regiment. At his emphatic request, there was no barbaric burial; his remains were cremated. Among his voluminous papers, only a tiny fragment of his manuscript history of the 154th New York survived. What happened to the rest of it is a mystery. Was it destroyed in the 1917 fire—or did the frustrated author burn it himself in a fit of pique?[46]

So it happened that, aside from brief accounts of the regiment and its members in county histories and other publications, the story of the 154th New York went unrelated. While E. D. Northrup squandered his chance to have his history published and then lost interest in the project, much of his potential audience passed away. "I have just been to the funeral today of an Old Soldier," Shepherd Thomas wrote to his comrade James Baxter in 1913. "So the Old Soldiers are dropping off—it will be you & I Before many years." A veteran of a Massachusetts regiment, writing to Alex Bird in 1910 to notify him of the death of Andrew Blood, conveyed the sadness inherent in the passing of a generation of soldiers:

> I had the privilege of attending with him your reunion, this year, and the many kindnesses shown me by the comrades of the famous 154th I shall never forget. Now it falls to my lot to apprize you that one of the noblest of men as well as a valiant soldier has passed over the river, there to await the grand reunion when every soldier of Jesus Christ shall receive their coronation. I trust that in that day the boys of the noble 154th N.Y. that wear the badge of honor here shall wear the crown of glory there. With you brave boys of his regiment I mourn. Soon the taps will be sounded as the last veteran of the war of 61–5 is laid away, then the nation may awake to the fact that at least it owed a debt of sympathy if not of gratitude to the boys in blue.[47]

As the veterans died, their service was commemorated one last time at their funerals, in their obituaries, and on their gravestones. Many of them were buried with full military honors in ceremonies conducted by the local GAR or American Legion post, complete with a volley by a rifle squad and a bugler playing "Taps." Most of the men's headstones (or the cenotaphs of men buried in the South) were inscribed with their company and regiment. Some told more detailed stories. In the Versailles Cemetery in Perrysburg, Cattaraugus County, for example, a gravestone was carved with a flag and an inscription: "William F. Chapman, Capt. of Co. K 154 Reg't N.Y. Vol. born June 5, 1843, died June 30, 1875, from the effects of wounds received in the battle of Chancellorsville, Va." In the headlines of their obituaries, "Taps Sounded" for the veterans, they "Answered the Last Roll Call" or "The Last Bugle Call," they were "Mustered Out" and "Passed to the Eternal Camping Ground." Virtually all of their obituaries summarized their military service, sometimes in considerable detail, and identified them as proud members of their regiment.[48]

The regiment's roster of survivors dwindled and expired in the early decades of the twentieth century. Lieutenant Colonel Dan Allen outlived all the other officers. When he died in 1934 at age ninety-five, it was reported that he had been the last surviving commander of a regiment that fought at Gettysburg. The last living member of the 154th New York might have been Private Jonathan M. Ames (brother of Homer and Edson Ames), who passed away in 1937. Ironically, Jonathan Ames had enlisted in April 1865 and had never served a day with the regiment.[49]

With E. D. Northrup's failure to publish his book, the 154th New York left no regimental history to posterity. As the Hardtacks died, their legacies passed to their families. Wartime letters, diaries, photographs, and relics, and postwar ribbons and badges, were tenderly preserved in homes throughout Cattaraugus and Chautauqua counties and across the country. Privately, descendants kept their ancestor's individual memory alive, but as the years passed, it seemed that collective remembrance of the 154th New York was fated for oblivion. Betrayed by E. D. Northrup, esprit de corps faded away with the last regimental comrades.

NOTES

INTRODUCTION: This Little Band

1. "Farewell Address To the 154th Reg't. N. Y. S. Volunteers," unidentified newspaper clipping, courtesy of Cattaraugus County Memorial and Historical Museum, Little Valley, N.Y. The address is reprinted in Mark H. Dunkelman, *Colonel Lewis D. Warner: An Appreciation* (Portville, N.Y.: Portville Historical and Preservation Society, 1990), 21–4.

2. Dunkelman, *Colonel Lewis D. Warner*, 3, 17–9; "Death of Col. L. D. Warner," *Olean Morning Times*, November 18, 1898, 1.

3. "Farewell Address To the 154th Reg't. N. Y. S. Volunteers."

4. Marcellus Warner Darling, *Events and Comments of My Life* (n.p., n.d.), unpaginated.

5. John Langhans to Julius Langhans, June 9, 1865.

6. *Ellicottville Post*, September 25, 1929, 1.

7. William Adams, ed., *Historical Gazetteer and Biographical Memorial of Cattaraugus County, N.Y.* (Syracuse: Lyman, Horton & Co., 1893), 594; *Presidents, Soldiers, Statesmen* (New York, Toledo and Chicago: H. H. Hardesty, 1899), 1501.

8. My definition of esprit de corps is from *Merriam-Webster's Collegiate Dictionary, Tenth Edition* (Springfield, Mass.: Merriam-Webster, 1995), 396.

9. Francis A. Lord, *They Fought for the Union* (New York: Bonanza Books, 1960), 59; E. B. Long with Barbara Long, *The Civil War Day by Day: An Almanac, 1861–1865* (Garden City, N.Y.: Doubleday, 1971), 716; Gerald J. Prokopowicz, *All for the Regiment: The Army of the Ohio, 1861–1862* (Chapel Hill: Univ. of North Carolina Press, 2001), 5.

10. William T. Sherman, *Memoirs of General William T. Sherman by Himself* (1875; reprint, Bloomington: Indiana Univ. Press, 1957), 2:385.

11. Gustavus A. Weber, *The Bureau of Pensions: Its History, Activities and Organization* (1923; reprint, New York: AMS Press, 1974), 19.

12. Bell Irvin Wiley, *The Life of Johnny Reb: The Common Soldier of the Confederacy* (1943; reprint, Baton Rouge: Louisiana State Univ. Press, 1993), 138–9; Bell Irvin Wiley, *The Life of Billy Yank: The Common Soldier of the Union* (1952; reprint, Baton Rouge: Louisiana State Univ. Press, 1993), 320. Works on the common soldier in the Civil War are enumerated and analyzed by William Garrett Piston, "Enlisted Soldiers," in Steven E. Woodworth, ed., *The American Civil War: A Handbook of Literature and Research* (Westport, Conn.: Greenwood Press, 1996), 454–65; and Reid Mitchell, "'Not the General but the Soldier': The Study of Civil War Soldiers," in James M. McPherson and William J. Cooper, eds., *Writing the Civil War: The Quest to Understand* (Columbia: Univ. of South Carolina Press, 1998), 81–95.

13. Lord, *They Fought for the Union*, 59.

14. Long, *The Civil War Day by Day*, 716; James I. Robertson Jr., *Soldiers Blue and Gray* (Columbia: Univ. of South Carolina Press, 1988), 21; Randall C. Jimerson, *The Private Civil*

War: Popular Thought During the Sectional Conflict (Baton Rouge: Louisiana Univ. Press, 1988), 182.

15. Gerald F. Linderman, *Embattled Courage: The Experience of Combat in the American Civil War* (New York: Free Press, 1987), 234–6; Larry M. Logue, *To Appomattox and Beyond: The Civil War Soldier in War and Peace* (Chicago: Ivan R. Dee, 1996), 42, 51.

16. Joseph T. Glatthaar, *The March to the Sea and Beyond: Sherman's Troops in the Savannah and Carolinas Campaigns* (New York: New York Univ. Press, 1985), 30–3, 38, 183, 186; Larry J. Daniel, *Soldiering in the Army of Tennessee: A Portrait of Life in a Confederate Army* (Chapel Hill: Univ. of North Carolina Press, 1991), 21, 23, 132.

17. Earl J. Hess, *The Union Soldier in Battle: Enduring the Ordeal of Combat* (Lawrence: Univ. Press of Kansas, 1997), 111, 117–22.

18. Joseph Allan Frank and George A. Reaves, *"Seeing the Elephant": Raw Recruits at the Battle of Shiloh* (Westport, Conn.: Greenwood Press, 1989), 2, 5–6, 20–2, 129–40; Joseph Allan Frank, *With Ballot and Bayonet: The Political Socialization of American Civil War Soldiers* (Athens: Univ. of Georgia Press, 1998), 57, 165.

19. Reid Mitchell, *Civil War Soldiers* (New York: Viking, 1988), 17; Reid Mitchell, *The Vacant Chair: The Northern Soldier Leaves Home* (New York: Oxford Univ. Press, 1993), 19–37, 158; James M. McPherson, *For Cause and Comrades: Why Men Fought in the Civil War* (New York: Oxford Univ. Press, 1997), 82–9, 131.

20. Prokopowicz, *All for the Regiment*, passim. Quotes from pages 5, 6, 28, 34, 188.

21. Prokopowicz, *All for the Regiment*, 5.

22. Mark H. Dunkelman and Michael J. Winey, *The Hardtack Regiment: An Illustrated History of the 154th Regiment, New York State Infantry Volunteers* (East Brunswick, N.J.: Fairleigh Dickinson Univ. Press, 1981); Mark H. Dunkelman, *Gettysburg's Unknown Soldier: The Life, Death, and Celebrity of Amos Humiston* (Westport, Conn.: Praeger, 1999).

CHAPTER 1: Demographics and Identity

1. "War Meeting in East Otto!" *Cattaraugus Freeman,* August 7, 1862.

2. John Quinn Imholte, *The Civil War Diary and Related Sources of Corporal Newell Burch 154th New York Volunteers Covering the Period August 25, 1862 to April 21, 1865,* unpublished manuscript, 1–2.

3. Mark H. Dunkelman, *Camp James M. Brown: Jamestown's Civil War Rendezvous* (Jamestown, N.Y.: Fenton Historical Society, 1996), passim; "By Telegraph!" *Cattaraugus Freeman,* August 26, 1862.

4. "All Hail! Old Perrysburgh Claims the Banner!" *Cattaraugus Freeman,* September 4, 1862.

5. "Volunteers from Salamanca," *Cattaraugus Freeman,* September 11, 1862; "From Camp James M. Brown," *Cattaraugus Freeman,* September 4, 1862; "Camp James M. Brown," *Cattaraugus Freeman,* September 11, 1862.

6. "War Meetings," *Jamestown Journal,* August 29, 1862.

7. Muster-in rolls, 154th New York, National Archives; "The Camp Brown Companies: Who Raised Them, and Where They Were Recruited," in Dunkelman, *Camp James M. Brown,* 33–6; Adams, *Historical Gazetteer and Biographical Memorial of Cattaraugus County,* 682.

8. Franklin Ellis, ed., *History of Cattaraugus County, New York* (Philadelphia: L. H. Everts, 1879), 107.

9. John Langhans to Julius Langhans, January 22, 1865; Edgar Shannon to Francelia Hunt, September 24, 1863; Thaddeus L. Reynolds to his family, May 20, 1863; George W. Newcomb to Ellen Newcomb, June 16, 1863, author's collection.

10. William L. Hyde, *History of the One Hundred and Twelfth Regiment N. Y. Volunteers* (Fredonia, N.Y.: W. McKinstry & Co., 1866), 14; "112 Regiment—Its Organization and Departure," *Cattaraugus Freeman*, September 18, 1862, reprinted article from the *Jamestown Journal*, September 12, 1862; Addison G. Rice to Adjutant General Thomas Hillhouse, September 15, 1862, Correspondence and Petitions, 1821–1896, New York State Adjutant General's Office, courtesy of New York State Archives, Albany.

11. Harold Holzer, ed., and Daniel Lorello, comp., *The Union Preserved: A Guide to Civil War Records in the New York State Archives* (New York: Fordham Univ. Press and the New York State Archives Partnership Trust, 1999), 124–5; Frederick Phisterer, *New York in the War of the Rebellion* (Albany: Weed, Parsons and Company, 1890), 308, 423.

12. "Departure of the 154th Regiment," *Cattaraugus Freeman*, October 2, 1862.

13. Philander W. Hubbard, poem, "The Friends I Left Behind Me"; Andrew G. Park, poem, "The Brave Soldier"; James Byron Brown, poem, "The Soldier's Farewell"; James Byron Brown, poem, "Army Song of the Cattaraugus Boys"; James Byron Brown, poem, "Army Song of the Chautauqua Boys."

14. Ellis, *History of Cattaraugus County*, 80; Andrew W. Young, *History of Chautauqua County, New York* (Buffalo: Printing House of Matthews & Warren, 1875), 666.

15. Descriptive books, 154th New York, National Archives.

16. Long, *The Civil War Day by Day*, 707; Descriptive books, 154th New York; William Charles letters, passim.

17. William Charles to Ann Charles, December 27, 1862.

18. Descriptive book, Company B, 154th New York, National Archives; Thomas R. Aldrich, "The Experience of Thomas R. Aldrich . . . while a Prisoner of War," manuscript reminiscence; Thomas R. Aldrich, interview notes, undated, Edwin Dwight Northrup Papers, #4190, Department of Manuscripts and University Archives, Cornell University Libraries, Ithaca, N.Y. (hereafter cited as E. D. Northrup Papers).

19. Discharge certificate, Jacob Winney, December 7, 1862, and affidavit of Isaac Bearfoot, November 21, 1901, Jacob Winney pension file, National Archives; Newcomb to Ellen Newcomb, December 9, 1862, author's collection. Although he was borne as Winney on the rolls, the family spells the name Winnie.

20. Descriptive books, 154th New York.

21. Hess, *The Union Soldier in Battle*, 133–8; Young, *History of Chautauqua County*, 99–101.

22. Descriptive books, 154th New York; Long, *The Civil War Day by Day*, 707; Records of Soldiers by Towns, Cattaraugus County Historical Museum, Little Valley, New York; Craig F. Senfield, ed., *Civil War Veterans Cemetery Locator, Volume I, Cattaraugus County, New York* (Olean, N.Y.: Twin Tier Civil War Roundtable, 1996), passim; "Old Soldier and Citizen Joins the Silent Majority," *Staples (Minnesota) World*, August 29, 1912; W. F. Beyer and O. F. Keydel, eds., *Deeds of Valor* (Detroit: Perrien-Keydel Co., 1907), 322–3.

23. Mark H. Dunkelman, "Senior Soldiers," *Military Collector & Historian* 44, no. 4 (winter 1992): 158–62; Bradford Rowland, Clark E. Oyer, and Esley Groat, interview notes, undated, E. D. Northrup Papers.

24. Records of Soldiers by Towns, Cattaraugus County Historical Museum; *Presidents, Soldiers, Statesmen,* passim; Adams, ed., *Historical Gazetteer and Biographical Memorial of Cattaraugus County,* passim; New York State Bureau of Military Statistics, Town and City Registers of Officers, Soldiers, and Seamen Composing the Quotas of Troops Furnished to the United States During the Civil War, 1861–1865, New York State Archives, Albany.

25. John C. Griswold to Susan Griswold, November 18, 1862.

26. Charles to Ann Charles, January 9, 1863. Father and son pairs were determined using a variety of sources, including published biographical sketches and the 1860 U.S. census.

27. Alva C. Merrill to Ruba Merrill, April 12, 1863; Barzilla Merrill to Ruba Merrill, April 12, 1863.

28. Darling, *Events and Comments of My Life.*

29. Corydon C. Rugg to Ruba Merrill, May 30, 1863.

CHAPTER 2: Lines of Communication

1. James D. Emmons to his sister Ann, October 28, 1862; Charles W. Abell to his mother, October 29, 1862; George A. Taylor to his parents, March 8, 1863; Taylor to Ellen Taylor, March 29, 1863.

2. Marion Plumb to Sarah Plumb, October 20, 1862; John Dicher to Sarah Frank, October 3, 1863, Doris Laing Collection; Richard J. McCadden to his mother and brother, November 8, 1863, Ron Meininger Collection; Marcellus W. Darling to his family, June 1, 1864; Jesse D. Campbell to his family, October 23, 1864; John Langhans to Julius Langhans, November 5, 1864.

3. Alva C. Merrill to Ruba Merrill, February 14, 1863; John C. Griswold to Susan Griswold, March 9, 1863; Edgar Shannon to Francelia Hunt, February 22, 1864; Emory Sweetland to Mary Sweetland, September 7, 1864; Taylor to Ellen Taylor, October 17, 1862.

4. Charles F. Allen to his parents, July 7, 1863.

5. Horace H. Howlett, undated poem to his sister.

6. Ira Wood to Hester Ann Wood, October 13, 1862; Thomas R. Aldrich to his mother, May 22, 1863; William Charles to Ann Charles, June 3, 1863; Henry Van Aernam to Amy Melissa Van Aernam, May 15, 1863.

7. Shannon to Francelia Hunt, March 9, 1863.

8. McCadden to his brother, December 7, 1862, Ron Meininger Collection; Darling to his family, January 7, 1863; James D. Quilliam to Rhoda Quilliam, May 31, 1863, January 10, 1864.

9. Martha James to Samuel R. Williams, October 12, 1862; Samuel R. Williams to Martha James, March 16, 1863.

10. Francelia Hunt to Edgar Shannon, May 1, 1864; Ann Eliza Jane Green to Stephen R. Green, March 29, 1864, author's collection.

11. Susan Griswold to John Griswold, May 5, 1863.

12. Mary Jane Chittenden to William F. Chittenden, circa November 1862; William F. Chittenden to Mary Jane Chittenden, December 8, 1862; Mary Jane Chittenden to William F. Chittenden, January 2, 1863.

13. Darling to his parents, December 6, 1862; Barzilla Merrill to Ruba Merrill, October 20, 1862, January 25, 1863, February 2, 1863, March 24, 1863.

14. Chittenden to William F. Chittenden, December 28, 1862.

15. "From the 154th Regiment," *Cattaraugus Freeman,* November 6, 1862.

16. Joel M. Bouton to Stephen E. Hoyt, May 22, 1862, and March 29, 1863; Amos Humiston to Philinda Humiston, December 2, 1862; "Letter from Major L. D. Warner," clippings from the *Olean Times* of letters dated May 21, June 1, June 17, June 21, July 1, July 8, July 14, July 28, 1864, Cattaraugus County Historical Museum; "Interesting letter from the 154th," *Fredonia Censor,* February 24, 1864; Sweetland to Mary Sweetland, October 26, 1862.

17. Thaddeus L. Reynolds to his family, February 14, 1863; Taylor to Ellen Taylor, November 14, 1862; Barzilla Merrill to Ruba Merrill, October 18, 1862; Eason W. Bull to Wyman Bull, January 29, 1863.

18. Henry A. Munger to Cassius Griswold, August 6, 1863; Bull to Wyman Bull, October 24, 1862; Bull to Lydia Bull, December 7, 1862; Alva C. Merrill to Ruba Merrill, February 14, 1863; Francis Strickland to Catherine Strickland, June 17, 1863; George W. Newcomb to Ellen Newcomb, March 1, 1863, author's collection; Harvey Earl to Alfred and Almina Earl, March 10, 1863; Lord, *They Fought for the Union,* 126.

19. Lyman Wilber to his uncle and aunt, January 29, 1864; Quilliam to Rhoda Quilliam, January 1, 1864; Humiston to Philinda Humiston, March 25, 1863.

20. Griswold to Susan Griswold, February 22, 1863; Levi D. Bryant to Cornelia Bryant, March 28, 1865.

21. Newton A. Chaffee to Norman F. Moore, April 6, 1864; Stephen R. Green, undated letter fragment, Phil Palen Collection; Wilber Moore to Emeline Moore, February 4, 1863; Van Aernam to his daughter Dora, January 19, 1863; Sweetland to Mary Sweetland, February 1, 1865; Shannon to Francelia Hunt, January 16, 1863; Newcomb to Ellen Newcomb, April 1, 1863, author's collection; Barzilla Merrill to Ruba Merrill, January 7, 1863.

22. Imholte, *The Civil War Diary . . . of Corporal Newell Burch,* 55; Barzilla Merrill to Ruba Merrill, November 21, 1862; Wilber Moore to Rosanna Porter Thorpe, July 20, 1863; Samuel Williams to Martha James, December 7, 1862; Chittenden to Mary Jane Chittenden, December 4, 1862.

23. Unknown writer to his uncle and aunt, October 11, 1862, Cattaraugus County Historical Museum; Chittenden to Mary Jane Chittenden, November 23, 1862; Nathaniel S. Brown to William F. Chittenden, November 25, 1862; Howlett to Ellen Newcomb, May 7, 1863.

24. Charles to Ann Charles, March 23, 1863; John N. Porter to Rosanna Porter Thorpe, February 2, 1863.

25. Abell to his mother, October 29, 1862; Bull to Wyman and Lydia Bull, December 26, 1862. The list of goods requested is drawn from twenty-seven letters.

26. Griswold to Susan Griswold, February 22, 1863; Salmon W. Beardsley to Ann Beardsley, February 25, 1863.

27. Taylor to Ellen Taylor, December 2, 1862; Charles to Ann Charles, February 4, 1864, and February 6, 1864.

28. Griswold to his niece, March 30, 1864.

29. "From the Soldiers in the Field," *Fredonia Censor,* April 6, 1864.

30. Patrick H. Jones to Ladies Aid Society, East Randolph, New York, March 25, 1864, regimental letter book, Ellicottville (N.Y.) Historical Society (hereafter cited as regimental letter book).

31. Charles to Ann Charles, February 19, 1864; Emmons to his sister Ann, March 13, 1863; Darling to his family, April 27, 1864, and undated fragment, circa September 15, 1864.

32. "A Valued Present," *Cattaraugus Freeman,* March 24, 1864; Sweetland to Mary Sweet-

land, April 10, 1864, January 25, 1865; Addison Shafer bullet, Edith Shafer Collection, Olean, New York; Asa S. Wing bullet, David B. Snyder Collection, Bay Village, Ohio; Charles E. Whitney diary, January 13, 1864; Matthew B. Cheney to E. D. Northrup, October 9, 1893, Charles E. Whitney, interview notes, December 27, 1890, John A. Bush, interview notes, undated, Leonard L. Hunt, Joseph Cullen, and Joseph Charlesworth, interview notes, February 21, 1893, Andrew G. Park, interview notes, March 1, 1893, all in E. D. Northrup Papers.

33. Humiston to Philinda Humiston, May 9, 1863; Dunkelman, *Gettysburg's Unknown Soldier,* passim.

34. Bradford Rowland, Clark E. Oyer, and Esley Groat, interview notes, E. D. Northrup Papers; Charles to Ann Charles, May 14, 1863.

35. Charles to Ann Charles, September 4, 1863, April 1, 1864; Sweetland to Mary Sweetland, May 27, 1863.

36. Charles to Ann Charles, September 5, 1863; Sweetland to Mary Sweetland, April 8, 1864; Van Aernam to Amy Melissa Van Aernam, March 29, 1864.

37. Photograph courtesy of William C. Welch, Allegany, New York. See also Mark Dunkelman and Michael Winey, "Precious Shadows: The Importance of Photographs to Civil War Soldiers, as Revealed by a Typical Union Regiment," *Military Images* 16, no. 1 (July–August 1994): 6–13.

38. Lord, *They Fought for the Union,* 124; McCadden to his mother, November 20, 1862, Ron Meininger Collection.

39. "The allotment Commissioners for the State of New York," *Westfield Republican,* December 17, 1862; Devillo Wheeler to William H. Wheeler, February 2, 1863.

40. Sweetland, undated letter fragment, circa June 15, 1863; Reuben R. Ogden diary; William D. Harper diary; Sweetland to Mary Sweetland, March 13, 1864; Charles to Ann Charles, September 13, 1863, January 12, 1864; Green to Ann Eliza Jane Green, April 15, 1863, author's collection; Green to Ann Eliza Jane Green, February 29, 1864, Phil Palen Collection.

41. Alva C. Merrill to his brother and sister, October 22, 1862.

42. Reynolds to his family, February 14, 1863; Lord, *They Fought for the Union,* 231–2; Stephen Welch diary, February 18, 1863.

43. Newcomb to Ellen Newcomb, March 6, 1863, Lewis Leigh Collection, U.S. Army Military History Institute, Carlisle Barracks, Pa. (hereafter cited as USAMHI); Taylor to his parents, March 8, 1863; Taylor to Ellen Taylor, March 19, 1863; Charles to Ann Charles, November 20, 1863.

44. Abell to his parents and siblings, December 31, 1863; Dwight Moore to his mother, May 22, 1863; Charles to Ann Charles, March 6, 1864.

45. Chittenden to William F. Chittenden, December 28, 1862.

46. Griswold to Susan Griswold, April 5, 1863; Darling to his mother and friends, March 4, 1863; James W. Washburn to his parents, May 24, 1863.

47. Charles to Ann Charles, June 3, 1863; Aldrich, "The Experience of Thomas R. Aldrich . . . while a prisoner of war"; Charles to Ann Charles, January 1, 1864; Whitney diary, December 16, 1864, and December 20, 1864; Sweetland to Mary Sweetland, April 11, 1864.

48. Ruba Cole Merrill diary, February 25, 1863; Alva Merrill to Ruba Merrill, February 22, 1863; Barzilla Merrill to Ruba Merrill, February 22, 1863, February 25, 1863, and March 7, 1863.

49. Lewis D. Warner diary, April 16, 1863; Shannon to Francelia Hunt, July 29, 1863.

50. Chittenden to Mary Jane Chittenden, September 9, 1862.

51. Taylor to Ellen Taylor, December 6, 1862; Chittenden to Mary Jane Chittenden, December 1, 1862.

52. Griswold to his friends, March 16, 1863; Newcomb to Ellen Newcomb, November 27, 1862, author's collection; Charles to Ann Charles, May 29, 1864; John W. Meloy to his parents and sisters, April 4, 1865.

53. Newcomb to Ellen Newcomb, January 12, 1863, author's collection; Newcomb to Ellen Newcomb, January 13, 1863, Phil Palen Collection; "Local and Miscellaneous," *Cattaraugus Freeman*, May 14, 1864; "The 154th Regiment," *Cattaraugus Union*, May 29, 1863; "The 154th New York," *Cattaraugus Freeman*, July 23, 1863.

54. Charles to Ann Charles, September 17, 1863.

55. Newcomb to Ellen Newcomb, March 16, 1863, author's collection.

56. Barzilla Merrill to Ruba Merrill, March 20, 1863, February 21, 1863; Griswold to Susan Griswold, April 5, 1863; Welch diary, March 31, 1863.

57. Adams, *Historical Gazetteer and Biographical Memorial of Cattaraugus County*, 733; Newcomb to Ellen Newcomb, circa February 9, 1863, author's collection; miscellaneous notes and Clark E. Oyer, interview notes, E. D. Northrup Papers.

58. Susan Griswold to John C. Griswold, May 5, 1863.

59. "Death of Lieut. John C. Griswold," *Fredonia Censor*, May 13, 1863; Susan Griswold to John C. Griswold, June 3, 1863; John Griswold to Susan Griswold, May 30, 1863.

60. Susan Griswold to John C. Griswold, June 3, 1863; John Griswold to Susan Griswold, June 8, 1863.

61. Susan Griswold to John C. Griswold, June 12, 1863.

CHAPTER 3: Friends and Foes

1. Mary Jane Chittenden to William F. Chittenden, October 28, 1862; William F. Chittenden to Mary Jane Chittenden, November 13, 1862.

2. William Charles to Ann Charles, January 18, 1864, May 1, 1864.

3. Charles W. Abell to his parents, June 15, 1863, February 18, 1863; Barzilla Merrill to Ruba Merrill, April 2, 1863; James W. Baxter to John Phillips, November 8, 1863.

4. Marcellus W. Darling to his mother, July 9, 1864; Charles to Ann Charles, December 24, 1863.

5. Martha James to Samuel R. Williams, December 1, 1862; Chittenden to William F. Chittenden, October 30, 1862; "Good!" *Cattaraugus Freeman*, May 28, 1863.

6. Isabella Shippy to the Commander of Convalescent Camp, undated, Shippy pension file, National Archives.

7. "The Soldier's Welcome," *Cattaraugus Freeman*, April 16, 1863.

8. "Mansfield Loyal League" and "Ellicottville Loyal League," *Cattaraugus Freeman*, May 7, 1863; "Loyal League of the Town of Freedom," *Cattaraugus Freeman*, May 28, 1863; Patrick H. Jones to Ladies Aid Society, East Randolph, New York, March 25, 1864, regimental letter book, Ellicottville (N.Y.) Historical Society; New York State Bureau of Military Statistics, Accounts Submitted by Local Officials Detailing Monies Raised and Expended and Men Furnished during the Civil War, 1861–1866, New York State Archives, Albany; Lemuel Moss, *Annals of the United States Christian Commission* (Philadelphia: J. B. Lippincott, 1868), 602–38.

9. Edgar Shannon to Francelia Hunt, April 21, 1864; James D. Quilliam to Rhoda Quil-

liam, April 23, 1864; "Letter from Lieut. Allanson Crosby," *Cattaraugus Freeman*, February 10, 1864; United States Sanitary Commission, Department of Arms and Trophies, Metropolitan Fair, *Catalogue of the Museum of Flags, Trophies and Relics* (New York: Charles O. Jones, 1864), 52, 55.

10. Ellis, *History of Cattaraugus County*, 280–2; "John Manley, Esq.," *Cattaraugus Freeman*, February 10, 1864.

11. "From Camp 'James M. Brown,'" *Cattaraugus Freeman*, September 11, 1862; "From the 154th Regiment," *Cattaraugus Freeman*, April 2, 1863; Regimental Order No. 37, March 16, 1863, 154th New York Miscellaneous Papers, National Archives; Stephen Welch diary, March 16, 1863; John N. Porter to Rosanna Porter Thorpe, April 2, 1863; "Ten Days with the Army," *Cattaraugus Freeman*, April 16, 1863.

12. Shannon to Francelia Hunt, April 10, 1863; Quilliam to Rhoda Quilliam, April 11, 1863; "From Washington," *Cattaraugus Freeman*, January 22, 1863, May 14, 1863, June 4, 1863, December 2, 1863, December 30, 1863, January 8, 1864, and February 17, 1864; "The Gallant 154th," *Cattaraugus Freeman*, December 2, 1863; "From our Volunteers," *Cattaraugus Freeman*, December 29, 1864.

13. Charles to Ann Charles, November 15, 1862; "Army Correspondence," *Gowanda Reporter*, undated clipping, Cattaraugus County Memorial and Historical Museum; Quilliam to Rhoda Quilliam, April 3, 1864.

14. "A Soldier's Opinion of Copperheads," *Fredonia Censor*, July 8, 1863.

15. Ibid.; Newton A. Chaffee to Norman F. Moore, August 29, 1864; "Letter from a Soldier," *Cattaraugus Freeman*, June 25, 1863; Devillo Wheeler to his parents, May 12, 1863.

16. Henry Van Aernam to Amy Melissa Van Aernam, July 30, 1863; Emory Sweetland to Mary Sweetland, July 17, 1863.

17. Barzilla Merrill to Ruba Merrill, March 24, 1863; "Letter from a Volunteer in 154th," *Cattaraugus Freeman*, July 18, 1863; Edgar Shannon to Francelia Hunt, November 4, 1863.

18. Chaffee to John R. Babcock, July 27, 1863.

19. "Cattaraugus County: Population of towns since 1860, and their Political Vote," chart courtesy of Kenneth C. Heller.

20. Ibid.; Chittenden to Mary Jane Chittenden, November 7, 1862; Charles to Ann Charles, November 12, 1862, November 15, 1862; "The 154th Regiment," *Fredonia Censor*, November 26, 1862.

21. "Military advice and Dictation," *Cattaraugus Union*, November 21, 1862.

22. "Military advice and Dictation," *Cattaraugus Freeman*, November 27, 1862.

23. "Home," *Cattaraugus Union*, February 20, 1863; "At Home," *Cattaraugus Freeman*, March 24, 1864.

24. George W. Newcomb to Ellen Newcomb, March 6, 1863, Lewis Leigh Collection, USAMHI; Quilliam to Rhoda Quilliam, December 27, 1863, February 4, 1864, February 22, 1864; Horace H. Howlett to his sister, December 28, 1863.

25. "Letter from a Soldier," *Cattaraugus Freeman*, June 25, 1863; Baxter to John Phillips, November 8, 1863.

26. Richard J. McCadden to his brother, April 10, 1863, Ron Meininger Collection; Barzilla Merrill to Ruba Merrill, April 10, 1863; Van Aernam to Amy Melissa Van Aernam, April 11, 1863; Mark H. Dunkelman and Michael J. Winey, "The Hardtack Regiment Meets Lincoln," *Lincoln Herald* 85, no. 2 (summer 1983): 95–9. For reactions in the regiment to Lincoln's

assassination, see Mark H. Dunkelman, "Alas! He Is Gone," *Lincoln Herald* 94, no. 2 (summer 1992): 46–8.

27. Baxter to John Phillips, November 8, 1863; Howlett to his sister, December 28, 1863; Sweetland to Mary Sweetland, March 20, 1864; David S. Jones to Edward Jones, March 27, 1864; Chaffee to A. W. W. Chaffee, September 13, 1864. See also William C. Davis, *Lincoln's Men: How President Lincoln Became Father to an Army and a Nation* (New York: Free Press, 1999), passim.

28. Sweetland to Mary Sweetland, September 4, 1864; "Good For the Captain!" *Cattaraugus Freeman*, June 30, 1864; Shannon to Francelia Hunt, September 15, 1864; "From the 154th Regiment," *Cattaraugus Freeman*, October 6, 1864; Charles to Ann Charles, October 25, 1864.

29. Lewis D. Warner to Nelson P. Wheeler, October 26, 1864, in W. Reginald Wheeler, *Pine Knots and Bark Peelers: The Story of Five Generations of American Lumbermen* (New York: Ganis and Harris, 1960), 66; Howlett to his sister, October 13, 1864; "The Soldiers' Vote," *Cattaraugus Freeman*, November 3, 1864; Horace Smith diary, November 1, 1864.

30. Smith diary, November 14, 1864. See also Mark H. Dunkelman, "Hurray For Old Abe! Fenton! and Dr. Van Aernam! The 1864 Election, as Perceived by the 154th New York Volunteers," *Lincoln Herald* 98, no. 1 (spring 1996): 12–22.

31. Andrew D. Blood to Wesley Blood, January 1, 1865.

32. Regimental muster rolls, National Archives.

33. James M. McPherson, *Battle Cry of Freedom: The Civil War Era* (New York: Oxford Univ. Press, 1988), 600–1.

34. McCadden to his brother, June 15, 1863, Ron Meininger Collection; Dwight Moore to his mother, June 4, 1863.

35. Stephen R. Green to Ann Eliza Jane Green, August 16, 1863, author's collection; Charles to Ann Charles, September 8, 1863; Abell to his parents, July 22, 1863; Oscar F. Wilber to Nathan Wilber, November 21, 1862, Beverly Geisel Collection.

36. McCadden to his sister, October 25, 1863, Ron Meininger Collection; McCadden to his mother and brother, November 8, 1863, Ron Meininger Collection; David Jones to his sister, March 13, 1864; James to Samuel R. Williams, November 2, 1862.

37. Dan B. Allen to Col. E. D. Townsend, February 8, 1864; Special Field Orders, No. 66, Headquarters Department of the Cumberland, March 6, 1864; Commodore P. Vedder to Maj. A. T. Diven, March 26, 1864; all in regimental papers, National Archives; Lewis D. Warner diary, April 17, 1864.

38. Roy P. Basler, ed., *The Collected Works of Abraham Lincoln* (New Brunswick, N.J.: Rutgers Univ. Press, 1953), 7:448–9; "Board of Supervisors—Extra Session" and "The Quota of Cattaraugus," *Cattaraugus Freeman*, August 4, 1864; "Proceedings of the Board of Supervisors—Extra Session," *Cattaraugus Freeman*, August 11, 1864.

39. Sweetland to Mary Sweetland, August 11, 1864.

40. Charles to Ann Charles, September 24, 1864.

41. Ibid., September 19, 1864.

42. Chaffee to A. W. W. Chaffee, September 13, 1864; Levi D. Bryant to Cornelia Bryant, October 30, 1864.

43. Darling to his family, December 16, 1864; John Langhans to Julius Langhans, January 22, 1865.

CHAPTER 4: Comrades, Cowards, and Survivors

1. John Langhans to Julius Langhans, November 5, 1864.

2. Marcellus W. Darling to his parents, October 11, 1862; Alva C. Merrill to Ruba Merrill, November 23, 1862.

3. Barzilla Merrill to Ruba Merrill, February 12, 1863, October 31, 1862.

4. Emory Sweetland to Mary Sweetland, January 1, 1863, April 10, 1864; Edwin R. Osgood to his brother, March 12, 1863.

5. Darling to his family, November 5, 1862; Andrew D. Blood diary, February 10, 1865.

6. Barzilla Merrill to Ruba Merrill, January 1, 1863; William Charles to Ann Charles, January 11, 1864; Marion Plumb to Sarah Plumb, October 20, 1862.

7. Barzilla Merrill to Ruba Merrill, January 9, 1863, March 17, 1863.

8. Alva Merrill to Ruba Merrill, November 8, 1862, November 23, 1862; George W. Newcomb to Ellen Newcomb, January 12, 1863, author's collection; Barzilla Merrill to Ruba Merrill, March 17, 1863.

9. James D. Emmons to his sister, March 13, 1863; Eason W. Bull to Wyman and Lydia Bull, November 19, 1862, December 8, 1862; Nathaniel S. Brown to Wyman Bull, February 20, 1863.

10. Barzilla Merrill to Ruba Merrill, December 4, 1862, January 29, 1863. Also miscellaneous notes; Clark E. Oyer, interview notes, undated; Bradford Rowland and Clark E. Oyer, interview notes, August 29, 1886, and August 21, 1893; Bradford Rowland, Clark E. Oyer, and Esley Groat, interview notes, undated; Charles Harry Matteson, interview notes, October 6, 1893; George C. Waterman to E. D. Northrup, February 5, 1896; all in E. D. Northrup Papers.

11. Robert Macoy, *The Masonic Manual* (New York: Clark, Austin, and Smith, 1857), inscribed on flyleaf, "Henry Loomis, 154th New York vols.," author's collection; E. P. Greer, "A Pioneer, a Gentleman and a Soldier," in *Souvenir Edition of the Winfield Courier* (Winfield, Kans.: Winfield Courier, 1901), 91–2; Charles W. Abell to his parents and siblings, March 21, 1864; Charles E. Whitney, interview notes, December 27, 1890, E. D. Northrup Papers.

12. George A. Taylor to Ellen Taylor, October 11, 1862, October 25, 1862, February 15, 1863, March 29, 1863.

13. Charles G. Sutton, interview notes, undated, E. D. Northrup Papers.

14. Newcomb to Ellen Newcomb, April 8, 1863, USAMHI; William F. Chittenden to his family, November 4, 1862; Chittenden to Mary Jane Chittenden, November 27, 1862; John C. Griswold to his family, March 16, 1863.

15. Charles to Ann Charles, November 27, 1862, May 14, 1863.

16. Chittenden to his family, October 10, 1862; Taylor to Ellen Taylor, December 6, 1862; Charles to Ann Charles, March 23, 1863.

17. Clark E. Oyer, interview notes, undated, E. D. Northrup Papers.

18. Emory Sweetland and Henry Bliton, interview notes, February 18, 1891, E. D. Northrup Papers.

19. John Farnham and Theodore Loveless, interview notes, undated, Clark E. Oyer, interview notes, undated, miscellaneous notes, E. D. Northrup Papers; muster rolls, Company H, February 29, 1864, and thereafter, National Archives.

20. Clark E. Oyer, interview notes, undated, E. D. Northrup Papers.

21. Sweetland to Mary Sweetland, January 26, 1863.

22. Sweetland to Mary Sweetland, April 10, 1864.

23. Griswold to Susan Griswold, October 18, 1862; Henry A. Munger to a friend, October 19, 1862; Plumb to Sarah Plumb, October 17, 1862; Taylor to Ellen Taylor, October 25, 1862.

24. Newcomb to Ellen Newcomb, November 16, 1862, USAMHI; Taylor to Ellen Taylor, November 14, 1862; miscellaneous notes, E. D. Northrup Papers; Newcomb to Ellen Newcomb, January 12, 1863, author's collection; Jerome Averill photographs and records courtesy of National Museum of Health and Medicine, Armed Forces Institute of Pathology, Washington, D.C.

25. Miscellaneous notes; Charles Harry Matteson, interview notes, October 6, 1893; George Eugene Graves, interview notes, August 17, 1895, all in E. D. Northrup Papers.

26. Miscellaneous notes, E. D. Northrup Papers; Company C muster roll, October 31, 1863, National Archives; Stephen Welch diary, February 28, 1863; Lewis D. Warner diary, May 13, 1863; Thaddeus L. Reynolds to his family, May 20, 1863; Griswold to Susan Griswold, February 20, 1864.

27. Alva Merrill to Ruba Merrill, December 26, 1862; Barzilla Merrill to Ruba Merrill, March 17, 1863.

28. "Letter From Col. A. G. Rice," *Cattaraugus Freeman,* October 23, 1862; Sweetland to Mary Sweetland, January 14, 1864; Company A muster rolls, 1864 and 1865, National Archives.

29. Alfred W. Benson diary, May 12, 1864, and May 23, 1864.

30. Charles to Ann Charles, October 26, 1863, and October 29, 1863; Lewis L. Jones to his father and mother, November 21, 1863, Jones pension file, National Archives; Charles to Ann Charles, January 7, 1864; W. W. Day, M.D., to Provost Marshall, April 21, 1865, Benjamin D. Morgan pension file, National Archives.

31. Stephen R. Green to Ann Eliza Jane Green, August 14, 1863, author's collection; Philo A. Markham, *Sketch of The Life & Army Service of P. A. Markham* (n.p., n.d.); Mark Dunkelman and Phil Palen, eds., "Philo Markham's Long Walk," *Civil War Times Illustrated* 34, no. 1 (March/April 1995): 26–30, 83; Green to Ann Eliza Jane Green, November 21, 1863, author's collection.

32. Green to Ann Eliza Jane Green, November 21, 1863, author's collection; Abell to his parents, July 13, 1863.

33. Bull to Wyman Bull, December 27, 1862; Amos Humiston to Philinda Humiston, January 29, 1863; Newcomb to Ellen Newcomb, January 27, 1863, USAMHI.

34. Chittenden to Mary Jane Chittenden, December 8, 1862; Darling to his family, circa August 1863; Bull to Wyman Bull, January 31, 1863; Sweetland to Mary Sweetland, January 20, 1863; Charles to Ann Charles, August 16, 1863.

35. Charles to Ann Charles, August 15, 1864.

36. Griswold to Susan Griswold, November 1 and December 2, 1863.

37. H. S. Merrill to Henry Van Aernam, October 5, 1863.

38. Francis M. Bowen diary, March 4, 1865.

39. Ambrose F. Arnold to Katie Arnold, April 29, 1864.

40. Charles to Ann Charles, April 13, 1863, July 3, 1863.

41. Munger to Cassius Griswold, February 5, 1863; Joseph H. Andrews diary, August 17, 1863; Griswold to Susan Griswold, June 23, 1863; Mervin P. Barber diary, September 7, 1864, September 13, 1864, September 17, 1864, September 20, 1864, October 7, 1864, and October

8, 1864; Bowen diary, February 26, 1865, March 14, 1865, and March 17, 1865; Francis M. Bowen to his wife, March 24, 1865.

42. Green to Ann Eliza Jane Green, May 26, 1863, author's collection; "A Letter From Capt. C. P. Vedder," *Cattaraugus Freeman*, June 25, 1863; Horace Smith diary, May 28, 1864, June 3, 1864, June 4, 1864, and June 5, 1864.

43. Griswold to Susan Griswold, August 6, 1863; Salmon W. Beardsley to his family, September 1, 1863.

44. James D. Quilliam to Rhoda Quilliam, October 25, 1863; Edgar Shannon to Francelia Hunt, January 1, 1864; Green to Ann Eliza Jane Green, March 29, 1863, author's collection; Charles to Ann Charles, March 3, 1865.

45. Darling to his mother, March 13, 1864; Darling to his family, April 5, 1864.

46. Henry Van Aernam to Amy Melissa Van Aernam, May 7, 1863.

47. George J. Mason to his sister, May 31, 1863; Newcomb to Ellen Newcomb, May 10, 1863, USAMHI; Newcomb to Ellen Newcomb, May 15, 1863, author's collection.

48. Green to Ann Eliza Jane Green, undated portion of letter, "Sheat No. 2," Phil Palen Collection.

49. Newton A. Chaffee to John R. Babcock, July 27, 1863; Mason to his mother, July 12, 1863; Charles to Ann Charles, July 17, 1863. For a complete breakdown of the regiment's Gettysburg losses, see Mark H. Dunkelman, "'We Were Compelled to Cut Our Way Through Them, and in Doing so Our Losses Were Heavy': Gettysburg Casualties of the 154th New York Volunteers," *Gettysburg Magazine*, 18 (January 1998): 34–56.

50. Welch diary, July 16, 1863; "Letter from a Volunteer in 154th," *Cattaraugus Freeman*, July 23, 1863, quoting letter of Colby M. Bryant, July 18, 1863; Shannon to Francelia Hunt, July 11, 1863.

51. "Letter from Major L. D. Warner," unidentified newspaper clipping, quoting letter of May 21, 1864, courtesy of Cattaraugus County Historical Museum, Little Valley, N.Y.; Sweetland to Mary Sweetland, June 3, 1864; Darling to his family, June 24, 1864, July 9, 1864; Milon J. Griswold to John C. Griswold, July 2, 1864; "From the 154th N.Y. Vol.," *Fredonia Censor*, September 28, 1864, quoting Griswold's letter of September 12, 1864.

52. Sweetland to Mary Sweetland, January 25, 1865. See also Mark H. Dunkelman, "Emory Sweetland Remembers November 19, 1863," *Lincoln Herald* 96, no. 2 (summer 1994): 44–50.

53. Regimental muster rolls, National Archives.

CHAPTER 5: Enduring Hardships

1. James D. Quilliam to Rhoda Quilliam, October 25, 1863; Barzilla Merrill to Ruba Merrill, December 23, 1862; Harvey Earl to his brother, October 19, 1862; Oscar F. Wilber to Nathan Wilber, November 21, 1862, Beverly Geisel Collection; Levi D. Bryant to Cornelia Bryant, October 4, 1864.

2. Unidentified writer to his uncle and aunt, added to letter of Henry Cunningham to a friend, October 11, 1862; William Charles to Ann Charles, December 25, 1863; James Monroe Carpenter to his friends, October 18, 1862.

3. Quilliam to Rhoda Quilliam, February 1, 1863; John N. Porter to Rosanna Porter

Thorpe, January 7, 1863; Eason W. Bull to Wyman Bull, October 24, 1862; Alva C. Merrill to Ruba Merrill, February 22, 1863.

4. William F. Chittenden to Mary Jane Chittenden, October 3, 1862; Barzilla Merrill to Ruba Merrill, October 18, 1862.

5. Emory Sweetland to Mary Sweetland, February 7, 1863; Dwight Moore to his mother, April 1, 1863; Sweetland to Mary Sweetland, December 7, 1862, December 22, 1862; Imholte, *The Civil War Diary . . . of Corporal Newell Burch* (hereafter cited as Burch diary), 44.

6. John C. Griswold to Susan Griswold, October 26, 1862; Alva C. Merrill to his brother and sister, October 22, 1862; Amos Humiston to Philinda Humiston, November 22, 1862; Charles to Ann Charles, December 27, 1862.

7. George W. Newcomb to Ellen Newcomb, December 22, 1862, author's collection; Barzilla Merrill to Ruba Merrill, December 7, 1862.

8. Newcomb to his father, December 8, 1862, USAMHI; Burch diary, 41.

9. James D. Emmons to his sister Ann, October 26, 1862; Humiston to Philinda Humiston, March 25, 1863; Alva C. Merrill to Ruba Merrill, January 27, 1863.

10. Alva C. Merrill to Ruba Merrill, April 12, 1863; Lewis D. Warner diary, December 12, 1863.

11. Griswold to his friends, March 16, 1863; Bull to Wyman Bull, undated; Barzilla Merrill to Ruba Merrill, April 10, 1863; Horace Smith diary, May 6, 1863.

12. Newcomb to Ellen Newcomb, May 18, 1863, author's collection.

13. "Interesting letter from the 154th," *Fredonia Censor,* February 24, 1864, quoting letter of Milon J. Griswold, December 24, 1863; Sweetland to Mary Sweetland, August 3, 1864; Bryant to Cornelia Bryant, November 8, 1864; John Farnham and Theodore Loveless, interview notes, undated, E. D. Northrup Papers.

14. Ira Wood to Hester Ann Wood, October 2, 1862; Hugh N. Crosgrove to his sister, March 27, 1864; John Dicher to Sarah Frank, December 17, 1862, Doris Laing Collection; Bryant to Cornelia Bryant, March 28, 1865.

15. Sweetland to Mary Sweetland, January 26, 1863; Porter to Rosanna Porter Thorpe, December 22, 1862; Martin D. Bushnell to his parents, January 29, 1864, Frank M. Bushnell Collection.

16. Barzilla Merrill to Ruba Merrill, February 21, 1863; Richard J. McCadden to his brother, June 15, 1863, Ron Meininger Collection.

17. Isaac N. Porter to Charles Murray Harrington, March 11, 1863; "The 154th Regiment," *Fredonia Censor,* November 26, 1862, quoting letter of Lewis D. Warner; Bull to Wyman and Lydia Bull, December 1862.

18. Dwight Moore to his mother, June 18, 1863; Emmons to his sister Ann, June 20, 1863; Charles to Ann Charles, circa June 19, 1863.

19. Charles to Ann Charles, December 17, 1863; "Interesting letter from the 154th," *Fredonia Censor,* February 24, 1864, quoting letter of Milon J. Griswold, December 24, 1863.

20. Edgar Shannon to Francelia Hunt, March 30, 1865; Emory Sweetland to Mary Sweetland, March 12, 1865; Richard J. McCadden to his mother and brother, March 29, 1865.

21. Thaddeus L. Reynolds to his family, February 14, 1863; John Langhans to Julius Langhans, November 5, 1864.

22. Quilliam to Rhoda Quilliam, January 23, 1863; Humiston to Philinda Humiston, January 2, 1862; Oscar F. Wilber to Nathan Wilber, February 2, 1863, Beverly Geisel Collection.

23. Lewis D. Warner to A. E. Fay, July 14, 1864, in unidentified newspaper clipping, Cattaraugus County Memorial and Historical Museum.

24. Stephen R. Green to Ann Eliza Jane Green, June 28, 1863, Phil Palen Collection; Chittenden to Mary Jane Chittenden, October 9, 1862; Charles to Ann Charles, September 17, 1863.

25. George A. Taylor to Ellen Taylor, December 6, 1862; Ira Wood to Hester Ann Wood, October 11, 1862; Earl to his family, March 3, 1863; Griswold to Susan Griswold, February 4, 1863; Griswold to his friends, March 16, 1863.

26. McCadden to his sister, February 14, 1863, Ron Meininger Collection; Martin Van Buren Champlin to Joel Crandall, October 17, 1862; Shannon to Francelia Hunt, November 4, 1863; Esley Groat to his friend, undated; Porter to Rosanna Porter Thorpe, October 11, 1862.

27. McCadden to his sister, February 14, 1863, Ron Meininger Collection; Dwight Moore to his mother, June 4, 1863; "Camp Correspondence," *Gowanda Reporter,* undated clipping, quoting letter of Orlando White of March 13, 1864, Cattaraugus County Memorial and Historical Museum; Shannon to Francelia Hunt, February 22, 1864; Newcomb to Ellen Newcomb, January 13, 1863, USAMHI; Dwight Moore to his brother, May 29, 1863.

28. McCadden to his mother, December 25, 1862, Ron Meininger Collection; Barzilla Merrill to Ruba Merrill, March 17, 1863; Griswold to Susan Griswold, April 26, 1863; Warner diary, June 21, 1863.

29. Charles to Ann Charles, June 4, 1863.

30. "Army Correspondence," *Gowanda Reporter,* undated clipping, quoting letter of Newton A. "Dell" Chaffee, Cattaraugus County Memorial and Historical Museum.

31. Bryant to Cornelia Bryant, March 28, 1865; Newton A. Chaffee to Norman F. Moore, January 17, 1864.

32. Charles to Ann Charles, June 27, 1864.

33. Bull to Lydia Bull, December 7, 1862; Landers Wright to his mother, March 30, 1863.

34. Griswold to his friends, March 16, 1863; Griswold to Susan Griswold, October 2, 1863.

35. Langhans to Julius Langhans, May 28, 1865; Bushnell to his parents, June 3, 1864, Frank M. Bushnell Collection.

36. Horace Howlett to his sister, July 8, 1863; Charles W. Abell to his family, June 2, 1865.

37. Barzilla Merrill to Ruba Merrill, January 13, 1863.

38. "Army Correspondence," *Gowanda Reporter,* undated clipping, quoting undated letter of William Charles, Cattaraugus County Memorial and Historical Museum; Charles to Ann Charles, June 27, 1864, March 20, 1863.

39. Marcellus W. Darling to his family, September 15, 1863; Darling to his mother, June 7, 1864; Darling to his family, September 19, 1864.

40. Newcomb to Ellen Newcomb, December 7, 1862, author's collection; Newcomb to Ellen Newcomb, April 8, 1863, USAMHI.

41. Charles to Ann Charles, May 14, 1863; Humiston to Philinda Humiston, November 22, 1862; Sweetland to Mary Sweetland, October 26, 1862; Edwin R. Osgood to his brother, March 12, 1863; Taylor to his wife and brother, February 21, 1863.

42. Taylor to Ellen Taylor, November 20, 1862; Humiston to Philinda Humiston, March 25, 1863, April 3, 1863.

43. *The Medical and Surgical History of the War of the Rebellion* (Washington: Government Printing Office, 1877), part 2, vol. 2, 117–8.

44. Marion Plumb to Sarah Plumb, November 12, 1862; Plumb to his wife and son, November 16, 1862; Plumb to Sarah Plumb, undated.

45. Chittenden to Mary Jane Chittenden, November 16, 1862; Chittenden to his family, November 24, 1862; Chittenden to Mary Jane Chittenden, December 2, 1862.

46. Green to Ann Eliza Jane Green, January 5, 1864, Phil Palen Collection; Wood to Hester Ann Wood, October 23, 1862.

47. Griswold to Susan Griswold, October 11, 1862, November 16, 1862; Homer A. Ames to Cassius Griswold, May 1, 1864, author's collection.

48. Mrs. Daniel Ball to Henry Van Aernam, M.D., August 4, 1864, USAMHI.

49. Henry Van Aernam to Amy Melissa Van Aernam, January 4, 1864.

CHAPTER 6: On the Battlefield

1. "Brave Boys in Blue," *Ellicottville Post,* September 5, 1888; John F. Wellman, "The Fun in Army Life," *Cattaraugus Republican,* September 19, 1902.

2. Thaddeus L. Reynolds, no salutation, undated; George W. Newcomb to Ellen Newcomb, October 3, 1862, USAMHI; Unidentified writer to his uncle and aunt, added to letter of Henry Cunningham to a friend, October 11, 1862.

3. John N. Porter to Rosanna Porter Thorpe, October 11, 1862; Marcellus W. Darling to his family, November 5, 1862; Reynolds to his family, October 19, 1862; "From the 154th Regiment," *Cattaraugus Freeman,* November 6, 1862, quoting letter of Alanson Crosby of October 23, 1862.

4. "Letter from the 154th," *Cattaraugus Freeman,* April 9, 1863, quoting letter of Alfred W. Benson of March 27, 1863.

5. William Charles to Ann Charles, November 12, 1862; John W. Badgero to George Ellery Badgero, October 11, 1862; "Death of Lieut. John W. Badgero," *Cattaraugus Freeman,* June 18, 1863.

6. Ambrose Arnold to his wife and sons, January 28, 1863.

7. Oscar F. Wilber to Sally D. Wilber, November 27, 1862, Wilber pension file, National Archives; Emory Sweetland to Mary Sweetland, April 9, 1863.

8. Dunkelman and Winey, *The Hardtack Regiment,* 53–60; Mark H. Dunkelman, "Main Address," in *Dedication of the Chancellorsville Monument to the 154th New York Volunteer Infantry* (154th New York Monument Fund, 1996), 10–21; Stephen Sears, *Chancellorsville* (Boston: Houghton Mifflin, 1996), 260–81, 475–91.

9. Richard J. McCadden to his mother, May 8, 1863, Ron Meininger Collection; James D. Quilliam to Rhoda Quilliam, May 11, 1863; Horace Smith diary, May 3, 1863; Darling to his family, June 12, 1863.

10. Truman Harkness to Andrew and Alfred, May 16, 1863; Porter to his brother-in-law, May 9, 1863; Newcomb to Ellen Newcomb, May 10, 1863, USAMHI.

11. Charles H. Field to Adrian Fay, June 8, 1863; Harvey Earl to his brother and sister, May 12, 1863; Charles to Ann Charles, May 8, 1863; Reynolds to his family, May 20, 1863.

12. Thomas R. Aldrich to his mother, May 6, 1863; George J. Mason to his sister Martha, May 1863; Smith diary, May 2, 1863, and May 4, 1863; Henry Van Aernam to Amy Melissa Van Aernam, May 7, 1863, May 15, 1863.

13. Lewis D. Warner diary, May 2, 1863.

14. Homer A. Ames to Susan Griswold, May 24, 1863, author's collection; Field to Adrian Fay, June 8, 1863; Dana P. Horton to Susan Griswold, May 23, 1863.

15. Isaac N. Porter to Charles Murray Harrington, May 13, 1863; Smith diary, May 2, 1863, and May 5, 1863.

16. James W. Washburn to his parents, May 12, 1863; Porter to his brother-in-law, May 9, 1863; Reynolds to his family, May 20, 1863; Newcomb to Ellen Newcomb, May 9, 1863, USAMHI.

17. Homer A. Ames to Susan Griswold, May 12, 1863, Fenton Historical Society, Jamestown, N.Y.; Newcomb to Ellen Newcomb, May 9, 1863, USAMHI; Field to Adrian Fay, June 8, 1863; Porter to his brother-in-law, May 9, 1863.

18. George A. Taylor to Ellen Taylor, May 20, 1863; Charles to Ann Charles, May 11, 1863.

19. Leonard L. Hunt, Joseph Cullen, and Joseph Charlesworth, interview notes, February 21, 1893, E. D. Northrup Papers.

20. "From Washington," *Cattaraugus Freeman*, May 14, 1863, quoting letter of John Manley of May 9, 1863.

21. "The Battle of Chancellorsville—Death of Adj't S. C. Noyes, Jr.," *Cattaraugus Freeman*, May 28, 1863.

22. Henry C. Loomis to John T. Sprague, May 19, 1863, in regimental letter book.

23. "From Washington," *Cattaraugus Freeman*, May 21, 1863, quoting letter of John Manley of May 14, 1863; Van Aernam to Amy Melissa Van Aernam, May 15, 1863.

24. "Losses in the 154th Regiment," *Cattaraugus Freeman*, May 21, 1863, quoting letter of Alanson Crosby of May 13, 1863.

25. Newcomb to Ellen Newcomb, May 8, 1863, USAMHI; Van Aernam to Amy Melissa Van Aernam, May 7, 1863; Amos Humiston to Philinda Humiston, May 9, 1863.

26. Dunkelman and Winey, *The Hardtack Regiment*, 71–7; Mark H. Dunkelman and Michael J. Winey, "The Hardtack Regiment in the Brickyard Fight," *Gettysburg Magazine* 8 (January 1993): 16–30; Dunkelman, "'We Were Compelled to Cut Our Way Through Them. . . .'" *Gettysburg Magazine* 18: 34–56.

27. Mason to his mother, July 12, 1863; Quilliam to William Quilliam, August 23, 1863; Smith diary, July 1, 1863.

28. "Letter from Lieut. Allanson Crosby," *Cattaraugus Freeman*, July 30, 1863, quoting letter of Alanson Crosby to Manley Crosby, July 17, 1863; "Interesting Narrative of the Escape of two Officers of the 154th Regt. N.Y.S. Vols. from the hands of the Rebels," *Jamestown Journal*, March 18, 1864, quoting letter of Alanson Crosby to Samuel G. Love, February 28, 1864; "From the Cattaraugus Regiment—154th," *Cattaraugus Union*, July 24, 1863, quoting letter of Dwight W. Day to his parents, July 8, 1863.

29. "Army Correspondence," *Gowanda Reporter*, undated clipping, quoting Newton A. "Dell" Chaffee to the editor, August 8, 1863, Cattaraugus County Historical Museum.

30. Dan B. Allen to John T. Sprague, July 1863, in regimental letter book, Ellicottville (N.Y.) Historical Society.

31. Lewis D. Warner to General John T. Sprague, December 24, 1863, in regimental letter book, Ellicottville (N.Y.) Historical Society; Dunkelman and Winey, *The Hardtack Regiment*, 62; Peter Cozzens, *The Shipwreck of Their Hopes: The Battles for Chattanooga* (Urbana and Chicago: Univ. of Illinois Press, 1994), 72; regimental return, October 1863, National Archives.

32. Warner diary, October 28, 1863.

33. James W. Baxter to John Phillips, November 8, 1863; Edgar Shannon to Francelia Hunt, November 4, 1863.

34. Martin D. Bushnell to Frank Congdon, November 6, 1863, Phil Palen Collection.

35. Shannon to Francelia Hunt, November 30, 1863; Charles to Ann Charles, November 27, 1863; McCadden to his sister, December 26, 1863, Ron Meininger Collection; "Interesting letter from the 154th," *Fredonia Censor*, February 24, 1864, quoting letter of Milon J. Griswold of December 24, 1863.

36. Salmon W. Beardsley to E. D. Northrup, October 5, 1893, E. D. Northrup Papers; Patrick H. Jones to General John T. Sprague, December 18, 1863, regimental letter book; U.S. War Department, *The War of the Rebellion: A Compilation of the Official Records of the Union and Confederate Armies*, 128 vols. (Washington: Government Printing Office, 1880–1901), series 1, vol. 31, part 2, 366–7 (hereafter cited as *OR*).

37. Dunkelman and Winey, *The Hardtack Regiment*, 101–22.

38. Colby M. Bryant diary, May 25, 1864.

39. Sweetland to Mary Sweetland, June 3, 1864, June 20, 1864; "Letter from Major L. D. Warner," undated newspaper clipping, quoting letter of Lewis D. Warner to A. E. Fay, July 1, 1864, Cattaraugus County Historical Museum.

40. Milon J. Griswold to John C. Griswold, July 2, 1864; "From the 154th N.Y. Vol.," *Fredonia Censor*, September 28, 1864, quoting letter of Milon J. Griswold of September 12, 1864; Addison L. Scutt to his mother-in-law, October 2, 1864.

41. Dunkelman and Winey, *The Hardtack Regiment*, 103–9.

42. Sweetland to Mary Sweetland, May 20, 1864; Darling to his family, May 21, 1864; "Letter from Major L. D. Warner," undated newspaper clipping, quoting letter of Lewis D. Warner to A. E. Fay, May 21, 1864, Cattaraugus County Historical Museum.

43. "Casualties in the 154th N.Y.V.," *Cattaraugus Freeman*, June 2, 1864; "Heroism in the 154th Regiment," *Cattaraugus Freeman*, August 18, 1864; "Letter from Col. P. H. Jones," *Cattaraugus Freeman*, July 7, 1864.

44. *OR*, series 1, vol. 38, part 2, 245–6.

45. Ibid., 246–53.

46. Marcellus W. Darling, *Events and Comments of My Life* (n.p., n.d.), unpaginated; Charles to Ann Charles, December 18, 1863; Quilliam to Rhoda Quilliam, January 1, 1864; Henry A. Munger to Cassius Griswold, August 6, 1863.

CHAPTER 7: The Wounded, Captured, and Dead

1. Andrew M. Keller to Mrs. Brown, May 24, 1863; William F. Chittenden to his family, May 20, 1863; Mary Jane Chittenden to William F. Chittenden, May 24, 1863; William Chittenden to his family, May 30, 1863; *Medical and Surgical History*, part 2, vol. 2, 310; Nathaniel S. Brown, "Claim for Invalid Pension," October 25, 1865, affidavit of Harrison Cheney, August 9, 1866, and affidavit of Milo M. Whiting, January 22, 1887, all in Brown pension file, National Archives.

2. Joseph R. Crowell to E. D. Northrup, September 1, 1889; Bradford Rowland, Clark E. Oyer, and Esley Groat, interview notes, undated, both in E. D. Northrup Papers.

3. Dunkelman and Winey, *The Hardtack Regiment*, 198; *Medical and Surgical History*, passim.

4. William Charles to Ann Charles, May 8, 1863.

5. Henry Van Aernam to Amy Melissa Van Aernam, May 7, 1863, July 30, 1863.

6. "From the Cattaraugus Regiment—154th," *Cattaraugus Union*, July 24, 1863, quoting letter of Dwight W. Day to his parents, July 8, 1863; *Medical and Surgical History*, 583–4; *Presidents, Soldiers, Statesmen*, 1526.

7. Miscellaneous notes of an undated interview with Truman D. Blowers; Clark E. Oyer, interview notes, August 30, 1886, and August 31, 1886; Emory Sweetland, interview notes, February 18, 1891; Emerson M. Wiltse, interview notes, undated, all in E. D. Northrup Papers.

8. Emory Sweetland to Mary Sweetland, May 15, 1863, May 19, 1863, July 17, 1863, July 22, 1863. See also Dunkelman, "Emory Sweetland Remembers November 19, 1863," 44–51.

9. Sweetland to Mary Sweetland, July 11, 1864.

10. Ibid., June 17, 1864.

11. Emory Sweetland, interview notes, February 18, 1891, E. D. Northrup Papers.

12. Thomas R. Aldrich and Byron A. Johnston, interview notes, undated; Bradford Rowland, Clark E. Oyer, and Esley Groat, interview notes, undated; William A. Farlee to E. D. Northrup, January 28, 1879, all in E. D. Northrup Papers.

13. Addison L. Scutt to his mother-in-law, October 2, 1864; Amos Humiston to Philinda Humiston, May 9, 1863; William D. Harper diary, October 28, 1863; Bradford Rowland, Clark E. Oyer, and Esley Groat, interview notes, undated, E. D. Northrup Papers; Homer A. Ames to his parents, July 11, 1864, Carolyn Ames Simons Collection.

14. "The 154th New York," *Cattaraugus Freeman*, July 23, 1863, quoting letter of James W. Phelps, July 19, 1863; James W. Phelps to Mr. Reynolds, July 24, 1863.

15. Stephen Welch diary, May 4–24, 1863; Colby M. Bryant diary, May 4–23, 1863.

16. Horace Smith diary, July 4–November 3, 1863; Burch diary; Aldrich, "The Experience of Thomas R. Aldrich . . . while a prisoner of war," passim (hereafter cited as Aldrich memoir).

17. Burch diary, 111–3, 116, 120, 127.

18. Smith diary, July 4, October 11, 25, 29–31, November 1, 1863.

19. Aldrich memoir; Leroy Litchfield, interview notes, August 28, 1895, E. D. Northrup Papers.

20. Charles W. Abell to his father, August 3, 1864; "Letter From Surgeon Van Aernam," *Cattaraugus Freeman*, August 18, 1863, quoting letter of Henry Van Aernam, August 3, 1864.

21. Marcellus W. Darling to his family, September 11, 1864.

22. Charles to Ann Charles, December 28, 1864; Lewis D. Warner to George L. Gile, April 3, 1865; Newton A. Chaffee to Norman F. Moore, April 23, 1865.

23. Edward R. Jones, poem, "The Starving Prisoners in Richmond."

24. Charles E. Whitney diary, May 8–November 19, 1864; Adams, *Historical Gazetteer and Biographical Memorial of Cattaraugus County*, 744; Charles E. Whitney, interview notes, December 27, 1890, E. D. Northrup Papers.

25. State of New York, Andersonville Monument Dedication Commission, *Dedication of Monument Erected by the State of New York at Andersonville, Georgia 1914* (Albany: J. B. Lyon Co., 1916), 90–1, 112, 144.

26. Lewis O. Saum, "Death in the Popular Mind of Pre–Civil War America," in David E. Stannard, ed., *Death in America* (Philadelphia: Univ. of Pennsylvania Press, 1975), 30–48; Drew Gilpin Faust, "The Civil War Soldier and the Art of Dying," in *The Civil War Soldier: A Historical Reader*, edited by Michael Barton and Larry M. Logue (New York: New York Univ. Press, 2002), 485–511.

27. "From the 154th Regiment," *Cattaraugus Freeman,* October 2, 1862, quoting letter of Henry Van Aernam of September 30, 1862; "Resolutions of Co. E, 154th Reg.," *Westfield Republican,* November 5, 1862; "Register of Deaths" in company descriptive books, National Archives; "Records of Soldiers by Towns," Cattaraugus County Historical Museum.

28. Chittenden to his family, October 20, 1862; Marion Plumb to Sarah Plumb, October 20, 1862; John C. Griswold to Susan Griswold, October 21, 1862; "Death in the 154th," *Cattaraugus Freeman,* November 6, 1862.

29. Chittenden to his family, October 20, 1862.

30. Ira Wood to Hester Ann Wood, October 21, 1862; "From the 154th Regiment," *Cattaraugus Freeman,* November 6, 1862, quoting letter of Alanson Crosby of October 23, 1862.

31. Abell to his mother, October 3, 1863.

32. *Presidents, Soldiers, Statesmen,* 1325; Truman A. St. John to William S. Sprague, March 1, 1863; William Kendall to William S. Sprague, March 2, 1863; Joseph B. Fay to William S. Sprague, March 2, 1863; St. John to William S. Sprague, March 16, 1863.

33. Nathaniel S. Brown to Wyman Bull, February 20, 1863.

34. Charles to Ann Charles, March 21, 1865; Barzilla Merrill to Ruba Merrill, April 9, 1863; Griswold to Susan Griswold, September 22, 1863; Sweetland to Mary Sweetland, October 30, 1864; Charles to Ann Charles, April 1864.

35. John N. Porter to Rosanna Porter Thorpe, April 2, 1863; "Letter from the 154th," *Cattaraugus Freeman,* April 9, 1863, quoting letter of Alfred W. Benson of March 27, 1863; James M. Gallagher to Emeline Moore, September 25, 1863.

36. "Died," *Fredonia Censor,* February 11, 1863; "Died in Hospital," *Cattaraugus Freeman,* February 19, 1863; "Death of Edward Schultz," *Cattaraugus Union,* March 6, 1863; "The remains of Edward Shults," *Cattaraugus Freeman,* March 12, 1863; Humiston to Philinda Humiston, January 11, 1863.

37. "Death of a Soldier," *Cattaraugus Freeman,* June 25, 1863, quoting letter of unidentified writer of June 12, 1863; Mrs. S. L. Mead to E. D. Northrup, March 15, 1893; H. C. Taylor to E. D. Northrup, January 15, 1895, both in E. D. Northrup Papers.

38. Regimental Order No. 34, March 6, 1863, in regimental order book, National Archives; memorandum in Harper diary, June 9, 1864; Edson D. Ames to his family, March 30, 1865; John M. Irvin to John L. Jones, June 3, 1864; "Cameron's a/c of Sam C. Noyes," in miscellaneous notes, E. D. Northrup Papers.

39. Alfred W. Benson to Dexter Campbell, December 20, 1864.

40. Gallagher to Emeline Moore, September 25, 1863.

41. Charles to Ann Charles, December 30, 1863.

42. Dwight Moore to his mother, May 22, 1863.

43. "The Roll of Honor. Death of Adj't Samuel C. Noyes, Jr.," *Cattaraugus Freeman,* May 21, 1863; "The Battle of Chancellorsville—Death of Adj't S. C. Noyes, Jr.," *Cattaraugus Freeman,* May 28, 1863; "Death of Adj't Samuel C. Noyes, Jr.," *Cattaraugus Union,* May 29, 1863.

44. "Death of Captain Allanson Crosby!" *Cattaraugus Freeman,* July 14, 1864; "Death of Capt. Crosby—Meeting of the Bar," *Cattaraugus Freeman,* July 21, 1864; "Capt. Crosby," *Cattaraugus Freeman,* July 21, 1864; "A Tribute to the Memory of the Late Capt. Allanson Crosby," *Cattaraugus Freeman,* August 11, 1864; "Letter From Capt. C. P. Vedder," *Cattaraugus Freeman,* August 18, 1864; "Letter from Major L. D. Warner," undated newspaper clipping, quoting letter of Lewis D. Warner to A. E. Fay, July 28, 1864.

45. "Resolutions passed by Co. E, 154th N.Y.V.," *Fredonia Censor,* April 6, 1864.

46. James D. Quilliam to Rhoda Quilliam, May 27, 1863; "John Wilson," *Fredonia Censor,* May 13, 1863; "The 154th Regiment—Losses of Co's E and F," *Fredonia Censor,* May 20, 1863; "The Romance of War," *Cattaraugus Freeman,* December 2, 1863; "Returned," *Cattaraugus Union,* August 24, 1865.

47. Mary Jane Chittenden to William F. Chittenden, May 24, 1863; Charles to Ann Charles, May 16, 1864; Ruba Cole Merrill diary, February 1, 1863; "Widow's Claim for Increase of Pension," November 1, 1866, William H. Seeker pension file, National Archives.

48. Army and Navy Record Company soldier's memorial, Gardner Walker Raistrick Collection, Greenhurst, New York; Currier & Ives, "The Soldier's Grave," lithograph, 1865, author's collection.

49. Charles to Ann Charles, August 8, 1864.

50. John F. Wellman, "The Fun in Army Life," *Cattaraugus Republican,* September 19, 1902; William A. Farlee to E. D. Northrup, January 28, 1879; John Farnham and Theodore Loveless, interview notes, undated; William Clark, interview notes, October 30, 1893; Bradford Rowland, Clark E. Oyer, and Esley Groat, interview notes, undated; Stephen Welch, interview notes, undated, all in E. D. Northrup Papers.

51. Betsey Phelps Howlett, poem, "On the Death of Barzillai and Alva Merrill."

52. David S. Jones, poem, "On the Death of Anson N. Park."

CHAPTER 8: In Camp and Beyond

1. Mark E. Neely Jr. and Harold Holzer, *The Union Image: Popular Prints of the Civil War North* (Chapel Hill: Univ. of North Carolina Press, 2000), 57; John N. Porter to Rosanna Porter Thorpe, October 11, 1862; John W. Badgero to George Ellery Badgero, October 11, 1862; L. N. Rosenthal, "Camp Seward, Va., 154th Regt. N.Y.S. Vol. Inf'ty.," engraving sent by Devillo Wheeler to William H. Wheeler, author's collection.

2. Henry Van Aernam to Amy Melissa Van Aernam, October 25, 1862; Edgar Shannon to Francelia Hunt, April 7, 1865.

3. George W. Newcomb to Ellen Newcomb, January 10, 1863, author's collection; Amos Humiston to Philinda Humiston, January 11, 1863; Barzilla Merrill to Ruba Merrill, January 7, 1863.

4. Van Aernam to Amy Melissa Van Aernam, January 27, 1863; James D. Emmons to his sister, February 4, 1863.

5. "Letter from the 154th," *Cattaraugus Freeman,* April 9, 1863, quoting letter of Alfred W. Benson of March 27, 1863; Newcomb to Ellen Newcomb, circa February 9, 1863, author's collection; Barzilla Merrill to Ruba Merrill, February 10, 1863.

6. James D. Quilliam to Rhoda Quilliam, December 26, 1863; Newton A. Chaffee to Norman F. Moore, January 17, 1864; William Charles to Ann Charles, December 30, 1863, January 20, 1864; Marshall A. Perkins to Dear Parents, February 21, 1864.

7. Charles W. Abell to his parents, February 18, 1863; Abell to his family, February 28, 1864; Emmons to his sister, March 13, 1863; Lyman Wilber to his uncle and aunt, January 29, 1864; Milon J. Griswold to his cousin and aunt, March 2, 1864.

8. Shannon to Francelia Hunt, November 20, 1862; Richard J. McCadden to his brother, December 7, 1862, Ron Meininger Collection; Lewis D. Warner diary, May 26, 1863; Regimen-

tal Order No. 55, May 30, 1863, regimental order book, National Archives; Quilliam to Rhoda Quilliam, May 31, 1863; George J. Mason to his sister, May 31, 1863; Regimental Order No. 75, December 24, 1863, regimental order book, National Archives; Dana P. Horton to John C. Griswold, January 8, 1864; "Letter From Captain Fay," *Fredonia Censor*, September 9, 1863; Lewis D. Warner diary, July 12, 1864.

9. Burch diary; Barzilla Merrill to Ruba Merrill, March 20, 1863; Bradford Rowland and Clark E. Oyer, interview notes, August 29, 1886, E. D. Northrup Papers.

10. Barzilla Merrill to Ruba Merrill, April 11, 1863; Homer A. Ames to his father and mother, April 17, 1864, Carolyn Ames Simons Collection; Joshua R. Pettit diary, April 16, 1864.

11. John F. Wellman, "The Fun in Army Life," *Cattaraugus Republican*, September 19, 1902; Bradford Rowland and Clark E. Oyer, interview notes, August 21, 1893, E. D. Northrup Papers.

12. Bradford Rowland, Clark E. Oyer, and Esley Groat, interview notes, undated, E. D. Northrup Papers; Wellman, "The Fun in Army Life," *Cattaraugus Republican*, September 19, 1902; Bradford Rowland and Clark E. Oyer, interview notes, August 29, 1886, E. D. Northrup Papers.

13. Bradford Rowland, Clark E. Oyer, and Esley Groat, interview notes, undated; Bradford Rowland and Clark E. Oyer, interview notes, August 29, 1886, and August 21, 1893; Thomas R. Aldrich and Byron A. Johnston, interview notes, undated, all in E. D. Northrup Papers.

14. Sweetland to Mary Sweetland, December 7, 1862; Oscar F. Wilber to Nathan Wilber, October 14, 1862, Beverly Geisel Collection.

15. Charles to Ann Charles, December 6, 1863.

16. Ellis, *History of Cattaraugus County*, passim.

17. Abell to his family, undated letter fragment, circa October 1862; Charles to Ann Charles, January 5, 1863; Emory Sweetland to Mary Sweetland, January 16, 1863.

18. Francis Strickland to Catherine Strickland, May 27, 1863; Philo A. Markham to his sister, January 13, 1864; Abell to his parents and siblings, March 15, 1863; Sweetland to Mary Sweetland, June 1, 1863, June 3, 1864.

19. Abell to his mother, October 29, 1862; Ira Wood to Hester Ann Wood, October 11, 1862, October 24, 1862.

20. Charles to Ann Charles, May 14, 1863.

21. Ellis, *History of Cattaraugus County*, 481; Barzilla Merrill to Ruba Merrill, October 19, 1862; Stephen R. Green to Ann Eliza Jane Green, August 15, 1863, author's collection.

22. Sweetland to Mary Sweetland, January 16, 1863, March 2, 1863, April 2, 1863, April 12, 1863; Charles to Ann Charles, August 16, 1863; Barzilla Merrill to Ruba Merrill, April 11, 1863; Henry D. Lowing to Colonel Patrick H. Jones, December 14, 1863, in regimental letter book; "Resignation of Rev. H. D. Lowing," *Cattaraugus Freeman*, February 10, 1864.

23. Moss, *Annals of the United States Christian Commission*, 480–1; Quilliam to Rhoda Quilliam, March 13, 1864; Abell to his family, February 21, 1864.

24. Lewis D. Warner to Nelson P. Wheeler, October 26, 1864, in Wheeler, *Pine Knots and Bark Peelers*, 70; William W. Norton to Frankie Norton, November 3, 1864, December 17, 1864, January 4, 1865.

25. Charles to Ann Charles, November 27, 1862; Emmons to his sister, February 4, 1863; Charles to Ann Charles, December 6, 1863; Abell to his sister, July 17, 1864; Sweetland to Mary Sweetland, July 27, 1864.

26. George A. Taylor to Ellen Taylor, October 11, 1862; Shannon to Francelia Hunt, November 20, 1862; Charles to Ann Charles, August 16, 1863; Barzilla Merrill to Ruba Merrill, March 8, 1863; Sweetland to Mary Sweetland, December 7, 1862, January 1, 1863.

27. Emmons to his sister Ann, October 28, 1862; Shannon to Francelia Hunt, February 13, 1864.

28. Francis M. Bowen diary, March 7, 1865; Wood to his family, November 13, 1862; Sweetland to Mary Sweetland, December 7, 1862, January 26, 1862; Porter to Rosanna Porter Thorpe, April 2, 1863.

29. Thomas R. Aldrich and Byron A. Johnston, interview notes, undated, E. D. Northrup Papers; Martin D. Bushnell diary, March 21, 1864; Sweetland to Mary Sweetland, January 20, 1865.

30. Levi D. Bryant to Cornelia Bryant, January 12, 1865; Thaddeus L. Reynolds to his family, February 5, 1863; Stephen Welch diary, April 26, 1863; Alexander Bird diary, January 31, 1863; Bradford Rowland, Clark E. Oyer, and Esley Groat, interview notes, undated, E. D. Northrup Papers; Pettit diary, April 4, 1865.

31. Barzilla Merrill to Ruba Merrill, January 1, 1863; Wood to Hester Ann Wood, October 21, 1862; Sweetland to Mary Sweetland, December 7, 1862, October 26, 1862; Alva C. Merrill to Ruba Merrill, December 26, 1862, January 27, 1863.

32. William F. Chittenden to Mary Jane Chittenden, October 9, 1862; Charles to Ann Charles, November 6, 1862; Chittenden to Mary Jane Chittenden, November 7, 1862.

33. Lewis D. Warner to Nelson P. Wheeler, October 26, 1864, in Wheeler, *Pine Knots and Bark Peelers,* 67; Bryant to Cornelia Bryant, March 28, 1865.

34. Chittenden to Mary Jane Chittenden, November 7, 1862; Mary Jane Chittenden to William F. Chittenden, November 13, 1863.

35. Sweetland to Mary Sweetland, January 20, 1865; Joel M. Bouton to Stephen E. Hoyt, March 29, 1863.

36. Warner to Nelson P. Wheeler, October 21, 1862, in Wheeler, *Pine Knots and Bark Peelers,* 64; Burch diary, 22; "From the 154th Regiment," *Cattaraugus Freeman,* December 18, 1862, quoting letter of Alanson Crosby of December 8, 1862.

37. Shannon to Francelia Hunt, April 10, 1863; Van Aernam to Amy Melissa Van Aernam, May 15, 1863; "From the 154th Regiment," *Gowanda Reporter,* undated clipping quoting undated letter of Allen L. Robbins, Cattaraugus County Historical Museum; Dwight Moore to his mother, May 8, 1863; Stephen Welch to his wife, June 12, 1863. For a more thorough assessment of the regiment's relationship with the Eleventh Corps Germans, see Mark H. Dunkelman, "Hardtack and Sauerkraut Stew: Ethnic Tensions in the 154th New York Volunteers, Eleventh Corps, during the Civil War," *Yearbook of German-American Studies* 36 (2001): 69–90.

38. Sweetland to Mary Sweetland, January 1, 1863; Levi L. Carr to his sister, December 26, 1862; George W. Barr to Vinnie, December 24, 1862; Shannon to Francelia Hunt, December 21, 1862; *Gowanda Reporter,* undated clipping, quoting letter of Newton A. "Dell" Chaffee of January 15, 1863, Cattaraugus County Historical Museum.

39. Alansing Wyant to his parents and siblings, February 24, 1863; Sweetland to Mary Sweetland, June 4, 1863; Horace Smith diary, June 13, 1863, and June 28, 1863; Shannon to

Francelia Hunt, March 22, 1865; Sweetland to Mary Sweetland, March 28, 1865; Patrick H. Jones, interview notes, undated, E. D. Northrup Papers.

40. Sweetland to Mary Sweetland, April 9, 1863; Newcomb to his father, December 8, 1862, USAMHI; Barzilla Merrill to Ruba Merrill, January 1, 1863.

41. Reynolds to his family, May 20, 1863; Charles E. Whitney, interview notes, December 27, 1890, and William Clark, interview notes, October 30, 1893, E. D. Northrup Papers.

42. Quilliam to Rhoda Quilliam, January 22, 1864; Sweetland to Mary Sweetland, February 28, 1864; Van Aernam, note, circa April 11, 1864, written on reverse of General Order #8, Howard's farewell to the Eleventh Corps, USAMHI.

43. Warner diary, November 2, 1863; Sweetland to Mary Sweetland, June 12, 1864, July 29, 1864; Quilliam to Rhoda Quilliam, April 10, 1864.

44. McCadden to his mother and brother, January 29, 1864, Ron Meininger Collection; Quilliam to Rhoda Quilliam, January 30, 1864; Martin D. Bushnell to his parents, January 29, 1864, Frank M. Bushnell Collection; Patrick H. Jones to E. D. Northrup, January 16, 1894, E. D. Northrup Papers.

45. Sweetland to Mary Sweetland, June 25, 1864, July 16, 1864, August 31, 1864; "From the 154th N.Y. Vol.," *Fredonia Censor*, September 28, 1864, quoting letter of Milon J. Griswold, September 12, 1864; Sherman, *Memoirs of General William T. Sherman*, 2:133.

46. Mason to his family, July 27, 1864; "From the 154th N.Y. Vol.," *Fredonia Censor*, September 28, 1864.

47. Marcellus W. Darling to his family, September 11, 1864; Sweetland to Mary Sweetland, August 31, 1864; William P. James, poem, "The White Star Division."

48. Charles W. McKay, "'Three Years or During the War,' With the Crescent and Star," *National Tribune Scrap Book*, 143; McCadden to his mother and brother, April 3, 1865, Ron Meininger Collection; Nathaniel Patterson, interview notes, undated, E. D. Northrup Papers.

49. Charles Harry Matteson, interview notes, October 6, 1893, E. D. Northrup Papers; Darling, *Events and Comments of My Life*; "One on Land and One on Sea," *Sioux City (Iowa) Journal*, February 23, 1891; "From the 154th N.Y. Vol.," *Fredonia Censor*, September 28, 1864; Sweetland to Mary Sweetland, October 2, 1864, April 10, 1865.

50. Sweetland to Mary Sweetland, December 22, 1862; Thaddeus Reynolds, fragment of letter, February 4, 1863.

51. Devillo Wheeler to William H. Wheeler, February 2, 1863; Barzilla Merrill to Ruba Merrill, January 7, 1863.

52. "From the Army," *Cattaraugus Freeman*, June 25, 1863, quoting letter of William H. H. Campbell, June 14, 1863; "Letter from Major L. D. Warner," undated clippings from the *Oleun Times*, quoting letters of Warner to A. E. Fay, July 14, 1864, and July 1, 1864.

53. Colby M. Bryant diary, May 3, 1863; Burch diary, 77–8; Smith diary, July 2, 1863; Charles to Ann Charles, May 17, 1863. For more on fraternization in the regiment, see Mark H. Dunkelman, "A Reflection of Their Own Image," *North & South* 3, no. 2 (January 2000): 74–80.

54. Taylor to his family, October 21, 1862; Eason Bull to Lydia Bull, November 14, 1862; Marshall O. Bond diary, February 5, 1863; Shannon to Francelia Hunt, March 30, 1865.

55. Barzilla Merrill to Ruba Merrill, January 1, 1863; Quilliam to Rhoda Quilliam, March 27, 1863; Charles to Ann Charles, July 17, 1864.

56. Van Aernam to Amy Melissa Van Aernam, November 5, 1862; "The 154th Regiment,"

Fredonia Censor, November 26, 1862, quoting undated letter of Lewis D. Warner; "From the 154th Regiment," *Cattaraugus Freeman,* December 18, 1862, quoting letter of Alanson Crosby of December 8, 1862.

57. Smith diary, April 16, 1863; Newcomb to his father, December 8, 1862, USAMHI; Charles to Ann Charles, June 27, 1864.

58. Sweetland to Mary Sweetland, June 27, 1863; Bryant diary, December 1, 1863.

59. Dwight Moore to his mother, June 19, 1863; Newcomb to Ellen Newcomb, June 20, 1863, USAMHI; Warner diary, July 23, 1863; Patrick Griffin military records, National Archives.

60. Andrew D. Blood diary, November 12, 1862; Alfred W. Benson diary, February 7, 1864, September 11, 1864; Bird diary, January 14, 1865; Abell to his family, January 22, 1865.

61. Sweetland to Mary Sweetland, August 3, 1864; Charles to Ann Charles, October 29, 1863, October 27, 1863.

62. John C. Griswold to Susan Griswold, November 10, 1863; Barzilla Merrill to Ruba Merrill, October 11, 1862; Green to Ann Eliza Jane Green, April 15, 1863, author's collection; Charles to Ann Charles, November 15, 1863.

63. Shannon to Francelia Hunt, October 16, 1862; Bull to Wyman Bull, November 1, 1862.

64. Samuel R. Williams to Martha James, May 9, 1863; Newcomb to Ellen Newcomb, January 27, 1863, USAMHI; Landers Wright to his mother, February 11, 1863; Bryant to Cornelia Bryant, March 28, 1865.

65. Harvey Earl to his brother, May 23, 1863; Isaac N. Porter to Charles Murray Harrington, March 11, 1863; Barzilla Merrill to Ruba Merrill, January 13, 1863.

66. Newcomb to Ellen Newcomb, January 19, 1863, USAMHI.

67. Quilliam to his father, January 27, 1864; Charles to his son, November 29, 1864.

68. Van Aernam to Amy Melissa Van Aernam, June 21, 1863.

69. Charles to his family, October 3, 1862; Quilliam to Rhoda Quilliam, May 18, 1863, May 17, 1863; Smith diary, April 16, 1863.

70. Asher Bliss Jr. to his mother, June 26, 1863; Horace H. Howlett to his sister, May 21, 1864; Bowen diary, March 24, 1865.

71. Charles to Ann Charles, April 24, 1864; Shannon to Francelia Hunt, April 21, 1864; Ariel H. Wellman military records, National Archives.

72. Sweetland, letter fragment, probably December 15, 1864; John Langhans to Julius Langhans, June 9, 1865; Shannon to Francelia Hunt, January 25, 1865.

73. Shannon to Francelia Hunt, March 22, 1865; Bowen diary, January 4, 1865; Bird diary, December 20, 1864.

74. George H. Davidson, interview notes, March 8, 1895, E. D. Northrup Papers; Clark E. Oyer, interview notes, undated, E. D. Northrup Papers.

75. William A. Farlee, "Mustering in Colored Troops," account accompanying letter to E. D. Northrup, January 28, 1879, E. D. Northrup Papers. For a broader treatment of the topic, see Mark H. Dunkelman, "Through White Eyes: The 154th New York Volunteers and African-Americans in the Civil War," *Journal of Negro History* 83, no. 3 (summer 2000): 96–111.

CHAPTER 9: Shoulder Straps and Courts-Martial

1. George A. Taylor to Ellen Taylor, February 1, 1863; Matthew B. Cheney to Capt. R. R. Crowley, September 3, 1893, E. D. Northrup Papers.

2. Barzilla Merrill to Ruba Merrill, April 11, 1863; Horace H. Howlett to his brother and sister, November 30, 1862; Taylor to his brother and sister, March 16, 1863; Levi D. Bryant to Cornelia Bryant, October 30, 1864; Taylor to Ellen Taylor, March 29, 1863; Francis M. Bowen diary, March 17, 1865.

3. Emory Sweetland to Mary Sweetland, January 1, 1863; "Local and Miscellaneous," *Cattaraugus Freeman*, August 6, 1863; Morris Keim to E. D. Northrup, January 12, 1896, E. D. Northrup Papers.

4. George W. Newcomb to Ellen Newcomb, March 7, 1863, USAMHI; John N. Porter to Rosanna Porter Thorpe, February 2, 1863.

5. "Camp 'James M. Brown,'" *Cattaraugus Freeman*, August 21, 1862, quoting letter of "Volunteer," August 14, 1862; "Camp 'James M. Brown,'" *Cattaraugus Freeman*, September 11, 1862, quoting letter of Richard J. McCadden, September 6, 1862; "From Camp 'James M. Brown,'" *Cattaraugus Freeman*, September 11, 1862, quoting letter of "D. R. B.," September 4, 1862; "From the 154th Regiment," *Cattaraugus Freeman*, November 6, 1862, quoting letter of Alanson Crosby, October 23, 1862; Charles W. Abell, undated letter fragment, circa October 1862.

6. Alansing Wyant to his parents and siblings, February 24, 1863; Abell, undated letter fragment, circa October 1862; James W. Washburn to his parents, May 24, 1863; Henry C. Loomis to Colonel Charles R. Coster, June 1, 1863, in regimental letter book.

7. Undated clipping, *Gowanda Reporter*, quoting letter of "D. K.," June 2, 1863; Horace Smith diary, July 4, 1864; Lewis D. Warner diary, September 22, 1864.

8. Adams, *Historical Gazetteer and Biographical Memorial of Cattaraugus County*, 359–60, 370. See also Mark H. Dunkelman, "Brigadier General Patrick Henry Jones," *Lincoln Herald* 89, no. 2 (summer 1987): 71–6.

9. Regimental Order No. 6, November 25, 1862; Patrick H. Jones to Capt. J. Alexander, November 29, 1862; Regimental Order No. 20, January 29, 1863; Regimental Order No. 21, January 29, 1863; Jones to General John T. Sprague, March 13, 1863; Jones to General Sprague, June 9, 1863; Regimental Order No. 79, December 31, 1863; Jones to General Sprague, January 22, 1864, all in regimental letter book.

10. Barzilla Merrill to Ruba Merrill, April 11, 1863; "From the 154th Regiment," *Cattaraugus Freeman*, December 18, 1862, quoting letter of Alanson Crosby, December 8, 1862; Truman Harkness to Andrew and Alfred, May 16, 1863; Washburn to his parents, May 24, 1863; "From Washington," *Cattaraugus Freeman*, May 14, 1863, quoting letter of John Manley, May 9, 1863.

11. Stephen R. Green to Ann Eliza Jane Green, December 28, 1863, Phil Palen Collection; Sweetland to Mary Sweetland, January 14, 1864; Smith diary, November 14, 1864.

12. Patrick H. Jones to General Lorenzo Thomas, January 14, 1864, Jones military file, National Archives; Reuben E. Fenton [and seventeen others] to the President of the United States, undated petition endorsed by Abraham Lincoln, March 17, 1864, John Hay Library, Brown University, Providence, R.I.; Reuben E. Fenton to Abraham Lincoln, October 11, 1864, Jones military file, National Archives; "Patrick H. Jones, Clerk of the Court of Appeals," in S. R. Harlow and H. H. Boone, *Life Sketches of the State Officers, Senators, and Members of the Assembly of the State of New York* (Albany: Weed, Parsons and Company, 1867), 46–9; Bowen diary, January 5, 1865; "Deserved Promotion," *Cattaraugus Freeman*, January 26, 1865; "Promoted," *Fredonia Censor*, February 1, 1865.

13. Patrick H. Jones to General John T. Sprague, June 9, 1863; Taylor to Ellen Taylor, March 6, 1863; Lewis D. Warner diary, May 26, 1863; Lewis D. Warner to General O. O. Howard, November 22, 1865, Oliver Otis Howard Papers, Bowdoin College Library, Brunswick, Me.; Matthew B. Cheney to E. D. Northrup, April 9, 1894, E. D. Northrup Papers.

14. "The New Recruits," *Cattaraugus Union*, August 22, 1862; Philander W. Hubbard to Colonel Patrick H. Jones, January 1, 1863, John R. Burdick to Colonel Jones, May 19, 1863, Orlando W. Avery to Patrick H. Jones, March 22, 1863, all in regimental letter book.

15. Baker Leonard Saxton to Colonel Patrick H. Jones, December 3, 1862, regimental letter book; Andrew D. Blood diary, December 3, 1862; Ira Wood to Hester Ann Wood, December 14, 1862; Saxton to Colonel Jones, March 3, 1863, Saxton pension file, National Archives.

16. Porter to Rosanna Porter Thorpe, October 11, 1862, January 7, 1863, April 3, 1863; Thaddeus L. Reynolds to his family, February 14, 1863; Taylor to Ellen Taylor, March 6, 1863; John F. Nelson to Colonel Patrick H. Jones, March 15, 1863, Patrick H. Jones to Paymaster General, U.S.A., March 19, 1863, both in regimental letter book; "Letter from the 154th," *Cattaraugus Freeman*, April 9, 1863, quoting letter of Alfred W. Benson, March 27, 1863.

17. Newcomb to Ellen Newcomb, March 6, 1863, Lewis Leigh Collection, USAMHI; Newcomb to Ellen Newcomb, February 28, 1863, Alexander G. Lynn Collection; Newcomb to Ellen Newcomb, April 8, 1863, USAMHI; George J. Mason to his sister Martha, October 3, 1863.

18. Taylor to Ellen Taylor, February 1, 1863, March 6, 1863; Taylor to his parents and siblings, March 8, 1863; Charles to Ann Charles, April 23, 1863; Henry Van Aernam, interview notes, August 4, 1890, E. D. Northrup Papers.

19. Susan Griswold to John C. Griswold, May 5, 1863, author's collection; Taylor to Ellen Taylor, May 31, 1863.

20. Newcomb to Ellen Taylor, February 1, 1863, author's collection.

21. Henry Martin cadet card, U.S. Military Academy Library, West Point, N.Y.; Charles A. McIntosh to E. D. Northrup, January 21, 1894; Salmon W. Beardsley to E. D. Northrup, October 22, 1895; Zeno Besecker, interview notes, undated; Bradford Rowland and Clark E. Oyer, interview notes, August 29, 1886; miscellaneous notes, all in E. D. Northrup Papers; Lewis D. Warner diary, August 9, 1864.

22. Griswold to Susan Griswold, April 19, 1863; Griswold to Cassius Griswold, December 26, 1862, November 26, 1862; Homer A. Ames to Susan Griswold, May 12, 1863, Fenton Historical Society; "From the Soldiers in the Field," *Fredonia Censor*, April 6, 1864, quoting letter of Milon J. Griswold, March 21, 1864.

23. Milon J. Griswold to Susan and Cassius Griswold, March 2, 1864; obituary of Mrs. Susan Griswold, *Fredonia Censor*, April 6, 1864; Milton D. Scott to William Scott, October 14, 1864.

24. Taylor to Ellen Taylor, November 14, 1862; Green to Ann Eliza Jane Green, August 14, 1863, author's collection; Bradford Rowland, interview notes, March 3, 1893, E. D. Northrup Papers; Richard J. McCadden to his mother, February 18, 1863, May 10, 1863, Ron Meininger Collection.

25. Marshall O. Bond diary, March 9, 1863.

26. Newton A. Chaffee to Norman F. Moore, April 6, 1864; Marcellus W. Darling to his mother, March 13, 1864; Edgar Shannon to Francelia Hunt, February 13, 1864; Shannon to Francelia Hunt, March 26, 1864.

27. Darling to his family, September 19, 1864; Shannon to Francelia Hunt, September 22, 1864.

28. Patrick H. Jones to Gen. Thomas Hillhouse, December 3, 1862; Officers of the 154th New York to Major Jacob H. Ten Eyck, January 2, 1863, and endorsement by Colonel Jones, January 4, 1863, all in regimental letter book.

29. Mark H. Dunkelman, "'A Just Right to Select Our Own Officers': Reactions in a Union Regiment to Officers Commissioned from Outside Its Ranks," *Civil War History* 44, no. 1 (March 1998): 24–34.

30. Wiley, *The Life of Billy Yank*, 128, 192–4, 197–206, 219, 293.

31. Blood diary, September 27, 1862; Wood to Hester Ann Wood, September 28, 1862.

32. 154th New York regimental muster rolls, National Archives; Stephen Welch diary, March 17, 1863; Blood diary, November 13, 1862; Wood to his family, November 13, 1862; Eason W. Bull to Lydia Bull, November 14, 1862; Alexander Bird diary, April 23–4, 1863; Smith diary, April 17, 1863; Welch diary, April 18, 1863.

33. Henry Van Aernam, interview notes, August 4, 1890, E. D. Northrup Papers; Blood diary, November 9–11, 1862; Matthew B. Cheney to E. D. Northrup, September 30, 1893, October 8, 1893, E. D. Northrup Papers.

34. Regimental Order No. 61, November 15, 1863; Regimental Order No. 22, January 30, 1863; Regimental Order No. 30, February 4, 1863, all in regimental letter book.

35. Joseph Cullen court-martial records, File LL274, folder 1, Record Group 153, Judge Advocate General (Army), National Archives (hereafter cited as RG 153, NA).

36. Asahel Hollister court-martial records, File LL3241, RG 153, NA.

37. George H. Davidson, interview notes, March 8, 1895, E. D. Northrup Papers.

38. Barzilla Merrill to Ruba Merrill, March 7, 1863; Bowen diary, January 18, 1865.

39. Clinton L. Barnhart court-martial records, File LL3240, folder 1, RG 153, NA; Harrison Cheney court-martial records, File NN972, RG 153, NA; Patrick H. Jones to Edwin M. Stanton, December 19, 1863, regimental letter book.

40. Green to Ann Eliza Jane Green, August 14, 1863, author's collection; General Order No. 35, Headquarters Second Division, Twentieth Army Corps, November 8, 1864, regimental letter book; William Merrell court-martial records, File LL3241, RG 153, NA; Wellman P. Nichols court-martial records, File LL2738, RG 153, NA.

41. Spencer Kelly court-martial records, Files LL1910, LL1911, and LL3031, RG 153, NA; Hiram Kelly court-martial records, File LL1911, RG 153, NA; General Order No. 40, Headquarters Second Division, Twentieth Army Corps, November 11, 1864, and "Report of enlisted men belonging to the 154th N.Y. Vols. whose term of service does not expire before the 1st day of October 1865," both in regimental papers, National Archives; Company H muster rolls, August 31, 1863, and thereafter, National Archives; Sweetland to Ellen Sweetland, January 14, 1864.

CHAPTER 10: Morale and Regimental Pride

1. William H. Keyes to Thomas Keyes, September 26, 1862; Andrew D. Blood diary, September 30, 1862; John C. Griswold to Susan Griswold, October 1, 1862.

2. Barzilla Merrill to Ruba Merrill, October 5, 1862; Charles W. Abell, undated letter fragment, circa October 1862; Eason W. Bull to Wyman Bull, November 1, 1862; Griswold to Susan Griswold, October 18, 1862; George W. Newcomb to Ellen Newcomb, October 21, 1862, author's collection; Lewis D. Warner to Nelson P. Wheeler, October 21, 1862, in Wheeler, *Pine Knots and Bark Peelers*, 65.

3. Bull to Wyman Bull, November 9, 1862; James D. Emmons to his sister, November 12, 1862.

4. Henry Van Aernam to Amy Melissa Van Aernam, December 17, 1862; Emory Sweetland to Mary Sweetland, December 22, 1862; Newcomb to Ellen Newcomb, December 22, 1862, author's collection; Amos Humiston to Philinda Humiston, January 2, 1863.

5. Sweetland to Mary Sweetland, January 16, 1863.

6. Barzilla Merrill to Ruba Merrill, January 1, 1863.

7. Ibid.

8. Van Aernam to Amy Melissa Van Aernam, June 30, 1863; Sweetland to Mary Sweetland, February 21, 1863; Barzilla Merrill to Ruba Merrill, March 20, 1863; James D. Quilliam to Rhoda Quilliam, March 27, 1863.

9. Richard J. McCadden to his mother, March 20, 1863, author's collection; "From the 154th Regiment," *Cattaraugus Freeman,* March 19, 1863, quoting letter of Alanson Crosby, March 9, 1863; "Letter from the 154th," *Cattaraugus Freeman,* April 9, 1863, quoting letter of Alfred W. Benson of March 27, 1863.

10. Thomas R. Aldrich to his mother, March 28, 1863.

11. Alansing Wyant to unknown recipient, March 6, 1863; Newcomb to Ellen Newcomb, April 1, 1863, author's collection.

12. Horace Smith diary, May 6, 1863; Van Aernam to Amy Melissa Van Aernam, May 7, 1863.

13. Smith diary, May 7, 1863; Homer A. Ames to Susan Griswold, May 12, 1863, Fenton Historical Society.

14. Dwight Moore to his mother, June 4, 1863; Van Aernam to Amy Melissa Van Aernam, June 8, 1863; Wyant to his parents, June 28, 1863.

15. Van Aernam to Amy Melissa Van Aernam, July 15, 1863.

16. Stephen R. Green to Ann Eliza Jane Green, August 16, 1863, author's collection; Van Aernam to Amy Melissa Van Aernam, September 3, 1863; George J. Mason to his sister Martha, August 27, 1863.

17. Griswold to Susan Griswold, October 2, 1863; McCadden to his sister, October 25, 1863, McCadden to his mother and brother, November 8, 1863, both Ron Meininger Collection; Van Aernam to Amy Melissa Van Aernam, December 4, 1863, January 12, 1864.

18. Philo A. Markham to his sister, January 13, 1864; Martin D. Bushnell to Franklin Congdon, January 25, 1864, Phil Palen Collection.

19. Charles F. Allen to his brother, April 12, 1864; Sweetland to Mary Sweetland, May 1, 1864.

20. McCadden to his mother and brother, May 3, 1864, Ron Meininger Collection; "Letter from Major L. D. Warner," undated clippings, quoting Warner to A. E. Fay, June 1, 1864, June 21, 1864.

21. "Letter from Col. P. H. Jones," *Cattaraugus Freeman,* July 7, 1864, quoting letter of June 24, 1864; "Letter from Major L. D. Warner," undated clipping, quoting Warner to A. E. Fay, July 8, 1864; Van Aernam to Amy Melissa Van Aernam, July 24, 1864; Abell to his sister Stella, August 21, 1864.

22. Sweetland to Mary Sweetland, September 4, 1864; Almon Deforest Reed to his sister, January 25, 1865.

23. Edgar Shannon to Francelia Hunt, April 7, 1865; Sweetland to Mary Sweetland, April 10, 1865.

24. McKay, "'Three Years or During the War,' With the Crescent and Star," 125; Bradford Rowland, Clark E. Oyer, and Esley Groat, interview notes, undated, E. D. Northrup Papers.

25. Martin Van Buren Champlin to his sister Louise, February 21, 1863; Newcomb to Ellen Newcomb, March 6, 1863, Lewis Leigh Collection, USAMHI.

26. McKay, "'Three Years or During the War,' With the Crescent and Star," 125; George A. Taylor to his parents, March 15, 1863; Dwight Moore to his mother, October 5, 1862; Newcomb to Ellen Newcomb, circa February 9, 1863, author's collection; Abell to his brother, July 23, 1864.

27. James W. Washburn to his parents, February 24, 1863; Emmons to his sister Ann, February 27, 1863; John Langhans to Julius Langhans, May 28, 1865.

28. Regimental Order No. 6, November 25, 1862, National Archives; "Camp Correspondence," *Gowanda Reporter,* undated clipping, quoting letter of Orlando White, March 13, 1864.

29. Benjamin F. H. Andrews to his father, October 3, 1862; William Charles to his family, October 8, 1862; Aldrich to his mother, October 28, 1862; "From our Cattaraugus Regiments," *Cattaraugus Union,* November 28, 1862; "From the 154th Regiment," *Cattaraugus Freeman,* December 18, 1862, quoting letter of Alanson Crosby, December 8, 1862.

30. Newton A. Chaffee to John R. Babcock, July 27, 1863; Martin D. Bushnell to Franklin Congdon, January 25, 1864, Phil Palen Collection; Sweetland to Mary Sweetland, January 14, 1864; Homer A. Ames to Cassius Griswold, May 1, 1864, author's collection.

31. "Departure of the 154th Regiment," *Cattaraugus Freeman,* October 2, 1862.

32. Frederick P. Todd, *American Military Equipage, 1851–1872* (New York: Charles Scribner's Sons, 1980), 297–301; Wiley, *The Life of Billy Yank,* 93–4; Lord, *They Fought for the Union,* 174.

33. Mark H. Dunkelman, *Brothers, Heroes, Martyrs: The Civil War Service of Lewis and George Bishop, Color Bearers of the 154th New York Volunteer Infantry* (Allegany, N.Y.: Allegany Area Historical Association, 1994), 1–12; Regimental Order No. 9, November 26, 1862, regimental records, National Archives; "The Battle of Chancellorsville—Death of Adj't S. C. Noyes, Jr.," *Cattaraugus Freeman,* May 28, 1863.

34. Quilliam to Rhoda Quilliam, May 31, 1863; McCadden to his mother, May 8, 1863, Ron Meininger Collection; Lewis D. Warner diary, May 2, 1863; Reuben E. Fenton to Color Sergeant Louis Bishop, June 1, 1863, in regimental letter book.

35. Dunkelman, *Brothers, Heroes, Martyrs,* 15; George W. Conklin, *Under the Crescent and Star: The 134th New York Volunteer Infantry in the Civil War* (Port Reading, N.J.: Axworthy Publishing, 1999), 111–2; E. D. Northrup, "Historical Sketch," in New York Monuments Commission for the Battlefields of Gettysburg and Chattanooga, *Final Report on the Battlefield of Gettysburg* (Albany: J. B. Lyon Company, 1902), 3:1055–56; James W. Bird to E. D. Northrup, May 20, 1891; Matthew B. Cheney to E. D. Northrup, October 9, 1893, and October 15, 1893; James W. Bird to Matthew B. Cheney, November 30, 1893, all in E. D. Northrup Papers.

36. "From the Cattaraugus Regiment," *Cattaraugus Union,* July 24, 1863, quoting letter of Dwight W. Day, July 7, 1863; George J. Mason to his mother, July 12, 1863; Matthew B. Cheney to E. D. Northrup, October 9, 1893, and October 15, 1893, E. D. Northrup Papers; Dan B. Allen to General John T. Sprague, July 1863, regimental letter book; *OR,* series 1, vol. 27, part 2, 468–70, 479–82, 483–7.

37. Dunkelman, *Brothers, Heroes, Martyrs,* 15–8; Warren Onan affidavit, undated, Lewis

Bishop pension file, National Archives; Alex Bird, "At Gettysburg," *Ellicottville Post,* September 16, 1908; James W. Bird to E. D. Northrup, November 30, 1893; Rev. F. J. F. Schantz, "Recollections of Visitations at Gettysburg after the Great Battle in July, 1863," in *Reflections on the Battle of Gettysburg,* vol. 13, no. 6, edited by Ralph S. Shay (Lebanon County, Pa.: Lebanon County [Pa.] Historical Society, 1963), 295; Sweetland to Mary Sweetland, July 28, 1863.

38. Dunkelman, *Brothers, Heroes, Martyrs,* 18–20; Van Aernam to Amy Melissa Van Aernam, January 16, 1864; O. O. Howard to Colonel Patrick H. Jones, January 13, 1864, regimental letter book; Sweetland to Mary Sweetland, January 14, 1864.

39. *OR,* series 1, vol. 38, part 2, 245, 247; "Heroism in the 154th Regiment," *Cattaraugus Freeman,* August 18, 1864; "Letter from Major L. D. Warner," *Olean Times* undated clipping, quoting letter of Warner, May 21, 1864; Ellis, *History of Cattaraugus County,* 116–7; Marcellus W. Darling to his family, May 21, 1864.

40. "Allen Williams Was Color Bearer," *Ellicottville Post,* November 30, 1910; Ellis, *History of Cattaraugus County, New York,* 122; Lewis D. Warner diary, May 30, 1865.

41. Alexander Bird diary, May 30, 1865; McCadden to his family, May 30, 1865, author's collection; McKay, "'Three Years or During the War,' With the Crescent and Star," 157.

42. Patrick H. Jones to General John T. Sprague, January 8, 1864, regimental letter book; Daniel Lorello, "The Bureau of Military Statistics," in Holzer and Lorello, *The Union Preserved,* 16–22.

43. Horatio Seymour to Colonel Patrick H. Jones, February 28, 1863, regimental letter book.

44. William Hotchkiss, autobiographical notes, courtesy of Donald L. Devendorf; *Third Annual Report of the Bureau of Military Record of the State of New York* (Albany: C. Wendell, 1866), 532, 571; photographs of Thomas K. Bambrick, Arthur Hotchkiss, Ephriam Hotchkiss, and Lewis D. Warner, Division of Military and Naval Affairs, New York State Adjutant General's Office, Albany, New York; "Individual Record of Personal History of Officers and Soldiers Belonging to Regiments from New-York in the Service of the United States" for Lewis D. Warner, September 3, 1863, John L. Spencer Collection; Lorello, "The Bureau of Military Statistics," 20–2.

45. Van Aernam to Amy Melissa Van Aernam, January 4, 1864; Alva C. Merrill to Ruba Merrill, April 12, 1863; Washburn to his parents, February 24, 1863; Emory Sweetland diary, March 30, 1865; William D. Harper to his family, August 31, 1864.

46. Charles H. Taylor to his father, March 22, 1863; Alva C. Merrill to Ruba Merrill, November 10, 1862.

47. Stephen Green camp sketch and notations, undated, Phil Palen Collection; drawing accompanying Charles to Ann Charles, January 20, 1864.

48. Unsigned sketch of Lookout Mountain and Valley, Charles Edmunds Collection; Van Aernam to Amy Melissa Van Aernam, November 18, 1863; Quilliam to Rhoda Quilliam, February 25, 1864; "Lookout Mountain and its vicinity, from the position of the Eleventh Army Corps," *Frank Leslie's Illustrated Newspaper,* December 5, 1863.

49. "Martin's Soldier's Record," author's collection. I also have an example made for Company E.

50. Green to Ann Eliza Jane Green, circa February 1864, author's collection.

51. Green to Ann Eliza Jane Green, December 7, 1862, author's collection.

52. Joseph R. Crowell to E. D. Northrup, September 1, 1889; George Eugene Graves, inter-

view notes, August 17, 1895, both in E. D. Northrup Papers; *Presidents, Soldiers, Statesmen,* 1363.

CHAPTER 11: E. D. Northrup and the Betrayal of Esprit de Corps

1. Linderman, *Embattled Courage,* 266–97; Hess, *The Union Soldier in Battle,* 158–90.

2. "Cattaraugus Soldiers' Union," *Cattaraugus Freeman,* September 15, 1864.

3. "Proceedings of the 32d Senatorial District 'United Service Society,' held at Great Valley, October 7th, 1865," *Cattaraugus Freeman,* October 11, 1865.

4. Ellis, *History of Cattaraugus County,* 123; Benedict R. Maryniak, "GAR Posts," *The Civil War Courier* (May 1999): 38.

5. Benedict R. Maryniak, "Cattaraugus County GAR Posts," typescript; "The name of S. C. Noyes post," *Ellicottville Post,* June 27, 1894.

6. The account of Post 232 is drawn from *Presidents, Soldiers, Statesmen* (New York, Toledo, and Chicago: H. H. Hardesty, 1899), 1621–22; "Application for Charter, S. C. Noyes Post, No. 232," Post Charter Applications, Grand Army of the Republic, Department of New York Records, New York State Archives, Albany; and numerous articles from the *Ellicottville Post* and *Ellicottville News.* The Noyes photograph presentation is in "Installation of Officers," *Ellicottville News,* January 15, 1885.

7. *Ellicottville Post* and *Ellicottville News, passim;* "G.A.R. Post Is No More," *Ellicottville Post,* December 10, 1924.

8. Marlynn M. Olson, *A Guide to Burial Sites, Cemeteries, and Random Stones in Cattaraugus County, New York* (Randolph, N.Y.: Register Graphics, 1996), 113, 124, 175, 255, 262, 263, 265, 279; epilogue by Clara Woodson Darling in Marcellus Warner Darling, *Events and Comments of My Life* (n.p., n.d.), unpaginated; "E. Randolph soldiers monument marks its 100th anniversary," unidentified newspaper clipping, author's collection.

9. "Application for Camp Charter," April 8, 1902, Fred C. Rider Collection; "There is a movement afoot to establish a camp of Sons of Veterans," *Ellicottville News,* March 28, 1896; "Patrick Jones Camp, No. 65, Sons of Veterans," *Ellicottville Post,* May 28, 1902; Thomas Pollock and Ronda Shaner Pollock, eds., *A History of the Town of Portville, 1805–1920* (Portville, N.Y.: Portville Historical and Preservation Society, 1986), 142; Adams, *Historical Gazetteer and Biographical Memorial of Cattaraugus County,* 643, 1020.

10. Robert G. Carroon and Dana B. Shoaf, *Union Blue: The History of the Military Order of the Loyal Legion of the United States* (Shippensburg, Pa.: White Mane Books, 2001), 3–25, 167, 186, 285, 370; Patrick Henry Jones MOLLUS record, Civil War Library and Museum, Philadelphia, Pa.

11. Cattaraugus County Ex-Union Prisoner of War Association charter, January 22, 1887, Franklinville (N.Y.) American Legion Post; "County Ex-Prisoners of War Association," *Ellicottville Post,* March 23, 1887; Aldrich memoir.

12. "The arrangement for celebrating the 4th," *Westfield Republican,* June 21, 1865; "The Fourth at East Ashford," *Cattaraugus Freeman,* July 19, 1865.

13. "Gen. P. H. Jones—The Union Candidate for Clerk of the Court of Appeals," *Cattaraugus Freeman,* September 27, 1865; Dunkelman, "Brigadier General Patrick Henry Jones," 75; Adams, *Historical Gazetteer and Biographical Memorial of Cattaraugus County,* 131–3, 379, 682,

757; *The Centennial History of Chautauqua County* (Jamestown, N.Y.: Chautauqua History Company, 1904), 2:839; "Death of Matthew Cheney," *Nebraska State Journal,* July 5, 1915; Alfred Henry Lewis, "Major Benson: A Sunflower Statesman," *Saturday Evening Post* 179, no. 8 (August 8, 1906), 3–4; "Fraternal Greeting. Exchange of Letters Between Senator Benson and Comrades of the 154th N.Y.V.," *Ellicottville Post,* July 25, 1906.

14. Manuscript minutes of Reunions of Co. E, Jean Schultz Collection; "The Co. E, 154th N.Y.V. Reunion," *Fredonia Censor,* October 14, 1867; "Reunion of Co. B, 154th Regt. N.Y.S.V.," *Cattaraugus Republican,* May 24, 1877; "Reunion of Co. K, 154th Regiment," *Cattaraugus Republican,* October 2, 1879.

15. "Attention Battalion!" *Cattaraugus Republican,* August 19, 1869; "Re-Union of the 154th and 64th Regiment," *Cattaraugus Republican,* September 9, 1869; "Soldiers Reunion," *Cattaraugus Republican,* August 28, 1879; "Soldiers & Sailors. Reunion of Veterans at Ellicottville," *Cattaraugus Republican,* September 12, 1879; *Ellicottville Post,* August 12, 1908.

16. Items regarding Cattaraugus County Memorial and Historical Building in *Ellicottville Post* of October 20, 1909, April 19, 1911, and September 20, 1911; "Dedication Ceremonies Of County Historical and Memorial Building," *Salamanca Republican Press,* September 8, 1914.

17. Stuart McConnell, *Glorious Contentment: The Grand Army of the Republic, 1865–1900* (Chapel Hill: Univ. of North Carolina Press, 1992), 143–53.

18. Shepherd N. Thomas to George C. Wickes, May 24, 1893, author's collection; "Soldiers should employ home agents," *Ellicottville News,* August 7, 1890; "T. R. Aldrich is having great success with his pension applicants," *Ellicottville News,* August 21, 1890; Patrick H. Jones, affidavit, October 4, 1865, James W. Baxter pension file, National Archives.

19. "Francis Patterson," unidentified newspaper clipping; "Another Case," *Buffalo Courier,* July 7, 1887; "Famous Pension Fraud," *Buffalo Daily Courier,* June 1, 1893, all in E. D. Northrup Papers.

20. "A permanent regimental organization," *Ellicottville Post,* September 21, 1887; "Brave Boys in Blue: First Annual Encampment and Reunion of the 154 Regiment New York Vols.," *Ellicottville Post,* September 5, 1888; Alfred W. Benson, address at first annual reunion of the 154th New York, August 30, 1888, Alfred W. Benson Papers, Kansas State Historical Society, Topeka.

21. Accounts of the various reunions in the *Cattaraugus Republican,* passim; "Reunion of Veterans Ends," *Salamanca Republican Press,* September 3, 1915; Shepherd N. Thomas to James W. Baxter, November 3, 1913, Baxter pension file, National Archives.

22. "Annual Reunion," *Ellicottville News,* June 10, 1897; "The G.A.R. in Buffalo," *Cattaraugus Republican,* August 27, 1893; "The Veteran Reunion," *Cattaraugus Republican,* September 3, 1893; "With the Boys in Blue," *Jamestown Evening Journal,* September 12, 1905.

23. "A Meeting of the Survivors of the 154th," *Randolph Register,* April 12, 1888; J. S. Whipple, "A Trip to Gettysburg," *Cattaraugus Republican,* July 11, 1890; "Speech of Hon. J. S. Whipple at the Dedication of the Soldier's Monument at Gettysburg, July 1st, 1890," *Ellicottville News,* September 25, 1890; Adams, *Historical Gazetteer and Biographical Memorial of Cattaraugus County,* 403–4; New York Monuments Commission for the Battlefields of Gettysburg and Chattanooga, *Final Report on the Battlefield of Gettysburg,* 3:1048–56.

24. "Turning back the calendar," *Olean Times Herald,* July 5, 1988; "Attention 154th N.Y.," *Ellicottville News,* April 20, 1893; Adams, *Historical Gazetteer and Biographical Memorial of Cattaraugus County,* 1020; *Ellicottville Post,* September 17, 1902; Alex Bird, "At Gettysburg," *Ellicot-*

tville Post, July 9, 1913; "C. E. Whitney, of Humphrey, was a pleasant caller at this office Friday," *Ellicottville News*, November 3, 1892.

25. "Headquarters 154th N.Y. Vols.," *Ellicottville Post*, August 10, 1910; "Peace Monument," *Ellicottville Post*, November 23, 1910; "Viewing Old Scenes," *Ellicottville Post*, November 23, 1910, reprinting undated story from the *Dalton (Ga.) Argus*; "The Blue and the Gray," *Ellicottville Post*, December 7, 1910, reprinting story of *The North Georgia Citizen*, November 24, 1910; John Langhans to Emma Langhans Dunkelman, postcards, November 15, 1910, and November 17, 1910, author's collection.

26. "Shep L. Thomas of Great Valley," *Ellicottville News*, January 12, 1899; Thomas Armory Lee, "Alfred Washburn Benson, L.L.D.," *Kansas State Historical Society Journal* 14:9–11; Alex Bird, "In the Southland," *Ellicottville Post*, August 26 and September 2, 1908; Alex Bird, "At Gettysburg," *Ellicottville Post*, September 16, 1908; State of New York, Andersonville Monument Dedication Commission, *Dedication of Monument Erected by the State of New York at Andersonville, Georgia, 1914* (Albany: J. B. Lyon Company, 1916), 144.

27. Charles H. Field to E. D. Northrup, October 10, 1893, E. D. Northrup Papers; "C. W. Smith Has Rare Relic of Civil War Days," *Silver Creek (N.Y.) News-Times*, January 13, 1938; Jack Berger, "Civil War Sketches Found in Basement of Randolph Library," *Jamestown (N.Y.) Post-Journal Tempo*, June 4, 1994, 6, 7; "We had the pleasure . . . of shaking hands with Capt. B. G. Casler," *Cattaraugus Freeman*, May 11, 1865; Aldrich memoir; Lee, *Alfred Washburn Benson*, 9.

28. "Alex Bird Answers Last Roll Call," *Ellicottville Post*, January 12, 1927; "East Otto," *Cattaraugus Republican*, September 8, 1882; "Comrades Assemble," unidentified newspaper clipping, October 6, 1893; unidentified writer to Alfred W. Benson, undated, Benson Papers.

29. Easel Monument Association soldier's record of Mervin P. Barber, John R. Burton Collection; *History of the Easel-Shaped Monument and a Key to the Principles and Objects of the Grand Army of the Republic and its Co-Workers* (Chicago: Dux Publishing Company, 1893), 66–9; *Presidents, Soldiers, Statesmen*, passim; Adams, *Historical Gazetteer and Biographical Memorial of Cattaraugus County*, passim.

30. I. R. Leonard, *Historical Sketch of the Village of Gowanda, N.Y.* (Buffalo: The Complete Art-Printing Works of the Matthews-Northrup Co., 1898), 71–81; Ellis, *History of Cattaraugus County, New York*, 3–4, 124–52, 107–22, facing 228, facing 255, 279, 293, 326, 494. See also Charles J. Shults, ed., *Historical and Biographical History of the Township of Dayton, Cattaraugus County, New York* (Buffalo: The Hausauer Press, 1901), 49–52; H. C. Taylor, *Historical Sketches of the Town of Portland* (Fredonia: W. McKinstry & Son, 1873), 270–1, 292–6; Butler F. Dilley, *Biographical and Portrait Cyclopedia of Chautauqua County, New York* (Philadelphia: John M. Gresham & Co., 1891), 108–9, 199, 446, 656–67.

31. Alex Bird, "My First Experience Under Fire," *Ellicottville News*, January 20, 1894; "March to the Sea," *Ellicottville Post*, November 25, 1914, December 2, 1914, December 9, 1914, and December 16, 1914; Markham, *Sketch of The Life & Army Service of P. A. Markham*; Darling, *Events and Comments of My Life*; Asa Brainard, *Reminiscences of the life of Asa Brainard as given by him in his own way at the First Reunion of the Brainard Family at the home of C. L. Brainard, Brocton, N.Y., July 11, 1914* (n.p., n.d.).

32. Charles W. McKay, "Bushbeck's Brigade," *National Tribune*, October 8, 1908; Emory Sweetland, "A Witness for Bundy," *National Tribune*, December 8, 1904; John M. Dawley, "Saw Stonewall Shot," *National Tribune*, May 12, 1904; McKay, "'Three Years or During the War,' With the Crescent and Star," *National Tribune Scrap Book*, 121–60; McKay, "Three Years

or During the War With the Crescent and Star," *Ellicottville Post,* serially from December 13, 1911, to March 30, 1912.

33. Application for Medals of Honor by Charles W. McKay, May 23, 1893; affidavit of Daniel M. Wright, October 25, 1893; Memorandum No. 384,924, Record and Pension Office, War Department, April 5, 1894; Col. F. C. Ainsworth to Stephen Welch, April 13, 1894, all courtesy of Allegany (N.Y.) Area Historical Association. See also McKay, " 'Three Years or During the War,' With the Crescent and Star," 144; Beyer and Keydel, *Deeds of Valor,* 1:322–3; Stephen Welch, interview notes, undated, E. D. Northrup Papers.

34. Aldrich memoir; Imholte, *The Civil War Diary . . . of Corporal Newell Burch,* 44; Emory Sweetland, undated speech to "Commander & Comrades of Fuller Post"; John F. Wellman, poem, "A Story of the 154 Regt. N.Y. Vols.," Alfred W. Benson Papers; Wellman, poem, "Story of a Regiment's First Fight"; Wellman to E. D. Northrup, March 18, 1894, E. D. Northrup Papers.

35. C. E. Dornbusch, compiler, *Military Bibliography of the Civil War* (New York: New York Public Library, 1975), vol. 1, part 2, 29–73; Phisterer, *New York in the War of the Rebellion,* passim.

36. The sources for these two paragraphs are the prefaces of thirty-three New York State regimental histories.

37. E. D. Northrup, "History of the 154th Regiment N.Y.S.V.," flyer, June 3, 1878, E. D. Northrup Papers.

38. E. D. Northrup Papers, passim; "History of the 154th," *Ellicottville Post,* August 5, 1885; "E. D. Northrup . . . ," *Ellicottville News,* October 6, 1894; "E. D. Northrup's history," *Ellicottville Post,* October 7, 1896; Newton A. Chaffee to E. D. Northrup, June 24, 1878, E. D. Northrup Papers.

39. E. D. Northrup Papers, passim.

40. E. D. Northrup to New York Monuments Commission, September 19, 1896; E. D. Northrup to Matthew B. Cheney, January 26, 1903, both in E. D. Northrup Papers; New York Monuments Commission for the Battlefields of Gettysburg and Chattanooga, *Final Report on the Battlefield of Gettysburg,* 3:1054–56.

41. Clark E. Oyer to E. D. Northrup, February 26, 1894; Earl Z. Bacon to E. D. Northrup, May 25, 1895; Simeon V. Pool to E. D. Northrup, March 15, 1893; Mrs. S. L. Mead to E. D. Northrup, February 25, 1893, all in E. D. Northrup Papers.

42. William E. Jones to E. D. Northrup, January 13, 1893, and June 6, 1893; A. A. Whipple to E. D. Northrup, March 30, 1891; Godfrey to E. D. Northrup, January 20, 1896, all in E. D. Northrup Papers.

43. E. D. Northrup, "The History of the One Hundred and Fifty-Fourth Regiment, New York Volunteers," flyer, circa August 1897, E. D. Northrup Papers.

44. A. C. Vandusen of the Courier Company to E. D. Northrup, August 27, 1897; E. D. Northrup to unidentified recipient, January 28, 1898; E. D. Northrup to the Courier Company, January 8, 1900; Courier Company to E. D. Northrup, January 12, 1900, all in E. D. Northrup Papers.

45. D. Appleton & Company to E. D. Northrup, November 26, 1897, and January 4, 1898; E. D. Northrup to Matthew B. Cheney, January 26, 1903; Charles E. Whitney to E. D. Northrup, April 29, 1904; E. D. Northrup to Whitney, January 2, 1905; Whitney to E. D. Northrup, January 10, 1905; and passim, E. D. Northrup Papers.

46. Whitney to E. D. Northrup, March 3, 1917; Northrup's obituary in the *Ellicottville Post*, February 5, 1919; and passim, E. D. Northrup Papers.

47. Thomas to Baxter, November 3, 1913; "Andrew D. Blood," *Ellicottville Post*, October 19, 1910.

48. Photograph of William F. Chapman's headstone by Phil Palen, Gowanda, New York; "Taps Sounded for W. W. Buck," *Randolph Register* 29, no. 43; "Alex Bird Answers Last Roll Call," *Ellicottville Post*, January 12, 1927, 1; and "Byron A. Johnston. Another Veteran Answers to the Last Roll Call and is Mustered Out," *Ellicottville Post*, March 18, 1903, are some of many examples of veterans' martial-toned obituary headlines.

49. "Gettysburg Veteran to be Buried Today," unidentified newspaper clipping, Medora Ball Collection; "Veteran Dies at Age of 91 Years," unidentified newspaper clipping, Carolyn Ames Simons Collection.

BIBLIOGRAPHY

Manuscript Sources

PRIVATE COLLECTIONS

Charles W. Abell Letters. Jean Schultz Collection, Westford, Vt.

Thomas R. Aldrich Letters and Memoir. "The Experience of Thomas R. Aldrich Late of Co. B 154th N.Y. Volls. while a prisoner of war from May 8, 1864 until February 22nd, 1865." Patricia Wilcox Collection, Fairport, N.Y.

Edson D. Ames Letters. Carolyn Ames Simons Collection, Phoenix, Ariz.

Homer A. Ames Letters. Author's Collection.

Homer A. Ames Letters and Diary. Carolyn Ames Simons Collection, Phoenix, Ariz.

Jonathan M. Ames Letter. Carolyn Ames Simons Collection, Phoenix, Ariz.

Joseph H. Andrews Diary. Rev. Robert Andrews Collection, Danville, Pa.

"Application for Camp Charter." Fred C. Rider Collection, Great Valley, N.Y.

Ambrose F. Arnold Letters. Mrs. Lawrence Urbshiet Collection, Fredonia, N.Y.

John W. Badgero Letters. Mrs. Burnell Marble Collection, New Port Richie, Fla.

Mervin P. Barber Diary. Paul A. Lockwood Collection, Newark, Ohio.

Mervin P. Barber Easel Monument Association Soldier's Record. John R. Burton Collection, Salt Lake City, Utah.

George W. Barr Letter. Phil Palen Collection, Gowanda, N.Y.

James W. Baxter Letter. Author's Collection.

Salmon W. Beardsley Letters. Author's Collection.

Alexander Bird Diary. Janet Bird Whitehurst Collection, Los Banos, Calif.

Asher Bliss Jr. Letters. William H. Petersen Collection, East Randolph, N.Y.

Andrew D. Blood Diary and Letter. Alan D. Henry Collection, Temperance, Mich.

Joel M. Bouton Letters. Maureen Koehl Collection, South Salem, N.Y.

Francis M. Bowen Diary and Letter. Ronald Bowen Collection, Brighton, Mich.

James Byron Brown Poem. "Army Song of the Cattaraugus Boys." William Petersen Collection, East Randolph, N.Y.

Nathaniel S. Brown Letter (February 20, 1863). Frances Ortwein Collection, Buffalo, N.Y.

Nathaniel S. Brown Letters. Author's Collection.

Colby M. Bryant Diary. Bruce H. Bryant Collection, Salamanca, N.Y.

Levi D. Bryant Letters. Cornelia Kopp Collection, Reading Center, N.Y.

Eason W. Bull Letters. Frances Ortwein Collection, Buffalo, N.Y.

Newell Burch Diary. John Quinn Imholte, *The Civil War Diary and Related Sources of Corporal Newell Burch 154th New York Volunteers Covering the Period August 25, 1862 to April 21, 1865.* Unpublished Manuscript. Author's Collection.

Augutus Burnham Letters. Jack Pearson Collection, Timonium, Md.

Martin D. Bushnell Letters. Phil Palen Collection, Gowanda, N.Y.

Martin D. Bushnell Letters and Diary. Frank M. Bushnell Collection, Napoli, N.Y.

Winfield S. Cameron Letter. Jerome H. Davis Collection, Corry, Pa.

Levi L. Carr Letter. Jerome H. Davis Collection, Corry, Pa.

Alonzo A. Casler Letters. Marjorie D. Hazen Collection, Ashland, Ohio.

Benjamin G. Casler Letter. Marjorie D. Hazen Collection, Ashland, Ohio.

Cattaraugus County Ex-Union Prisoner of War Association Charter. American Legion Post Collection, Franklinville, N.Y.

"Cattaraugus County: Population of towns since 1860, and their Political Vote." Chart. Kenneth C. Heller Collection, Bradford, Pa.

Newton A. Chaffee Letters. Howard Stearns Collection, Fairhope, Ala.

Martin Van Buren Champlin Letter (March 30, 1863). Richard D. Champlin Collection, Bountiful, Utah.

Martin Van Buren Champlin Letter (October 17, 1862). Donald K. Ryberg Jr. Collection, Westfield, N.Y.

Martin Van Buren Champlin Letters. Louise Crooks Collection, Shinglehouse, Pa.

William Charles Letters. Jack Finch Collection, Freedom, N.Y.

Mary Jane Chittenden Letters. Author's Collection.

William F. Chittenden Letters. Author's Collection.

Hugh N. Crosgrove Letters. J. E. Stockman Collection, Mill Creek, Wash.

Job B. Dawley Letter (April 24, 1863). Author's Collection.

Job B. Dawley Letter (January 9, 1864). Phil Palen Collection, Gowanda, N.Y.

John Dicher Letters. Doris Laing Collection, East Otto, N.Y.

John Dicher Letters. Scott Frank Collection, Cheektowaga, N.Y.

Thomas Donnelly Letter. Author's Collection.

Fayette Dutcher Letter. Celia M. Krieger Collection, Little Valley, N.Y.

Harvey Earl Letters. Marguerite Whitcomb Collection, Great Valley, N.Y.

James D. Emmons Letters. Leslie R. Page Collection, Auburn, N.Y.

Charles H. Field Letter. Patrick Gallagher Collection, Sunnyvale, Calif.

Ann Eliza Jane Green Letter. Author's Collection.

Stephen R. Green Letters. Author's Collection.

Stephen R. Green Letters and Sketches. Phil Palen Collection, Gowanda, N.Y.

John C. Griswold Letter (March 30, 1864). Vince Martonis Collection, Hanover, N.Y.

Milon J. Griswold Letters. Author's Collection.

Susan Griswold Letters. Author's Collection.

Esley Groat Letter. Arthur Olin Collection, Ellicottville, N.Y.

William D. Harper Diary and Memoir. Raymond Harper Collection, Dunkirk, N.Y.

Dana P. Horton Letter (July 9, 1863). Jerome H. Davis Collection, Corry, Pa.

Dana P. Horton Letters. Author's Collection.

William Hotchkiss Autobiographical Notes. Donald L. Devendorf Collection, East Lansing, Mich.

Betsey Phelps Howlett Poem. "On the Death of Barzillai and Alva Merrill." William H. Petersen Collection, East Randolph, N.Y.

Horace Howlett Letter (May 7, 1863). Author's Collection.

Horace Howlett Letters and Poem. Eugene Johnson Collection, North Ridgeville, Ohio, and Douglas W. Johnson Collection, Perrysburg, N.Y.

Philander Hubbard Poem. "The Friends I Left Behind Me." Author's Collection.

Amos Humiston Letters. Allan L. Cox Collection, Medford, Mass.

Francelia Hunt Letters. Timothy T. Shaw Collection, Cheektowaga, N.Y.

Martha James Letters. Jack Finch Collection, Freedom, N.Y.

William P. James Poem. "The White Star Division." Charles Edmunds Collection, Farmersville, N.Y.

David S. Jones Letters. Clara Jones Collection, Salamanca, N.Y.

David S. Jones Poem. "On the Death of Anson N. Park." William H. Petersen Collection, East Randolph, N.Y.

Edward R. Jones Poem. "The Starving Prisoners in Richmond." William H. Petersen Collection, East Randolph, N.Y.

Lewis L. Jones Letters. Barbara R. Henry Collection, Canandiagua, N.Y.

William E. Jones Letter. Barbara R. Henry Collection, Canandiagua, N.Y.

John Langhans Letters. Floris Sarver Collection, Getzville, N.Y.

John Langhans Postcards. Author's Collection.

Henry C. Loomis Letter. Author's Collection.

Benedict R. Maryniak. "Cattaraugus County GAR Posts." Typescript. Author's Collection.

George J. Mason Letters. Juliet Mason Collection, Russell, Pa.

Richard J. McCadden Letters. Author's Collection.

Richard J. McCadden Letters. Ron Meininger Collection, Gaithersburg, Md.

John W. Meloy Letter. Fred C. Rider Collection, Great Valley, N.Y.

Alva C. Merrill Letters. Doris Williams Collection, Orange City, Fla.

Barzilla Merrill Letters. Doris Williams Collection, Orange City, Fla.

Ruba Cole Merrill Diary. Gerald Merrill Collection, South Dayton, N.Y.

Minutes of Reunions of Company E. Jean Schultz Collection, Westford, Vt.

Dwight Moore Letter (November 17, 1862). Phil Palen Collection, Gowanda, N.Y.

Wilber Moore Letter (July 20, 1863). Francis N. T. Diller Collection, Fairview, Pa.

Peter P. Mount Letters. Evelyn E. Row Collection, Alden, Pa.

Henry A. Munger Letters. Author's Collection.

Boyd D. Myers Diary. David L. Myers Collection, Erie, Pa.

George W. Newcomb Letter (January 13, 1863). Phil Palen Collection, Gowanda, N.Y.

George W. Newcomb Letters. Alexander G. Lynn Collection, Chicago, Ill.

George W. Newcomb Letters. Author's Collection.

George W. Newcomb Letters. Michael W. Schaefer Collection, Gettysburg, Pa.

William W. Norton Letters. Author's Collection.

Reuben R. Ogden Diary. Bradley J. Eide Collection, Chesterfield, Va.

Clark E. Oyer Letters. Phyllis Oyer Collection, Rochester, N.Y.

Andrew G. Park Poem. "The Brave Soldier." Francis T. Diller Collection, Fairview, Pa.

Joshua R. Pettit Diary. Mary C. Ranney Collection, Ellicottville, N.Y.

Marion Plumb Letters. Kenneth F. Plumb Collection, Vienna, Va.

John N. Porter Letters. Francis N. T. Diller Collection, Fairview, Pa.

James D. Quilliam Letters. Edithe Nasca Collection, Fredonia, N.Y.

Almon D. Reed Letter. Donald K. Ryberg Jr. Collection, Westfield, N.Y.

Corydon C. Rugg Letter. Louise Koenig Collection, Olean, N.Y.

Milton D. Scott Letter. Richard DeBell Collection, Falconer, N.Y.

Addison L. Scutt Letter. Jerry L. Scutt Collection, Portville, N.Y.

Edgar Shannon Letters (August 1862–February 1864). Alberta McLaughlin Collection, Frews-burg, N.Y.

Edgar Shannon Letters (March 1864–April 1865). Timothy T. Shaw Collection, Cheektowaga, N.Y.

James P. Skiff Diary. Scott N. Hilts Collection, Arcade, N.Y.

John Adam Smith Diary. Donald J. Gould Collection, South Dayton, N.Y.

Francis Strickland Letter (May 27, 1863). Virginia Strickland Judd Collection, Inverness, Fla.

Francis Strickland Letters. Charles L. Strickland Collection, Templeton, Calif.

Emory Sweetland Letters, Diary, and Speech. Lyle Sweetland Collection, South Dayton, N.Y.

John Wesley Sweetland Letters. Margaret N. Smith Collection, Williamsport, Pa.

Shepherd N. Thomas Letter. Author's Collection.

Mile Tupper Letters and Memorandum. May Stephan Collection, Allegany, N.Y.

Unsigned Sketch of Lookout Mountain and Valley. Charles Edmunds Collection, Farmersville, N.Y.

Lewis D. Warner Diary (1863) and "Individual Record of Personal History. . . ." John Lewis Spencer Collection, Canandaigua, N.Y.

Lewis D. Warner Diary (1864–65). Charles H. Warner III Collection, Santa Rosa, Calif.

Lewis D. Warner Letter and Deposition (April 12, 1864). Louise Crooks Collection, Shingle-house, Pa.

James W. Washburn Letters (November 16, 1862; March 30, 1863). Cathy Wingebach Collec-tion, Diamond Bar, Calif.

Stephen Welch Diary and Letter. Carolyn Stoltz Collection, Tonawanda, N.Y.

John F. Wellman Poem. "Story of a Regiment's First Fight." John M. Wellman Jr. Collection, California City, Calif.

Charles E. Whitney Diary. Elizabeth Maher Collection, Mayville, N.Y.

Byron Wiggins Letter. Fred Cadwell Collection, Buffalo, N.Y.

Lyman Wilber Letter. Beverly Geisel Collection, Hamburg, N.Y.

Oscar F. Wilber Letters. Beverly Geisel Collection, Hamburg, N.Y.

David J. Williams Letter. William G. Mather III Collection, Vienna, Va.

Samuel R. Williams Letters. Jack Finch Collection, Freedom, N.Y.

Jacob Winney Pension Papers. Arnold (Barney) Waterman Collection, Irving, N.Y.

George L. Winters Letter. Phil Palen Collection, Gowanda, N.Y.

Daniel M. Wright Deposition (April 12, 1864). Louise Crooks Collection, Shinglehouse, Pa.

REPOSITORIES

Allegany Area Historical Association, Allegany, N.Y.

Papers Relating to the Medal of Honor of Stephen Welch and Charles W. McKay

Bowdoin College Library, Brunswick, Me.

Oliver Otis Howard Papers

Brown University, John Hay Library, Providence, R.I.

Reuben E. Fenton Petition

Cattaraugus County Memorial and Historical Museum, Little Valley, N.Y.

James Monroe Carpenter Letter
Henry Cunningham Letter
Andrew M. Keller Letter
Records of Soldiers by Towns
Francis Strickland Letter (June 17, 1863)
Unknown Writer's Letter (October 11, 1862)
Various Unidentified Newspaper Clippings
Ira Wood Letters

Chautauqua County Historical Society, Westfield, N.Y.

George A. Taylor Letters

Civil War Library and Museum, Philadelphia, Pa.

Patrick H. Jones MOLLUS Record

Cornell University, Ithaca, N.Y.

Edwin Dwight Northrup Papers, #4190, Department of Manuscripts and University Archives

Division of Military and Naval Affairs, New York State Adjutant General's Office, Albany, N.Y.

Photographs

Ellicottville Historical Society, Ellicottville, N.Y.

154th New York Regimental Letter Book

Fenton Historical Society, Jamestown, N.Y.

Homer A. Ames Letters (with John C. Griswold Letters)
John C. Griswold Letters

Gowanda Area Historical Society, Gowanda, N.Y.

Newton A. Chaffee Letters (July 27, 1863; September 13, 1864)
Philo A. Markham Letters

Kansas State Historical Society, Topeka, Kans.

Alfred W. Benson Diary and Address at First Annual Reunion
John F. Wellman Poem, "A Story of the 154 Regt. N.Y. Vols," Alfred W. Benson Papers

Mazomanie Historical Society, Mazomanie, Wisc.

Horace Smith Diary

National Archives, Washington, D.C.

Charles F. Allen Letters, Allen Pension File
Timothy A. Allen Letter, Hamilton Longcore Pension File
Benjamin F. H. Andrews Letters, Andrews Pension File
James W. Baxter Pension File
Alfred W. Benson Letter, Jesse D. Campbell Pension File
Lewis Bishop Pension File
Nathaniel S. Brown Pension File
Jesse D. Campbell Letters, Campbell Pension File
Calvin T. Chamberlain Letters, Chamberlain Pension File
Descriptive Books, 154th New York
Joseph B. Fay Letter, William H. Sprague Pension File
James M. Gallagher Letters, Wilber Moore Pension File
Patrick Griffin Military Records
Danford L. Hall Letter, Oscar F. Wilber Pension File
Truman Harkness Letter, Harkness Pension File
John M. Irvin Letter, Lewis L. Jones Pension File
Byron A. Johnston Letter, Hamilton Longcore Pension File
Lewis L. Jones Letters, Jones Pension File
Patrick Henry Jones Military Records
William Kendall Letter, William H. Sprague Pension File
William H. Keyes Letters, Keyes Pension File
Hamilton Longcore Letters, Longcore Pension File
Duane Marsh Letters, Marsh Pension File
Miscellaneous Papers, 154th New York
Dwight Moore Letters, Moore Pension File
Wilber Moore Letters, Moore Pension File
Benjamin D. Morgan Pension File
S. H. Morrison Letter, Marshall A. Perkins Pension File
Muster Rolls, 154th New York
Edwin R. Osgood Letter, Osgood Pension File
Order Book, 154th New York
Marshall A. Perkins Letters, Perkins Pension File
James W. Phelps Letter, Thaddeus L. Reynolds Pension File
Record Group 153, Judge Advocate General (Army), Court-Martial Records
Returns, 154th New York
Thaddeus Reynolds Letters, Reynolds Pension File
Baker Leonard Saxton Pension File
William H. Seeker Pension File
Isabella Shippy Letter, Augustus A. Shippy Pension File
Edward Shults Letter, Shults Pension File
Philander B. Sickler Letter, Sickler Pension File

William H. Sprague Letters, Sprague Pension File
Truman A. St. John Letters, William H. Sprague Pension File
Charles H. Taylor Letter, Taylor Pension File
Lewis D. Warner Letter (April 3, 1865), Almon L. Gile Pension File
James W. Washburn Letters, Washburn Pension File
Ariel H. Wellman Military Records
Devillo Wheeler Letters, Wheeler Pension File
Milo L. Wilber Letters, Oscar F. Wilber Pension File
Oscar F. Wilber Letters, Wilber Pension File
Landers Wright Letters, Wright Pension File
Alansing Wyant Letters, Wyant Pension File

National Museum of Health and Medicine, Armed Forces Museum of Pathology, Washington, D.C.

Jerome Averrill Photograph and Records

New York State Archives, Albany, N.Y.

Correspondence and Petitions, 1821–1896, New York State Adjutant General's Office
Grand Army of the Republic Department of New York Records
Post Charter Applications
New York State Bureau of Military Statistics, Accounts Submitted by Local Officials Detailing Monies Raised and Expended and Men Furnished during the Civil War, 1861–1866
New York State Bureau of Military Statistics, Town and City Registers of Officers, Soldiers, and Seamen Composing the Quotas of Troops Furnished to the United States During the Civil War, 1861–1865

New York State Library, Albany, N.Y.

Marshall O. Bond Diary

State University of New York College at Fredonia, Reed Library, Local History Collection, Fredonia, N.Y.

James Byron Brown Poem, "Army Song of the Chautauqua Boys"
Isaac N. Porter Letters

U.S. Army Military History Institute, Carlisle Barracks, Pa.

Mrs. Daniel Ball Letter (in Henry Van Aernam Letters)
James Byron Brown Poem, "The Soldier's Farewell"
H. S. Merrill Letter (in Henry Van Aernam Letters)
George W. Newcomb Letter (March 6, 1863), Lewis Leigh Collection, Book 36, #90
George W. Newcomb Letters
Henry Van Aernam Letters

U.S. Military Academy Library, West Point, N.Y.

Henry Martin Cadet Card

University of Iowa Library, Iowa City, Iowa

Marcellus W. Darling Letters and Diary

Published Sources

NEWSPAPERS

Buffalo Courier
Buffalo Daily Courier
Cattaraugus Freeman, Ellicottville, New York
Cattaraugus Republican, Salamanca, New York
Cattaraugus Union, Ellicottville, New York
Ellicottville (New York) News
Ellicottville (New York) Post
Frank Leslie's Illustrated Newspaper
Fredonia (New York) Advertiser
Fredonia (New York) Censor
Gowanda (New York) Reporter
Jamestown (New York) Evening Journal
Jamestown (New York) Journal
Jamestown (New York) Post-Journal Tempo
Mayville (New York) Sentinel
National Tribune, Washington, D.C.
Nebraska State Journal, Lincoln, Nebraska
Olean (New York) Morning Times
Olean (New York) Times
Olean (New York) Times Herald
Potter Journal, Coudersport, Pennsylvania
Randolph (New York) Register
Salamanca (New York) Republican Press
Silver Creek (New York) News-Times
Sioux City (Iowa) Journal
Staples (Minnesota) World
Westfield (New York) Republican

BOOKS AND ARTICLES

Adams, William, ed. Historical Gazetteer and Biographical Memorial of Cattaraugus County, N.Y. Syracuse: Lyman, Horton & Co., 1893.
Basler, Roy P., ed. The Collected Works of Abraham Lincoln. New Brunswick, N.J.: Rutgers Univ. Press, 1953.

Beyer, W. F., and O. F. Keydel, eds. *Deeds of Valor*. Detroit: Perrien-Keydel Co., 1907.

Brainard, Asa. *Reminiscences of the life of Asa Brainard as given by him in his own way at the First Reunion of the Brainard Family at the home of C. L. Brainard, Brocton, N.Y., July 11, 1914*. N.p., n.d.

Carroon, Robert G., and Dana B. Shoaf. *Union Blue: The History of the Military Order of the Loyal Legion of the United States*. Shippensburg, Pa.: White Mane Books, 2001.

The Centennial History of Chautauqua County. Jamestown, N.Y.: Chautauqua History Company, 1904.

Conklin, George W. *Under the Crescent and Star: The 134th New York Volunteer Infantry in the Civil War*. Port Reading, N.J.: Axworthy Publishing, 1999.

Cozzens, Peter. *The Shipwreck of Their Hopes: The Battles for Chattanooga*. Urbana and Chicago: Univ. of Illinois Press, 1994.

Daniel, Larry J. *Soldiering in the Army of Tennessee: A Portrait of Life in a Confederate Army*. Chapel Hill: Univ. of North Carolina Press, 1991.

Darling, Marcellus Warner. *Events and Comments of My Life*. N.p., n.d.

Davis, William C. *Lincoln's Men: How President Lincoln Became Father to an Army and a Nation*. New York: Free Press, 1999.

Dilley, Butler F. *Biographical and Portrait Cyclopedia of Chautauqua County, New York*. Philadelphia: John M. Gresham & Co., 1891.

Dornbusch, C. E., comp. *Military Bibliography of the Civil War*. New York: New York Public Library, 1975.

Dunkelman, Mark, and Phil Palen, eds. "Philo Markham's Long Walk." *Civil War Times Illustrated* 34, no. 1 (March/April 1995): 26–30, 83.

Dunkelman, Mark H. "'A Just Right to Select Our Own Officers': Reactions in a Union Regiment to Officers Commissioned from Outside Its Ranks." *Civil War History* 44, no. 1 (March 1998): 24–34.

———. "A Reflection of Their Own Image." *North & South* 3, no. 2 (January 2000): 74–80.

———. "Alas! He Is Gone." *Lincoln Herald* 94, no. 2 (summer 1992): 46–8.

———. "Brigadier General Patrick Henry Jones." *Lincoln Herald* 89, no. 2 (summer 1987): 71–6.

———. *Brothers, Heroes, Martyrs: The Civil War Service of Lewis and George Bishop, Color Bearers of the 154th New York Volunteer Infantry*. Allegany, N.Y.: Allegany Area Historical Association, 1994.

———. *Camp James M. Brown: Jamestown's Civil War Rendezvous*. Jamestown, N.Y.: Fenton Historical Society, 1996.

———. *Colonel Lewis D. Warner: An Appreciation*. Portville, N.Y.: Portville Historical and Preservation Society, 1990.

———. "Emory Sweetland Remembers November 19, 1863." *Lincoln Herald* 96, no. 2 (summer 1994): 44–50.

———. *Gettysburg's Unknown Soldier: The Life, Death, and Celebrity of Amos Humiston*. Westport, Conn.: Praeger, 1999.

———. "Hardtack and Sauerkraut Stew: Ethnic Tensions in the 154th New York Volunteers, Eleventh Corps, during the Civil War." *Yearbook of German-American Studies* 36 (2001): 69–90.

———. "Hurray For Old Abe! Fenton! and Dr. Van Aernam! The 1864 Election, as Perceived by the 154th New York Volunteers." *Lincoln Herald* 98, no. 1 (spring 1996): 12–22.

——. "Main Address." In *Dedication of the Chancellorsville Monument to the 154th New York Volunteer Infantry.* 154th New York Monument Fund, 1996.

——. "Senior Soldiers." *Military Collector & Historian* 44, no. 4 (winter 1992): 158–62.

——. "Through White Eyes: The 154th New York Volunteers and African-Americans in the Civil War." *Journal of Negro History* 83, no. 3 (summer 2000): 96–111.

——. "'We Were Compelled to Cut Our Way Through Them, and in Doing so Our Losses Were Heavy': Gettysburg Casualties of the 154th New York Volunteers." *Gettysburg Magazine* 18 (January 1998): 34–56.

Dunkelman, Mark H., and Michael J. Winey. *The Hardtack Regiment: An Illustrated History of the 154th Regiment, New York State Infantry Volunteers.* East Brunswick, N.J.: Fairleigh Dickinson Univ. Press, 1981.

——. "The Hardtack Regiment in the Brickyard Fight." *Gettysburg Magazine* 8 (January 1993): 16–30.

——. "The Hardtack Regiment Meets Lincoln." *Lincoln Herald* 85, no. 2 (summer 1983): 95–9.

——. "Precious Shadows: The Importance of Photographs to Civil War Soldiers, as Revealed by a Typical Union Regiment." *Military Images* 16, no. 1 (July–August 1994): 6–13.

Ellis, Franklin, ed. *History of Cattaraugus County, New York.* Philadelphia: L. H. Everts, 1879.

Faust, Drew Gilpin. "The Civil War Soldier and the Art of Dying." In *The Civil War Soldier: A Historical Reader,* edited by Michael Barton and Larry M. Logue. New York: New York Univ. Press, 2002.

Frank, Joseph Allan. *With Ballot and Bullet: The Political Socialization of American Civil War Soldiers.* Athens: Univ. of Georgia Press, 1998.

Frank, Joseph Allan, and George A. Reaves. *"Seeing the Elephant": Raw Recruits at the Battle of Shiloh.* Westport, Conn.: Greenwood Press, 1989.

Glatthaar, Joseph T. *The March to the Sea and Beyond: Sherman's Troops in the Savannah and Carolinas Campaign.* New York: New York Univ. Press, 1985.

Greer, E. P. "A Pioneer, a Gentleman and a Soldier [Henry C. Loomis]." In *Souvenir Edition of the Winfield Courier.* Winfield, Kansas: Winfield Courier, 1901.

Harlow, S. R., and H. H. Boone. *Life Sketches of the State Officers, Senators, and Members of the Assembly of the State of New York.* Albany: Weed, Parsons, and Company, 1867.

Hess, Earl J. *The Union Soldier in Battle: Enduring the Ordeal of Combat.* Lawrence: Univ. Press of Kansas, 1997.

History of the Easel-Shaped Monument and a Key to the Principles and Objects of the Grand Army of the Republic and its Co-Workers. Chicago: Dux Publishing Company, 1893.

Holzer, Harold, ed., and Daniel Lorello, comp. *The Union Preserved: A Guide to Civil War Records in the New York State Archives.* New York: Fordham Univ. Press and the New York State Archives Partnership Trust, 1999.

Hyde, William L. *History of the One Hundred and Twelfth Regiment N.Y. Volunteers.* Fredonia, N.Y.: W. McKinstry & Co., 1866.

Jimerson, Randall C. *The Private Civil War: Popular Thought during the Sectional Conflict.* Baton Rouge: Louisiana State Univ. Press, 1988.

Lee, Thomas Armory. "Alfred Washburn Benson, L.L.D." *Kansas State Historical Society Journal* 14 (1918): 4–22.

Leonard, I. R. *Historical Sketch of the Village of Gowanda, N.Y.* Buffalo: The Complete Art-Printing Works of the Matthews-Northrup Co., 1898.

Lewis, Alfred Henry. "Major Benson: A Sunflower Statesman." *Saturday Evening Post* 179, no. 8 (August 8, 1906): 3–4.

Linderman, Gerald F. *Embattled Courage: The Experience of Combat in the American Civil War.* New York: Free Press, 1987.

Logue, Larry M. *To Appomattox and Beyond: The Civil War Soldier in War and Peace.* Chicago: Ivan R. Dee, 1996.

Long, E. B., with Barbara Long. *The Civil War Day by Day: An Almanac, 1861–1865.* Garden City, N.Y.: Doubleday, 1971.

Lord, Francis A. *They Fought for the Union.* New York: Bonanza Books, 1960.

Macoy, Robert. *The Masonic Manual.* New York: Clark, Austin, and Smith, 1857.

Markham, Philo A. *Sketch of the Life & Army Service of P. A. Markham.* N.p., n.d.

Maryniak, Benedict R. "GAR Posts." *The Civil War Courier* (May 1999): 38.

McConnell, Stuart. *Glorious Contentment: The Grand Army of the Republic, 1865–1900.* Chapel Hill: Univ. of North Carolina Press, 1992.

McKay, Charles W. "'Three Years or During the War,' With the Crescent and Star." In *The National Tribune Scrap Book,* 121–60. N.p., n.d.

McPherson, James M. *Battle Cry of Freedom: The Civil War Era.* New York: Oxford Univ. Press, 1988.

———. *For Cause and Comrades: Why Men Fought in the Civil War.* New York: Oxford Univ. Press, 1997.

McPherson, James M., and William J. Cooper, eds. *Writing the Civil War: The Quest to Understand.* Columbia: Univ. of South Carolina Press, 1998.

The Medical and Surgical History of the War of the Rebellion. 2 vols. Washington, D.C.: Government Printing Office, 1870–83.

Mitchell, Reid. *Civil War Soldiers.* New York: Viking, 1988.

———. *The Vacant Chair: The Northern Soldier Leaves Home.* New York: Oxford Univ. Press, 1993.

Moss, Lemuel. *Annals of the United States Christian Commission.* Philadelphia: J. B. Lippincott, 1868.

Neely, Mark E., Jr., and Harold Holzer. *The Union Image: Popular Prints of the Civil War North.* Chapel Hill: Univ. of North Carolina Press, 2000.

New York Monuments Commission for the Battlefields of Gettysburg and Chattanooga. *Final Report on the Battlefield of Gettysburg.* Albany: J. B. Lyon Company, 1902.

Olson, Marlynn M. *A Guide to Burial Sites, Cemeteries, and Random Stones in Cattaraugus County, New York.* Randolph, N.Y.: Register Graphics, 1996.

Phisterer, Frederick. *New York in the War of the Rebellion.* Albany: Weed, Parsons and Company, 1890.

Pollock, Thomas, and Ronda Shaner Pollock, eds. *A History of the Town of Portville, 1805–1920.* Portville, N.Y.: Portville Historical and Preservation Society, 1986.

Presidents, Soldiers, Statesmen. New York, Toledo and Chicago: H. H. Hardesty, 1899.

Prokopowicz, Gerald J. *All for the Regiment: The Army of the Ohio, 1861–1862.* Chapel Hill: Univ. of North Carolina Press, 2001.

Robertson, James I., Jr. *Soldiers Blue and Gray.* Columbia: Univ. of South Carolina Press, 1988.

Saum, Lewis O. "Death in the Popular Mind of Pre–Civil War America." In *Death in America,* edited by David E. Stannard, 30–48. Philadelphia: Univ. of Pennsylvania Press, 1975.

Schantz, Rev. F. J. F. "Recollections of Visitations at Gettysburg after the Great Battle in July, 1863." In *Reflections on the Battle of Gettysburg*, vol. 13, no. 6, edited by Ralph S. Shay, 285–303. Lebanon County, Pa.: Lebanon County (Pa.) Historical Society, 1963.

Schults, Charles J., ed. *Historical and Biographical History of the Township of Dayton, Cattaraugus County, New York*. Buffalo: Hausauer Press, 1901.

Sears, Stephen. *Chancellorsville*. Boston: Houghton Mifflin, 1996.

Senfield, Craig F., ed. *Civil War Veterans Cemetery Locator, Volume I, Cattaraugus County, New York*. Olean, N.Y.: Twin Tier Civil War Roundtable, 1996.

Sherman, William T. *Memoirs of General William T. Sherman by Himself*. 1875. Reprint, Bloomington: Indiana Univ. Press, 1957.

State of New York, Andersonville Monument Dedication Commission. *Dedication of Monument Erected by the State of New York at Andersonville, Georgia 1914*. Albany: J. B. Lyon Co., 1916.

Taylor, H. C. *Historical Sketches of the Town of Portland*. Fredonia, N.Y.: W. McKinstry & Son, 1873.

Third Annual Report of the Bureau of Military Record of the State of New York. Albany: C. Wendell, 1866.

Todd, Frederick P. *American Military Equipage, 1851–1872*. New York: Charles Scribner's Sons, 1980.

United States Sanitary Commission, Department of Arms and Trophies, Metropolitan Fair. *Catalogue of the Museum of Flags, Trophies and Relics*. New York: Charles O. Jones, 1864.

U.S. War Department. *The War of the Rebellion: A Compilation of the Official Records of the Union and Confederate Armies*. 128 volumes. Washington: Government Printing Office, 1880–1901.

Weber, Gustavus A. *The Bureau of Pensions: Its History, Activities and Organization*. 1923. Reprint, New York: AMS Press, 1974.

Wheeler, W. Reginald. *Pine Knots and Bark Peelers: The Story of Five Generations of American Lumbermen*. New York: Ganis and Harris, 1960.

Wiley, Bell Irvin. *The Life of Billy Yank: The Common Soldier of the Union*. 1952. Reprint, Baton Rouge: Louisiana State Univ. Press, 1993.

———. *The Life of Johnny Reb: The Common Soldier of the Confederacy*. 1943. Reprint, Baton Rouge: Louisiana State Univ. Press, 1993.

Woodworth, Steven E., ed. *The American Civil War: A Handbook of Literature and Research*. Westport, Conn.: Greenwood Press, 1996.

Young, Andrew W. *History of Chautauqua County, New York*. Buffalo: Printing House of Matthews & Warren, 1875.

Index

West Salamanca, N.Y., 253
Wheeler, Devillo, 25, 45, 60, 171, 193
Wheeler, John, 82
Wheelock, Perry, 118
Wheelock, Theodore, 77
Whipple, Henry F., 253, 262, 273
Whipple, James S., 262
White, Orlando, 110, 236–7
Whitford, Howard, 82–3
Whitney, Charles E., 42, 48, 79, 152–3, 263,
    264, 275
Wiggins, Byron A., 161, 273
Wilber, Lyman, 37, 173–4
Wilber, Oscar F., 68, 84, 99, 107, 122, 176
Wiley, Bell Irvin, 7–8, 220–1
Williams, Allen, 162, 241, 242
Williams, David J., 47, 54, 77
Williams, George, 26
Williams, George, Jr., 27
Williams, Samuel R., 34, 38, 55, 69, 115, 200
Williams, William, 81–2

Willis, Thomas S., 159
Wilmington, N.C., 264
Wilson, James, 161
Wilson, John, 166
Winey, Michael J., 11
Wing, Asa S., 42
Winney, Jacob, 24, 26
Wisconsin regiments, 183, 189
Wood, Hester Ann, 178
Wood, Ira, 33, 104, 108, 118, 154–5, 178, 182,
    184, 213, 221
Woodard, Robert J., 153, 264
Wounded, care of, 113, 142–7, 148
Wright, Abraham, 24
Wright, Landers, 112, 200
Wright, Ora, 24
Wyant, Alansing, 188, 208, 230, 231

Yelsey, Martin, 159
Yorkshire, N.Y., 35, 49, 54
Young, Monroe, 40, 46–7, 80